The Presence of God in the World

European University Studies
Europäische Hochschulschriften
Publications Universitaires Européennes

Series XXIII
Theology

Reihe XXIII   Série XXIII
Theologie
Théologie

Vol./Band 844

PETER LANG

Bern · Berlin · Bruxelles · Frankfurt am Main · New York · Oxford · Wien

Steven G. Ogden

The Presence of God in the World

A Contribution to Postmodern Christology based on the Theologies of Paul Tillich and Karl Rahner

PETER LANG

Bern · Berlin · Bruxelles · Frankfurt am Main · New York · Oxford · Wien

Bibliographic information published by Die Deutsche Bibliothek
Die Deutsche Bibliothek lists this publication in the Deutsche Nationalbibliografie;
detailed bibliographic data is available on the Internet at
‹http://dnb.ddb.de›.

British Library Cataloguing-in-Publication Data:
A catalogue record for this book is available from *The British Library*, Great Britain

Library of Congress Cataloging-in-Publication Data

Ogden, Steven G., 1955-

The presence of God in the world : a contribution to postmodern Christology
based on the theologies of Paul Tillich and Karl Rahner / Steven G. Ogden.

p. cm. -- (European university studies. Series XXIII, Theology, ISSN 0721-3409 ;
v. 844 = Europäische Hochschulschriften. Reihe XXIII, Theologie ; Bd. 844)

Includes bibliographical references (p.   ).
ISBN 978-3-03-911303-3 (alk. paper)

1. Jesus Christ--History of doctrines--20th century. 2. Postmodernism--Religious aspects--Christianity.
3. Tillich, Paul, 1886-1965. 4. Rahner, Karl, 1904-1984. I. Title.

BT198.O365 2007

231.7--dc22

2007031843

ISSN 0721-3409
ISBN 978-3-03911-303-3

© Peter Lang AG, European Academic Publishers, Bern 2007
Hochfeldstrasse 32, Postfach 746, CH-3000 Bern 9, Switzerland
info@peterlang.com, www.peterlang.com, www.peterlang.net

Printed in Germany

Acknowledgements

Over the years, I have been fortunate to have many good people take an interest in my life. The period of the production of this thesis is no exception. I am grateful to my supervisors the Revd Dr Andrew Dutney and Dr Stephen Downs. From the outset they were open to the idea of the project. Throughout, they have been a constant source of critical insight and goodwill. I am very grateful for their enthusiasm, learning and support. Lee Parker, friend and mentor, his timely wisdom and encouragement were invaluable. He went the extra mile. Many others have also helped along the way with their encouragement: friends, colleagues and members of St Peter's Cathedral.

Above all, there is my wife Anne Ogden. Anne is the most generous person I know. It is her nature to want those she loves to soar. Since we first met, Anne has only wanted the best for me. To that end, she has sacrificed countless days off and holidays as I have wrestled with the project: always encouraging, always believing.

I dedicate this thesis to Annie.

Table of Contents

Abstract

The presumption of the absence of God is prevalent in Western scholarship. Consequently, this study addresses the problem of the presence of God in the world. The study's thesis is that the presence of God in the world can be affirmed, if presence is understood in relation to absence and within the context of experience. Accordingly, it argues that the experience of God in the world is ambiguous and that it consists of presence and absence. While the idea of interpreting experience from the perspective of presence and absence is not new, the sustained application of this interpretation to the theological systems of Tillich and Rahner provides new insights. The overall aim of this study is to make a contribution to postmodern Christology by re-interpreting their theologies in relation to postmodernity.

There are important theological differences between Tillich and Rahner, their theologies however can be described as theologies of presence in that for them God-is-in-the-world. For Tillich, presence is the human awareness of its participation in Divine life. For Rahner, presence is humankind's experience of the awareness of the closeness of God's self. For both, Christ is the definitive expression of presence. All the same, presence is problematic for contemporary scholarship because of its metaphysical associations. Hence, the study's intention is to redefine presence in a postmetaphysical manner.

Chapter 1 outlines the study's problem and thesis. It establishes the rationale for using Tillich and Rahner and defines the study's method and key terms. It assumes the importance of a particular concept of experience in which experience is ambiguous, consisting of presence and absence. This is examined in Chapter 4 which is the study's leading chapter. On the basis of the assumption that experience is ambiguous, the aim of the study is to make a contribution to postmodern Christology by focusing on the themes of the Incarnation and the Death-Resurrection event. This chapter employs theological insights derived from the theologies of Tillich and Rahner as outlined in chapters 2 and 3. Chapter 5 outlines the conclusions, limitations and implications of the study.

Abbreviations

Tillich

ATR	*Against the Third Reich*
BRUR	*Biblical Religion and the Search for Ultimate Reality*
CEWR	*Christianity and the Encounter of World Religions*
CHR	*The Construction of the History of Religion in Schelling's Positive Philosophy*
DF	*The Dynamics of Faith*
EN	*The Eternal Now*
HCT	*A History of Christian Thought*
IRCM	*The Irrelevance and Relevance of the Christian Message*
LPJ	*Love, Power and Justice*
MSFA	*My Search for Absolutes*
OTB	*On the Boundary: An Autobiographical Sketch*
PPT	*Perspectives on 19th and 20th Century Theology*
SS	*The System of the Sciences*
ST	*Systematic Theology*
TCB	*The Courage to Be*
TNB	*The New Being*
TOC	*Theology of Culture*
TPE	*The Protestant Era*
TSF	*The Shaking of the Foundations*
UC	*Ultimate Concern: Tillich in Dialogue*

Rahner

BT	*Belief Today*
CS	*The Church and the Sacraments*
ES	*Encounters with Silence*
ET	*Encyclopedia of Theology*
FCF	*Foundations of Christian Faith*
HW	*Hearer of the Word*
IR	*I Remember: An Autobiographical Interview with Meinhold Krauss*
OH	*On Heresy*
OP	*On Prayer*
PL	*Prayers for a Lifetime*
SM	*Sacramentum Mundi*
SW	*Spirit in the World*
TGCY	*The Great Church Year*
TI	*Theological Investigations*
TT	*The Trinity*

Chapter 1: The Problem of the Presence of God in the World

The aim of this section is to introduce the study's problem, thesis and major themes. The study's problem relates to presence. In sections of Western scholarship, the presumption of the absence of God is prevalent.[1] Absence is arguably a given in postmodernity. Thus, the study addresses the problem of the presence of God.[2] Its thesis is that the presence of God can be affirmed, if presence is understood in relation to absence and in the context of experience. In particular, the experience of God in the world is ambiguous and consists of presence and absence. Presence and absence represent two distinct meanings of the experience of God, where presence and absence cannot be separated from experience or each other as if they were discrete entities. The idea of interpreting experience from the perspective of presence and absence is not new, but the application of this construal to the theologies of Tillich and Rahner provides significant new insights. Moreover, Tillich and Rahner argue for the presence of God, though their theologies are primarily oriented toward modernity. The overall aim of this study is to make a contribution to postmodern Christology by re-interpreting their work in relation to postmodernity.

Theologians and philosophers alike have debated the meaning of presence and interest in absence has fuelled that debate. This study sees the absence of God as a theological and philosophical symptom of the process of the marginalisation of God.[3] The marginalisation of God be-

---

1   E.g. theology, philosophy, literary studies, cf. P.L. Berger, "The desecularization of the world: A global overview" in P.L. Berger ed., *The Desecularization of the World: Resurgent Religion and World Politics*, (Grand Rapids, Michigan: Eerdmans, 1999), p. 10.

2   The terms *presence* and *presence of God* are used in this study as shorthand forms of *the presence of God in the world*. Similarly, *absence* and *the absence of God* are used as shorthand forms of *the absence of God in the world*.

3   In this study, the term marginalisation is used in the sense of being displaced from the centre and moved to the edge, cf. D. Edwards, "secularization" A. Bullock and

gan in the Late Middle Ages, accelerated under the influence of Descartes, Locke and others, and developed during the Enlightenment in tandem with the emergence of modernity. Its denouement occurred with Nietzsche pronouncing the epitaph that God is dead.[4] With the emergence of postmodernity, the nature of the marginalisation changed. In modernity, God is displaced from the world. In postmodernity, God is displaced from other domains as well as the world (e.g. text, syllabus, university). There are also other gods and religions with their own truth claims (i.e. pluralism). A defining feature of modernity is the presumption of an unbridgeable gap between the material and the spiritual. This is the prime cause of modernity's displacement of God. Tillich and Rahner accept the gap as a given. For them, the gap is part of the modern worldview. They assert that the problem of gap can be transcended by virtue of an inherent God-given capacity in the world, which is experienced as presence. While there are differences between Tillich and Rahner, both their theologies can be described as theologies of presence, in that for them, God-is-in-the-world. In Tillich, presence is human awareness of its participation in Divine life (2.2.1). In Rahner, presence is human experience of the awareness of the closeness of God's self (3.2.1). For both theologians, humankind experiences God in relation to and by means of the material world. For both, God is the creator who is involved in an ever-evolving creative salvific historical process. However, God is neither contained by nor confined to the world: God is God even without a world, though a world of sorts is required for humankind to know God as God or by another name. Ultimately, Christ is the definitive expression of the presence of God in the world for both Tillich and Rahner. What they say about Christ hinges largely on the themes of the Incarnation and the Death-Resurrection event. In this study, these themes form the basis of an incremental contribution to postmodern Christology in a Western context at the beginning of the twenty first century.

This is a theological study that is informed by the theologies of Tillich and Rahner; it is not unreservedly committed to either of their positions. For instance, Tillich and Rahner understand presence largely in

---

S. Trombley eds., *The New Fontana Dictionary of Modern Thought*, 3rd ed., (London: Harper Collins, 1977, 1988, 1999), pp. 778-779.

4   F. Nietzsche, *The Gay Science* [1882, 1887, p. 125], and *Beyond Good and Evil* [1886, p. 53], in P. Novak ed., *The Vision of Nietzsche*, (Rockport, Massachusetts: Element, 1996), pp. 57-59.

16

metaphysical terms and this is a problem in a postmodern setting. Their reliance on universals and speculative methods warrants a degree of hermeneutical suspicion.[5] Thus, the study's intention is to redefine presence in a postmetaphysical manner. It concentrates on the theological writings of Tillich and Rahner. While its method is principally theological, it uses insights from other methods, not privileging one method over another. It relies on argumentation and incorporates interrelated strategies of philosophical reasoning, historiography, conceptual critique and comparative analysis. The overall aim is to make a contribution to postmodern Christology. The study's epistemological strategy limits that aim to achieving an incremental contribution to Christological knowledge, where the acquisition of knowledge is understood in cumulative terms as part of an ongoing conversation, which is expressed in terms of probability. The study does not address explicitly the issue of religious pluralism, though the issue is present implicitly by virtue of the study's interest in postmodernity. The study seeks to make an incremental contribution in the context of the Western Christian tradition. It is not attempting to make absolute or universal truth claims on behalf of other cultures or religions. Nor is it taking what Haack describes as a "tribalist" position.[6] That is, the study is not saying its contribution applies solely to the Western Christian tradition; it is saying that outside this context is beyond the scope of the study. It presumes the ambiguous nature of experience as presence and absence. It presumes theology is provisional, meaning that each era and every faith community has to perform its own theological reflection.[7] However, it affirms the existence of theological constants (e.g. Jesus of Nazareth) that have to be re-interpreted in new

5   D.M. Armstrong "universals" in J. Kim and E. Sosa eds., *A Companion to Metaphysics*, (Oxford: Blackwell, 1995), pp. 502-506, the meaning of universals is debated. There is a narrow use of the term that can be found in relation to the debate about universal and particulars (e.g. the referent to red). In this study, the term is used in a general way to apply to abstract, metaphysical principles, which are asserted to apply regardless of context (e.g. Tillich's latent church; Rahner's anonymous Christian).

6   S. Haack, *Evidence and Inquiry: Towards Reconstruction in Epistemology*, (Oxford: Blackwell, 1993, 1995), p. 192.

7   The term *faith community* is used rather than church; there is nothing wrong with the term church, but not all Christian traditions use the term (e.g. Society of Friends). The term *faith community* has a postmodern pluralist nuance too, which seems fitting in this study.

settings and re-appropriated by new faith communities. The study is not an exercise in pastoral theology, but it assumes that theology is written out of the experience and for the benefit of faith communities. Therefore, the study asserts that the experience of faith communities, along with other factors, has a place in epistemic justification.

1.1. Rationale for Using Tillich and Rahner

Tillich and Rahner have been selected as primary sources for four reasons. First, their work is amenable to an interpretation based on the themes of experience, presence and absence. Second, Christ for them is the definitive expression of the presence of God in the world. In their engagement with modernity, they say something positive about Christology. Third, the claim that God is present in the world is a guiding assumption in their theological visions. This is not a startling claim, as other theologians have also laid claim to this; but not every theologian has seen merit in modernity and used it as creatively as they have. Their spirited engagement with modernity represents a theological precedent as well as an invitation to subsequent generations of students of theology to engage with postmodernity with equal endeavour. Fourth, little has been done to compare Tillich and Rahner in a detailed and comprehensive way.

In recent years, there has been a revival of interest in Tillich, especially in America. R.F. Bulman and F.J. Parella claim, "Catholic theologians, and indeed the Churches of all traditions, are fortunate to have Tillich as a prophetic colleague and friend, and his theological system as a source of wisdom in the journey to come".[8] Similarly, Rahner's influence is pervasive.[9] Like Tillich, Rahner is one of the great figures of

---

8   R.F. Bulman and F.J. Parella, "Introduction" in R.F. Bulman and F.J. Parella eds., *Paul Tillich: A New Catholic Assessment*, (Collegeville, Minnesota: The Liturgical Press, 1994), p. 7.

9   A. Dulles, *The Craft of Theology: From Symbol to System* (New York: Crossroad, 1992); J. Macquarrie, *Jesus Christ in Modern Thought*, (London: SCM Press, 1990); Ruether, R.R. *Sexism and God-Talk: Towards A Feminist Theology*, (London: SCM Press, 1983).

18

twentieth century theology. In biographical terms, there are a number of differences between the two theologians.

– Tillich came from an upper class Prussian Lutheran home, whereas Rahner from a middle class Alemanian Catholic home.
– Tillich was eighteen years older than Rahner.
– Tillich experienced warfare firsthand.[10]
– Tillich enjoyed celebrity status, Rahner was comparatively reserved.[11]
– Tillich was free of the constraints of the *magisterium*, Rahner believed a conception ought not refute the *magisterium*.[12]

Yet there is a family resemblance between the two theologians.[13] This exists partly because they emerge from a similar European intellectual milieu.[14] They witnessed similar historical events (e.g. rise of National Socialism). They shared theological and philosophical interests: the turn to the subject, the importance of experience, the influence of existentialism and an appreciation of the concept of symbol.[15] They used similar sources. For example, Heidegger's emphasis on the questioning nature of humanity, "In Rahner's philosophical theology the world of revelation

10 W. Pauck and M. Pauck, *Paul Tillich: His Life and Thought*, (San Francisco: Harper and Row, 1989), p. 41, Tillich's participation in the First World War as chaplain and ambulance officer had a profound effect on him.
11 T.F. O'Meara, *A Theologian's Journey*, (New York: Paulist Press, 2002), p. 241, O'Meara was a student of Rahner, "Rahner was unassuming, approachable, and direct. He did not fit the type of the *Herr Professor*. He had no interest in prestige, in power, and certainly not in money".
12 K. Rahner, "Dogmatic reflections on the knowledge and self-consciousness of Christ", TI 5, p. 199.
13 L. Wittgenstein, *Philosophical Investigations*, G.E.M. Anscombe trans., (Oxford: Blackwell, 1974), p. 32, "I can think of no better expression to characterize these similarities than 'family resemblances'; for the various resemblances between members of a family: build, features, colour of eyes, gait, temperament, etc. etc. overlap and criss-cross in the same way. – And I shall say: 'games' form a family".
14 O'Meara, *Journey*, p. 228, "I could see that Rahner and Paul Tillich had some similarities. Though not of the same age, both had neo-Kantian and existentialist mentors, both sought a theology that left room for the gospel amid modernity, and both theologians stimulated positive appreciations of the world religions".
15 In this study, the term *the turn to the subject* is a short hand term used to describe a broad and complex paradigmatic shift of focus in intellectual inquiry from an *external* God to the human *subject*. Its genesis lies in part in the work of Descartes and Kant.

cannot be the reversal of man's philosophical conclusions. The divine answer is anticipated by the question, just as in Tillich's method of correspondence".[16] Above all, they were influenced by and responded to modernity; "Both were profoundly influenced by their respective encounters with secularity. In an effort to overcome the dichotomy between orthodoxy and the Enlightenment, they each attempted to speak to our century about the sacred present in the profane and each assumed an anthropological starting-point to do so".[17] In different ways, they shared similar apologetic and kerygmatic concerns as they tried to respond to the challenge of modernity. However, while they shared a family resemblance, the similarities as well as differences have not been explored comprehensively in recent theological literature.

Tillich and Rahner are often mentioned in discussions about the history of theology.[18] Their names appear together in discussions on Christology, anthropology, sacramental theology, existentialist theology and religious pluralism.[19] Generally, these references are either general allusions or specific references which are subordinate to larger purposes, for instance, S. Cowdell, R. Haight and W.J. Wildman.[20] In Cowdell there are references to both theologians but there is no explicit comparison. In Wildman there are a few explicit comparisons, but they are very much subservient to his thesis. With Haight there are many references and some comparisons, but they are general in nature and subordinate to other concerns. Overall, these scholars refer to Tillich and Rahner thoughtfully but in passing. There are exceptions.[21] F.J. van Beeck has a

16   G. Vass, *A Theologian in Search of a Philosophy: Understanding Karl Rahner*, Vol. 1, (Westminster, London: Christian Classics, Sheed and Ward, 1985), p. 124.

17   R. Modras, "Catholic substance and the Catholic church today" in Bulman and Parrella, p. 42.

18   Dulles, *Craft*, p. 52.

19   B.R. Hill, P. Knitter and W. Madges, *Faith Religion and Theology: A Contemporary Introduction*, Rev ed. (Mystic, CT: Twenty-Third Publications, 1990, 1997, 1998), p. 168.

20   S. Cowdell, *Is Jesus Unique? A Study of Recent Christology*, (New York: Paulist Press, 1996); R. Haight, *Jesus Symbol of God* (New York: Orbis Books, 1999); W.J. Wildman, *Fidelity with Plausibility: Modest Christologies in the Twentieth Century*, (New York: State University of New York Press, 1998).

21   R. Haight, *Dynamics of Theology*, (Mahwah, NJ: Paulist Press, 1990); J.A. Lamm, "'Catholic substance' revisited: reversals of expectations in Tillich's doctrine of God" in R.F. Bulman and F.J. Parrella, *Paul Tillich: A New Catholic Assessment* (Collegeville, Minnesota: The Liturgical Press, 1994), pp. 48-72. D. Tracy, *The*

worthwhile but limited comparison. In contrast, Haight's treatment of Tillich and Rahner is more comprehensive than van Beeck's but not as rigorous. Regarding Tillich and Rahner, Haight claims that, "I see no fundamental antithesis between these two theologies of symbol" and in the same breath he admits, "This is not the place to develop a full critique of Rahner's or Tillich's theology of symbol or their christology".[22] Clearly, Haight's analysis of the individual theologians, as well as his comparison of the two, is subservient to his interest in developing a comprehensive theology of revelation.[23] Moreover, like this study, Haight is interested in the presence of God and places a premium on human experience.[24] However, Haight does not treat explicitly the issue of absence, "The problem then is not that of the possibility of revelation, nor of the absence of revelation; the problem is the many manifestations of it".[25] In contrast, this study is concerned about absence. It is interested in the ambiguity of experience as presence and absence, and this is explored in the context of the theologies of Tillich and Rahner. The similarities and differences that exist between them are particularly important in terms of exploring the meaning of presence and absence.[26] Unlike Haight, this study is not interested in developing a comprehensive theology of revelation. Certainly, there are insights into the nature of revelation, but they are subservient to the Christological aim. Moreover, the study's use of presence and experience cannot be understood without the concept of absence. In conclusion, the similarities and differences between Tillich and Rahner are frequently noted, but they are not pursued at length; as O'Meara observes, "few studies comparing Rahner and

---

Analogical Imagination: Christian Theology and the Culture of Pluralism, (London: SCM Press Ltd, 1981), pp. 418-9. F.J. van Beeck, *Christ Proclaimed: Christology as Rhetoric*, (New York: Paulist Press, 1979), pp. 217-223.

22   Haight, *Dynamics* p. 259, n.17.

23   *Ibid.* p. 51.

24   *Ibid.* pp. 79, 96.

25   *Ibid.* p. 65.

26   J. D. Caputo "The experience of God and the axiology of the impossible" in M.A. Wrathall ed. *Religion after Metaphysics*, (Cambridge: Cambridge University Press, 2003), pp. 123-145. Caputo's essay has different research interests to this study (i.e. Caputo's God of the impossible). However, the experience of God is a given in both studies, given in the sense that as humans we try and deal with our *experience* of God (or lack thereof).

Tillich (their similarities could occupy many books) have appeared".[27] There are no substantial references in Tillich or Rahner to the other.[28]

1.2. Outline, Limitations and Questions

1.2.1. Outline of the Study

Historically, the presence of God has been accepted as a given by theologians. However, in certain quarters of the contemporary Western intellectual world, the contention is that absence is a given. In that context, the onus is on theology to justify the presence of God in the world. To that end, Chapter 1 outlines the study's problem and thesis, establishes the rationale for using Tillich and Rahner and defines the study's method and key terms. It assumes the importance of a particular concept of experience in which experience is ambiguous, consisting of presence and absence. This concept of experience is examined in Chapter 4, which is the foremost chapter in the study. On the basis of the assumption that experience is ambiguous, the study aims to make a contribution to postmodern Christology by focusing on the themes of the Incarnation and the Death-Resurrection event (4.4; 4.5). Chapter 5 outlines the study's limitations, implications and contribution.

Chapters 2 and 3 examine the theologies of Tillich and Rahner. They are substantial chapters for two reasons. First, the theological works of Tillich and Rahner are substantial in terms of size, scope and complexity. While it is not possible to cover all their work, Chapters 2 and 3 represent critical analyses of their theological visions. Second, the study's contribution to Christology in Chapter 4 depends in part on the reliability of the insights derived from Chapters 2 and 3. Chapters 2 and 3 examine similar issues like method, theology and Christology, though there are variations in the way each chapter addresses these issues. This is partly a reflection of the differences that exist between the methods and the the-

27 O'Meara, "Paul Tillich in Catholic thought" p. 22.
28 Rahner, "Observations on the doctrine of God", TI 9, p. 141, has a passing reference to Tillich.

ologies of Tillich and Rahner. In addition, a general comparison is made between Tillich and Rahner and modernity throughout Chapters 2 and 3 respectively. A specific comparison is made between Tillich and Rahner and postmodernity in the final sections of Chapters 2 and 3 respectively. In short, Chapters 2 and 3 are critical analyses, which are composed for the purpose of exploring experience, presence and absence in relation to the themes of the Incarnation and the Death-Resurrection event in Chapter 4.

The aim in Chapter 4 is to make a contribution to postmodern Christology (4.3). This entails bringing together theological insights from Tillich and Rahner and a theology of presence (4.2). The study's theology of presence is premised on a particular concept of experience (4.1). This concept of experience has a role in epistemic justification, providing experience is interpreted in conjunction with reason, and coheres with other beliefs. This view of experience is implicitly intersubjective, not only because the study adopts a postmodern approach to the subject, but also because public and social grounds have a role in the study's epistemology (4.1.1). In other words, while individual or corporate experience is important, no one individual or faith community has privileged epistemological status. Therefore, it is important to establish a working definition of experience and to demonstrate its epistemic credibility (4.1). Further, the study's epistemological strategy means that its Christological aim will be restricted to achieving an incremental contribution to Christological knowledge, where the acquisition of knowledge is understood in cumulative terms as part of an ongoing conversation and is expressed in probability statements. The term *incremental* is used in a postmetaphysical sense of not seeking to make new, or revert to old, universal or absolute claims.[29] The term *cumulative* is used in the sense of seeing the acquisition of knowledge as an incremental process, which is played out over time and in conversation with other voices (cf. C.S. Peirce; J. Armstrong; S. Haack).[30] The term *conversation* is used in the sense that the process of the accumulation of knowledge necessarily

---

29   Wildman, *Fidelity* p. xix.

30   C.S. Peirce, "Consequences of four incapacities" in C. Hartshorne and P. Weiss eds., *Collected Papers of Charles Sanders Peirce*, Vol. 5. (Cambridge, Mass.: Harvard University Press, 1934, 1935, 1960), p. 157 [265]; J. Armstrong, *Looking at Pictures: An Introduction to the Appreciation of Art*, (London: Duckworth, 1996), p. 151; Haack *Evidence and Inquiry*, p. 2; cf. Cowdell, *Unique* pp. 283, 289.

involves dialogue with other voices and not just the theological and the philosophical voices, but also ecclesial and societal voices. All the epistemological claims are expressed in terms of *probability* statements and this means that an element of doubt is unavoidable.[31] This is consistent with the study's presumption that theology is provisional. In short, having established a credible epistemology, the credibility of the concept of presence needs to be addressed.

In a postmetaphysical context, presence is contentious and so the credibility of the concept of presence needs to be addressed before proceeding to the development of a theology of presence (4.2). This presumes a long and complex debate about what it means to speak meaningfully about the presence of God.[32] There are many issues at stake such as the attributes or the agency of God. Besides the philosophical problems, there is a plethora of perspectives on God ranging from scholastic to feminist. Clearly, concerns in the debate have changed. For instance, the presumption of a metaphysical basis for theology has been challenged. Hence, if modernity can be depicted as the problem of the gap between the world and God, then postmodernity can be depicted as the problem of speaking about God.[33] In that context, presence has come under attack as part of a philosophical movement away from ontotheology (4.2). This movement can be seen in the use of relatively new jargon like totalisation, metanarratives, logocentrism and Archimedean points.[34] In this study, the main criticism of presence relates to its metaphysical underpinnings. Historically, presence has been condemned as outmoded because of its reliance on metaphysical schema (e.g. Heidegger prefigured some of the challenges to presence). More recently, Derrida challenged the so-called metaphysics of presence, "There is nothing outside

31 W.D. Hamlyn, "epistemology, history of", T. Honderich ed., The Oxford Companion to Philosophy, (Oxford, New York: Oxford University Press, 1995), hereafter OCP, p. 245.

32 P.C. Hodgson, *Winds of the Spirit: A Constructive Christian Theology*, (Louisville, Kentucky: Westminster/John Knox Press, 1994), p. 65.

33 It is the problem of discriminating between the gods and religions of the world. This is an important issue, which will be mentioned, but a full treatment of the topic is beyond the scope of the present study.

34 K.B. Osborne, *Christian Sacraments in a Postmodern World: A Theology for the Third Millennium*, (New York: Paulist Press, 1999), p. 57.

24

of the text".[35] However, postmodernism and deconstructionism in particular have their critics, as "deconstruction is not a novel procedure made possible by a recent philosophical discovery. Recontextualisation in general, and inverting hierarchies in particular, has been going on for a long time".[36]

Lastly, the theology of presence becomes the basis for a construal of the themes of the Incarnation and the Death-Resurrection event in Tillich and Rahner (4.3). These themes embody for them the definitive expression of the presence of God. The challenge in Chapter 4 is to adapt their themes without incorporating their metaphysical underpinnings. Moreover, the debate about the status of metaphysics in theology has not been fully resolved. With the jury out, this makes the way clear for re-defining the concept of presence (4.2). Specifically, the study does not rely explicitly on being as a form of epistemic justification.

1.2.2. Limitations and Questions

The limitations and questions in this study concern the following issues:

–   Historical periodisation.
–   Working definitions of modernity and postmodernity.
–   Characterisations of the theologies of Tillich and Rahner.
–   Definitions and use of experience, presence and absence.
–   The nature of the contribution to postmodern Christology.

The limitations concern periodisation, definitions and the nature of the study's contribution to postmodern Christology. Historical periodisation is a methodological issue that has theological implications. Metaphorically, periodisation is about where the line is drawn and on what basis. In that context, periodisation is provisional because the line can always be re-drawn as criteria change. In this study, the issue of periodi-

35   J. Derrida, *Of Grammatology*, G.C. Spivak trans., (Baltimore and London: John Hopkins University Press, 1967, 1974, 1976, 1997), p. 158.
36   R. Rorty, *Contingency, Irony and Solidarity*, (Cambridge, UK: Cambridge University Press, 1989), p. 134; cf. G. Steiner, *Real Presences*, (Chicago: University of Chicago Press, 1989), p. 129 and L. Spencer "Postmodernism, modernity, and the tradition of dissent" in S. Sim ed. *Postmodern Thought*, (Cambridge: Icon Books, 1998), p. 162.

sation surfaces in two major areas. First, in terms of the theological works of Tillich and Rahner, there is the question of the period of study. Second, in terms of comparing their period with today, there is the question of the distinction between modernity and postmodernity. In terms of Tillich and Rahner, 1933-1984 has been selected as the period of study. The period has been selected for various reasons (1.3.1). However, the period of study, the range of works and the number of historical *facts* could be expanded or interpreted in other ways. It is a partly a question of the scope of the study, but it is also a question of the determination of reliable criteria for defining a period. This problem surfaces in another form in relation to the task of defining modernity and postmodernity. The study's definitions of modernity and postmodernity are working definitions (1.4). The term *working definition* implies that there is something provisional about the definition of a historical period (e.g. modernity). In brief, the limitation is the recognition that any periodisation scheme is provisional; it will disclose some things and conceal others. The key question here concerns criteria for defining modernity and postmodernity as distinct historical periods.

There are also hermeneutical problems associated with describing and defining the systems of Tillich and Rahner. Each of their systems is a complex amalgam of philosophical, theological, ethical, spiritual, homiletical and pastoral insights. The complexity raises the issue of determining an appropriate way of describing or characterising their work. Over time their work evolves somewhat abruptly and this further complicates the task of characterisation. In short, the limitation is that any characterisation will be provisional. Further, the task of characterising their work is related to the task of comparing their theologies, which is partly based on the provisional task of characterisation. Certainly, there are similarities between Tillich and Rahner (e.g. Kant as a source) but there are differences too. They are different people (cf. war experience), from different traditions (i.e. Protestant; Catholic) with different methods (cf. correlation; transcendental). This raises the question of the nature of the differences. In this study, Tillich and Rahner will be compared specifically in relation to the issues of experience, presence and absence in a Christological context. The key difference to emerge from the comparison relates to their different understandings of human existence.

Lastly, there is a debate about the meaning and status of experience in philosophy. The question is about finding a definition of experience that

26

has epistemic credibility. There is also a debate about the meaning of presence. This concerns the possibility of defining and using presence in a postmetaphysical way. In theology, the place of presence has been challenged because of presence's apparent dependency on the concept of being as a means of epistemic justification. Further, the study's construal of the ambiguity of experience as presence and absence will be used to explore the meaning of the Christological themes of the Incarnation and the Death-Resurrection. The limitation is that these two Christological themes, while significant parts of their theologies, represent aspects of their vast theologies and the burgeoning field of Christology. In terms of the study's contribution, the key question concerns what can be gleaned from the analysis of the Christological themes.

1.3. Method

The method is primarily argumentation, which incorporates interrelated strategies, namely, philosophical reasoning, historiography, conceptual critique and comparative analysis. In general, the study's terms will be interpreted from the perspective of thematic analysis rather than content analysis (i.e. word studies). The principal themes of experience, presence and absence will be dealt with specifically in Chapter 4. In this context, history and philosophy are important interpretive tools because they place the issues in context, offer new perspectives and fill in knowledge gaps. In particular, philosophy is used to develop the concept of experience and the theology of presence. History is used in three ways. First, history is used to show that postmodernity is a different historical period to modernity on the basis of the discontinuities that exist between the two periods. The difference is significant critically but it is not absolute. Its critical significance lies in the fact that it makes possible a comparative analysis between the era of Tillich and Rahner and today. Second and related to the first, history is used to show that Tillich and Rahner were primarily oriented toward modernity. Third, history is used to define the period of study (1933-1984). This is the period in which they produced their major works and received recognition from their peers, the Church and wider society. While there are some lines of continuity between them and postmodernity, they were primarily moderns. Never-theless, in the end this is a theological study.

1.3.1. Range, Scope and Terms

Concerning the range of the study, the period selected includes primarily works published after 1932. Any periodisation of a scholar's work is provisional, but there are historical, biographical and practical reasons for this periodisation. Concerning Tillich, the year 1933 is a clear turning point. At the macro level of analysis, Hitler became Chancellor on 30th January 1933. At the micro level, Tillich was suspended by the Nazi government 13th April 1933 and subsequently migrated to America. This event had theological impact, "Up to the time of his coming to the States most of Tillich's writings were of a philosophical character rather than systematically theological".[37] Moreover, "Even a cursory examination of Tillich's writings reveals that his scholarship had different orientations before and after his emigration to America".[38] For example, the differ-ence in Tillich's thinking between *The System of the Sciences* (1923) and his *Systematic Theology* (1951, 1957, 1963) reflects a movement from finding a place for theology among other forms of knowledge, in particu-lar theology as part of the science of religion, to an understanding of theology that deals with ultimate concern and sciences that deal with preliminary concerns.[39] Finally, Tillich's quintessential works were pub-lished in the said period, namely *On the Boundary* (1936), *The Protes-tant Era* (1948), *Systematic Theology* I (1951), *The Courage to Be* (1952), *Systematic Theology* II (1957) and *Systematic Theology* III (1963). Concerning Rahner, the year 1933 does not constitute the dra-matic turning point for him as it did for Tillich. In a pragmatic sense, the turning point in Tillich's life is a convenient demarcation point for a

37   J.L. Adams, *Paul Tillich's Philosophy of Culture, Science and Religion*, (New York: Harper and Row, 1965), p. 259.

38   I.E. Thompson, *Being and Meaning: Paul Tillich's Theory of Meaning, Truth and Logic*, (Edinburgh: Edinburgh University Press, 1981), p. 9.

39   P. Weibe, "From system to systematics: the origin of Paul Tillich's theology" in J.J. Carey ed. *Kairos And Logos: Studies in the Roots and Implications of Tillich's Theology*, (Mercer: Mercer University Press, 1978, 1984), p. 116. There are also elements of continuity, e.g. typological understanding of God, p. 117.

28

comparison with Rahner. In 1932, Rahner was ordained priest. In 1933, Rahner began his tertianship and in the following year he undertook doctoral studies. Moreover, he wrote *Spirit in the World* between 1934-36 and the majority of his important works were published after 1933, namely, *Spirit in the World* (1939), *Hearer of the Word* (1941),[40] *Theological Investigations* I (1954), *Quaestiones Disputatae* (1958-84), *Sacramentum Mundi* (1967-69) and *Foundations of Christian Faith* (1976).

The scope of the study is primarily theological. For example, the problem of the absence of God relates to the process of the marginalisation of God. From a sociological perspective, this raises ideological issues. The term *ideology* is used in a value-neutral sense to mean the process by which ideas emerge and how they are expressed and legitimated. Invariably, ideas express the interests of individuals and/or groups (e.g. Western intellectual elites, Christian theologians). While an individual or a group may assert that God is marginalised for ideological reasons, the extent to which God is actually marginalised is another question. In like vein, the apparent religious revival of the late twentieth and early twenty-first centuries does not add weight to the claim that God is actually present in the world. In global terms, the revival may only mean more people practice religion now than in the time of Tillich and Rahner; whether this is true or not in lies outside the scope of the study. In this study, the problem of the absence of God is used to encompass the theological problem that modernity poses for Tillich and Rahner. Likewise, the thesis that God is present in the world is used to encompass the positions of Tillich and Rahner. This has two implications. In the context of modernity, it is the validity of their arguments about the presence of God, which is under scrutiny and not God's location. In the context of postmodernity, it is the validity of the concept of presence, which is under scrutiny. Further, the study's interest in presence could be seen as an aspect of a theology of revelation, but the study does not intend to develop a theology of revelation *per se*; its focus is narrower. The study is philosophically informed, but it is not a philosophy of presence. Ultimately, the terms presence and absence are used as theological terms. Moreover, presence is associated with sacramental

---

40   The study uses Donceel's edition, which is *Hearer of the Word*, Metz's edition is *Hearers of the Word*.

theology, but this is not a study in sacramental theology.[41] Finally, Tillich and Rahner often wrote in a rhetorical style in order to persuade the reader in matters of faith.[42] They were visionaries. They wrote from conviction. This does not take away from their erudition; neither does it imply criticism of other styles (cf. Pannenberg). It says something about how they wrote and why. Hence, the study uses the term *guiding theological vision* or simply *vision* to capture the impetus behind the formation of their theological systems.

The terms God, world and Christ are understood in this study theologically and symbolically. For instance, God is a symbol of Tillich's ground of being or Rahner's incomprehensible one. G.D. Kaufman refers to the terms God, world, humanity and Christ as the four principal symbols from which Christians construct their world-view.[43] In this study, terms like God, world and Christ are critical, but they are used without Kaufman's constructivist assumptions. For Kaufman, theology is God-talk and as such it is a human construct.[44] According to him, the only way to do theology is to reflect on our talk about God. Overall, Kaufman is reacting against the notion that some, or even all, religious knowledge could be considered as unmediated and this is a point on which both Tillich and Rahner would agree with Kaufman. But for Kaufman, unlike Tillich and Rahner, imaginative constructs are the only means available of doing justice to the concept of God.[45]

41   B.J. Cooke, *The Distancing of God: The Ambiguity of Symbol in History and Theology,* (Minneapolis: Fortress Press, 1990), p. 358, "Divine presence is not a matter of 'God being somewhere'; rather presence, as an awareness of an 'other's' self-giving in communication, occurs as a constitutive element of consciousness. Moreover, while there may be 'peak experiences' of this presence that occur in ritual or in exceptional moments of religious awareness, the basic continuing and matrix of divine presence is people's day-by-day experience of being Christian."

42   Thompson, *Being*, pp. 12-13.

43   G.D. Kaufman, "Religious diversity, historical consciousness, and christian theology" in J.H. Hick and P.F. Knitter eds., *The Myth of Christian Uniqueness: Toward a Pluralist Theology of Religions*, (Maryknoll, New York: Orbis Books, 1987), p. 10.

44   G.D. Kaufman, *An Essay on Theological Method*, rev. ed. (Montana: Scholars Press, 1975, 1979).

45   *Ibid.* p. 34.

1.3.2. Historiography

In this study, the primary role of history is to bring greater substance and clarity to the comparisons between the work of Tillich and Rahner and postmodernity. It is about re-contextualising their work. However, history does not solve all of a theologian's problems. Historiography has a mixed status in theological and biblical studies. In some cases, the implicit assumption has been made that recourse to history will remedy deficiencies in knowledge. That is, if there is a theological gap (e.g. resurrection) then the right piece of historical evidence will fill it (e.g. empty tomb). In other cases, an over-reliance on history can be seen to undermine the credibility of orthodox beliefs. That is, if history can explain everything then there is no room for faith (e.g. miracle stories dismissed). Moreover, the field of history has been subject to hermeneutical problems similar to those that have assailed theology. In history, there is wide recognition of problems associated with the nature of historical facts, the interpretation of facts and the development of narratives. However, this study is not going to the other extreme of arguing that historical facts cannot be established and that it is all a matter of different readings of the text, "Even consciously postmodernist reconstructionists are trying to help us to form *better* beliefs about what they think actually happened".[46] So it is important at this juncture to clarify the limits of history.

Even a short survey of historiography will show the limits of history and the hermeneutical problems it shares with theology. In his classic study, E.H. Carr cast a critical eye over historiography.[47] Specifically, Carr questioned the efforts of certain nineteenth century historians who searched for historical facts.[48] He questioned claims like:

- Facts as readily identifiable.
- Facts speak for themselves.
- History is an accumulation of facts.

---

46   C. Butler, *Postmodernism: A Very Short Introduction*, (Oxford: Oxford University Press, 2002), p. 35.

47   E.H. Carr, *What is History?* (Hampshire: Palgrave, 1961, 1986, 2001). Based on a series of radio lectures. Carr (1892-1982) was a bureaucrat, diplomat and journalist, as well as historian, who worked for the British foreign office and a national newspaper (p. x).

48   *Ibid.* p. 3.

In particular, Carr was critical of static or empirical approaches to history. In contrast, he offers a dynamic view of interpretation.[49] His view is based on a number of interactive relationships between fact and interpretation and between past, present and future.[50] In this context, he claims that the historian is part of history.[51] Thus, it is important to understand the historian and the historian's social and historical context.[52] Further, the historian needs to establish standards and tests of significance, because interpretation entails selection on the historian's part and selection is based on historical significance as assigned by the historian.[53] Consequently, "History requires the selection and ordering of facts about the past in the light of some principle or norm of objectivity accepted by the historian, which necessarily includes elements of interpretation. Without this, the past dissolves into a jumble of innumerable isolated and insignificant incidents, and history cannot be written at all".[54] Since the publication of Carr's book, recognition of the role of the interpreter has grown, regardless of whether the interpreter is an historian, a theologian or a philosopher. This raises some problems. For J. Scott, "History is in the paradoxical position of creating the objects it claims only to discover. By creating, I don't mean making things up, but rather constructing them as legitimate and coherent objects of knowledge".[55] Some scholars have taken this further. For M. Oakeshott, the past is understood as a construction based on the present. That is, it is a reading of the present on the basis of the past.[56] The past is not simply appropriated by the present.[57] According to Oakeshott, historiography is a type of thinking or an attitude towards history that produces its own peculiar form of discourse. Unlike scientific discourse, historical discourse cannot establish necessary and sufficient conditions for truth

---

49   *Ibid.* p. 24.
50   *Ibid.* 114.
51   *Ibid.* p. 38.
52   *Ibid.* pp. 34, 38.
53   *Ibid.* pp. 118-119.
54   *Ibid.* p. lxi, from Carr's notes for the proposed second edition.
55   J. W. Scott, "After History?" *History and the Limits of Interpretation: A Symposium,* (Draft: Rice University, Feb 20, 1996), p. 1.
56   M. Oakeshott, "The activity of being an historian" in P. King ed., *The History of Ideas: An Introduction to Method,* (London: Croom Helm, 1983), pp. 69-95.
57   *Ibid.* p. 84.

statements. History deals with occasions and so it has to wrestle with contingent truths.

P. Burke claims that there is a new kind of history writing emerging in which culture is one of the driving forces,

> The cultural relativism implicit here deserves to be emphasized. The philosophical foundation of the new history is the idea that reality is socially or culturally constituted ... This relativism also undermines the traditional distinction between what is central in history and what is peripheral.[58]

Issues in the new history include defining culture and cultural relativism. The so-called new history is plausible but for internal and external reasons alike it is reasonable to speak of the crisis of the traditional paradigm of historical writing. However, "the new paradigm also has its problems: problems of definition, problems of sources, problems of method, problems of explanation".[59] Clearly, there are new hermeneutical problems that need to be addressed and these problems often require a reading between the lines by the interpreter, but on what basis can this reading be conducted? Burke concludes that, "The discipline of history is now more fragmented than ever before".[60] In sum, "new history" or "critical history" offers new ways of seeing. History is text and text can be re-written and re-interpreted.

1.3.3. Philosophical Reasoning

In this study, philosophy is used in three areas: experience, sources and concepts. First, philosophy is used to develop a concept of experience that has epistemological credibility (4.1). Second, the major philosophical sources used by Tillich and Rahner are outlined in order to understand more fully their theological systems (2.1.2; 3.1.1). This is not an easy task because Tillich and Rahner draw on the work of many philosophers. Moreover, they re-work the source material and as a result the sources are often deeply embedded within their theological systems. In addition, they do not consistently name their sources. Third, it is neces-

---

58 P. Burke, "Overture: the new history, its past and its future" in P. Burke ed., *New Perspectives in Historical Writing*, (Cambridge: Polity Press, 1991), pp. 3-4.

59 *Ibid.* p. 9.

60 *Ibid.* p. 18.

sary to think philosophically about certain concepts (e.g. presence, onto-theology). Subsequently, a discussion on the nature of philosophy will highlight some of the problems philosophy holds in common with other disciplines and reinforce the need for the use of constituent strategies in this study.

In broad terms, "philosophy is rationally critical thinking, of a more or less systematic kind about the general nature of the world (metaphysics or theory of existence), the justification of belief (epistemology or theory of knowledge), and the conduct of life (ethics or theory of value)".[61] Philosophy is a form of critical thinking and as such philosophy is one academic discipline among many (e.g. history). Like other scholars, philosophers work in collaboration and in competition with their peers in an attempt to establish their positions. However, traditionally philosophy has been regarded as different from other disciplines because of the specific object of its version of critical thinking, in that a philosopher reflects upon the nature and process of thinking itself as well as related concepts of reason, truth, mind, matter and the like. In terms of its own history, philosophy helped to create the Enlightenment and modern philosophy is in large part a product of the Enlightenment. For instance, philosophy in tandem with the newly emerging confidence in science helped foster the Enlightenment's optimism in human reason and until recently, a critical understanding of reason was regarded as belonging almost exclusively to the domain of philosophy. Today, thinking itself is studied within psychology, neurology and computer studies and new fields have developed that cross over traditional boundaries (e.g. cognitive science). Consequently, in certain quarters, philosophy is experiencing the impact of hermeneutics in general and deconstruction in particular. Arguably, philosophy is undergoing a kind of "splintering".[62] Philosophy can be construed as one reading of a text among other possible and equally valid readings.[63] That is, under the impact of hermeneutics, philosophy cannot claim a privileged position. Of course, this raises

---

61   A. Quinton, "Philosophy" OCP, p. 666.

62   J. Lyotard, The *Postmodern Condition: A Report on Knowledge*, G. Bennington and B. Massumi trans., (Minnesota: University of Minneapolis, 1979, 1984), p. 41.

63   J. Lyotard, "Apostil on narratives" in *The Postmodern Explained: Correspondence 1982-1985*, J. Pefanis and M. Thomas trans. ed. and D. Barry, B. Maher, J Pefanis, V Spate and M Thomas trans., (Minneapolis and London: University of Minnesota Press, 1988, 1992), pp. 17-18.

34

other issues, such as whether or not the notion of multiple readings of a text is a philosophical or literary issue in the first place. Thus, the task of arriving at an adequate definition of philosophy has been complicated by the almost universal impact of hermeneutical developments.

In terms of sources, this is a complex problem. If philosophy is "thinking about thinking",[64] then Tillich and Rahner worked philosophically. They thought about thinking and categories of thought. In the process, they use a variety of sources, many of which stem from philosophy. The task of clearly delineating and accurately describing their philosophical sources is difficult because of the way they integrated them into their theological systems. Concerning Tillich's use of Otto, Heywood Thomas observes: "This is an interesting example of the way in which the number and variety of Tillich's points of contact with the history of philosophy and theology make it almost impossible to analyse exactly his relation to this or that particular figure."[65] Positively, the task of identifying the philosophical sources can help explain some of the nuances in the theological systems of Tillich and Rahner, but there are limits as to what can be gleaned of the sources from their theological systems. The extent of these limits relates primarily to how they interpret and incorporate philosophies and philosophers into their systems. Clearly, they worked and re-worked their sources. In the process, specific sources have been melded together with other elements within their systems. By analogy, attempts to isolate clinically the sources of Tillich and Rahner are reminiscent of the German form-critical school's attempts to isolate the authentic (or primary) level within biblical texts. While that movement had its measure of success, many of its exponents pushed the technique beyond reasonable limits into the realm of speculation.[66]

In summary, this is a theological study that concentrates on the theological writings of Tillich and Rahner published from 1933. The aim is to make an incremental contribution to postmodern Christology. It assumes that experience has a role in epistemic justification. It assumes

---

64   Quinton, "philosophy", p. 666.

65   J. Heywood Thomas, *Tillich*, (London and New York: Continuum, 2000), p. 17.

66   H.W. Wolff, *Joel and Amos*, W. Janzen, S.D. McBride and E.A. Muenchaw trans., S.D. McBride ed. (Philadelphia: Fortress Press, 1969, 1977), Wolff posits six levels of redaction, with the first level containing the so-called authentic words of the prophet Amos.

that theology is provisional, existence is contingent and experience is ambiguous. Thus, theological constants have to be re-interpreted in new settings by new faith communities.

1.4. Modernity and Postmodernity

1.4.1. Modernism and Modernity

The aim of this section is to establish working definitions of modernity and postmodernity for the purpose of comparing Tillich and Rahner with the present era.[67] The four related terms of modernity, postmodernity, modernism and postmodernism are hard to define precisely.[68] Typically, modernism and postmodernism refer to what can be described as a variegated cultural movement of values, ideas and philosophical positions, which are expressed in many forms (e.g. architecture, art, literature), whereas the terms modernity and postmodernity refer to "a period concept".[69] In short, the study is adopting working definitions where modernity and postmodernity refer to historical periods, while modernism and postmodernism refer to broad cultural movements. Clearly, they are working definitions, which means there is an element of provisionality, but working definitions make it possible to make critical comparisons. Moreover, there are reasons for making these definitions, which will be presented in this section.

---

67   H. Küng, *Global Responsibility: In Search of a New World Ethic*, J. Bowden trans., (London: SCM Press, 1990, 1991), p. 3, and the study's definitions are heuristic devices (i.e. "search-term").

68   F.L. Cross and E.A. Livingstone eds. *The Oxford Dictionary of the Christian Church*, 3rd ed., (Oxford, New York: Oxford University Press, 1997), hereafter ODCC, pp. 1098-1099. For example, within art the term modernism is a relatively late phase. Within the Catholic tradition, there is a movement known as Modernism. This was an eclectic movement of the nineteenth century, which embraced attitudes symptomatic of modernity (e.g. attitude to scripture, history). Pius X condemned it in 1907. In this study, the term modernism is used as a generic term embodying a broad cultural movement.

69   G. Ward "Introduction" in G. Ward ed. *The Postmodern God: A Theological Reader*, (Oxford: Blackwell Publishing, 1997), p. xxiv.

36

The word *modernity* comes from the Latin *modernus*, from the adverb *modo* (equivalent to *nunc* meaning *now*). It involves perceptions and judgements about the past. Modernity is inherently self-reflexive. For instance, *we are moderni* whereas *they were antiqui.* These judgements entail a distancing from the past because the past is considered, by comparison with the present, as *passé*.[70] Ted Peters views this distancing as the central characteristic of modernity, which gives rise to the development of critical consciousness; "the essence of critical consciousness is distance. Distance takes the forms of objectification, nonparticipation, and alienation".[71] The roots of modernity are found in the thirteenth century, but modernity proper emerges with the development of the Enlightenment. Ideas associated with modernity include reason, progress, tolerance, individualism, secularisation, nationalism, urbanisation and land consolidation.[72] Küng claims that modernity, as a historic period, begins in earnest with Descartes and ends within the years encompassed by 1918 and the end of World War II.[73] For Küng, the seventeenth century is a turning point because "the new becomes normative".[74] Scientific theory is no longer the aim but "the means of realizing a (rational) practice".[75] The question of a basis for certainty becomes paramount and by relying on methodical, radical and universal doubt, "the fact of one's

---

70 G. Benavides, "Modernity" in M.C. Taylor ed., *Critical Terms for Religious Studies*, (Chicago: University of Chicago Press, 1998), p. 187.

71 T. Peters, *God-the World's Future: Systematic Theology for a Postmodern Era*, (Minneapolis: Fortress Press, 1992), p. 9.

72 D. Allen, *Christian Belief in a Postmodern World: The Full Wealth of Conviction*, (Louisville, Kentucky: Westminster/John Knox Press, 1989), p. 6. Allen argues that there is an integral connection between modernity and the Enlightenment. He identifies four principles of the Enlightenment, which become the foundations of modernity. First, the idea that God is superfluous is taken for granted within intellectual circles. Second, morality is based on reason and religion is not required. Third, science, technology and education become the basis for confidence in social progress. Fourth, knowledge is inherently good.

73 Küng, *Global Responsibility*, p. 3.

74 Küng, *Christianity: The Religious Situation of Our Time*, (London: SCM Press, 1994, 1995), p. 651; cf. S. Toulmin *Cosmopolis: The Hidden Agenda of Modernity*, (Chicago: University of Chicago Press, 1990, 1992), p. 12, Toulmin claims that most scholars see the period encompassing Galileo and Descartes as formative for the concept of modernity.

75 Küng, *Christianity*, p. 671.

own existence is the foundation of all certainty".[76] Subsequently, a distinction is made between *res extensa* (extension, body, matter, external world) and *res cogitans* (thought, spirit, self, internal world). This distinction becomes the basis for the modern dualisms of subject/object and humanity/nature. A materialistic world-view emerges in which value is ascribed to the human capacity to interpret phenomena in terms of mathematical computations. Overall, reason is prized because it enables individuals to think and act *correctly*. Consequently, the human being is considered primarily as rational and the spiritual aspect is relegated or even dismissed because it is seen as non-rational or non-sensible. The social development of individualism waxes as the influence of organised religion wanes and the locus of certainty shifts from God (i.e. marginalisation) to the self and human reason (i.e. turn to the subject).[77]

Emerging from the Enlightenment, modernity accepts the idea that there is an unambiguous division between the *material* and *spiritual*. In practice, modernity focuses its attention on the material to the exclusion of the spiritual. It is based on what Charles Taylor describes as a closed world structure,

> I want to explore here the constitution in modernity of what I shall call "closed" or "horizontal" worlds. I mean by this shapes of our "world" in Heidegger's sense which leave no place for the "vertical" or "transcendent," but which in one way or another close these off, render them inaccessible, or even unthinkable.[78]

In addition, modernity presumes a mechanistic view of the material world (i.e. world as machine). The mechanistic view is in part a corollary of the original division between the material and the spiritual. Ironically, the acceptance of a mechanistic view tacitly reinforces the acceptance of the idea of a division between the material and the spiritual as a statement of *fact*. Concurrently, modernity employs a more restricted and technical use of reason to study the world that is linked to the facts and expects a version of mathematical precision. Modernity achieves this with a degree of cultural, economic, technological and scientific success.

---

76   *Ibid.*

77   The development of historical critical method (e.g. Reimarus) parallels the development of modernity, where the rational is used to account for and in some instances dismiss non-rational aspects in biblical texts (e.g. miracles).

78   C. Taylor, "Closed World Structures" in M.A. Wrathall ed., *Religion After Metaphysics*, (Cambridge: Cambridge University Press, 2003), p. 47.

38

Throughout, modernity accords privileged epistemological status to the outcomes of the use of this type of reason (e.g. *hard* science) over and above the potential benefits of other types of reason (e.g. Tillich's intuitive reason). Further, the material, the methods and outcomes of the analysis of the material, are construed as objective and the term objective is invested with positive moral value. That is, the objective or striving for the objective is seen as virtuous, at least in an instrumental way. The attribution of positive moral value occurs because the objective is amenable to the technical form of reason and in some instances is open to empirical verification. Finally, the attribution of positive moral value hinges on the presumption of the equation of objectivity and truth. That is, if something is objective then it is true, or it is a fact, and facts are true. All told, the objective, or acting objectively, is highly regarded and sought after in modernity. Toulmin describes this in terms of decontextualisation, that is, the search for abstract and universal rules or norms.[79] Significantly, Toulmin claims that many philosophers in the 1930's and 1940's argued that modernity started with the era of Galileo and Descartes and in keeping with Descartes they searched for decontextualised principles (i.e. abstract, universal, ahistorical).[80] In many ways Tillich's and Rahner's perceptions of modernity support Toulmin's thesis in that there is a tendency in their work toward the development of abstract, universal, even ahistorical principles. Nevertheless, like Toulmin, they also critiqued the prevailing view of modernity (Chapters 2 and 3).

The gap between the material and the spiritual is characteristic of modernity; this, combined with a new understanding of causality, led to the situation where the development of modernity implied the absence of God. For instance, historically the cause of the plague had been attributed to the wrath of God. However, there was no major outbreak of the

---

79 Toulmin, *Cosmopolis*, p. 75.
80 *Ibid.* pp. ix, 104, for Toulmin, "decontextualization" occurs when processes of human reason are divorced from historical and cultural contexts. The key example in Toulmin is Descartes. Toulmin argues two things in relation to Descartes. First, it is incorrect to assume that Descartes was immune to his historical and cultural context. For instance, the instability of the thirty years war and the accompanying existential need for certainty is transmogrified in Descartes into a philosophical (rational) quest for certainty. Second, Descartes failed to provide a perfect foundation for certainty.

plague in Western Europe after 1720 because of the control and quarantine of the migration of infected communities,[81]

> Within two centuries after Newton, the secularity of the modern outlook had fully established itself. Mechanistic materialism had dramatically proved its explanatory power and utilitarian efficacy. Experiences and events that appeared to defy accepted scientific principles – alleged miracles and faith healings, self-proclaimed religious revelations and spiritual ecstasies, prophecies, symbolic interpretations of natural phenomena, encounters with God or the devil – were now increasingly regarded as the effects of madness, charlatanry, or both.[82]

In effect, the absence of God could be described as the secularisation of the Western world.

Secularisation has been seen as part of the heritage of the Enlightenment and as a defining feature of modernity. Sociologist Peter Berger challenges the assumption that we live in a secularised world. This has been a long-term interest of Berger's. In an earlier work Berger refers to the process in terms of "The alleged demise of the supernatural".[83] More recently, he describes the thinking behind secularisation as "secularization theory".[84] For Berger, the central idea in secularisation theory stems from the Enlightenment and the presumed correlation between the development of modernity and the marginalisation of God. Berger claims the relationship between modernity and religion is more complex than this *either/or* scenario.[85] Berger does not offer a solution or imply there is one. For Berger, it is a difficult task to define secularisation, let alone assess the extent to which secularisation has occurred and it is an equally difficult task to compare religions in terms of their relationship to modernity.[86] Further, Berger argues that interest in Christianity *per se* appears to have waned in Europe (e.g. falling church attendance) and that there has been significant growth in some religions (e.g. Islam; evangelical Christianity). However, Berger claims that the situation in Europe has not been satisfactorily researched and that interest in religion may

---

81 J.M. Roberts, *The Triumph of the West*, (London: British Broadcasting Company, 1985), p. 259.

82 R. Tarnas, *The Passion of the Western Mind*, (London: Pimlico, 1991), p. 303.

83 P.L. Berger, *A Rumor of Angels: Modern Society and the Rediscovery of the Supernatural*, (Garden City, New York: Anchor Books, 1969), p. 1.

84 Berger, *Desecularization*, pp. 1-18.

85 *Ibid.* p. 3.

86 *Ibid.* p. 13.

have become diffused rather than diminished. In other words, the changes in Europe reflect "a shift in the institutional location of religion".[87] Likewise, Benavides contends that secularisation is in many ways not the disappearance of religion but its differentiation and consolidation.[88]

In conclusion, the claim that God is absent from the world is not necessarily invalidated by empirical evidence, which attests that proportionally more people believe in God now than in a previous era. Even if *everyone* believed in God, this does not necessarily mean God is present. Conversely, even if *no one* believed in God, this does not necessarily mean God is absent. The current claims about God's absence appear to rest more with suspicion of institutional religion and its metanarratives than empirical evidence. Indeed, Berger surmises that secularisation theory is in part a product of "a globalized *elite* culture".[89] He speculates that a Western-influenced "international subculture", which advocates Enlightenment ideas and values, may be responsible for promulgating secularisation theory.[90] Similarly, Hodgson speculates that "elite intellectual circles" are responsible for *God is absent* arguments.[91] Likewise Caputo, "since religion was reported missing mostly by the intellectuals; no one outside the academy thought that it had gone anywhere at all".[92] Nevertheless, Berger is speculating. Even if arguments about the absence of God derive solely from these so-called elites, the arguments exist and need to be addressed because they are part of a globalised intellectual

---

87 *Ibid.* p. 10.
88 Benavides, "Modernity", p. 196.
89 Berger, *Desecularization*, p. 10.
90 *Ibid.* pp. 10-11; cf. Carr, "What is History?" p. 111, "it is significant that almost all our latter-day prophets of decline, our sceptics who see no meaning in history and assume that progress is dead, belong to that sector of the world and to that class of society which have triumphantly played a leading and predominant part in the advance of civilization for several generations".
91 Hodgson, *Winds of the Spirit*, p. 56.
92 J.D. Caputo, *On Religion*, (London and New York: Routledge, 2001), p. 66, written for popular consumption, it has some insightful assessments of postmodern issues; cf. P. van Inwagen, "Quam Dilecta" in T.V. Morris ed., *God and the Philosophers: The Reconciliation of Faith and Reason*, (New York and Oxford: Oxford University Press, 1994), p. 36, on a personal note, van Inwagen states, "I know that sneers directed at God and the church, which – I hope I am not giving away any secret here – are very common in the academy, were becoming increasingly intolerable to me".

culture. In brief, sociological insights are useful, in that they clarify the nature of claims about the absence of God. However, this study seeks to make a theological response to the absence of God. Clearly, the very nature of modernity has been bound to the notion of the absence of God and the issue now is the nature of absence in postmodernity.

1.4.2. Postmodernism and Postmodernity

For Tillich and Rahner, modernity posed a challenge for Christianity. Today, postmodernity poses new challenges:

> No unmoved mover, no gods, no prophetic longing for righteousness, no Jesus restlessly healing and teaching and running risks. The passionless arrogance of the post-modernist style makes 'post-modernist religion' oxymoronic. The post-modernists don't care much for 'purpose' or 'meaning' or searches for them. That is why they give us such large chunks of Nietzsche.[93]

There are many possible responses to the challenge of postmodernity. Some scholars see it as an opportunity to overcome modernity's problems, rather than as a problem to be eradicated.[94] Others refute the existence of postmodernity as a distinct historical period in defense of more orthodox theological and philosophical positions.[95] Others recognise the challenge it holds under the banner of high modernity, late modernity or the end of modernity (i.e. "the last gasp of the past"), but do not necessarily see postmodernity as a distinct period.[96] In all these, the existence of postmodernity as a distinct historical period is downplayed or refuted.[97] Postmodernity, as a distinct historical period, is difficult to establish precisely or conclusively,

---

93   W. Hamilton, *A Quest for the Post-Historical Jesus*, (London: SCM Press, 1993), p. 17.

94   Peters, *God-the World's Future*, p. 15; Ward, "Introduction", pp. xxi-xxii.

95   The words postmodern and postmodernity are absent from the index of particular scholars, e.g. J. Thornhill, *Modernity: Christianity's Estranged Child Reconstructed*, (Cambridge, U.K.: Wm. B. Eerdmans, 2000).

96   M.C. Taylor, *About Religion: Economies of Faith in Virtual Culture*, (Chicago, London: University of Chicago Press), p. 21.

97   Benavides, "Modernity", p. 200. Thornhill, *Modernity*, pp. 54-55.

42

'Postmodernity' is a problematic concept, to be sure, and is more an expression of confusion than a definition for a new world epoch which does not yet have a name of its own, but now towards the end of the century people generally are becoming increasingly aware of it. For me, too, postmodernity is neither a magic word nor an omnibus word which explains everything, nor is it a taunt or a slogan, but a term which, while open to misunderstanding, is heuristically unavoidable: it is a 'search-term' which needs to be defined more closely and which provides the structure for a problem, the analysis of what distinguishes our epoch from the modern period.[98]

In this study, the term postmodernity is a heuristic device. It is used in the sense of a constellation or syndrome, where a syndrome is a set of recurring characteristics.[99] Further, the recurring characteristics that constitute the syndrome (or constellation) of postmodernity include the rejection of grand theory, questioning of older cause and effect explanations, the rejection of the notion of continuous development, a willingness to focus on difference and discontinuity, a desire to deconstruct or change what is already known and a increasing concern to give voice to the marginalised.

In specific terms, this study is using three identifying characteristics associated with pluralism, language and intersubjectivity, along with historical discontinuity, to establish postmodernity as a distinct period. Clearly, there is an element of circularity in that postmodern characteristics are used to establish postmodernity as a distinct period, which in turn encompasses postmodernism. Hence, historiography is important here as a means of establishing independent grounds for treating postmodernity as a distinct historical period. Moreover, these historical grounds are supported by new philosophical critiques (e.g. Lyotard). To sum up, in conjunction with the three recurring characteristics, there are historical and philosophical grounds in favour of establishing postmodernity as a distinct historical period, but the process of making a boundary is always provisional (cf. periodisation). The purpose of establishing postmodernity as a distinct period is to make possible a critical comparison with Tillich and Rahner in relation to their period.

98   Küng, *Global Responsibility*, p. 3.
99   New SOED.

1.4.3. Defining Characteristics of Postmodernity

In this study, the distinguishing characteristics of postmodernity represent key points of discontinuity (i.e. pluralism, language, subject). The characteristics indicate a change of mood with different questions, which in turn supports the assertion it is a different period. This approach is in keeping with postmodern interest in discontinuity. Scott, for example, focuses on discontinuity instead of linear development, "Historical investigation locates the breaks, describes them as the deviations they are from established norms, and attempts to account for their emergence – not in terms of general principles of development, but in terms of the specificity of their occurrence".[100] For Scott, discontinuity posits "differences" between past and present. These differences are decisive and not simply a means of contrast: for instance, postmodernity deals with issues that were marginal or lacking during modernity (e.g. cloning). Likewise, Allen concludes, with a degree of poetic license, that,

> A massive intellectual revolution is taking place that is perhaps as great as that which marked off the modern world from the Middle Ages. The foundations of the modern world are collapsing, and we are entering a postmodern world. The principles forged during the Enlightenment (c. 1600-1780), which formed the foundations of the modern mentality, are crumbling.[101]

In addition to the three distinguishing characteristics, there are historical and philosophical grounds for seeing postmodernity as a distinct historical period.

Historical and Philosophical Grounds for Establishing
a Distinctive Period

The beginning of the transition from modernity to postmodernity is not clear. The critical factor here is the establishment of reasonable historical grounds for the discernment of significant discontinuity between the two periods. The antecedents of postmodernity are evident in Nietzsche and his perspectivism, which prefigures postmodern suspicion of metanarratives in general and the Christian metanarrative in particular, certainly as

100   Scott, "After History?" p. 8.
101   Allen, *Christian Belief*, p. 2.

44

understood in relation to classical theism.[102] Further, Küng on historical grounds considers the end of modernity and the beginning of postmodernity as occurring between 1918 (e.g. immense loss of life, new treaties and borders) and the end of World War II (e.g. holocaust, Hiroshima; Cold War). Undoubtedly, the two World Wars played a major role in changing lives, nations and ideas and influenced a growing mood of disenchantment with modernity's faith in reason and progress. The mood of disenchantment has been described as a loss of innocence.[103] This change of mood is one point of discontinuity between the two periods, embodying a shift of consciousness away from post-Enlightenment self-confidence and the unqualified belief in human progress. Specifically, the period between the two wars is a significant transition phase. Interestingly, while the ground is being prepared for postmodernity, there is in some quarters a revival of modernity.[104] The horrors of the Great War (1914-1918) and the impact of the Great Depression (1929-1933) led certain scholars to seek Cartesian-like universal, abstract truths (e.g. return to formalism), in the hope that the vicissitudes of post-war existence might be transcended.[105] Nonetheless, this rather specific revival was out of kilter with the more general change of mood,

> I would argue that the project of modernity (the realization of universality) has not been forsaken or forgotten but destroyed, "liquidated." There are several modes of destruction, several names that are symbols for them. "Auschwitz" can be taken as a paradigmatic name for the tragic "incompletion" of modernity".[106]

Postmodernity emerges as a distinctive period during the 1960's; "it was in the sixties that the tide began to turn".[107] The 1960's witnessed the beginnings of major social, political and cultural transformations in Western culture. The danger here is that the sixties is a period of signifi-

---

102 Nietzsche, *Beyond Good and Evil*, [1886, p. 53], in *Vision of Nietzsche*, pp. 59-60.

103 A.C. Thiselton, *Interpreting God and the Postmodern Self: On Meaning, Manipulation and Promise*, (Edinburgh: T and T Clark, 1995), p. 11.

104 Toulmin, *Cosmopolis*, pp. 156-157.

105 *Ibid.* p. 153.

106 Lyotard, "Apostil", p. 18

107 Ward, "Introduction", p. xxxviii. Toulmin, *Cosmopolis*, p. 162, claims the sixties is a significant period of transition. He prefers to describe the new phase as the "third phase of modernity" (p. 203) rather than postmodernity. He does not see the distinction between the terms *third phase of modernity* and *postmodernity* as significant, the significance is that a new historical phase begins in the sixties.

cance for *baby boomer* scholars, thus running the risk of overemphasising the importance of their own formative era and experiences. Nonetheless, a series of developments took place that changed Western consciousness ranging from the Bay of Pigs (1961) and the assassinations John F. Kennedy (1963) and Martin Luther King (1968) to Vatican II (1962-5), Beatlemania and the rise of Pop culture (1963-7), birth control, the sexual revolution, the Stonewall Inn resistance and the lunar landing (1969). Moreover, the Tet offensive (1968) disturbed American and Western self-confidence and led eventually to the Paris Peace accords (1973). The student and worker riots in Paris (1968) fostered the growing postmodernist movement in France. All these developments represented significant symbolic as well as historical changes. There was a parallel upheaval in theological circles and ecclesial traditions with the advent of the so-called death of God theology (e.g. Vahanian's *The Death of God*).[108] In addition, in the eyes of many Catholics and interested onlookers, the impact of *Humanae Vitae* (1968) implicitly undermined both the authority of the Christian metanarrative and the authority of the ecclesial *legislators* (Lyotard's term),

> The 'long 1960's,' ending around 1973, was not at all the frivolous decade it is so often painted. A good claim can be made for saying that it was the most important postwar period, the most pivotal, when man's basic condition – the nature of his very freedom – came under threat and under scrutiny, for the reason that his psychology, his self-awareness, was changing. The shift from a class-based sociology to an individual psychology, the rise of new groups to identify with (race, gender, students) changed not only self-awareness but politics.[109]

Since the sixties, social changes have taken place almost exponentially. The political map has continued to change. The dismantling of the Berlin Wall (1989) and the apartheid system in South Africa (1991) represent major political as well as symbolic changes. There have been ground breaking developments in fields like cosmology, genetics, computer technology and reproductive medicine. In addition, the full emergence of

---

108 G. Vahanian, *The Death of God: The Culture of Our Post-Christian Era*, (New York: George Braziller, 1957, 1959, 1960, 1961); W. Hamilton, "Death of God theology" in D.W. Musser and J.L. Price eds., *A New Handbook of Christian Theology*, (Nashville: Abingdon Press, 1992), pp. 120-121. It goes back to a media event in 1965, in the *New York Times* and *Time* magazine.

109 P. Watson, *A Terrible Beauty: The People and Ideas that Shaped the Modern Mind*, (London: Phoenix Press, 2000), pp. 551-552.

a hermeneutics of suspicion has meant Western intellectual approaches themselves have undergone changes. Consequently, individuals who have been schooled in the Western intellectual tradition and others who have been influenced by them are wary of metanarratives. Just as proponents of the Enlightenment project were suspicious of the authority of the Church in matters of faith, reason and liberty, there is now suspicion of grand schemes in theological, philosophical and political domains, that is, schemes that claim a privileged epistemological position,

> The thesis proposed here, on the basis of an analysis of cyberspace as a cultural metaphor for postmodernism, is that modernism is linked to specific conceptions of time, space, and substance, and that postmodernism explodes the myths and ideologies constructing these conceptions.[110]

In summary, postmodernity represents a new period in history, that is, the next historical period after modernity. The boundary between the two periods cannot be defined precisely. Thus, Hodgson uses the term postmodern "as a way of indicating a broad historical passage".[111] It is more appropriate to describe the difference between two periods as the result of historical transition in which significant points of discontinuity emerge than as the existence of a sharp division between two periods. In other words, there are significant differences between the two periods and these emerged over time. The argument in favour of these significant differences is supported on historical and philosophical grounds, in conjunction with the three postmodern characteristics relating to pluralism, language and the intersubjectivity.

Pluralism

In this study, pluralism is a defining characteristic of postmodernity,

> Postmodernity in the strict sense … seeks to describe the developments which really leave behind ('post-') them a modernity that has become questionable, without challenging the achievements of modernity in a pessimistic view of culture. There will be no going back here to a uniform interpretation of the world.[112]

110 Ward, "Introduction", p. xvii.
111 Hodgson, *Winds of the Spirit*, p. 55.
112 Küng, *Christianity*, pp. 773-4.

In particular, the phenomenon of religious pluralism is not new: what is
new is the heightened awareness of the epistemological and ethical implications of religious pluralism, especially within Western intellectual
circles. An implicit judgement here, which is part of the new awareness,
is that all religions are of equal value and no one religion can lay claim
to a privileged epistemological position. Indeed, the effect of the awareness of pluralism is the challenge it poses to a Christianity that claims to
be in possession of a privileged epistemological position. Generally,
world religions present such a claim in the form of legitimising metanarratives (cf. crisis of representation).[113] For Lyotard, the two myths of
legitimation are, "the liberation of humanity and ... the speculative unity
of all knowledge".[114] In Lyotard, the appeal to a metanarrative is a feature of modernity: "Simplifying to the extreme, I define *postmodern* as
incredulity toward metanarratives".[115] His critique includes the Christian
metanarrative,

> The "metanarratives" I was concerned with in *The Postmodern Condition* are those
> that have marked modernity: the progressive emancipation of reason and freedom,
> the progressive or catastrophic emancipation of labor ... the enrichment of all hu-
> manity through the progress of capitalist technoscience, and even – if we include
> Christianity itself in modernity ... – the salvation of creatures through the conver-
> sion of souls to the Christian metanarrative of martyred love.[116]

However, Lyotard has been criticised for inconsistency, as "Lyotard's
own account nonetheless remains indebted to what he identifies as – in
order to distance himself from – the Enlightenment metanarrative of
knowledge as emancipatory".[117]

In a theological context, A.E. McGrath sees postmodernity as a reaction to the totalising effects of the Enlightenment, "Nevertheless, it is
possible to identify its leading general feature, which is the deliberate

---

113 Lyotard, *Postmodern Condition*, p. 8, his interest is in "the legitimation of the
legislator"; cf. "Apostil", p. 20, the later Lyotard expands on his understanding of
narrative to accommodate a more highly nuanced understanding of human existence.

114 *Postmodern Condition*, p. ix (from the foreword by Fredric Jameson).

115 *Ibid.* p. xxiv.

116 Lyotard, "Apostil", pp. 17-18

117 D. J. Herman ,"Modernism versus Postmodernism: Towards an Analytic Distinction" in J. Natoli and L. Hutcheon eds. *The Postmodern Reader*, (Albany: State
University of New York, 1993), p. 163.

and systematic abandonment of centralizing narratives".[118] Generally, the term totalisation is used in postmodern literature in the negative sense of the homogenisation of differences.[119] For example, the danger of the Christian metanarrative is that it reduces or eliminates the differences that exist between it and other religions. Further, attention in postmodernism has been directed toward the significance of the interpreter in relation to metanarratives and the construction of narratives in general. J.B. Miller observes that the postmodern world is evolutionary and humanity is "a contingent (i.e., not necessary) product of universal natural processes".[120] The world is now "relative, indeterminate, and participatory".[121] In historiography, Ankersmit argues that the new focus on the interpreter and the interpretation process does not eliminate the need for critical discrimination. Indeed, there is a need to focus on signification and the distinction between the interpretation and the interpreter.[122] In summary, postmodernity, as a new historical period, includes a growing awareness of religious pluralism, the impact of legitimising narratives and the hermeneutical significance of the interpreter. Moreover, there is also the apparent failure of the old metaphysical systems, "the philosophical counterpart of the sociological dictum that grand stories have lost their credibility".[123]

Language

In this study, language plays a role in identifying postmodernity as a new period. The focus on language is a significant aspect of postmodernity, whether it reflects concerns about metanarratives or problems of refer-

118 A.E. McGrath, *Christian Theology: An Introduction*, 3rd ed., (Oxford: Blackwell, 2001), p. 112.

119 K. Hart, *The Trespass of the Sign: Deconstruction, Theology and Philosophy*, (New York: Fordham University Press, 1989, 2000), p. 24, in the context of Derrida's deconstruction, Hart describes totalising as attempts "to delimit wholly and homogeneously" textual meaning.

120 J.B. Miller, "The Emerging Postmodern World" in F.D. Burnham ed., *Postmodern Theology: Christian Faith in a Pluralist World*, (San Francisco: Harper Collins, 1989), p. 8.

121 *Ibid.* p. 9.

122 Ankersmit, "Historicism", p. 155.

123 G. De Schrijver "Postmodernity and the withdrawal of the divine: A challenge for theology", in L. Boeve and L. Leijssen eds., *Sacramental Presence in a Postmodern Context*, (Leuven: Leuven University Press, 1997), p. 44.

ence, meaning and truth. This interest in language has its precursors like Heidegger's *Poetry, Language, Thought*.[124] Similarly, Wittgenstein turned his attention to language as it is used in everyday activities (e.g. language games), "the meaning of a word is its use in the language".[125] More recently, the concept of *language games* is an important aspect of Lyotard's work. He argues that it can only be understood on the basis of his theory agonistics.[126] Significantly, this approach entails more than focusing on the meaning of words as it includes a different way of philosophising,

> From the point of view of both *Philosophical Investigations* and *Being and Time*, the typical error of traditional philosophy is to imagine that there could be, indeed that there somehow *must* be, entities which are atomic in the sense of being what they are independent of their relation to any other entities (e.g., God, the transcendental subject, sense-data, simple names).[127]

The issue of language is also related to pluralism. For example, pluralism leads to: the awareness of difference and relativity, problems associated with metanarratives (Lyotard), power associated with discourse (Foucault) and the problem of reference (Derrida).[128] In the light of this, language like the latent Church (Tillich) or the anonymous Christian (Rahner) can be construed as a metanarrative that leads to the devaluation of other religions. Interestingly, Lindbeck addresses the use of language as a model for understanding Christianity; "though postliberal antifoundationalism need not imply relativism or fideism, the question remains of how to exhibit the intelligibility and possible truth of the religious message to those who no longer understand the traditional

---

124 M. Heidegger, "Building dwelling thinking," in *Poetry, Language, Thought*, A. Hofstadter trans. and introduction, (New York: Harper and Row, 1971), p. 146, "Man acts as though *he* were the shaper and master of language, while in fact *language* remains the master of man".

125 Wittgenstein, *Philosophical Investigations*, p. 20, cf. p. 11, "Here the term 'language-*game*' is meant to bring into prominence the fact that the *speaking* of a language is part of an activity, or a form of life".

126 Lyotard, *Postmodern Condition*, p. 10, which is Lyotard's language game.

127 R. Rorty, "Wittgenstein, Heidegger, and the reification of language" in C. Guigon ed., *The Cambridge Companion To Heidegger*, (Cambridge: Cambridge University Press, 1993), p. 347.

128 In short, the problem of reference is concerned about the relationship between language and reality.

50

words".[129] Lindbeck endorses a cultural-linguistic model, which emphasises form over matter, form over experience, code over encoded. In this approach, experience is derivative.[130] He likens the issue of categorial adequacy to the use of a map. True religion is like having the true map; it depends on how the map is used. For the cultural-linguistic model, meaning is found in the use of language and not behind it, hence the importance of description. However, Lindbeck implicitly treats the Biblical text as metanarrative.[131] Further, postmodernism presents a specific theological challenge,

> The challenge of postmodernity, I contend, is to "speak meaningfully" of God's presence and action in the world. The presence of God may indeed be a function of our ability to speak meaningfully of God. When language fails, so also presence fails since language is the means by which what is not empirically immediate is made present. Through language we call into being a whole world of near and distant things, events, ideas, values. In this sense the presence of God is a language-event since God is not an empirical, ostensible, worldly object.[132]

Consider Rorty, an analytic philosopher, who presumes the "sheer contingency" of language and whose work on language fits the syndrome of postmodernism.[133] He is critical of the search for some source of external truth, which manifests itself in the process of replacing God with an alternative divinity,

> Beginning in the seventeenth century we tried to substitute a love of truth for a love of God, treating the world described by science as a quasi divinity. Beginning at the end of the eighteenth century we tried to substitute a love of ourselves for a love of scientific truth, a worship of our own deep spiritual or poetic nature, treated as one more quasi divinity.[134]

---

129 G. Lindbeck, *The Nature Of Doctrine: Religion And Theology In A Postliberal Age*, (Philadelphia: Westminster Press, 1984), p. 132. Lindbeck, who has been influenced by Wittgenstein, uses language as a model for understanding Christianity (pp. 129). His approach can be summarised as "religions, like languages, can be understood in their own terms, not by transposing them into alien speech" (p. 129). An individual learns a religion like learning a language, by participating in it.

130 *Ibid.* p. 35.

131 W.C. Placher, "Postmodern theology" in Musser and J.L. Price, p. 374.

132 Hodgson, *Winds of the Spirit*, p. 65.

133 Rorty, *Contingency* p. 22.

134 *Ibid.* p. 22.

This study has sympathy with Rorty's argument that the truth is not "out there" or "in here".[135] Likewise, spatial metaphors alone, while illustrative, are limited in trying to articulate something of God. While Rorty would be the first to admit that he uses these terms metaphorically, his unrelenting use of these terms suggests that Rorty has one particular (extreme) theistic model of God in view. Rorty's image of God tends to be a stereotypical God who is "out there". Moreover, this study sees merit in what Rorty has to say about language (but it does not share his anti-epistemological attitude, 4.1).[136] Nevertheless, his understanding of language at the least is a challenge to re-think theology. In the end, this is partly why this study focuses on the experience of God rather than God *per se*.

Intersubjectivity

The concept of the subject has lost credibility in some quarters; "the site of subjectivity has its own ambiguities, among which are its foundationalism, its conception of the self, its anthropocentrism, and its elitism".[137] However, a new understanding of the subject is characteristic of postmodernity. Now, the subjective usually connotes the intersubjective. At the risk of simplification, a contrast will help to show the change in usage and meaning. In modernity, the subject in contrast to the object is largely an abstract, individualised, atomistic concept. The modern conception of the subject goes back to Descartes' *cogito, ergo sum*, "But what then am I? A thing which thinks. What is a thing which thinks? It is a thing which doubts, understands, [conceives], affirms, denies, wills, refuses which also imagines and feels".[138] Descartes does not in fact establish that there is this thinking thing. The meaning of Descartes' *I* seems to be related to awareness or consciousness, but those concepts raise other issues of meaning. R.C. Solomon follows the rise and fall of

135 *Ibid.* p. 5.
136 Cf. Haack, *Evidence and Inquiry*, p. 182.
137 F.S. Fiorenza, "Being, Subjectivity, Otherness", in J.D. Caputo, M. Dooley, M.J. Scanlon eds., *Questioning God*, (Bloomington and Indianapolis: Indiana University Press, 2001), p. 349.
138 Second meditation from "Meditations on the first philosophy in which the existence of God and the distinction between mind and body are demonstrated" in E. Chávez-Arvizo ed. and E.S. Haldane and G.R.T. Ross trans. *Descartes: Key Philosophical Writings*, (Hertfordshire: Wordsworth Editions, 1997), p. 143.

52

the timeless, universal and transcendental self (or subject). For Solomon, the debate begins in earnest with Kant and his idea of the transcendental implying necessary and universal.[139] Solomon concludes that, "The underlying presumption is that in all essential matters everyone, everywhere, is the same".[140] In addition to these philosophical considerations, there are also social factors. In everyday speech, the concept of subject and subjectivity is a way of referring to the idea of self in relation to others and the world; implicit in this is a notion of intersubjectivity in which identity and meaning are socially constructed,

> The creation of meaning is an active process, the result of INTENTIONALITY, and each individual proposes his own interpretation of the world, through his language and actions, to a world of countersubjects. Thus a world of intersubjectivity is continuously built up and held in being … Intersubjectivity is thus very much a local cultural creation.[141]

In postmodernity, the subject is understood in relation to other subjects as largely a concrete, corporate, holistic concept. The shift reflects historical changes. However, there is a change in perspective, that is, from philosophical critique to consideration of social usage and from an atomistic to a holistic understanding of humankind,[142]

> In its deconstruction of the modern self, postmodernism returns us to the decentered self, deficient by modern standards but ripe for a rehabilitated rhetoric that can serve public discourse and, for our purposes, public theology. Fallible, feeble, finite, tentative, revisable as is our chastened rationality, effective in public theology, it may still be as God uses the weak to confound the strong.[143]

---

139 R.C. Solomon, *Continental Philosophy Since 1750: The Rise and Fall of the Self*, (Oxford, New York: Oxford University Press, 1988), p. 31.

140 *Ibid.* p. 6.

141 R. Poole "Intersubjectivity" in A. Bullock and S Trombley eds., *The New Fontana Dictionary of Modern Thought*, (London: Harper Collins, 1977, 1988, 1999, 2000), p. 442.

142 N. Everitt and A. Fisher, *Modern Epistemology: A New Introduction*, (London: McGraw-Hill, 1995), p. 203.

143 M.J. Scanlon, "The humiliated self as the rhetorical self" in J.D Caputo, M.D. Dooley and M.J. Scanlon eds., *Questioning God*, (Bloomington, Indianapolis: Indiana University Press, 2001), p. 272.

Thus, "The self involves a becoming that emerges in social experience".[144] Subjectivity is intersubjectivity.[145] Admittedly, the concept of intersubjectivity has limitations, "Is what philosophers call 'intersubjectivity' or 'common or shared subjectivity' possible?"[146] Nonetheless, the use of the concept of intersubjectivity moves away from the idea of the transcendent self and in the process it accommodates important social factors like human identity and the notion that ideas and values are shaped by social interaction and cultural factors. This is consonant with the study's epistemology, which recognises the importance of social and public dimensions in epistemic justification (4.1).

In Conclusion

If totalisation means the homogenisation of difference, then ironically, postmodernity runs the risk of trivialising difference,

> It will thus be clear that there is an inbuilt precommitment to relativism or pluralism within postmodernism in relation to questions of truth. To use the jargon of the movement, one could say that postmodernism represents a situation in which the signifier has replaced the signified as the focus of orientation and value.[147]

Indeed, there are many critics of postmodernity and postmodernism,

> Whereas the modern mind's conviction of superiority derived from its awareness of possessing in an absolute sense more knowledge than its predecessors, the postmodern mind's sense of superiority derives from its special awareness of how little knowledge can be claimed by any mind, itself included. Yet precisely by virtue of that self-relativizing critical awareness, it is recognized that a quasi-nihilist rejection of any and all forms of "totalization" and "metanarrative" – of any aspiration toward intellectual unity, wholeness, or comprehensive coherence – is itself a position not beyond questioning, and cannot on its own principles ultimately justify itself any more than can the various metaphysical overviews against which the postmodern mind has defined itself. Such a position presupposes a metanarrative of

---

144 F.S. Fiorenza, "Being", p. 357.

145 Osborne, *Christian Sacraments*, pp. 76-77.

146 "Objective/Subjective", J. Baggini and P.S. Fosl, *The Philosopher's Toolkit: A Compendium Of Philosophical Concepts And Methods*, (Oxford: Blackwell Publishing, 2003), p. 161.

147 McGrath, *Christian Theology*, p. 113. McGrath may have overstated his case here, but there is merit in his claim.

its own, one perhaps more subtle than others, but in the end no less subject to deconstructive criticism.[148]

Keeping these cautionary comments in mind, this study posits that postmodernity represents a new period in history. While the boundary line between modernity and postmodernity cannot be staked out in absolute terms, there are important differences between the two periods. The differences have been established here on the strength of historical factors, three postmodern characteristics related to pluralism, language and the subject as well as newer philosophical construals (4.1; 4.2). Consequently, on the basis of construing postmodernity as a new period, it is possible to make a critical comparison with Tillich and Rahner who are primarily oriented toward modernity.

In summary, Chapter 1 has outlined the study's problem and thesis, established the rationale for using Tillich and Rahner and defined the study's method and key terms. The study assumes that experience is ambiguous, consisting of presence and absence. On the basis of this assumption, the study aims to make a contribution to postmodern Christology by focusing on the themes of the Incarnation and the Death-Resurrection event (4.4; 4.5). This involves the use theological insights derived from the theologies of Tillich and Rahner. Hence, it is important to explore now the guiding theological visions of Tillich and Rahner.

148 Tarnas, *Passion*, pp. 401-2.

Chapter 2: Tillich

This chapter is a critical analysis of the theology of Tillich; it represents the context for understanding Tillich's view of the presence of God in the world, which will be explored further in Chapter 4. Presence is a major theme in Tillich's theology. In part, presence is his response to the problem of the relationship between the finite and the infinite. Tillich refers to this problem as "the gap" between the finite and the infinite.[1] This is a major problem for Tillich, whereby "The infinite distance between God and man is never bridged; it is identical with man's finitude".[2] Moreover, "There is no proportion or gradation between the finite and the infinite. There is an absolute break, an infinite 'jump'".[3] For Tillich, the problem of the gap is related to the nature of God; this is "the gap between the unrestricted and the conditioned which no ontological or ethical self-elevation can bridge".[4] However, Tillich challenges the Kantian construal of the gap between the finite and the infinite. According to Tillich, the problem of the gap has been exacerbated by Kant's distinction between the sensible and the supersensible.[5] Consequently, there is no access to the presence of God in modernity because of the gap and the problem of the gap cannot be resolved solely by rational means. Further, if God the unconditioned is construed as supersensible, then absence is partly the logical outcome of designating presence as inaccessible.[6] In contrast, Tillich's theology is directed toward making a positive theological statement about presence in modernity.

This chapter examines in sequence the following three aspects of his work: method, theology and Christology. The significance of these aspects will be outlined here. First, Tillich's method is a sophisticated combination of philosophical concepts, theological themes and multiple

1   "Realism and faith", TPE, p. 86.
2   ST III, p. 239.
3   ST I, p. 237.
4   "Realism and faith", TPE, p. 76.
5   *Ibid.* p. 70, i.e. "prison of finitude".
6   Thompson, *Being*, p. 28, Tillich is critical of being forced into choosing either supernaturalism or naturalism; for Tillich it is a false dichotomy that leads nowhere.

sources. Tillich's precise method is not always apparent because, in addition to its complexity, his method of argument is often inconsistent and the meaning of his concepts is often unclear. Second, Tillich's theology is a creative, but not an entirely consistent argument in favour of the presence of God in the world. For Tillich, the presence of God in the world is the uniquely human awareness of its own participation in Divine life, where participation is premised on the concept of self-transcendence, which is the means by which the gap between the finite and the infinite is transcended. From the outset, experience is vital to Tillich's theology.[7] He recognises the ambiguous nature of experience.[8] Moreover, Tillich makes numerically more references to presence than to absence, but absence is nearly always implicitly present, because absence is a characteristic of estrangement.[9] Third, the gap between the finite and the infinite is overcome by participation in Divine life through the power of self-transcendence. An experience of presence enables humankind to transcend but not remove the problem of the gap and Christ is the definitive expression of presence.

2.1. Theological Method

The aim of this section is to outline Tillich's theological method. This entails examining his use of philosophy, sources, understanding of reason and revelation and ontological perspective. Unfortunately, "clarity and consistency are often lacking in Tillich".[10] Further, philosophy is important for Tillich. He is well versed in philosophy and many of his sources are philosophical in nature. He wants theology to answer the

---

7   ST I, pp. 40-46.

8   ST III, p. 32.

9   OTB, p. 52, absence has strong personal associations for Tillich. Specifically, World War I made a lasting impression on his life and theology, "The experience of those four years of war revealed to me and to my entire generation an abyss in human existence that could not be ignored"; cf. Pauck and Pauck, p. 51, "In one sense, Tillich never fully recovered from his intense suffering in the face of death".

10   A. Thatcher, *The Ontology of Paul Tillich*, (Oxford: Oxford University Press, 1978), p. 23.

existential questions of the day and philosophy represents for him an important means of addressing these questions. Throughout his work there is a tension between the disciplines of theology and philosophy. Tillich sees the dialectical interplay between the two disciplines as essential to the theological process. Ironically, this tension is part of the appeal of Tillich's work. However, Tillich's emphasis of the importance of this tension promises much but does not always deliver, in that the reader is often left with conflicting approaches or unresolved issues (e.g. his use of paradox).

2.1.1. Theology and Philosophy

Tillich uses many sources, but he is especially interested in those philosophers who shaped modernity. Arguably, Kant is the primary philosophical influence on Tillich, followed by Schelling. Kant provides Tillich with a *modern* perspective for understanding the problem of the gap between the infinite and the finite and Schelling provides Tillich with a process that links God, history and humanity (by means of Schelling's notion of consciousness). For Tillich, the use of philosophy in theology is inevitable, "We cannot avoid philosophy, because the ways we take to avoid it are carved out and paved by philosophy".[11] Tillich defines philosophy as "that cognitive endeavor in which the question of being is asked".[12] Because it asks the ultimate question, philosophy is not restricted to "logical analysis and epistemological inquiry."[13] However, Tillich sees philosophy in tension with theology.[14] This tension is the result of the boundary situation that exists between theology and philosophy.[15] For Tillich, theology is not concerned about being as such, but as it is in actuality. So the primary source for theology is not the universal *logos*, but the concrete *logos* in the world.[16] For Tillich, "Theol-

11   BRUR, p. 10.
12   *Ibid.* p. 5.
13   *Ibid.*
14   "Philosophy and theology", TPE, an address delivered by Tillich on his assumption
      to the chair of Professor of Philosophical Theology at Union Theological Seminary
      (1933).
15   OTB, p. 56.
16   ST I, p. 24.

ogy deals with what concerns us inescapably, ultimately, unconditionally. It deals with it not as far as it *is* but as far as it is *for us*. In no theological statement can the relation *to us* be omitted."[17] This means the theologian, unlike the philosopher, cannot remain detached.[18] This is a dilemma for Tillich, "As a theologian I have tried to remain a philosopher, and vice versa. It would have been easier to abandon the boundary and to choose one or the other. Inwardly this course was impossible for me. Fortunately, outward opportunities matched my inward inclinations."[19] The dilemma helps explain why Tillich describes his theology as philosophical theology.

For Tillich, the term *philosophical theology* embodied the holding-in-tension of two disciplines, "PHILOSOPHICAL theology is the unusual name of the chair I represent. It is a name that suits me better than any other, since the boundary line between philosophy and theology is the centre of my thought and work."[20] Philosophical theology addresses the existential question of being and the answer is God. Philosophical theology addresses the problem of existence and the answer is Christ, who is the decisive manifestation of the presence of God in the world.[21] The strength of Tillich's use of the term philosophical theology is that it holds in tension his twin concerns of being and existence. However, the precise nature of the relationship between being and existence is not clear in Tillich. Also, the nature of the relationship between philosophy and theology is not clear. On the one hand, theology and philosophy are in tension. On the other hand, they have no common basis, "Thus there is no conflict between theology and philosophy, and there is no synthesis either – for exactly the same reason which insures that there will be no conflict. A common basis is lacking".[22] Further, Tillich's inability to resolve the tension is reflected in the fact that it is difficult to work out whether Tillich is writing as philosopher, theologian or philosophical

17 "Philosophy and theology", TPE, p. 98.
18 ST I, p. 23.
19 OTB, p. 58.
20 "Philosophy and theology", TPE, p. 93.
21 *Ibid.* p. 103, "the philosophical theologian, as a Christian, tries to show in his work that the existential situation of the Christian Church is, at the same time, the place where the meaning of being has appeared as our ultimate concern. In other words, he tries to show that Jesus as the Christ is the logos."
22 ST I, p. 27.

theologian.[23] Certainly, Tillich's view of the relationship between theology and philosophy changed following his migration to America.[24] Subsequently, his work became more overtly theological.[25] This is true in terms of content. However, at the same time he extended his claim for what philosophy could achieve, as philosophy is now responsible for asking about the concrete *logos*.[26] These tensions in Tillich are never resolved.

2.1.2. Sources and Premises

The aim of this part is to review Tillich's use of his philosophical sources.[27] These sources provide insights into his understanding of presence in particular and his theological system in general. His sources include Spinoza, Kant, Fichte, Hegel, Schelling, Schopenhauer, Kierkegaard, Nietzsche and Heidegger.[28] In terms of their importance for Tillich, it is difficult to rank the sources as the task of separating them out is complicated by the fact that he re-worked the material over an

23   Adams, *Philosophy*, pp. 262-263.

24   *Ibid.* p. 260; cf. TSOS p. 208, "Theology is theonomous systematics. This definition in principle excludes the *empirical view* of religion and of Christianity from theology".

25   Adams, *Philosophy*, p. 259.

26   ST I, p. 20, "Philosophy asks the question of reality as a whole; it asks the question of the structure of being".

27   The focus is on philosophical sources, but it would be remiss not to mention Augustine and Schleiermacher. Tillich is indebted, though not uncritically, to Augustine (HCT, p. 111). This is particularly evident in his essay "The two types of philosophy of religion" (TOC). Schleiermacher offers Tillich an alternative to the rational theology of the Enlightenment. For Schleiermacher, intuition and feeling are the basis of religion and this is independent of dogma. The highest possible experience is union with the infinite. For Tillich, Schleiermacher's concept of feeling has been misunderstood, feeling "in Schleiermacher should not really be understood as subjective emotion. Rather, it is the impact of the universe upon us in the depths of our being which transcends subject and object" (PPT, p. 96). Tillich argues that Schleiermacher means the "feeling of unconditional dependence" (PPT, p. 97, cf. OTB, p. 48). Other influences include M. Kähler and A. Ritschl. Indeed, Tillich's interests were extensive as he was also concerned about art, music and psychoanalysis. While these interests do not constitute sources *per se*, they were important influences.

28   Cf. OTB, p. 46 ff., also Karl Marx influenced Tillich's writings on society.

extended period of time. In some instances, the profusion of sources makes it hard to understand what exactly Tillich means.[29] Nonetheless, in Tillich's view, Kant in particular and Schelling stand out (2.4.2). Further, the central concern in Tillich is the gap between the finite and the infinite. Tillich posits two approaches to the problem, which he describes in terms of the principles of identity and contrast.[30] He claims scholars like Kant presupposed a principle of contrast, where the finite is construed as separate and distinct from the infinite. Scholars like Spinoza presupposed a principle of identity, where there is no separation or distinction between the finite and the infinite.[31] In response, Tillich pursued the idea of the co-inherence of the infinite and the finite. This idea forms the basis of his transcendental union. For Tillich, the transcendental union goes back to the tradition of the "inner light", which Tillich intuits is premised on a mystical experience of, and religious conviction about, co-inherence.[32] For Tillich, mysticism affirms that the gap can be transcended. Schelling provides Tillich with a means of expressing this mystical connection in philosophical terms. Tillich adapts Schelling's philosophy of religion which has human consciousness as its medium, to free theology from the impact of heteronomy, formalism and idolatry.

It is important to expand on the philosophical origins of Tillich's central concern because this helps to explain his response to the challenge of modernity and the problem of the gap. To begin, Descartes and Kant challenged the naïve realism of pre-modern theology. In particular, Descartes presumed that the external world could not be reliably inferred from the perception of objects, "we must confess that the life of man is very frequently subject to error in respect to individual objects, and we must in the end acknowledge the infirmity of our nature".[33] Descartes sought a reliable method for establishing knowledge. The world could only be reclaimed by a particular kind of rational awareness (i.e. *Cogito*).

---

29 Thatcher, *Ontology*, p. 10, e.g. the ontological question.

30 PPT, p. 74.

31 *Ibid.* p. 75, for Tillich, Schelling tried to deal with the tension between the principles of distance or contrast and identity by attempting "the great synthesis of Kant and Spinoza".

32 PPT, p. 77.

33 Descartes "Sixth Meditation" in E Chavez-Arvizio ed., E.S Haldane and G.R.T. Ross trans., *Descartes: Key Philosophical Writings*, (Hertfordshire: Wordsworth Editions Limited, 1997), p. 190.

The focus on the *I* as a means of acquiring knowledge, with its relegation of the non-essential body and external world, led to the emergence of Cartesian dualism (eg. mind/matter, internal world/external world, person as mind/body as non-essential). In contrast, Kant reclaimed the external world by means of the mind. Kant presumed knowledge was dependent on the appearance of things (i.e. phenomenal) because there was no access to things, as they exist in themselves (i.e. noumenal).[34] Sensible things can only be apprehended by the mind in this way. Pure reason alone cannot access the supersensible.[35] So according to Tillich, Kant sets the parameters of the modern problem of the gap between the finite and the infinite.

For Kant, the Enlightenment was "man's leaving his self-caused immaturity. Immaturity was the incapacity to use one's intelligence without the guidance of another."[36] Kant was concerned about how knowledge was derived. Kant's solution was to give priority to the mind's role in shaping perceptions of reality. He accepted that this took place in the world and that "all our knowledge begins with experience".[37] For Kant, the world is rationally ordered. Reason is the capacity of the human mind to give meaning to the world, it is not passive; this is the core notion in his concept of transcendental idealism.[38] Kant asserts,

> I apply the term *transcendental* to all knowledge which is not so much occupied with objects as with the mode of our knowledge of objects, so far as this mode of knowledge is possible *a priori*. A system of such concepts would be called *Transcendental Philosophy.*[39]

In his view, for objects to be known, they have to conform to the mind. The mind gives *content* to the appearance of the object through the forms of sensibility (i.e. time and space). The *form* of object is imposed by the

---

34 E.L. Mascall, *The Openness of Being: Natural Theology Today*, (London: Darton, Longman and Todd, 1971), p. 64; how do you account for the noumenal?

35 Admittedly, Kant had a practical alternative to pure reason (i.e. moral imperative).

36 I. Kant "What is Enlightenment?" in C.J. Friedrich ed. and trans. *The Philosophy of Kant: Immanuel Kant's Moral and Political Writings*, (London: Random House, 1949), p. 132.

37 *Ibid.* p. 30.

38 H. Caygill, "transcendental" in *A Kant Dictionary*, (Oxford: Blackwell Publishers, 1995), pp. 399-400, and a transcendental is a universal property of the mind with the capacity to shape our perception of reality.

39 Kant, *Critique of Pure Reason*, p. 43.

mind through the categories of understanding. The mind shapes reality; to be precise, the mind shapes the perceptions of the appearances of reality. It does this in a pre-determined way, pre-determined on the basis of its own *a priori* categories. In brief, Kant's metaphysical epistemology is designed to explain the relationship between the mind and the world. It is premised on a particular view of God and the world, namely, that God is purposeful and rational and God has ordered the world in a meaningful way. Hence, the world is accessible to human inquiry. However, God is not accessible in the same way.[40] God is not amenable to the forms of apprehension. Therefore, rational propositions about God are meaningless.

Tillich identifies with the voluntarist tradition as mediated by Schelling. *The Will* is a central theme in the later philosophy of Schelling; "The old proposition is here once again in place: the original being is will, and will is not merely the beginning but also the *content* of the first emergent being".[41] The supra-material aspect of the soul is a will, which is "its own act".[42] For Schelling, the divine is suprahistorical yet intelligible *(a posteriori)*, as God becomes God in the world (as witnessed through the world religions). The theogonic process is best described using Schelling's metaphor, where the universe is depicted as an emerging self (i.e. God as *the* emerging self). In Schelling's view, the other gods are related to God as individual moments are related to the whole; they contribute to the birth of the whole. These themes are reflected in the early Tillich,

> Only when God can really be distinguished as positing and posited can aseity become actual and living and God become spirit and personality ... The process by which God becomes personal is the world process. The beginning, that is, the separation of God from his nature, is the beginning of the development of consciousness in God. The stages of the world process are the stages by which he becomes per-

---

40 J. Macquarrie, "The continuing relevance of Kant" in *Stubborn Theological Questions*, (London: SCM Press, 2003), p. 200, "probably for much of his life Kant thought of God in a way that was typical of the eighteenth century, that is to say, after the manner of the deists".

41 F.W.J. Schelling "The Second Book" in V.C. Hayes trans. *Schelling's Philosophy Of Mythology And Revelation*, (Armidale: AASR, 1995), p. 172.

42 *Ibid.* p. 181.

sonal and conscious. Only in man do they reach perfection. In him God becomes self-consciousness and spirit.[43]

Schelling links revelation and human consciousness, so that revelation is worked out in human religious history. Reality is grounded in God the great unconscious (i.e. the ungrounded abyss). The conscious rises from the unconscious but the former is always aware of the latter. The abyss is dialectically at odds with itself; this tension generates the cosmic fall. Schelling links the fall to the origin of the finite world. Furthermore, the culmination of the process of revelation is Christianity and Christ is the end (goal and climax) of revelation; "On the day of deliverance, the true God will cease to be merely the one who appears, the one who reveals himself ... revelation will come to an end. And this actually happened in Christ, for Christ is the *End (Ende)* of revelation".[44] This is similar to Tillich's Christ as the *final* revelation. In this context, "MAN IN HIS ORIGINAL ESSENCE has no other significance than to be the being-who-posits-God".[45] Schelling's Christology is speculative. He understands Christ in two ways; there is an earthly view and a higher view. The higher view is the driving force behind Schelling's Christology. According to Schelling, the pre-existence of Christ refers to the higher history of the second divine potency. That is, Christ "existed as natural potency before he appeared as divine personality".[46] In Tillich, Christ is the incarnate *Logos*, where the *Logos* is "a principle of order and structure in all realities".[47]

Schelling's concept of potencies influenced Tillich's system in terms of the latter's polarities in particular and his dialectical approach in general. The concept of *potency* is related to the power to posit.[48] Schelling identifies three potencies. *The first potency* is the ground of all that is. It is the material cause and the principle of individuation of real objectivity, which resists thought. It is the irrational will to selfhood. It is non-

---

43   CHR, pp. 56-57.
44   Schelling, p. 105.
45   *Ibid.* p. 108.
46   *Ibid.* p. 127.
47   PPT, p. 30; cf. Schelling, p. 274, he focuses more on the person than the work of Christ. His Christology is expressed in speculative terms reminiscent of Pauline Kenoticism and Johannine *Logos* Christology. In terms of the Incarnation, it is not the divine nature that changes, but "the divine subject which is posited outside the divine".
48   CHR, p. 58.

being *(me on)* and through self-positing it comes to be. *The second potency* is the formal and efficient cause of being. It is complete selflessness and the principle of love. It must overcome the first potency by the negation of universality; this leads to the existence of the manifold. Christ is the highest form of the second potency that surrenders to the wrath of the first potency. *The third potency* is spirit (i.e. final cause). Spirit is unity of the first and second potencies. The first potency is posited as pure potency. The second potency is posited as pure act. The third potency must be posited to be free of the one-sidedness of the first two, "Whereas the first potency is what can be, and the second is what must be, the third is the goal, what ought to be or what shall be. It is the potency of monotheism".[49] In Tillich, potencies (i.e. polarities) are more methodological than speculative. In *Systematic Theology*, potencies are the principles of the doctrine of being in the self-world polarity; they are articulated in individualisation and participation, dynamics and form, freedom and destiny.[50] The self-world polarity stands in opposition to the first and second potencies. The separated potencies have become the structure of estrangement.[51] The New Being becomes possible through Christ the Incarnation of second potency.[52]

In conclusion, theological reflection is a quest for Tillich, which takes place on the boundary. The decisive bearing is being-itself; only being-itself can enable the theologian to transcend the anxiety of the quest. The boundary is the setting in which essential elements are simultaneously distinguished and held together in tension. Consequently, the boundary is a precarious region because the theologian has to grapple with tensions: life and death, faith and doubt, being and non-being. These elements-in-tension represent the all-important polarities of Tillich's system. Indeed, Tillich's theology is characterised by dialectical tensions. He interprets the tensions as polarities. The polarities are part of the structure of being. They make the quest possible as "They provide us with the ontological safety without which neither thinking nor acting would be possible".[53]

---

49   *Ibid.* pp. 53-54.
50   ST I, pp. 168-186.
51   ST II, pp. 62-66.
52   There are differences. For Tillich, the first potency is the Abyss *(Abgrund)*, that is, God is the ground. For Schelling, the first potency can be construed as the ground of God's existence.
53   MSFA, p. 77.

The concept of polarity represents the metaphysical heart of his system, "its vitality, its lifeblood, its inner character".[54] Schelling's concept of potencies influenced Tillich polarities. In sum, Kant's construal of the problem of the gap (i.e. prison of finitude) had a profound and lasting influence on Tillich's world-view. Late in his career, Tillich moves away from the direct influence of Schelling. This is due to other influences.[55]

2.1.3. Apologetic Concern

For Tillich, the task of theology is to answer the questions of the day. In particular, the purpose of a theological system is to make the Christian message relevant; "A theological system is supposed to satisfy two basic needs: the statement of the truth of the Christian message and the interpretation of this truth for every new generation".[56] In this context, Tillich is attempting to critique modernity and rehabilitate reason. In his view, the essence of the Enlightenment is the free and mature use of reason.[57] However, Tillich claims that reason was not used in the Enlightenment in today's analytic sense.[58] He distinguishes four types of reason: universal, critical, intuitive and technical. Universal reason refers to the *Logos*, which is "a principle of order and structure in all realities".[59] Critical reason, more effective in some areas than the *Logos* concept of reason, involves a passionate belief in and a revolutionary commitment to the *Logos* structure of reality. Intuitive reason refers to the phenomenological; it presumes that the mind is able to discern essences intuitively.[60] It is descriptive and non-analytic. Significantly, technical reason is associ-

---

54   PPT, p. 115; OTB, p. 51.

55   Dulles, *Craft*, p. 125; cf. Heywood Thomas, *Tillich*, pp. 11-12; Heywood Thomas asserts that the so-called movement away from Schelling is debatable.

56   ST I, p. 3.

57   PPT, p. 24 ff., to understand the Enlightenment, Tillich employs four basic concepts: autonomy, reason, nature and harmony. With *autonomy*, Tillich begins with Kant. According to Tillich, Kant defined the Enlightenment as overcoming immaturity, where immaturity is the inability to use reason.

58   *Ibid.* p. 29.

59   *Ibid.* p. 30.

60   *Ibid.* p. 32.

ated with the pragmatic; the problem with modernity is that the use of technical reason came to predominate over the other uses of reason.[61]

Tillich explores the impact of the domination of technical reason on modernity in his *The Irrelevance and Relevance of the Christian Message.*[62] For Tillich, the major issue is the fate of the vertical in modernity. He uses the metaphor of the *vertical* to represent the infinite (beyond time and space), whereas the *horizontal* represents the finite (the realm of time and space). Tillich asserts that if existential questions are to be answered then the determining principles of the modern mind need to be identified. Four principles emerge:

- Horizontal emphasis
- Intention to control nature
- Reduction of reason to calculating reason
- Transformation of everything into calculable objects described in numbers

Tillich sees this as the end of an old development that stems from the Renaissance. The key transformation is from the ideals of the Greek contemplative (i.e. metaphor of the *circle*) and Medieval transcendent (i.e. metaphor of *vertical line*) to the ideal of "actively controlling and shaping the world", that is, the *horizontal line.*[63] Tillich explains the horizontal in terms of hope. The modern era is not without hope, on the contrary, modernity redefines hope, "hope now became, not fulfilment above, but in time and space".[64] In modernity, the sense of the vertical has been lost and the loss has been reinforced by cosmology and the treatment of human beings as objects.[65] The change reflects a "Christian humanism" that neglects "the problem and the anxiety of guilt".[66] What

61   J.D. Caputo, *Radical Hermeneutics: Repetition, Deconstruction, And The Hermeneutic Project*, (Bloomington and Indianapolis: Indiana University Press, 1987), p. 228, "Reason today has been institutionalized".

62   IRCM, p. 13 ff. three examples of irrelevance are Christian language, the content of Christian thinking and traditionalism (as distinct from tradition); cf. p. vii, D. Foster (ed.) states that the work is based on Tillich's Earl Lectures and that "The largely extempore exposition had been rife with divagations, entanglements, and elusive utterances".

63   *Ibid.* p. 27.

64   *Ibid.* p. 29.

65   *Ibid.* p. 31.

66   *Ibid.* p. 33.

is more, a salvific function is attributed to technical control as God is marginalised.[67]

Tillich's view of modernity can be gleaned from his view of existentialism,

> Existentialism is a diagnosis of the situation of the modern personality, of the negativity of a world determined only by the horizontal line, by calculating reason and objectifying control. It shows that there is something else: namely our finitude, anxiety, guilt, loneliness, and meaninglessness.[68]

Tillich contrasts existentialism positively with the attitude associated with controlling nature, calculating reason and forwardism.[69] However, he argues that existentialism does not go far enough in its critique of modernity. In contrast, he asserts that Christianity can answer the questions that existentialism raises. The Church has a paradoxical nature in that it represents and conceals the kingdom of God; "The churches represent this Spiritual Community which is hidden and manifest at the same time".[70] This is the Church in essence and existence. Its essence is found in its origin in the vertical; its existence is expressed in the horizontal. Thus, Christianity is able to take into itself the horizontal line. That is, Christianity participates in the horizontal but knows that it is ultimately grounded in the vertical. In the individual Christian, this leads to self-acceptance, this is grace and grace is "the actual paradox in which we live".[71]

In the face of modernity and the loss of the vertical, the purpose for Tillich of the theological system is to establish the relevance of the Christian message as a matter of ultimate concern. This requires the use of the method of correlation.[72] The method of correlation is based on the two poles of message and situation.[73] The method is "a way of uniting message and situation".[74] Tillich is not dismissing the importance of

---

67   *Ibid.* p. 34.
68   *Ibid.* p. 40.
69   *Ibid.* p. 44.
70   *Ibid.* p. 48.
71   *Ibid.* p. 56.
72   STI, p. vii.
73   *Ibid.* p. 4.
74   *Ibid.* p. 8, cf. p. 60, "The method of correlation explains the contents of the Christian faith through existential questions and theological answers in mutual interdependence"; cf. p. 4, the message is contained in but is not identical with the Bible.

kerygmatic theology; both kerygmatic and apologetic theologies are necessary. He is reinforcing the seriousness of the questions implied by the situation and the need for theology to answer these questions.[75] Tillich interprets the situation through his concept of culture, which is a medium of revelation; "Since the split between a faith unacceptable to culture and a culture unacceptable to faith was not possible for me, the only alternative was to attempt to interpret the symbols of faith through expressions of our own culture. The result of this attempt is the three volumes of *Systematic Theology*."[76] Further, Tillich admits that the method of correlation is a "theological assertion".[77] Nonetheless, the validity of the method is established in practice. This means the method is by nature "circular".[78] That is, existential questions and theological answers are interdependent and the interdependence is worked out within the theological circle.[79] The theological circle means the theologian acts as a theologian on the basis of intentional and personal commitment to ultimate concern.[80] Like the philosopher of religion, the theologian acknowledges the impact of *a priori* factors, but unlike the philosopher of religion, the theologian "adds to the 'mystical *a priori*' the criterion of the Christian message".[81] In summary, the rationale behind the system is Tillich's aspiration to discern the basis of a synthesis between situation and message, question and answer, culture and theology, the finite and the infinite, the particular and the universal.

2.1.4. Reason and Revelation

Tillich links presence and reason and the key to this link is his understanding of the primal relation between reason and mystery. Reason is grounded in the mystical *a priori*, the transcendent union. In philosophical terms this is based on the union of being and knowing. Indeed,

75   STI, p. 6.
76   ST III, pp. 4-5.
77   STI, p. 8.
78   *Ibid.* pp. 9, 135.
79   *Ibid.* p. 11.
80   *Ibid.* p. 10.
81   *Ibid.* p. 9.

70

"Knowing is a form of union".[82] While Tillich critiques modernity, he embraces elements of it, for example, the importance of reason. He accepts that "According to the classical philosophical tradition, reason is the structure of the mind which enables the mind to grasp and to transform reality".[83] He interprets this reality by means of the self-world polarity (2.1.5). The self-world polarity is "the basis of the subject-object structure of reason".[84] Rational thinking is built on this polarity. In turn, reason makes the world a structured whole and the self a structure of centredness, whereby the mind functions to actualise the rational structure of the self. Further, there is an ontological dimension to this understanding of reality and reason. For Tillich, being has priority over intellect because the depth of reason, "precedes reason and is manifest through it".[85] The idea of the depth of reason stems from Tillich's ontological construal of reason. Furthermore, Tillich makes a distinction between ontological reason and technical reason. His concern is dehumanisation, which occurs when reason is reduced to its technical function.[86] Tillich also makes a distinction between controlling knowledge and receiving knowledge. Controlling knowledge is a product of the application of technical reason, where receiving knowledge is not a product but a gift of revelation; "revelation is the manifestation of the ground of being for human knowledge".[87] In terms of truth statements controlling knowledge is verified experimentally whereas receiving knowledge is verified experientially.[88] Controlling knowledge does not require participation by the individual whereas receiving knowledge demands participation. Participation points to the mystical *a priori* aspect of reason because participation involves intuition.[89]

Alongside reason, revelation is an important part of Tillich's epistemology. They are not in competition because reason is grounded in revelation. For Tillich, revelation means "removing the veil" from something

82   *Ibid.* p. 94.
83   *Ibid.* p. 72.
84   *Ibid.* p. 171.
85   *Ibid.* p. 79.
86   *Ibid.* p. 73.
87   *Ibid.* p. 94.
88   *Ibid.* p. 102.
89   *Ibid.* p. 103.

that is hidden.[90] The mediums of revelation are nature, history, groups, individuals, word and inner word. The word is a necessary dimension in all the forms of revelation. Tillich makes a distinction between original and dependent revelation; "An original revelation is a revelation which occurs in a constellation that did not exist before".[91] For Tillich, the coming of the New Being in Christ is the original revelation and everything else is dependent revelation (e.g. Scriptures, tradition) given to a group through an individual in a concrete situation.[92] Further, revelation is mystery that has been hidden and the paradox of religion is the assertion that mystery is revealed,

> The genuine mystery appears when reason is driven beyond itself to its "ground and abyss," to that which "precedes" reason, to the fact that "being is and nonbeing is not" (Parmenides), to the original fact *(Ur-Tatsache)* that there is *something* and not *nothing.*[93]

Mystery has a negative as well as a positive side. The negative side is experienced in the awareness of finitude, the shock of non-being and confrontation with the abyss. The positive side is experienced in revelation where "the mystery appears as ground and not only as abyss".[94] In the concrete situation, "revelation is the manifestation of what concerns us ultimately".[95] Mystery is the objective side of revelation; the subjective side is experienced as ecstasy.[96] In everyday speech, ecstasy has negative connotations. For Tillich, ecstasy is not the same as enthusiasm; "ecstasy is not a negation of reason; it is the state of mind in which reason is beyond itself, that is, beyond its subject-object structure".[97] Ecstasy occurs when the mind is grasped by mystery and there is no revelation without the experience of ecstasy,

90   *Ibid.* p. 108.
91   *Ibid.* p. 126.
92   *Ibid.* p. 127.
93   *Ibid.* p. 110.
94   *Ibid.*
95   *Ibid.*
96   *Ibid.* p. 111.
97   *Ibid.* pp. 112, 118.

Ecstasy as a state of mind is the exact correlate to self-transcendence as the state of reality. Such an understanding of the idea of God is neither naturalistic or supra-naturalistic. It underlies the whole of the present theological system.[98]

In short, Tillich's epistemology is premised on an ontological view of reason, "Epistemology, the 'knowledge' of knowing, is a part of ontology, the knowledge of being, for knowing is an event within the totality of events. Every epistemological assertion is implicitly ontological".[99] The depth of reason points to the mystical provenance of all knowledge. Even controlling knowledge is premised on this, this means the capacity to think cannot be divorced from the union between being and knowing. Moreover, in principle philosophical truth is about the structure of being. It is expressed conceptually. In contrast, the truth of faith is about ultimate concern.[100] It is expressed symbolically, "Faith cannot guarantee factual truth. But faith can and must interpret the meaning of facts from the point of view of man's ultimate concern. In doing so it transfers historical truth into the dimension of the truth of faith".[101]

2.1.5. Ontological Basis

Tillich's theological system is based on ontology.[102] This becomes a critical factor in this study when the issue of ontotheology is addressed (4.2.1). In particular "Tillich identifies God with Being, Deus with Esse. The identity is the keystone of his whole ontological-theological system, and the basis of the complex interplay between philosophy and theology".[103] Tillich examines most things from an ontological perspective. In particular, he uses ontology to explain how presence enables humankind to transcend the gap between the finite and the infinite and overcome estrangement,

98   ST II, p. 8.
99   ST I, p. 71.
100   DF, p. 96.
101   *Ibid.* p. 86.
102   PPT, p. 217, "there are always ontological presuppositions in every epistemology"; cf. Heywood Thomas, *Tillich*, p. 47, concerning LPJ, "It is always the case with Tillich that at whatever point he begins his argument, no matter how concrete, the direction of the argument is towards the abstraction of ontology".
103   Thatcher, *Ontology*, p. 25.

> For this inquiry I like to use the word "ontology", derived from *logos* ("the word")
> and *on* ("being"); that is, the word of being, the word which grasps being, makes its
> nature manifest, drives it out of its hiddenness into the light of knowledge. Ontol-
> ogy is the center of all philosophy.[104]

For Tillich, the study of ontology begins with an analysis of human experience; "Ontology presupposes a conversion, an opening of the eyes, a revelatory experience. It is not a matter of detached observation, analysis, and hypothesis".[105] An analysis of experience raises existential concerns, "Why is there something, why not nothing?"[106] Moreover, "What is being itself?"[107] The answer is God: God is being-itself, the ground of being and the power of the structure of being that makes existence possible,[108]

> If man is that being who asks the question of being, he has and has not the being for
> which he asks. He is separated from it while belonging to it. Certainly we belong to be-
> ing – its power is in us – otherwise we would not be. But we are also separated from it;
> we do not possess it fully. Our power of being is limited. We are a mixture of being and
> nonbeing. This is precisely what is meant when we say that we are finite.[109]

Tillich's ontology can be looked at in terms of four levels of ontological concepts:

– The basic ontological structure
– The elements of the ontological structure
– The characteristics of being which are the conditions of existence
– The categories of being and knowing

The first level is the basic ontological structure, it is premised on the subject-object structure of being and it "cannot be derived. It must be accepted".[110] It begins with human awareness. This involves an awareness of the self as self and the world as world and of the self as separated

---

104 BRUR, p. 6.
105 *Ibid.* p. 65.
106 ST I, p. 163.
107 *Ibid.*
108 "We live in two orders", TSF, pp. 24-32, Tillich's sermon is a good example of how his ontological thinking pervades his theology.
109 BRUR, p. 11.
110 ST I, p. 174.

from but connected to the world. Reason enables humankind to sense this self-world polarity. The self-world polarity is actually "the basis of the subject-object structure of reason".[111] What is called *rational* thinking is built upon this polarity and vice versa. Reason makes the world a structured whole and the self a structure of centredness. That is, the mind functions to actualise the rational structure of the self. God is not part of the subject-object structure. All told, the basic ontological structure is premised on the self-world polarity.

The second level of Tillich's ontological concepts involves the constitutive elements, consisting of three pairs: individuality and universality, dynamics and form, freedom and destiny; "In these three polarities the first element expresses the self-relatedness of being, its power of being something for itself; while the second element expresses the belongingness of being, its character of being a part of a universe of being".[112] With the first pair of elements, individuality is "a *quality* of everything".[113] There is no sense of selfhood without individuality. Selfhood and individualisation "are different conceptually, but actually they are inseparable".[114] Individuality only makes sense in polar relation to universality. An individual is an individual in relation to others in two ways – in resistance to others and in relationship with others. This implies an individual is capable of participation. Tillich asserts that individualisation and participation are "interdependent on all levels of being".[115] With the second pair, form should not be contrasted to content. Form is related to *essentia*.[116] In terms of *essentia*, form refers to "its definite power of being".[117] To be something means to have a form and "Every form forms something".[118] This is its dynamics. Thus, form and dynamics are in polar relation and there is no being without form. Dynamics is "the *me on*, the potentiality of being, which is nonbeing in contrast to things that have a form, and the power of being in contrast to pure nonbeing".[119]

---

111 *Ibid.* p. 171.
112 *Ibid.* p. 165.
113 *Ibid.* pp. 174-175.
114 *Ibid.* p. 175.
115 *Ibid.* p. 177.
116 MFSA, pp. 72-73.
117 ST I, p. 178.
118 *Ibid.* p. 179.
119 *Ibid.*

Dynamics and form appear in experience as vitality and intentionality.[120] With the third pair, the freedom of an individual is not a function but an aspect of human identity that is "experienced as deliberation, decision, and responsibility".[121] This freedom is not unlimited, as destiny sets down the conditions and limits of freedom.[122] In the process, the individual transcends biological necessity and social determinism, as the individual is confined but not captive to the limits of existence.[123]

The third level of ontological concepts involves the characteristics of being.[124] Tillich uses the term *being* to explain the nature of God, the world and the God-world relationship.[125] For Tillich, being means "the whole of human reality, the structure, the meaning, and the aim of existence".[126] According to Tillich, being is defined in relation to non-being, where being is the negation of non-being. However, non-being is not easily defined, as "one can only experience its threat".[127] This is the ontological shock, which occurs with the threat of non-being.[128] Thus, non-being and being are in polar relation. In anthropological terms, existential being is essential being that has been limited and distanced by the threat of non-being. The distorting effects of non-being form the basis of Tillich's concept of finitude. Finitude is the awareness of limits, which means that humankind falls short of essential being and this is the cause of ontological anxiety. Only being-itself can enable existential being to transcend the anxiety of finitude.[129] Further, Tillich claims both existentialist and essentialist perspectives are necessary,[130]

120 *Ibid.* p. 180.
121 *Ibid.* p. 184.
122 *Ibid.* p. 185.
123 *Ibid.* p. 182.
124 *Ibid.* p. 165, they express "the power of being to exist and the difference between essential and existential being".
125 E.J. Lowe, "being", OCP, p. 82. Being is the subject of ontology; it involves the study of the nature of beings, entities or things and refers to concepts like existence and reality. It tries to address the question of why is there something and not nothing (and what is something?). The subject of being invokes the history of philosophy from Plato to Heidegger.
126 ST I, p. 14.
127 MSFA, p. 81.
128 ST I, pp. 113, 163.
129 MSFA, p. 74.
130 PPT, p. 245; ST I, p. 204, "A complete discussion of the relation of essence to existence is identical with the entire theological system".

A complete discussion of the relation of essence to existence is identical with the entire theological system. The distinction between essence and existence, which religiously speaking is the distinction between the created and the actual world, is the backbone of the whole body of theological thought. It must be elaborated in every part of the theological system.[131]

For Tillich, the root meaning of the word existence means to "stand out" and humankind exists, stands out, in the face of non-being.[132] With echoes of Schelling, Tillich writes, "The world is the self-realization of the divine mind; existence is the expression of essence and not the fall away from it".[133] Essence is hard to define because it cannot be isolated from existence, "the state of essential being is not an actual stage of human development".[134] Certainly, Tillich uses existentialist insights, and shares something of existentialism's "protest against Hegel's essentialism".[135] According to Tillich, Kierkegaard, in response to Hegel, thought that reconciliation is theoretically possible within the system of essences, but we do not live in a system of essences.[136] However, while existentialism is an important element in Tillich's system, it is premised on "a vision of the essential structure of reality".[137] In other words, Tillich gives priority to essentialism over and above existentialism.[138]

The fourth level of ontological concepts consists of the categories of being and knowing "Categories are the forms in which the mind grasps and shapes reality".[139] They are "forms of finitude".[140] They unite affirmative and negative elements. They address the affirmative and negative from outside and inside. The categories are time, space, causality and substance. Time is "the central category of finitude"[141] and "striving

131 *Ibid.* p. 204.
132 ST II, p. 20.
133 *Ibid.* p. 24.
134 *Ibid.* p. 33.
135 PPT, p. 122, cf. p. 245.
136 *Ibid.* p. 164.
137 *Ibid.* p. 142.
138 ST II, p. 4, Tillich claims the movement from Vol. 1 to Vol. 2 of *Systematic Theology*, "mirrors the leap from man's essential nature to its distortion in existence". For Tillich, it is important to understand the essential nature first.
139 ST 1, p. 192.
140 *Ibid.*
141 *Ibid.* p. 193.

for space is an ontological necessity".[142] Causality is ambiguous and existence is contingent, as we do not have aseity.[143] Substance is associated with the traditional substance/accidents distinction, more importantly, for Tillich it is related to identity,

> The four categories are four aspects of finitude in its positive and negative elements. They express the union of being and nonbeing in everything finite. They articulate the courage which accepts the anxiety of nonbeing. The question of God is the question of the possibility of this courage.[144]

In conclusion, a problem remains concerning Tillich's definition and use of being. For Tillich, being is defined in relation to non-being.[145] He uses the prefix *non* in non-being in the sense of *not* being (i.e. "radical negation") rather than as *no* being (i.e. nothingness).[146] Moreover, with echoes of Plato, Tillich employs a distinction between relative or dialectical non-being *(me on)* and absolute or non-dialectical non-being *(ouk on)*.[147] In Tillich's ontology, being is in a dialectical relationship with relative non-being. He uses relative non-being to interpret the significance of the experience of finitude.[148] Finitude is the awareness of anxiety and anxiety is a reverberation from the shock of non-being. Furthermore, Tillich asserts that there is no metaphysical parity between being and non-being, as "being, limited by nonbeing, is finitude … [b]ut nonbeing is literally nothing except in relation to being. Being precedes nonbeing in ontological validity, as the word 'nonbeing' itself indicates".[149] Paradoxically, non-being has a positive function within the context of its polar relation with being, because non-being functions analogously like a catalyst in chemistry, in that non-being evokes from *a* being the power of self-transcendence, "non-being drives being out of its seclusion, it forces it to affirm itself dynamically".[150] For Tillich, this power of self-affirmation is crucial to what it means to be. The power of self-

---

142 *Ibid.* p. 194.
143 *Ibid.* p. 196.
144 *Ibid.* p. 198.
145 MFSA, pp. 80-81.
146 ST I, p. 186, n. 5; cf. Heywood Thomas, *Tillich*, p. 74.
147 ST I, p. 188.
148 *Ibid.* p. 189.
149 *Ibid.*
150 TCB, p. 174.

affirmation can be understood as the power for humankind to grasp that it belongs to being-itself, in spite and because of the shock of non-being.[151] Even with God,

Non-being makes God a living God. Without the No he has to overcome in himself and in his creature, the divine Yes to himself would be life-less. There would be no revelation of the ground of being, there would be no life.[152]

However, while Tillich defines non-being in relation to being, in practice he refers to non-being as though it is *a* being. Admittedly, no one has solved the problem of defining being. Clearly, Heidegger influences Tillich's understanding of being.[153] Tillich acknowledges this influence.[154] For Heidegger, the word being is indefinable, grammatically and etymologically; "the word 'being' is empty and its meaning a vapour".[155] Moreover, metaphysics does not deal directly with being.[156] Its focus is on the ontological analysis of entities.[157] According to Heidegger, being cannot have "the character of an entity"[158] and the being of entities "'is' not itself an entity".[159] So, being is hard to define; but it demands an inquiry.[160] But there is a tension in Heidegger, in that, being is the being

151　ST I, p. 191, Tillich describes this power as "the power of infinite self-transcendence".
152　TCB, p. 174.
153　J.D. Caputo, "Heidegger and theology" in C. Guignon ed., *The Cambridge Companion to Heidegger*, (Cambridge: Cambridge University Press, 1993), p. 275, Tillich draws on motifs from *Being and Time*; cf. Pauck and Pauck, p. 98; "Heidegger's thought made a profound impression on Tillich, at first unconsciously. There are some who feel that had it not been for Heidegger's *Being and Time*, Tillich would never have developed his ontology as he did".
154　OTB, p. 48, LPJ, p. 36, ST I, p. 168.
155　Heidegger, *An Introduction to Metaphysics*, R. Mannheim trans., (New York: Anchor Books, 1961), p. 61.
156　"The way back into the ground of metaphysics" in W. Kaufman ed. and trans., *Existentialism: From Dostoevsky to Sartre*, revised and expanded, (New York: New American Library, 1965, 1975), pp. 268-269.
157　M. Heidegger, *Being and Time*, J. Macquarrie and E. Robinson trans., (Oxford and Cambridge: Blackwell Publishers, 1962), p. 22, metaphysics deals with entities as a whole and this is not to be equated with being, "The 'universality' of Being '*transcends*' any universality of genus".
158　*Ibid.* p. 23.
159　*Ibid.* p. 26.
160　*Ibid.* p. 24.

of entities and so entities inevitably become the focus of inquiry. Thus, Tillich is in good company with regard to his inability to solve the problem of being, non-being and their interrelations.[161]

2.2. The Presence of God in the World

The purpose of this section is to begin to explore Tillich's understanding of the presence of God in the world. Tillich affirms the presence of God in the world, where presence is human awareness of its participation in the Divine by means of self-transcendence. Tillich sees presence as an answer to the existential questions posed by modernity because it enables humankind to transcend the experience of the gap between the finite and the infinite.[162] Presence is part of human experience and experience is ambiguous as presence is bound to absence. They are in polar relation.

2.2.1. Presence

Presence is a major theme in Tillich's theology. It is his response to the problem of the relationship between the finite and the infinite. In other words, Tillich is responding to modernity's defining problem (i.e. the gap).[163] Presence is the key. While Tillich does not use the expression *the presence of God in the world* as such, the theme of the presence of God is an integral part of his theology. In Tillich, the concept of presence means human awareness of its own participation in Divine life. It is experienced as ultimate concern.[164] It presumes the possibility of the co-

---

161 Thatcher, *Ontology*, p. 34; cf. p. 39, Thatcher concludes that Tillich has two versions of God as being-itself: an ontological concept and a theological symbol.
162 ST I, p. 237; cf. p. 172, "If God is brought into the subject-object structure of being, he ceases to be the ground of being and becomes one being among others (first of all, a being beside the subject who looks at him as an object). He ceases to be the God who is really God".
163 "Realism and faith", TPE, p. 86.
164 UC, pp. 7, 11, 26-27.

inherence of the infinite and the finite, the unconditional and the conditional; the vertical and the horizontal; the spiritual and the material. This co-inherence means it is possible to transcend the gap between the finite and the infinite. Above all, Christ is the definitive expression of presence,

> The divine Spirit was present in Jesus as the Christ without distortion. In him the New Being appeared as the criterion of all Spiritual experiences in past and future. Though subject to individual and social conditions his human spirit was entirely grasped by the Spiritual Presence; his spirit was "possessed" by the divine Spirit or, to use another figure, "God was in him." This makes him the Christ, the decisive embodiment of the New Being for historical mankind.[165]

Tillich uses various terms for presence.[166] He expresses it implicitly with terms like love,[167] holiness,[168] the word of God,[169] and mysticism.[170] He expresses it explicitly with terms like omnipresence,[171] sacramental presence,[172] the Spirit,[173] the Divine Spirit,[174] and Spiritual Presence.[175] Notably, he uses the terms the Spirit, divine Spirit and Spiritual Presence more than Holy Spirit. According to Tillich, this is because the term Holy Spirit is not used widely in modern culture and modern culture no longer understands the significance of the Spirit. Further, Tillich tries to avoid traditional biblical and theological language as he attempts to construct "a theological system for our period".[176] He prefers to use philosophical, psychological and sociological concepts because he is writing to an audience for whom "traditional language has become irrelevant".[177] Tillich's main terms for presence are Spirit, Divine Spirit and Spiritual

165 *Ibid.* p. 144.
166 BRUR, p. 22, "Everything can become a medium of revelation, a bearer of divine power".
167 ST III, p. 137.
168 ST I, p. 215.
169 BRUR, p.78.
170 PPT, p. 22.
171 ST I, pp. 276-278.
172 *Ibid.* p. 278.
173 *Ibid.* pp. 249-252; ST III pp. 139, 162-163.
174 ST III, pp. 111-138, 162 ff.; UC pp. 17, 79.
175 ST III, pp. 111-161; 162-182.
176 ST II, p. viii.
177 ST III, p. 4.

Presence. Overall, they are used synonymously for manifestations of presence:

> We should become fully aware of the Spiritual Presence, around us and in us, even though we realize how limited our experience of "God present to our spirit" may be. For this is what Divine Spirit means: God present to our spirit. Spirit is not a mysterious substance; it is not a part of God. It is God Himself: but not God as the creative ground of all things and not God directing history and manifesting Himself in its central event, but as God present in communities and personalities, grasping them, inspiring them, and transforming them.[178]

The difference between implicit and explicit expressions of presence in Tillich is not absolute. For example, love is a unity linked to presence and so *agape* is an "ecstatic manifestation" of Spiritual Presence.[179] Similarly, *eros* is related to the Spirit or described by Tillich in terms comparable to the way he describes the work of the Spirit. Thus, *eros* is "the moving power of life".[180] It has "the greatness of a divine-human power".[181] It entails "the drive towards the unity of the separated".[182] The holy is related to presence, as "The holy and the divine must be interpreted correlatively".[183] Concerning the word,

> His Word is an event created by the divine Spirit in the human spirit. It is both driving power and infinite meaning. The Word of God is God's creative self-manifestation and not a conversation between two beings. Therefore, the Word is one of the aspects of God himself; it is God manifesting himself to himself.[184]

With mysticism, the "mystical element is the inward participation in and experience of the presence of the divine".[185] For Tillich, mysticism forms a bond between rationalism and piety. In particular, rationalism emerged from the mystical experience of the "inner light".[186] In fact, "The rationalists were all philosophers of the inner light, even though this light later

178 "Spiritual Presence", EN, p. 84; ST III, p. 107.
179 ST III, p. 137.
180 LPJ, p. 25.
181 *Ibid.* p. 117.
182 *Ibid.* p. 25.
183 ST I, p. 215.
184 BRUR, p. 78.
185 PPT, p. 22.
186 *Ibid.* p. 19.

82

on became cut off from its divine ground".[187] The interior experience of
the inner light is consonant with the exterior experience of the Word of
God,[188] because the Spirit is "the mediating power which overcomes the
conflict between outside and inside".[189] In this process, the conflict between *inside* (interior life, subjectivity) and *outside* (external world, objectivity) is overcome by means of the "mystical union".[190] Behind all
this, Tillich sees a union between reason and presence.

For Tillich, the rational and mystical co-exist within human subjectivity, as "Mysticism means inwardness, participation in the Ultimate Reality through inner experience".[191] Reason gives form, while "Spirit as a
dimension of life includes more than reason – it includes *eros*, passion,
imagination – but without *logos*-structure it could not express anything".[192] An encounter with the presence of God is an experience of the
mystical union. The mystical union finds full expression in Tillich's
theonomous vision of the world. For Tillich, theonomy is a leading theological concept and it is related to but surpasses the significance of mysticism. Theonomy is the ultimate expression of the mystical union; it is
"an autonomy informed by a religious substance".[193] It is "the substance
and meaning of history" where autonomy is "the dynamic principle of
history",[194]

> Theonomy goes beyond autonomy, which is empty critical thought. It goes beyond
> heteronomy, which means authoritarianism and enslavement. Theonomy is the un-
> ion of what is true in autonomy and in heteronomy, the fulfilment of a whole soci-
> ety with the spiritual substance, in spite of the freedom of the autonomous
> development, and in spite of living in the great traditions in which the Spirit has
> embodied himself.[195]

Tillich links theonomy with reason arguing that there is a tension between heteronomous reason (i.e. external, imposed) and autonomous
reason (i.e. internal, not grounded in its own depth), where theonomous

187 HCT, p. 185.
188 ST I, p. 123; BRUR, p. 78.
189 PPT, p. 21.
190 *Ibid.* p. 120; cf. ST III, p. 129, "transcendental union".
191 PPT, p. 22.
192 ST III, p. 24.
193 OTB, p. 38.
194 "Kairos", TPE, p. 51.
195 PPT, p. 238.

reason "means autonomous reason united with its own depth".[196] The
tension between autonomy and heteronomy is creative because it is conducive to the search for a new theonomy,

> The permanent struggle between autonomous independence and heteronomous re-
> action leads to the quest for a new theonomy, both in particular situations and in the
> depth of the cultural consciousness in general. This quest is answered by the impact
> of the Spiritual Presence on culture. Wherever this impact is effective, theonomy is
> created, and wherever there is theonomy, traces of the impact of the Spiritual Pres-
> ence are visible.[197]

These are *kairos* moments.[198]

Tillich does not always define his terms for presence consistently or
explain their interrelations clearly.[199] He attributes this in part to the cost
of trying to create a deductive system of theology (ironically, this approach is symptomatic of the modernity he critiques).[200] Typically, Tillich introduces a seminal theme like the Spirit.[201] He defines the theme
and pursues tangents, which stem from his original definition, for the
benefit of new insights but at the expense of clarity.[202] For instance, the
distinction between spirit and Spiritual Presence is crucial in Tillich,

> We have dared to use the almost forbidden word "spirit" (with a small "s") for two
> purposes: first, in order to give an adequate name to that function of life which
> characterizes man as man and which is actualized in morality, culture and religion;
> second, in order to provide the symbolic material which is used in the symbols "di-
> vine Spirit" or "Spiritual Presence." The dimension of spirit provides this mate-
> rial.[203]

---

196 ST I, p. 85, "there is no complete theonomy under the conditions of existence".
197 ST III, p. 252.
198 "Kairos", TPE, p. 53, cf. "Philosophy and fate", TPE, p. 31, following the apostle
    Paul, *kairos* is the "definitive" time, "a center of history" from which all times find-
    ing their bearings.
199 Thatcher, *Ontology*, p. 23.
200 P. Tillich, "Reply to interpretation and criticism" in C.W. Kegley and R.W. Bretall
    eds., *The Theology of Paul Tillich*, Vol. 1, (New York: MacMillan, 1961), p. 330.
201 Heywood Thomas, *Tillich* pp. 35-36, "Characteristic of Tillich's method of argu-
    ment throughout his whole work is this intuitive grasp of a principle which then be-
    comes the basis for further assertions, all of which are perfectly valid assertions as
    inferences from that basic premiss".
202 Adams, *Philosophy*, p. 261.
203 ST III, p. 111.

Tillich contends that the word "spirit" has traditionally been reserved "for religion and attributed to God and divine things alone".[204] He laments that this has meant that humankind has been "deprived of spirit".[205] Therefore, he proposes a solution,

> Perhaps one of the ways in which we can try to overcome such difficulties is by re-introducing the concept of spirit, with a small "s" and not use this term for God alone with a capital "S". For if you cannot experience what spirit is in yourself, you cannot apply it symbolically or analogically to God either.[206]

The distinction between spirit and Spirit is vital in his theology of presence. First of all, spirit is specifically human spirit.[207] For Tillich, spirit is "the unity of power and meaning".[208] The word "spirited" retains something of this dynamic nuance.[209] Significantly, an understanding of human spirit helps to explain the meaning of divine Spirit and an understanding of Spirit enables humankind to discern that its spirit is intimately linked to the Divine.[210]

Hegel's philosophical synthesis forms part of the background to Tillich's understanding of the spirit/Spirit relationship. Tillich interpreted Hegel's synthesis in two ways: first, as a synthesis of cultural elements in Western culture and second, as a synthesis of polarities in religious thought expressed in the doctrine of absolute and relative mind *(Geist)*. In many ways, this seems an oversimplification of Hegel's use of the term *Geist*, as it is difficult to translate.[211] Nonetheless, Tillich uses spirit

---

204 PPT, p. 119.

205 *Ibid.*

206 *Ibid.*

207 ST III, p. 21, Tillich claims that *spirit* has been replaced in the English language by *mind* but it is not an adequate replacement, p. 38; spirit has moral dimensions, "morality is the function of life by which the realm of the spirit comes into being. Morality is the constitutive function of spirit. A moral act, therefore, is not an act in which some divine or human law is obeyed but an act in which life integrates itself in the dimension of the spirit, and this means as personality within community" (p. 38).

208 ST I, p. 249, cf. ST III, pp. 22, 24; "The Eternal Now", EN, p. 89, spirit as "revolutionary power".

209 ST III, p. 22, Tillich regards the term *spiritual* as beyond redemption.

210 PPT, p. 13, the spirit makes faith possible.

211 M. Inwood, "spirit" in *A Hegel Dictionary*, (Oxford: Blackwell Publishers, 1992), pp. 274-277.

and reinterprets the distinction between absolute and relative *Geist* as between *Spirit* (absolute, divine, infinite) and *spirit* (relative, human, finite). Knowing God means a union of spirit and Spirit. This is more than knowledge because it is an experience of the mystical union. Moreover, it highlights Tillich's distinction between the human and the divine. Tillich tries to hold the two in tension. On the one hand, he tries to preserve the gap between finite and the infinite. On the other hand, he tries to show it is possible to claim that the presence of God is in the world without jeopardising the distinction between the human and the divine. Moreover, human awareness is decisive; "the dimension of the spirit actualizes itself within the dynamics of self-awareness and under its biological conditions".[212] Momentarily, it offers an experience of unambiguous life,[213]

> The spirit, a dimension of finite life, is driven into a successful self-transcendence; it is grasped by something ultimate and unconditional. It is still the human spirit; it remains what it is, but at the same time, it goes out of itself under the impact of the divine Spirit. "Ecstasy" is the classical term for this state of being grasped by the Spiritual Presence. It describes the human situation under the Spiritual Presence exactly.[214]

However, Tillich recognises that the contrast between spirit and Spirit runs the risk of being dismissed as a dualism.[215] He explores ways of accounting for this problem. For Tillich, it is not possible to compare the finite to the infinite. We can only use metaphors to talk about the infinite. Thus, he tries to affirm that the finite is grounded in the infinite or the infinite is the "depth" of all that is finite. Subsequently, he describes the experience of presence as a fragment, where the fragment is whole and unambiguous; "There is always participation in the transcendent union of unambiguous life. But this participation is fragmentary".[216] Therefore, the human experience of life is ambiguous, "appearing under the conditions of finitude but conquering both estrangement and ambiguity".[217] This includes the experience of absence.

212 ST III, p. 118.
213 *Ibid.* p. 112.
214 *Ibid.*
215 *Ibid.* p. 113.
216 *Ibid.* p. 140.
217 *Ibid.* p. 150.

For Tillich, absence is an important theme. It is an experience that can be understood from three perspectives: ontological, anthropological and sociological. From an ontological perspective, absence is a distorting effect of relative non-being.[218] As a symptom of the ontological shock, absence does not mean God is absent in reality, but it does mean humankind experiences the absence of God. From an anthropological perspective, absence is symptomatic of finitude.[219] As such, it is a measure of estrangement where "the Spirit of God hides God from our sight".[220] Estrangement refers to the existential state of humankind after the Fall,

> When I speak in any college about estrangement, everybody knows what I mean, because they all feel estranged from their true being, from life, from themselves especially. But if I spoke of their all being sinners, they would not understand at all. They would think, "I haven't sinned; I haven't drunk or danced," as in some fundamentalist churches … But estrangement is a reality for them. Yet estrangement is what sin means – the power of estrangement from God. And that is all it means.[221]

From a sociological perspective, absence is symptomatic of the profanisation associated with modernity.[222] Specifically, absence is symptomatic of the emptiness of profanisation. In short, Tillich describes absence metaphorically as the space that evokes a longing for the presence of God.[223] For Tillich, this space is God's space and the term *space* implies a vacuum because only God can fill it:

> We live in an era in which the God we know is the absent God. But in knowing God as the absent God, we *know* of Him; we feel His absence as the empty space that is left by something or someone that once belonged to us and has now vanished from our view. God is always infinitely near and infinitely far. We are fully aware of Him only if we experience both of these aspects. But sometimes, when our

218 ST I, p. 113.
219 ST II, p. 44, for Tillich, the Fall is more than a biblical story; it represents the transition from essence to existence made possible by finite freedom, "The state of existence is the state of estrangement. Man is estranged from the ground of his being, from other beings, and from himself. The transition from essence to existence results in personal guilt and universal tragedy".
220 "Spiritual Presence", EN, p. 88.
221 UC, p. 98.
222 *Ibid.* p. 5, Tillich prefers the term profanisation to secularisation, as profanisation is "a process of becoming more and more empty or materialistic without any ultimate concern"; cf. demonisation occurs when ultimacy is granted to the conditioned.
223 "Spiritual Presence", EN, p. 88.

awareness of Him has become shallow, habitual … He becomes the absent God. The Spirit has not ceased to be present. The Spiritual Presence can never end. But the Spirit of God hides God from our sight. No resistance against the Spirit, no indifference, no doubt can drive the Spirit away. But the Spirit that always remains present to us can hide itself, and this means that it can hide God. Then the Spirit shows us nothing except the absent God, and the empty space within us which is *His* space.[224]

The significance of absence in Tillich is clear from his discussions on estrangement, a major theme in his work.[225] In this regard, Tillich refers to a fundamental ontological category in his system, namely, the ontological structure of self-world polarity. For Tillich, humankind has a world and exists in that world. The term *world* in Tillich means more than the planet earth or the known physical environment, "The world is a structural whole which includes and transcends all environments".[226] Thus, estrangement means the loss of the self and "with the loss of self, man loses his world".[227] Without a world there is no presence, because presence is mediated presence, that is, presence is mediated by the world and so the absence of God is a symptom of self-loss. It is a measure of finitude.[228] It is a consequence of estrangement.[229] Tillich is not asserting that God is absent, only that humankind experiences absence in existential estrangement; "one must say that even in the state of separation God is creatively working in us – even if his creativity takes the way of destruction. Man is never cut off from the ground of being, not even in the state of condemnation".[230] The experience of the absence of God in the world as estrangement can be explained in terms of the shock of (relative) non-being.[231] Namely, absence is an experience and expression the shock of non-being.

Using the language of Otto,[232] Tillich describes the experience of the ontological shock as simultaneously "preserved in the annihilating power

224 *Ibid.*
225 ST II, p. 44 ff.
226 ST I, p. 170.
227 ST II, p. 61.
228 *Ibid.* p. 73.
229 *Ibid.* pp. 68-69.
230 *Ibid.* p. 78.
231 ST I, p. 189, "finitude, or creatureliness, is unintelligible without the concept of dialectical nonbeing".
232 DF, p. 13.

of the divine presence *(mysterium tremendum)*" and "overcome in the elevating power of the divine presence *(mysterium fascinosum)*".[233] Absence is then the experience of the negative side of mystery, which is experienced as the awareness of finitude, the shock of non-being and confrontation with the abyss,

> This negative side is always potentially present, and it can be realized in cognitive as well as in communal experiences. It is a necessary element in revelation. Without it the mystery would not be mystery. Without the "I am undone" of Isaiah in his vocational vision, God cannot be experienced (Isa 6:5). Without the "dark night of the soul," the mystic cannot experience the mystery of the ground.[234]

The abyss is "the depth of the divine life, its inexhaustible and ineffable character",[235] and "the abyss of possible nonbeing".[236] Thus, absence in Tillich is the experience of an encounter with the abyss. Further, the negative and positive sides of this encounter with mystery do not represent a binary opposition in Tillich as, "the ground of being is at the same time the abyss of any definite being".[237] Moreover,

> The positive side of the mystery – which includes the negative side – becomes manifest in actual revelation. Here the mystery appears as ground and not only as abyss. It appears as the power of being, conquering nonbeing. It appears as our ultimate concern. And it expresses itself in symbols and myths which point to the depth of reason and its mystery.[238]

In Tillich, presence and absence represent the experience of God as ground and abyss. They represent the existential side of mystery: the human side of mystery. The terms ground and abyss represent Tillich's attempts to describe in metaphorical terms the God side of mystery. Thus, absence is an experience of "the annihilating power of divine presence",[239] and presence is an experience of "the elevating power of divine

---

233 ST I, p. 113.
234 *Ibid.* p. 110.
235 *Ibid.* p. 156.
236 *Ibid.* p. 164.
237 "Symbol and knowledge: a response by Paul Tillich" in J. Clayton ed., *Paul Tillich: Mainworks*, Vol. 4, (Berlin and New York: *De Gruyter-Evangelisches Verlagswerk GmbH*, 1987), p. 273, cf. ST III, p. 11, by inference, presence and absence reflect something of "the polarity of life and death".
238 ST I, p. 110.
239 *Ibid.* p. 113.

presence".[240] In mystical terms, this God is "the transpersonal *One*, the ground and abyss of everything personal".[241] In ontological terms, this means "Non-being is the negation of being within being itself".[242] So just as being and non-being have their unity in being, presence and absence have their unity in the human experience of God in the world, "The God above the God of theism is present, although hidden, in every divine-human encounter".[243]

In conclusion, Tillich's theme of presence can be critiqued in terms of its theology and its internal structure. First, concerning theology, Van Beeck criticises Tillich because there is no sense of the wonder of creation in Tillich's work, as all creation is estranged.[244] For Van Beeck, there is no sense of the magnanimous grace of God in Tillich, only a foreboding sense of judgement.[245] All the good is on one side, the divine side, "The infinite distance between God and man is never bridged; it is identical with man's finitude".[246] Certainly, Van Beeck is half right, as Tillich does not have a sense of the created goodness of the world as it is, and this is because it exists under the weight of estrangement. Admittedly, Tillich's focus on the impact of estrangement is relentless and at times exhausting. Nevertheless, Van Beeck is half wrong, for while Tillich does not use explicitly and consistently the language of grace, the presence of God functions implicitly in his theological system as the grace of God in the world. In Tillich, gracious presence alleviates the impact of estrangement. Second, concerning structure, the experience of God in Tillich is ambiguous. It is experienced as presence and absence and the experience of presence and absence reflects something of the nature of God.[247] In particular, there is a correlation between absence as "the negative side of the mystery" where mystery is "the abysmal element" and presence as "the positive side of the mystery" where mystery is ground *and* abyss.[248] Moreover, absence in Tillich is implicitly of God;

240 *Ibid.*
241 BRUR, p. 26.
242 LPJ, p. 38.
243 TCB, p. 180.
244 Van Beeck, *Christ Proclaimed*, pp. 214-216.
245 *Ibid.* p. 211.
246 ST III, p. 239.
247 ST I, p. 113.
248 *Ibid.* p. 110.

90

"even negative experiences are experiences of God – they reveal his character as abyss".[249] However, the relationship between ground and abyss is hard to understand,

> What I mean is that the ground of being is at the same time the abyss of any definite being; and conversely that the abyss of being which transcends all special beings is at the same time the creative ground of all forms of existence. They are all conditioned by it; but it itself is not conditioned by anything; they are all contained in it but it itself is not exhausted in their infinity.[250]

The relation between ground and abyss can be described as a polarity.[251] But the precise meaning of polarity is not clear. It seems to apply to the micro-level of analysis (e.g. essential relations), where the related term *dialectic* applies more to the macro-level of analysis (e.g. world history). Nevertheless, in general, there is no expression of presence in Tillich without at least an implicit understanding of absence, that is, without the presence of absence, because presence and absence are in polar tension, "as everywhere in the whole of being, non-being is dependent on being, the negative on the positive, death on life".[252]

2.2.2. God and the World

Self-transcending Realism

This part explores Tillich's concepts of God and world and the relationship between the two, in order to understand better his theology of presence. Ultimately, Tillich describes the relationship between God and the world in terms of self-transcending realism, which is the speculative basis of both his theological system and his Christology. To begin with, God's separation from the world, that is, the gap between the finite and the infinite, is fundamental to the way Tillich envisages the God-world relationship.[253] Indeed, Tillich's theology is premised on this concept of separation. The concept is consistent with the way he understands both

---

249 Thatcher, *Ontology*, p. 57.
250 "Symbol and Knowledge", p. 273.
251 Thatcher, *Ontology*, p. 55; ST I, p. 60, a polarity is a form of correlation that entails "the logical interdependence of concepts".
252 ST II, p. 60.
253 ST I, p. 237.

the nature of revelation and God. That is, Tillich's God is experienced in the finite world, as revelation is mediated but God is infinite. Subsequently, there is an inherent tension in Tillich between the concepts of God and world; this is the conflict between "the concreteness and the ultimacy of the religious concern".[254] The source of this tension is Tillich's abiding concern about treating God as a thing in the world, which exists alongside other things. For Tillich, that God is not part of the subject-object structure is decisive.[255] Recalling that participation is the basis of his concept of presence, the problem for Tillich is to hold in tension God's *separation* from the subject-object structure with God's participation in the world and human awareness of its *participation* in Divine life. For Tillich, participation in Divine life is restricted by finitude. Finitude is a defining element of what it means to be human as our existence "is determined not only by the omnipresence of the divine but also by our separation from it".[256] Consequently, Tillich claims that a disclosure of God's self in a personal life is needed for humankind to transcend the gap and know God (2.3). Consequently, Tillich posits a Christological solution, which holds in tension God's separation from the subject-object structure with God's participation in the world and human awareness of its *participation* in Divine life. Tillich's Christological solution is articulated in terms of the concept of symbol and justified on the basis of self-transcending realism. For Tillich, Jesus Christ is *the* symbol of Divine presence.[257]

Tillich claims that God's participation in the world and human participation in Divine life cannot be expressed in spatial or temporal terms, only in symbols.[258] Even God is a symbol for God,[259]

> But faith, understood as the state of being ultimately concerned, has no language other than symbols. When saying this I always expect the question: Only a symbol? He who asks this question shows that he has not understood the difference between signs and symbols nor the power of symbolic language, which surpasses in quality

254 *Ibid.* p. 211.
255 TCB, p. 180, "the God above the God of theism"; cf. ST I, p. 172.
256 "Nature and sacrament", TPE p. 123.
257 ST I p. 136, DF p. 98.
258 ST I, p. 245, ST II, p. 9.
259 DF, p. 46; HCT, p. 189.

and strength the power of any nonsymbolic language. One should never say "only a symbol," but one should say "not less than a symbol."[260]

For Tillich, symbols have something in common with signs, namely, signs and symbols point beyond themselves.[261] Unlike the sign, the symbol "participates in the reality which is symbolized".[262] Symbols are forms of human consciousness.[263] They have a consciousness-raising function as they open up new levels of reality.[264] They grow and die.[265] They cannot be invented. Notably, a symbol's creation, maintenance and demise are related to culture. In this cultural context, human beings are partners in the symbol-making process.[266] Clearly, the link between symbol and culture is crucial in Tillich.[267] Further, the test of a symbol is its adequacy for the meaning of faith. Living symbols have adequacy of expression and this is related to "the power of expressing an ultimate concern in such a way that it creates reply, action, communication".[268] Religious symbols share general characteristics with non-religious symbols, but they also possess their own "peculiar characteristics".[269] For Tillich, the characteristics are figurative and represent perceptibility, innate power and acceptability, with innate power as the most important.[270] Religious symbols are distinguished from non-religious symbols by means of the former's capacity to point "beyond the conceptual sphere … to what concerns us ultimately".[271] All told, symbols are the

260 DF, p. 45.
261 *Ibid.* p. 41.
262 ST II, p. 9.
263 DF, p. 50.
264 "The nature of religious language", TOC, pp. 58-59.
265 UC, pp. 147-148.
266 H. Carse, "Simple water, consuming flame: nature, sacrament and person in Paul Tillich", *Theology*, 99 (1996), p. 24.
267 ST III, pp. 4-5; cf. F.W. Dillistone *The Power of Symbols*, (London: SCM Press, 1986), p. 125; Tillich does not satisfactorily explain the relationship between symbol and culture.
268 DF, p. 96.
269 "Religious Symbol", p. 75.
270 *Ibid.* p. 76.
271 *Ibid.* p. 77.

only means of referring to ultimate-reality[272] and "the fundamental symbol of our ultimate concern is God".[273]

There are problems with Tillich's understanding of symbols over and above his inconsistent use of terms. For instance, the distinction between non-religious and religious symbols is not always clear, especially as all symbols can point beyond the present sphere because they are dependent on being-itself. It seems that what makes a symbol specifically a religious symbol in Tillich has to do with the consciousness and intention of the individual (i.e. through faith). Similarly, the difference between symbol and analogy is not always clear in Tillich. Further, his definition of symbol can appear as merely a psychological abstraction.[274] Nevertheless, there is a consistent theme in all this; that is, Tillich continually uses the concept of symbol in conjunction with the notion of innate power. The meaning of innate power is to be found in his notion of transcendent realism.[275] This helps him explain the meaning of the experience of presence as well as the concept of innate power. In theory, humankind can transcend the gap, because finite reality is able to participate in Divine life by means of the power of self-transcendence.[276] However, only humankind is aware of the experience of participation. For Tillich, presence means more than just participation, as all beings participate in being-itself by virtue of the power of being, presence is the *uniquely human awareness* of its participation in Divine life.[277]

The concept of self-transcendence is part of this transcendent realist perspective. Tillich identifies three types of realism: technological, mystical and historical. He prefers historical realism, which focuses on the finite in the present.[278] It entails a personal investment in "the concrete historical situation" and thus, the limitations of the real are transcended.[279] Tillich describes the ontological basis of transcendent realism in this way, "Can a segment of finite reality become the basis for an as-

272 ST II, p. 9, the problem of "the symbolic knowledge of God".
273 DF, p. 45.
274 DF, p. 50.
275 "Religious Symbol", p. 89.
276 DF, p. 44, no finite reality can express ultimacy.
277 "Religious language", TOC, p. 59, participation in the divine is not the same as identity with God.
278 "Realism and faith", TPE, pp. 85-88, historical realism becomes self-transcending realism when it points beyond itself to the ultimate ground.
279 *Ibid.* p. 85.

sertion about that which is infinite? The answer is that it can, because
that which is infinite is being-itself and because everything participates
in being-itself".[280] Ultimately, the power of being-itself is the basis for
Tillich's confidence that the problem of the gap can be *solved*,

> Being-itself infinitely transcends every finite being. There is no proportion or gra-
> dation between the finite and the infinite. There is an absolute break, an infinite
> "jump". On the other hand, everything finite participates in being-itself and in its
> infinity. Otherwise it would not have the power of being.[281]

Tillich's transcendent realism presumes a particular view of the natural
world, on the basis of which "everything participates in being-itself".
This is evident in his work on sacraments, where he posits a necessary
relationship between "the idea and the material element".[282] Moreover,

> The power of nature must be found in a sphere prior to the cleavage of our world
> into subjectivity and objectivity. Life originates on a level which is "deeper" than
> the Cartesian duality of *cogitatio* and *extensio* ("thought" and "extension").[283]

Tillich places nature within the framework of the history of salvation.[284]
Thus, "natural objects can become bearers of transcendent power and
meaning".[285] Theoretically, all natural objects can be the bearers of
power, "Any object or event is sacramental in which the transcendent is
perceived to be present".[286] However, while objects may be the bearers,
they are not the makers of "sacramental power".[287] Likewise, humankind
is a bearer of divine power but it is not its maker. Thus, transcendent
realism is Tillich's metaphysical view of the relation between nature and
being-itself, and innate power exists in the world because of this relation.

---

280 ST I, p. 239. DF, p. 46, "in the notion of God we must distinguish two elements: the
    element of ultimacy, which is a matter of immediate experience and not symbolic in
    itself, and the element of concreteness, which is taken from our ordinary experience
    and symbolically applied to God".
281 ST I, p. 237.
282 "Nature and sacrament", TPE p. 107.
283 *Ibid.* p. 113, the sphere that is prior, to the cleavage of our world into objectivity
    and objectivity, is ontologically and not chronologically prior.
284 *Ibid.* p. 114.
285 *Ibid.*
286 *Ibid.* p. 120.
287 *Ibid.* p. 122.

In summary, transcendent realism means that there is an inherent capacity in the world for bearing "transcendent power and meaning".[288] Tillich refers to this capacity as the power of infinite self-transcendence.[289] Self-transcendence involves self-affirmation and the power of self-affirmation is the power of humankind to grasp that it belongs to being-itself.[290] For Tillich, the two-sided notion of self-transcendence/self-affirmation "underlies the whole of the present theological system".[291] Significantly, self-transcendence means it is possible for humankind to experience the presence of God in the world, that is, to participate in Divine life. Only humankind is aware of its participation (i.e. consciousness). This means presence is the uniquely human awareness of its participation in Divine life. However, God cannot be described as participating in human life because God as being-itself is not an entity.[292] Thus, Tillich claims that God can only be described symbolically.[293]

Critique of Self-Transcending Realism

Tillich's concept of self-transcendence has an important role in his theology. It is premised on historical realism. Historical realism becomes self-transcending realism when it points beyond itself to the ultimate ground (i.e. the unconditional).[294] The ultimate ground is "the power of a thing", "the power of reality" or "the really real".[295] Historical realism focuses on the present and entails a personal investment in "a concrete historical situation",[296] whereas idealism idealises rather than transcends

288 *Ibid.* p. 114.
289 ST I, p. 191; cf. ST II, p. 8.
290 TCB, p. 174, this is where non-being evokes the power of self-transcendence from being; cf. ST II, p. 9, participation is experienced in this instance as ultimate concern.
291 ST II, p. 8, "the idea of God is neither naturalistic or supranaturalistic".
292 S. Ogden, *The Reality of God And Other Essays*, (London: SCM Press, 1963, 1965, 1967), pp. 54-55, he argues that Tillich's being-itself is an attempt to claim the best of pantheism and theism and, in so doing, surpass their problems. But does it achieve this or leave a nonrelative, changeless God?
293 ST II, p. 9.
294 "Realism and faith", TPE, pp. 85, 87.
295 *Ibid.* pp. 77, 85.
296 *Ibid.* p. 87.

the real.[297] For Tillich, faith and realism belong-together-in-tension.[298] However, Tillich's striving for the unconditioned ground and his view of God as being-itself make it hard to characterise his theology as realist. His tendency to draw out ontological implications, from almost every aspect of his theology, creates the impression that his underlying view is more Neo-Platonic than realist. Hence, Tillich's apparent realism is a metaphysical realism.[299] Moreover, it is hard to see how he could establish a plausible non-speculative basis for making truth statements. For Alston, Tillich has a nonrealist position based on a form of conceptual transcendence.[300] The core idea in Alston's conceptual transcendence is "otherness (*difference* from creatures)".[301] Alston asserts that the problem with extreme forms of conceptual transcendence is how to refer to God and this is the case with Tillich. Tillich claims God is not *a* being and so all references to God are of necessity symbolic, but he also claims that the statement that God is being-itself is a nonsymbolic statement. It is hard to discern what these two claims and the relationship between them mean. In practical terms Tillich's "God above God is finally indifferent to the details of how we live together on the earth".[302] There is some truth in this charge.

297 *Ibid.* p. 76.
298 *Ibid.* p. 76, "idealism relativizes, self-limiting realism denies, but self-transcending realism accepts the tension". Tillich defines idealism as self-transcendence that is not realistic and self-limiting realism as realism without self-transcendence (cf. positivism, pragmatism, empiricism).
299 W.P. Alston, "Realism and the Christian faith", *International Journal of Philosophy of Religion*, 38 (1995), p. 37, "Traditionally realism is a metaphysical position", Alston describes his own view as alethic realism. On the basis of treating theology as a body of discourse, Alston develops theses that have a "correspondence" dimension and presume a "cognition-independent realism" in order to determine truth statements (p. 39).
300 *Ibid.* p. 53; cf. p. 37, n.1, Alston "uses the terms 'nonrealism' and 'irrealism' interchangeably".
301 *Ibid.* p. 51.
302 C. Heyward, "Heterosexist theology: Being above it all", *Journal of Feminist Studies in Religion*, 3 (1987), p. 34, Heyward is concerned about the "moral bankruptcy" of the liberal position, where the heterosexist perspective dominates. Her yardstick is the actual experience of women, and the gay and lesbian community. Tillich's theology, and his ontology in particular, fails to take into account the relational nature of *actual* human experience (p. 31).

Tillich's God above the God of theism can be dismissed as opaque and outdated metaphysical dualism, which is beyond conceptualisation (e.g. Alston) and out of touch with *real* human experience (e.g. C. Heyward). However, Tillich has also been defended in recent years. In terms of dualism, Lamm contends that Tillich goes beyond Kant by repositioning Kant in a non-dualistic world-view.[303] Similarly, Morrison, while recognising there is *a* duality in Tillich (i.e. ontic/ontology), sees Tillich as putting forward a non-dualist position, which Morrison understands as a dialectical form of monism.[304] According to Morrison, the focus of Tillich's ontology is directed beyond the ontic categories. For Morrison, the ontic includes "the categories, principles, attitudes, and value judgments that constitute Kant's notion of theoretical reason".[305] In Morrison, ontology refers to a deeper reality, "beyond the ontic categories and metaphorically 'prior' to the subject-object distinction that makes ontic thinking possible".[306] Hence, Morrison contends that Tillich adopts a different kind of logic,

> The dialectical component of Tillich's method involves the introduction of a non-methodical logic. Tillich distinguished between formal logic that obeys the law of noncontradiction and dialectical logic that precedes or transcends the law of noncontradiction. He defended formal logic, but limited it to its "legal use". He then argued that God as a living God must be described in dialectical statements. Technically stated, Tillich's dialectical logic demands the de-absolutizing of the law of noncontradiction.[307]

In Morrison's view, Tillich acknowledges the merits of the methodical line but adopts the nonmethodical line (e.g. inner light). While Morrison's assertion of the priority of the ontological over the ontic in Tillich's work is evident from even a cursory reading of Tillich's theology, his assertion that Tillich employs a "dialectical logic" to replace a "formal logic" is an unconvincing attempt to justify Tillich's ontological approach. Moreover, while there may be an internal dialectical logic or

303 Lamm, "Revisited", p. 53.
304 R.D. Morrison, "Tillich, Einstein, and Kant: Method, Epistemology, and the Personal God", J.J. Carey ed. *Theonomy and Autonomy*, (Macon: Mercer University Press, 1984), p. 54. It is not clear in this article what Morrison means by ontologically real (pp. 40, 55).
305 *Ibid.* p. 39.
306 *Ibid.* p. 40.
307 *Ibid.* p. 59.

pattern in Tillich's theological system, how that logic refers to God's self and the real world is an open question. Morrison shifts the problem rather than solves it.

To reiterate, the problem for Tillich is to hold in tension God's *separation* from the subject-object structure with God's participation in the world and human awareness of its *participation* in Divine life. Morrison tried to solve the problem by re-configuring formal logic. Now, even if Morrison's attempt is right, there is still the issue of agency. Alston explores God's agency.[308] Initially, Alston challenges the idea that direct action by God is impossible. He then raises the issue that because God works through natural causes this does not mean that a notion of divine agency is unwarranted,

> Merely by the use of natural causes God carries out His purposes and intentions with respect to creatures, and this surely counts as genuine action toward them. If God speaks to me, or guides me, or enlightens me by the use of natural causes, He is as surely in active contact with me as if He had produced the relevant effects by a direct fiat.[309]

For Alston, Tillich is wary of talking about God operating outside the natural order and he explains knowledge of God in terms of the ecstatic. Alston's point is that there is no reason why the ecstatic cannot constitute God's action. For Alston, Tillich's use of God as being-itself restricts Tillich from talking cogently about the agency of God, "Tillich keeps Being-Itself in the background as an objective referent for religious affirmations, even though the conceptual and cognitive inaccessibility of Being-Itself prevents us from assessing those affirmations as true or false of Being-Itself in a realist sense".[310] Alston is not coming from an avowedly postmodern perspective, yet his criticism of Tillich echoes the postmodern critique of ontotheology (4.2.1) in that both perspectives criticise attempts to solve theological problems by resorting to

---

308 W.P. Alston, "God's Action in the World" in W.P. Alston ed., *Divine Nature and Human Language*, (Ithaca and London: Cornell University Press, 1989), p. 198, "I think of God as literally a personal agent". Alston contends that, even where God is not the agent, it could be argued that the effects are in keeping with God's intentions.

309 *Ibid.* p. 217.

310 Alston, "Realism", p. 42.

being.[311] Therefore, the issue of the dualistic or non-dualistic nature of Tillich's theology has not been resolved. Moreover, attempts to interpret Tillich's approach as non-dualist are not convincing.

In conclusion, the paradoxical nature of Tillich's theology becomes evident in his attempts to understand God, world and their interrelation. On the one hand, humankind can participate in the Divine life, through an experience of the presence of God in the world. However, God cannot be described as participating in the world because the gap between the finite and infinite cannot be bridged. If the gap is bridged then God becomes part of the subject/object structure and God becomes a tyrannical being; this is the God of theological theism.[312] On the other hand, Tillich does advocate a God-above-God, but the "God above the God of theism is present, although hidden, in every divine-human encounter".[313] Thus, Tillich's self-transcendent realism is an attempt to explain his own paradox. As an explanation it is persuasive and it makes sense of Tillich's view of presence, symbol and salvation. The problem with the explanation is its speculative foundations. In short, Tillich envisages the possibility of a Trinitarian explanation of "the problem of the unity between ultimacy and concreteness in the living God".[314] But his Trinitarian explanation is built on a speculative basis. Within Tillich's own historical context, the use of a speculative basis is not uncommon (cf. Rahner). Besides, Tillich is aware of the limitations of his theological system.[315] Consideration of this and related issues will be given at the end of the chapter (2.4).

311 R.H. Bryant, "An evaluation of the christological dimensions of Tillich's theology of culture" in J.J. Carey ed., *Kairos and Logos: Studies in the Roots and Implications of Tillich's Theology*, (Mercer: Mercer University Press, 1978, 1984), p. 263, cf. p. 267, Bryant claims that problems arise because Tillich has not adequately addressed, even conceptually, the problem of "the dichotomy between universal Being and particular existence".

312 TCB, pp. 178-179.

313 *Ibid.* p. 180.

314 ST I, p. 228.

315 ST III, p. 5.

100

2.2.3. Anthropology: From Essence to Existence

In Tillich, presence is the uniquely human awareness of its participation in Divine life. This presumes a certain kind of anthropology. The key to understanding this anthropology is the movement from essential being to existential being. Accordingly, Tillich's anthropology will be examined as it throws light on his view of presence. To begin, Tillich's anthropology is seemingly inconsistent as humankind is capable of great courage and faith, yet humankind is fallen.

On the one hand, Tillich has a *high* view of humankind as humankind is "the highest being within the realm of our experience".[316] Other beings may possess centredness, which is a quality of individualisation, but humankind is the highest being because of its "definiteness" of centre.[317] Unlike other beings, humankind has a world (as well as an environment).[318] Unlike other beings, humankind has a capacity for faith.[319] Unlike other beings, humankind has spirit, where spirit is the particularly human dimension of life.[320] With human beings, there is a new psychological dimension, which is related to the emergence of self-awareness.[321] Thus, humankind is able to ask the ontological question and the answer to the question is partially found within humanity itself, because humankind "experiences directly and immediately the structure of being and its elements".[322] On the other hand, Tillich's anthropology is best understood from the perspective of the Fall as a movement from essential to existential being, where human being is existential being and existential being is fallen being.[323] Existential being is essential being, which has been limited by the threat of non-being. The idea of the distorting effects of non-being is the basis for his concept of finitude. The awareness of finitude is the awareness of the limited nature of existence and this awareness informs existential being that it has fallen short of essential being. Further, existential being grapples with ontological anxi-

---

316 *Ibid.* p. 17.
317 *Ibid.* p. 36.
318 *Ibid.* p. 38.
319 DF, p. 83.
320 ST III, p. 21.
321 *Ibid.* p. 37.
322 ST I, p. 169.
323 ST II, p. 36.

ety. However, humankind has the potential to transcend the limits of existence because humankind belongs to being-itself.[324] Tillich defines existence in terms of the idea of *standing out*.[325] Humankind *stands out* from non-being; "if we say that something exists, we say that it has left the state of mere potentiality and has become actual. It stands out of mere potentiality, out of relative non-being".[326] Thus, to exist for Tillich means to experience estrangement from our essential nature, which entails a loss of true essentiality. Furthermore, Tillich interprets essence on the basis of his second level of ontological concepts and the constitutive elements of dynamics and form (2.1.5). For Tillich, form is related to *essentia*.[327] Therefore, if the experience of absence is symptomatic of estrangement, and estrangement is a consequence of the movement from essential to existential being, then absence entails a loss of essentiality.

The Fall reveals much about the tone and character of Tillich's anthropology. It explains symbolically the significance of the movement from essence to existence. In Tillich's theology, the Fall is more than a biblical story or an insightful narrative, which it is; it is his anthropological explanation of the gap between the finite and the infinite. Humankind "is integrated only fragmentarily and has elements of disintegration or disease in all dimensions of his being".[328] It is finite and aware of its finitude. Tillich describes the awareness of finitude in terms of anxiety, which is the driving force in the transition from essence to existence, where humankind "decides for self-actualization, thus producing the end of dreaming innocence".[329] The key anthropological theme here is that humankind belongs to what it has become estranged from. Further, Tillich sees a connection between estrangement and original sin and actual sins. Original sin needs to be interpreted existentially.[330] It is related to universal estrangement.[331] Subsequently, the concept of estrangement in Tillich does not supplant sin; on the contrary, "Sin expresses most

---

324 ST I, p. 191.
325 ST II, p. 20, which is the root meaning of *existere*.
326 *Ibid.* pp. 20-21.
327 MFSA, pp. 70-75; ST I, p. 178, form referring to "its definite power of being".
328 DF, p. 108, cf. p. 110.
329 ST II, p. 36, cf. p. 33, innocence stands for "non-actualized potentiality" and the "state of essential being is not an actual stage of human development".
330 *Ibid.* p. 41, Tillich rejects "the idealistic separation of an innocent nature from guilty man".
331 *Ibid.* p. 56.

sharply the personal character of estrangement over against its tragic side".[332] Furthermore, Tillich considers that the concept of hubris is critical in relation to both sin and estrangement, construing it as the self-elevation of humankind "into the sphere of the divine".[333] In contrast to *sins*, hubris as *sin* "in its total form, namely, the other side of unbelief or man's turning away from the divine center to which he belongs … its main symptom is that man does not acknowledge his finitude".[334] Therefore, the absence of God, which is symptomatic of estrangement, is an existential consequence of original sin and an existential expression of actual sins.

In conclusion, the experience of the absence of God in the world entails a loss of essentiality, which evokes a yearning for the infinite as humankind "is driven toward faith by his awareness of the infinite to which he belongs".[335] That is, humankind's capacity for faith is related to its awareness of finitude. This awareness leads to an uncertainty, which has to be accepted by means of courage; "the daring self-affirmation of one's own being in spite of the powers of 'nonbeing'".[336] He describes this kind of faith as absolute faith.[337] It is "the state of being ultimately concerned".[338] It is "passionate concern".[339] It is symptomatic of the capacity for self-transcendence. However, human resistance is a stumbling block to self-transcendence. For Tillich, the power of self-transcendence is harnessed through an act of self-affirmation (which is not the same as self-elevation) and this requires an act of self-negation. Significantly, only Christ is capable of a genuine act of self-negation.

332 *Ibid.* p. 46, in Tillich, *sins* (plural) are expressions of sin, whereas *sin* (singular) refers to the nature of the relationship between humankind and God.
333 *Ibid.* p. 50.
334 *Ibid.* pp. 50-51.
335 DF, p. 9.
336 *Ibid.* p. 17; cf. p. 21.
337 TCB, p. 179.
338 DF, p. 1, cf. p. 4, "Faith as ultimate concern is an act of the total personality. It happens in the center of the personal life and includes all its elements. Faith is the most centered act of the human mind. It is not a movement of a special section or a special function of man's total being. They are all united in the act of faith".
339 *Ibid.* p. 106.

2.3. Christology

The aim of this section is to present both an overview of Tillich's Christology and an examination of his theology of the Incarnation and the Death-Resurrection event, in preparation for Chapter 4. Tillich's Christology has been criticised for not being overtly Christian or biblical.[340] It lacks a clear sense of the Jesus of history, his "words and deeds", his experience of suffering and "the actual historical events".[341] However, it is important to remember that he is chiefly interested in the impact of the New Being in the here and now. Indeed, he sought to discern the saving presence of God in Christ in the contemporary situation. Thus, Tillich tends to sacrifice methodological rigour for existential relevance. Ironically, he laments that,

> This sentimental Jesus has nothing to say to the strong in our period. But beyond this, the word "Jesus" does not communicate in depth anymore. And the word "Christ", which originally meant the anointed one sent by God to bring the new aeon, has become ununderstandable. It is used as a proper name, instead of the paradox of a climactic function given to a human being.[342]

Some of these criticisms are fairly levelled at Tillich's work. Nonetheless, history is important for Tillich and he wants his Christ to be grounded in history, because only Jesus the Christ is capable of the fundamentally necessary act of self-negation.

Tillich's Christology is linked to his anthropology and his soteriology. In relation to anthropology, Tillich claims that there is a connection between Christ and the human predicament. He envisages the human predicament as an on-going, all-consuming struggle, which is "a symptom of the ambiguity of life in all realms".[343] He describes the predicament in terms of "disruption, conflict, self-destruction, meaninglessness, and despair in all realms of life".[344] For Tillich, the struggle is symptomatic of the state of estrangement and the anxiety of finitude (2.2.3).

340 Macquarrie, *Jesus Christ*, p. 303.
341 Van Beeck, *Christ Proclaimed*, pp. 208-210.
342 IRCM, pp. 15-6.
343 ST III, p. 53.
344 ST I, p. 49.

104

However, the anxiety of finitude is not the same for the Christian as the despair of self-destruction,

> Christianity sees in the picture of Jesus as the Christ a human life in which all forms of anxiety are present but in which all forms of despair are absent. In the light of this picture it is possible to distinguish "essential" finitude from "existential" disruption, ontological anxiety from the anxiety of guilt which is despair.[345]

Humankind sees in Christ the possibility of existential being living as essential being, because Christ has inaugurated a new salvific era and overcome the human predicament.[346] This new reality means the resolution of "the conflict between essential being and distorted existence".[347] In contrast to the fractured nature of the human predicament, the New Being is characterised by "the undisrupted unity of the center of his being with God".[348] This unity is maintained even in the midst of estrangement and it is manifested as self-surrendering love.[349] In relation to soteriology, Tillich claims that salvation requires new being, for only a New Being can produce a new action.[350] The meaning of salvation is partly found in the idea of healing.[351] Salvation also has cosmic dimensions, but the cosmic sweep of salvation is grounded in a particular personal life, namely the life of Jesus the Christ, "he is the ultimate criterion of every healing and saving process".[352] So,

> "Where is this New Being manifest?" Systematic theology answers this question by saying: "In Jesus the Christ." This answer also has presuppositions and implications which it is the main purpose of the whole system to develop. Only this must be said here – that this formula accepts the ancient Christian baptismal confession of Jesus as the Christ. He who is the Christ is he who brings on the new eon, the new reality.[353]

---

345 *Ibid.* p. 201.
346 ST II, p. 119.
347 IRCM, p. 53.
348 ST II, p. 138.
349 IRCM, p. 54, n. 6, years later the order is changed with Tillich placing more emphasis on the self-surrendering love and the cross.
350 ST II, p. 79.
351 *Ibid.* p. 166; IRCM, p. 56.
352 ST II, p. 168.
353 ST I, p. 49.

2.3.1. New Being: History, Scripture, Biblical Picture of Christ

Tillich is interested in the impact of Christ the New Being. This orients the way he expresses his Christology. He is critical of the traditional methodological distinction of the person and work of Christ. He abandons this distinction on the basis that "the being of the Christ is his work and that his work is his being, namely, the New Being which is his being".[354] Unfortunately, Tillich does not fully define the concept of the New Being.[355] Nonetheless, something of its character can be gleaned from his descriptions of the impact of the New Being in history.

The Christ event in Tillich takes place in history, thus, "history has received a meaning and a center".[356] For Tillich, "the Greek word *historia* means primarily inquiry, information, report, and only secondarily the events inquired about and reported".[357] This prefigures his two-sided view of history,

> Human history … is always a union of objective and subjective elements. An "event" is a syndrome (i.e., a running-together) of facts and interpretation. If we now turn from the semantic to the material discussion, we find the same double structure in all occurrences which deserve the name "historical event".[358]

The central event in history is the advent of the New Being.[359] Christ inaugurates a new reality, which is an event in history that takes root in the life of the disciples,

> This is an event *which has happened*, an event which consists of two parts: the fact of a personal life, and the reception of this life by a group called disciples or followers. This is the event on which everything else is dependent. I repeat, the event has two sides: the factual side and the receiving side; and both are necessary".[360]

---

354 ST II, p. 168.
355 Heywood Thomas, "Tillich", p. 107, Heywood Thomas is emphatic about Tillich's repeated failure to define terms clearly and/or consistently, (e.g. "unfortunately he never explains what exactly he means by this concept").
356 BRUR, p. 41.
357 ST III, p. 300.
358 *Ibid.* p. 302.
359 *Ibid.* p. 364.
360 IRCM, p. 46; cf. ST III, p. 308.

106

As an event in history, it includes fact and reception.[361] The fact is the personal life of Jesus of Nazareth. The reception is the recognition bestowed upon Jesus by the disciples of the salvific significance of Jesus as the Christ. Thus, the disciples constitute for Tillich the all-important "history-bearing" group.[362] For Tillich, Christianity began not with the birth of Jesus, but with the assertion by a disciple that "Thou art the Christ" (i.e. Caesarea Philippi).[363] This becomes important in relation to the Death-Resurrection event (2.3.3). Overall, his view of history is hard to fathom. On the one hand, he has a macro view of history, that is, history on the world stage. With echoes of Schelling, Hegel and Marx, Tillich tries to spell out the universal significance of the impact of the New Being.[364] On the other hand, he has a micro view of history, that is, history as it pertains to the discipline of historiography, especially in the context of the relationship between Scripture and the historical Jesus. Clearly, Tillich sees an important relationship between the two levels of historical analysis; the problem is trying to spell out the nature of that relationship. In spite of these methodological problems, he is adamant that Christ is the centre history. The significance of Christ in Tillich can be summed up in the idea that Christ is able to make the necessary act of self-negation.

The significance of the New Being can be understood in terms of the gap between the finite and the infinite. Humankind cannot transcend the gap because of the sin of hubris. The capacity to sin has its *origins* in the Fall and the subsequent genesis of the awareness of finitude. The awareness of finitude is a source of anxiety and the anxiety of finitude is a force in the transition from essence to existence.[365] In this context, sin expresses the profound nature of the experience of estrangement.[366] Subsequently, hubris is an obstacle, which prevents humankind from making the necessary act of self-negation and overcoming estrangement. Hubris is self-elevation where humankind presumes it is capable of its own sal-

---

361 UC, p. 154.
362 ST III, p. 308.
363 ST II, p. 97, cf. UC, p. 25, Tillich sees this as the most revealing story in the synoptic gospels (Matt 16:21-23), as it reveals ultimate concern and idolatry.
364 PPT, pp. 130-133.
365 ST II, p. 36.
366 *Ibid.* p. 46.

vation.[367] It is the refusal to acknowledge reality and the impact of finitude. It is humankind's "turning away from the divine center".[368] Hubris is more than a caprice as sin is expressed in and reinforced by "the bondage of the will".[369] Thus, salvation requires new being because, "New being precedes new acting".[370] Only a New Being is capable of making the necessary act of self-negation,

> In the image of Christ we find the traits of this new power. What we see is the astonishing fact – the paradoxical fact – that in the midst of human existence we find an image of essential humanity. It is not an "ideal", something merely hoped for or prophetically announced, as in the Old Testament ... it is seen as a *reality* which radiates through Jesus' image, as that was remembered by the disciples when they received it.[371]

Tillich argues that this unique personal act of self-negation cannot be achieved by means of a group, because a group cannot be the bearer of the final revelation.[372] Unlike an individual, a group is not capable of the *centredness* required for such an act; where centredness is "a quality of individualization, in so far as the indivisible thing is the centered thing".[373] A social group does not possess a "natural, deciding center".[374] In contrast, Jesus is completely centred and so his personal life is able to represent existence as a whole.[375] He achieves this because he is completely self-possessed, that is, he is fully united with the ground of being.[376] Therefore, Jesus is able to make the necessary act of self-negation, where self-negation involves an act of freedom and freedom is realised in the context of destiny.[377] Thus Jesus, in an act of freedom,

---

367 *Ibid.* p. 50.
368 *Ibid.* p. 51.
369 *Ibid.* p. 80, the temptation of religion is to turn revelation into self-salvation.
370 *Ibid.* p. 79.
371 IRCM, p. 53.
372 ST II, p. 120, cf. 95, "The basic answer to these questions is given in the concept of essential man appearing in a personal life under the conditions of existential estrangement".
373 ST III, pp. 32, 68, in humankind, centredness is essentially given but it is actualised in freedom through destiny by means of a moral act.
374 ST II, p. 58.
375 *Ibid.* p. 98.
376 ST I, p. 135, two important aspects about Jesus the Christ, as depicted in the New Testament, are his unity with God and his sacrificial disposition.
377 *Ibid.* p. 200.

chooses to sacrifice himself completely and in so doing fulfills his destiny.[378]

The idea of the significance of salvation being concentrated in one personal life is pivotal to Tillich's Christology:[379]

> If there were no personal life in which existential estrangement had been overcome, the New Being would have remained a quest and an expectation and would not be a reality in time and space. Only if the existence is conquered in *one* point – a personal life, representing existence as a whole – is it conquered in principle, which means "in beginning and in power".[380]

There are four concerns here about attributing salvific significance to one personal life. First, in relation to Tillich's concept of centredness, the distinction between the group and the individual seems reasonable. That is, only an individual has a "natural, deciding center".[381] But it is not clear what that is; besides this is at odds with his description of history bearing groups, where the group rather than the individual has a centre that makes it capable of bearing history.[382] If there is a distinction, then the distinction is not clear. Second, assuming Jesus was truly centred, it is still not clear *how* the salvific event actually takes place in one personal life. That is, it is not clear how Jesus' essential unity with God, which is the basis of his act of self-negation, is the means of salvation.

> In his key christological statement, namely that the normative revelation of God is that of "essential manhood" in Jesus as the Christ, Tillich fails to argue convincingly how such an abstract concept could or did constitute a particular historical revelation of God, or how it did unite with a particular person, Jesus of Nazareth.[383]

Third, it is not clear why salvation can only occur in *one* personal life. Apparently, this presumption is a non-negotiable in Tillich. This may be the result of his over-reliance on Schelling's Christology, where Christi-

---

378 *Ibid.* p. 136; cf. BRUR, p. 85.
379 ST II, p. 120, "The New Being has appeared in a personal life, and for humanity it could not have appeared in any other way; for the potentialities of being are completely actual in a personal life alone."
380 *Ibid.* p. 98.
381 *Ibid.* p. 58.
382 ST III, p. 308.
383 Bryant, "Evaluation", p. 267, for Bryant, Tillich could not see how finitude was not a deficiency in God, and that it enabled God to participate. For Bryant, God does not have to be *the God above God* to be God.

anity is the culmination of the process of revelation and Christ is the end
and climax,

> On the day of deliverance, the true God will cease to be merely the one who ap-
> pears, the one who reveals himself ... revelation will come to an end. And this actu-
> ally happened in Christ, for Christ is the *End* (*Ende*) of revelation.[384]

This incorporates the notion that there is an end point in history, namely,
a singularity requiring one personal life to embody it. Further, Tillich
appeals to existence itself as a form of justification, which reveals that
the story of salvation is expressed in and through one personal life,
namely Jesus the Christ. It is related to Tillich's assumption that the biblical picture of Christ reveals that Christ is unique, because he is not
estranged from God. Clearly, there are romantic elements in Tillich, who
questioned the Church's tradition but was sympathetic to certain phases
of the tradition.[385] In spite of his assertions, none of this necessarily excludes the possibility that other personal lives may have enjoyed undif-
ferentiated unity with God. Fourth, Tillich asserts that his Christological
focus is on one personal life, but in practice, it is on the picture of the
one personal life.[386] Tillich virtually grants autonomy to this picture,
independent of the personal life that lies behind it.[387] Further, in places
Tillich's distinction between *the person* and *the picture* of Christ seems
like a theological sleight of hand. One possible response is that the picture of Christ in Tillich functions as a symbol of the person and thus the
picture manifests power symbolically. This seems more convincing than
Tillich's own reliance on the *analogia imaginis*. However, the concept of
the biblical picture of Christ needs to be explored, as he attributes a great
deal of significance to the concept.

Tillich uses the concept of the biblical picture of Christ because it allows him to address historical and hermeneutical problems without being
captive to either history or text. Consequently, he sacrifices some historical and exegetical rigour in order to speak of the ongoing existential
impact of the New Being. Certainly, Tillich is informed about historical-

384 Schelling, p. 105.
385 HCT, p. 29 ff.
386 OTB, p. 50, cf. UC p. 145.
387 ST II, pp. 114-115, 117, 136, 151.

110

critical and biblical-hermeneutical matters.[388] He acknowledges the significance of the contribution of historical studies.[389] Even so, he argues that research into the historical Jesus has failed. For Tillich, Christianity "is based on the witness to the messianic character of Jesus by people who were not interested at all in a biography of the Messiah".[390] The reality of the Christ-event is actualised by faith through human participation and not by means of "historical argument".[391] After all, it is not possible to get *behind* biblical texts via historical criticism to the historical Jesus, because the Jesus in the texts is the Christ of faith.[392] Therefore, Tillich makes the considerable claim that, "The foundation of Christian belief is the biblical picture of Christ, not the historical Jesus".[393] According to Tillich, historical research has shown that the historical events behind the biblical picture can only be established on the basis of probability.[394] While the character of some biblical material can be decided by historical research with a high degree of probability (e.g. infancy narratives as myth), only faith can say something about, "the reality which is manifest in the New Testament picture of Jesus as the Christ has saving power for those who are grasped by it, no matter how much or how little can be traced to the historical figure who is called Jesus of Nazareth".[395] All this is persuasive, but it hinges on the dubious concept of the biblical picture of Christ.

388 *Ibid.* p. 101, "The historical method unites analytical-critical and constructive-conjectural elements".
389 *Ibid.* p. 113, "the preceding evaluation of the historical approach to the biblical records led to a negative and a positive assertion. The negative assertion is that historical research can neither give nor take away the foundation of the Christian faith. The positive assertion is that historical research has influenced and must influence Christian theology, first, by giving an analysis of the three different semantic levels of biblical literature … second, by showing in several steps the development of the christological symbols … and, finally, by providing a precise philological and historical understanding of the biblical literature by means of the best methods developed in all historical work".
390 *Ibid.* p. 105.
391 *Ibid.* p. 114.
392 *Ibid.* pp. 114-115.
393 OTB, p. 50.
394 DF, p. 87.
395 *Ibid.* p. 88. Later, Tillich prefers *image* to *picture*, though it is not clear why (e.g. UC, p. 154).

Before proceeding to look closely at the concept of the biblical picture of Christ, it is important to consider his underlying assumptions in order to see what Tillich is trying to achieve. His concept of the biblical picture of Christ is an attempt to simultaneously ground Christ in the Jesus of Nazareth, while maintaining Christ's ongoing unity with God, without making God captive to the Jesus of history. Christ's unity with God is a prime assumption in Tillich; while Christ "has only finite freedom under the conditions of time and space, he is not estranged from the ground of his being".[396] This New Being is a new reality because it is "the undistorted manifestation of essential being within and under the conditions of existence".[397] Thus, Tillich affirms Christ's unity with God. Further, Tillich uses "dynamic-relational concepts" to describe Christ,[398] rejecting the use of the static term "human nature" for Christ, in favour of "the dynamics of his life".[399] He envisages the unity between Christ and God as a dynamic process, rather than as a static event in history. Furthermore, Tillich claims that this God can only be referred to by means of analogy, in particular, he relies on the analogy of being, "The *analogia entis* gives us our only justification of speaking at all about God. It is based on the fact that God must be understood as being-itself".[400] Analogical predication involves the use of similarities and differences.[401] With theological analogies the validity of a set of similarities and differences depends in part on premises about the nature of God and God's relationship with the world. *Similarities* make it possible to speak about God, that is, similarities make for human understanding of God (i.e. cataphatic theology). Simultaneously, this means that God-talk is indirect as there is no direct or immediate access to God. Implicitly, the analogous nature of God-talk is a reminder that God is different (i.e. other). Like the similarities, the *differences* involved in analogical predication make for human understanding of God (i.e. apophatic theology). Moreover, Tillich is aware of the limits of analogies.

396 ST II, p. 126.
397 *Ibid.* p. 119.
398 *Ibid.* p. 148.
399 *Ibid.* pp. 146-148, likewise his preference for "eternal God-man-unity".
400 ST I, p. 240.
401 "Analogies", Baggini and Fosl, p. 46.

112

If the knowledge of revelation is called "analogous," this certainly refers to the classical doctrine of the *analogia entis* between the finite and the infinite. Without such an analogy nothing could be said about God. But the *analogia entis* is in no way able to create a natural theology. It is not a method of discovering truth about God; it is the form in which every knowledge of revelation must be expressed. In this sense *analogia entis*, like "religious symbol," points to the necessity of using material taken from finite reality in order to give content to the cognitive function in revelation.[402]

However, Tillich's central theological premise is the unbridgeable difference (i.e. the gap) between the finite and the infinite, that is, God is other, the transcendent, unconditioned being-itself. Therefore, knowledge of the unity of Christ with God, which is a gift of divine revelation, can only be described analogically (or symbolically). In short, the concept of the biblical picture of Christ is an analogous way of referring to the unity of Christ and God, which is grounded in but not restricted to Jesus of Nazareth. Nevertheless, the use of the concept does not resolve major theological problems. Tillich concedes that it is not a method of knowing but a way of "speaking of God".[403]

As indicated, there are problems with Tillich's concept of the biblical picture of Christ. To begin, Tillich claims that, "The foundation of Christian belief is the biblical picture of Christ, not the historical Jesus".[404] Only faith can say something about the reality that is expressed through the biblical picture of Christ.[405] But there is an unresolved tension in all this. In terms of the various pictures of Christ in Scripture, Tillich acknowledges the diversity and claims that the "substance" is the same in each and every instance.[406] However, the precise nature of this common "substance" is not clear. He may mean that the transforming power evoked by each and every biblical picture of Christ is the source of continuity. Subsequently, he makes a distinction between an imaginary picture and a real picture.[407] The imaginary picture has no power to transform; only the real picture has the power, because it is grounded in and is an expression of a new reality.[408] However, Tillich's distinction

---

402 ST I, p. 131.
403 ST II, p. 115.
404 OTB, pp. 48-50.
405 DF, p. 88.
406 ST II, p. 138.
407 *Ibid.* p. 115.
408 IRCM, p. 53, "In the image of Christ we find traits of this new power".

between real and imaginary pictures is not convincing.[409] The problem is that he is trying to express in the biblical picture of Christ something of the ongoing significance of the presence of God-in-Christ in the world as well as maintain God's separateness from finitude. In an effort to express the existential significance of the New Being, he has not addressed key theological problems. Lastly, Tillich has been accused of reducing Christ to *only* a symbol and failing to distinguish clearly "between symbolic or metaphorical and analogical speaking of God",[410] or confusing symbolic modes.[411] This is a reasonable criticism not the least because Tillich is inconsistent with his use of terminology.[412] In fairness to Tillich, however, this last critique requires more consideration, which is beyond the scope of the present study.

2.3.2. The Incarnation

The concept of the biblical picture of Christ represents Tillich's attempt to affirm his view of the Incarnation in the context of dealing with the complicated hermeneutical issue of the relationship between the Jesus of history, the biblical text and the Christ of faith. This part of the study deals with three general theological issues associated with the Incarnation. First, the theme of the Incarnation has an important but implicit function in Tillich's Christology. Second, Tillich uses the concept of paradox, with limited success, in an attempt to resolve some of the broader problems associated with the Incarnation. Third, Tillich's *Logos* interpretation of the Incarnation emphasises the universal nature of Christ as the New Being.

The Incarnation has an important role in Tillich's Christology. Admittedly, as noted his Christology is open to criticism, for example, "Til-

---

409 Heywood Thomas, *Tillich*, pp. 114-115; Macquarrie, *Jesus Christ*, p. 303.
410 F.I. Gamwell, "Speaking of God after Aquinas", *The Journal of Religion* 81 (2001), p. 201.
411 D.R. Weisbaker, "Aesthetic elements in Tillich's theory of symbol" in J. J. Carey ed. *Kairos and Logos: Studies in the Roots and Implications of Tillich's Theology*, (Mercer: Mercer University Press, 1984), p. 253. J. Macquarrie *Principles of Christian Theology*, rev. ed., (London: SCM Press, 1966, 1977), p. 135, n. 10.
412 Heywood Thomas, *Tillich*, pp. 33-36

114

lich shows a surprising lack of interest in the historical life of Jesus".[413] There is a strong sense in which Tillich's Christ is abstract, as he seems more interested in the idea of the Incarnation than its concrete expression. However, this is in part due to his abstract style of argumentation and expression, his understanding of historical critical studies and the fact that the significance of the Incarnation in Tillich is understated. For example, Tillich is concerned about the danger of "the monophysitic distortion of the picture of Jesus as the Christ".[414] He wants to affirm the full humanity of Christ. In particular, it is fundamental to Tillich's theological vision that Jesus experiences finitude. Hence, the accounts of the temptation of Jesus are important for him.[415] The temptation stories imply desire and desire is not in itself wrong; it is part of the risk of the polarity of dynamics and form, "The unity with God is not the negation of the desire for reunion of the finite with the infinite".[416] While the New Testament describes Jesus in mythical language, "A real, individual life shines through all his utterances and actions".[417] Therefore, Tillich's claim that Christ experiences finitude is in fact an emphatic statement of a general incarnational principle. Further, he rejects the use of "sinlessness" as an appellation for Christ. For Tillich, sinlessness misses the point of the Incarnation, as "Finitude implies openness to error, and error belongs to the participation of the Christ in man's existential predicament".[418] Consequently, Christ participates in the ambiguities of human existence and as a result the negativities of existence are incorporated into his unity with God. In brief, Tillich's theology of incarnation is implicit, general and yet central to his guiding theological vision.

The concept of paradox has an important place in Tillich's theological system in general and in his incarnational theology in particular. For Tillich, *Jesus the Christ* as a theological designation is a paradox; "the appearance of the New Being under the conditions of existence, yet

413 Van Beeck, *Christ Proclaimed*, p. 208.
414 ST II, pp. 128, 141-146; HCT, p. 81 ff. G. Newlands, "Monophysitism" in A. Richardson and J. Bowden, *A New Dictionary of Christian Theology*, (London: SCM Press, 1983), hereafter NDCT, p. 381; monophysitism claimed that the incarnate Christ consisted of "one single nature", associated with Eutyches and condemned at Chalcedon.
415 UC, p. 137.
416 ST II, p. 129.
417 *Ibid.* p. 151.
418 ST II, p. 131; cf. UC, p. 143.

judging and conquering them, is the paradox of the Christian message. This is the only paradox and the source of all paradoxical statements in Christianity".[419] Now Tillich's use of the concept of paradox has two interrelated aspects. First, the metaphysical aspect is that the universal and the particular meet in Christ.[420] Second, the existential aspect is the self-negation of Christ.[421] Therefore, the paradox in Tillich is *de facto* an article of faith, as those who profess Jesus is the Christ must assert the paradox that he who overcame existential estrangement also participated in it.[422] Further, in Tillich, paradox does not mean dualism.[423] He denies any notion of dualism, asserting an essentialist understanding of unity.[424] The source of the unity is to be found in his principle of the multidimensional unity of life, though life is experienced as ambiguous, "it unites essential and existential elements".[425] Thus, for Tillich, paradox is more a means of describing the revelatory experience of the disciples than the strict application of a philosophical concept. For example, Tillich affirms that the acceptance of this paradox is not the acceptance of the absurd, but is the state of being grasped by the power, which breaks into our experience from above; it is "a new reality and not a logical riddle".[426]

419 ST II, p. 92, cf. IRCM, p. 49, "In the records we have reports of the fight of Jesus with the apostles about the meaning of his mission and his death. Only through his death can he be the Messiah. This is the basic paradox of Christianity over against the unparadoxical, religiously primitive attitude of the disciples".
420 ST II, p. 100, "The Christ is God-for-us!"
421 ST I, p. 133, (i.e. "negating itself without losing itself"), cf. ST II, p. 94, "In *one* personal life essential manhood had appeared under the conditions of existence without being conquered by them".
422 ST II, p. 97; cf. p. 126, the paradox can be expressed as Jesus the Christ is the universal *Logos* expressed in the (concrete) incarnate *Logos*, "the paradoxical character of his being consists in the fact that, although he has only finite freedom ... he is not estranged from the ground of his being".
423 "paradox" in S. Blackburn, *The Oxford Dictionary of Philosophy*, (Oxford, New York: Oxford University Press, 1996), hereafter ODP, p. 276, "A paradox arises when a set of apparently incontrovertible premises gives unacceptable or contradictory conclusions". In Tillich, the paradox is how the universal (God) can be found in the particular (Jesus the Christ).
424 "essentialism", ODP, p. 125, "The doctrine that it is correct to distinguish between those properties of a thing, or kind of thing, that are essential to it, and those that are merely accidental". In Tillich, these essential properties are invariably metaphysical.
425 ST III, p. 29.
426 ST II, p. 92.

116

Nonetheless, Tillich is aware of some of the philosophical nuances of the concept of paradox. To that end, he claims the paradox does not defy the laws of formal logic.[427] Thus, on the basis of paradox, the concept of Incarnation needs to be revised.[428] Subsequently, Tillich asserts that it is nonsensical to say, "God has become man".[429] He claims that the words "God has become man" cannot be taken at face value; otherwise this means God becomes that which God is not and ceases to be God. However, this detracts from Tillich's commitment to the concept of Christ's participation in estrangement. In short, his use of paradox is persuasive, but in fact it does not advance the analysis of the Incarnation. In this context, Tillich's *Logos* construal is important for his theological vision.

In Tillich, the Incarnation is the definitive expression of the absolutely concrete and the absolutely universal. To explain the meaning of this paradox, he applies a *Logos* construal to the Incarnation,

> The incarnation is a once-for-all event; and it is not a particular element or characteristic of God which becomes incarnate. Rather, it is the very center of divinity which becomes incarnate, and to express this the idea of the Logos was used.[430]

The *Logos* is an integral part of Tillich's Christology as Christ is the Word *(Logos)* of God. For Tillich,

> "Logos" is the principle of the divine self-manifestation in God as well as in the universe, in nature as well as in history. "Flesh" does not mean a material substance but stands for historical existence. And "became" points to the paradox of God participating in that which did not receive him and in that which is estranged from him.[431]

The original and final revelation of the presence of God in the world is made manifest in Christ the incarnate *Logos*.[432] The *Logos* is "a principle of order and structure in all realities".[433] Tillich contends that the *Logos*

---

427 *Ibid.* p. 91.
428 *Ibid.* p. 95, "The unqualified use of the term 'Incarnation' in Christianity creates pagan, or at least superstitious, connotations".
429 *Ibid.* p. 94.
430 HCT, p. 32.
431 *Ibid.* p. 95.
432 ST I, p. 126.
433 PPT, p. 30.

doctrine is the foundation of all Christian theology.[434] For Tillich, the *Logos* is the universal *Logos*, which is coupled to reason and the Spirit. It is a touchstone in philosophy and theology as even "The name 'Jesus the Christ' implies an ontology".[435] Further, if biblical personalism finds its fulfillment in Christ the *Logos*, then ontology explains the nature of the *Logos*. In other words, the idea of the incarnate *Logos* is only meaningful in the context of an understanding of the universal *Logos*. They are one and the same *Logos*, "the Logos universal and the Logos as the power of a personal life are one and the same Logos".[436] Nonetheless, Christ as the *Logos* raises two issues. First, Christ as *Logos* produces a Trinitarian problem, that is, the problem of explaining how the universal (the infinite) is manifested in the concrete (the finite).[437] Tillich is adamant that God is holy, other and separate and that the gap between the infinite and the finite cannot be bridged because God as being-itself cannot participate in human existence.[438] Second, Christ as the *Logos* provides an answer to the Trinitarian problem and this goes back to Tillich's idea of self-transcendence (i.e. an attempt to explain how human life participates in divine life). It is possible because one particular personal life, which is Jesus of Nazareth, participates fully in divine life. So Tillich concludes that Christianity is *the* theology because "it is based on the tension between the absolutely concrete and the absolutely universal",[439] embodied by the *Logos* doctrine.[440] Thus, Tillich has simultaneously underlined the universal significance of Christ and grounded the universal *Logos* in the life of Jesus.

Tillich is a child of modernity, as seen from the perspective of his love of reason and *Logos* theology. Though not without its problems, Tillich manages to combine modernity's preoccupation with the rational and the church's veneration of the *Logos* tradition in his theology of the Incarnation. The Incarnation is a crucial theme in Tillich, where its importance is implicit and pervasive. For example, Tillich's ideal view of the human condition could be described broadly as incarnational, "the

434 ST I, p. 17.
435 BRUR, p. 76.
436 *Ibid.* p. 75.
437 ST I, p. 228.
438 *Ibid.* p. 237.
439 *Ibid.* p. 16.
440 *Ibid.* p. 17.

118

ideal of non-religion and non-secular, the identity of workday and Sunday, the manifestation of the divine in everything in which we live".[441] However, Tillich's use of analogy and paradox, while illuminating in parts, does not resolve the presenting theological problems. In conclusion, Tillich's commitment to the theme of the Incarnation manifests itself in his wholehearted emphasis on the significance of Christ's participation in estrangement, "Though subject to individual and social conditions his human spirit was entirely grasped by the Spiritual Presence; his spirit was 'possessed' by the divine Spirit or, to use another figure, 'God was in him'".[442]

2.3.3. Death-Resurrection Event

The aim in this part of the study is to explore the theme of the Death-Resurrection event in Tillich. For Tillich, the death and resurrection of Christ are interdependent symbols.[443] Initially, the significance of the cross will be treated separately from the resurrection, although they are part of the one salvific process in human history. For Tillich, atonement is part of the salvific process; it is "the effect of the New Being in Jesus as the Christ on those who are grasped by it in their state of estrangement".[444] It has subjective and objective sides.[445] These two sides are there to maintain both the involvement and the otherness of the divinity: "The replacement of the concept of substitution by the concept of participation seems to be a way to a more adequate doctrine of atonement, in which the objective and the subjective sides are balanced".[446] Tillich rejects substitutionary theories of atonement.[447] He emphasises that the

---

441 IRCM, p. 51.

442 ST III, p. 144.

443 ST II, p. 153, cf. ST I, p. 60.

444 ST II, p. 170.

445 *Ibid.* p. 170, "a divine act and a human reaction".

446 *Ibid.* p. 173.

447 *Ibid.* p. 176; cf. C. Gunton, *The Actuality of Atonement: A Study of Metaphor, Rationality and the Christian Tradition*, (Edinburgh: T and T Clark, 1988). Gunton, on the basis of metaphor, has a place for a substitutionary approach. For Gunton, metaphor has a greater truth claim than so-called *pure* language. Metaphors provide insight into part (but not the whole) of reality. They have a revelatory role (pp. 51,

atoning processes come from God, which means there is no conflict between God's love and justice.[448] Further, God's removal of guilt and
punishment acknowledges the reality of estrangement, but the idea of the
atoning processes of God means God-in-Christ participates in human
estrangement. Christ experiences finitude. Thus, humankind is able to
participate in God's atoning processes through the death of Christ.

Tillich is not interested in developing a new theology of atonement;
"I did not develop a new doctrine myself because we are in a transition
period concerning a symbol which has almost died and probably cannot
be restored in the original sense".[449] For Tillich, the death of Christ is
construed from within the context of the God-world relationship,

> God's atoning activity must be understood as his participation in existential es-
> trangement and its self-destructive consequences. He cannot remove these conse-
> quences; they are implied in his justice. But he can take them upon himself by
> participating in them and transforming them for those who participate in his partici-
> pation. Here we are in the very heart of the doctrine of atonement and of God's act-
> ing with man and his world.[450]

That is, the death and the atonement in Tillich have to be interpreted
from the perspective of salvific effects of God's participation in human
estrangement within the history of the world. In this perspective, the
cross is a vital symbol.[451] It is the definitive expression of God's participation in the estrangement of human existence. However, though God
participates in estrangement, unity with God is not destroyed.[452] Further,
the cross is *the* finite reality, which manifests the saving power of God.
Manifestations are effective expressions as well as communications. A
manifestation affects or causes something. For Tillich, the cross of Christ
is the decisive manifestation. It is the central actualisation and criterion
of all other manifestations of the presence of God in the world.[453] Lastly,
the death on the cross cannot be separated from the resurrection, except

---

62, 113, 137-138). Gunton asserts that this role is more than a subjective experience
(p. 46) and that Jesus is more than an exemplar.

448 ST II, pp. 173-6.
449 UC, p. 147, cf. ST III, p. 5, Tillich recognises that he could have done more on the
theme of the atonement in his *Systematic Theology*.
450 ST II, p. 174.
451 DF, p. 104.
452 ST I, p. 136.
453 ST II, p. 175.

120

artificially. Thus, the term Death-Resurrection event is used in this study to show the unity that both Tillich and Rahner see as essential to Christology.

Tillich considers the cross and the resurrection as interdependent symbols.[454] For example, "Easter becomes living where a genuine Passiontide, a genuine Good Friday, has preceded it".[455] For Tillich, these two symbols are interdependent because Christ entered into and transcended existence, that is, the cross is Christ's subjection to existence and the resurrection is Christ's conquest of existence.[456] Thus, the Death-Resurrection event constitutes a form of unity-in-difference. Tillich admits that his reflections on the resurrection are comparatively theoretical;[457] "even now he is accused of forfeiting the Jesus of history for a mythical Christ. The mischievous joke is still around that when told Jesus' bones were found, disproving the Resurrection, Tillich exclaimed, 'Then he really lived!'"[458] Yet Tillich asserts that "a real experience" lies behind the resurrection stories,

> A real experience made it possible for the disciples to apply the known symbol of resurrection to Jesus, thus acknowledging him definitely as the Christ. They called this experienced event the "Resurrection of the Christ," and it was a combination of event and symbol.[459]

Tillich claims the resurrection itself "is the ecstatic confirmation of the indestructible unity of the New Being and its bearer, Jesus of Nazareth".[460] He sees the resurrection as an indivisible event in history consisting of the resurrected Christ and the experience of the disciples. He cautiously describes this view as "restitution theory":

454 *Ibid.* p. 153.
455 "The Ancient and Eternal Message of Easter", ATR p. 242.
456 ST II, p. 153, in Tillich, the process of linking symbol *and* reality is part of the function of myth.
457 *Ibid.* p. 158; cf. p. 153, the cross is a symbol linked to reality, it is historically observable, whereas the resurrection is a symbol, which is linked to reality that is veiled in mystery.
458 D. Foster ed., IRCM, p. xx.
459 ST II, p. 154.
460 *Ibid.* p. 157, cf. p. 160, for Tillich, in the context of pre-existence and post-existence, the birth of Jesus in Bethlehem corroborates the symbol of the cross and the virgin birth corroborates the symbol of the resurrection.

The Resurrection is the restitution of Jesus as the Christ, a restitution that is rooted in the personal unity between Jesus and God and in the impact of this unity on the minds of the apostles. Historically, it may well be that the restitution of Jesus to the dignity of the Christ in the minds of the disciples may precede the story of the acceptance of Jesus as the Christ by Peter. The latter may be a reflex of the former; but, even if this is the case, the experience of the New Being in Jesus must precede the experience of the Resurrected.[461]

Tillich also claims that the resurrection includes the disciples' reception of the resurrected Christ and that the resurrected Christ has "the character of spiritual presence".[462] Thus, the resurrection is an indivisible event consisting of the fact of resurrection and its reception by the disciples.[463] This is based on his concept of historic event as fact and reception.[464] Clearly, Tillich is anxious to prevent the resurrection from being reduced to purely a psychological explanation. So rather than reducing the resurrection to a psychological experience, Tillich makes the experience of the disciples the existential stage on which the resurrection drama is played out. In other words, it seems that Tillich has undervalued the importance of his own understanding of symbol, as the experience of the disciples is the tangible aspect of the sign which confers the presence of the resurrected Christ. The resurrected Christ is the meaning of the symbol and the source of transcendence conferred by the symbol. Therefore, the relationship between the resurrected Christ and the disciples is a symbolic event.[465] This is an implicit but recurring theme in Tillich. In the following example, he refers to historical personalities who have become the object of faith:

It is therefore correct to say that Christ or the Buddha, for example, in so far as the unconditioned transcendent is envisaged in them, are symbols. But they are symbols that have at the same time an empirical, historical aspect, and in whose symbolic meaning the empirical is involved. Therefore both aspects, the empirical and the transcendent, are manifest in this kind of symbols [sic] and their symbolic power depends upon this fact.[466]

461 *Ibid.* pp. 157-158.
462 *Ibid.* p. 157.
463 IRCM, p. 46, cf. ST III, p. 308.
464 UC, p. 154.
465 DF, p. 45, in Tillich, there is no such thing as "only a symbol".
466 "The Religious Symbol", pp. 92-93.

122

In conclusion, Tillich's failure to justify his concept of centredness is a flaw in his Christology. To a degree, this weakness is balanced by the cosmic sweep of his salvific theology. For Tillich, it is crucial that the resurrection is seen as an integral part of the salvific process of the presence of God in the world in human history. At this macro-level of analysis, Tillich has a process-like view of history that reflects Schelling's influence; "the content of revelation is nothing but a higher history which goes back to the beginning of things and on to the end".[467] Further, the death and resurrection of Christ in Tillich is the decisive revelation of God in history and this event "goes back to the beginning of things" and "on to the end". Tillich interprets the Death-Resurrection event as the final revelation; where *final* means decisive, fulfilling, unsurpassable, the criterion of all others.[468] The final revelation takes place because of Jesus' power of self-negation.[469] He has this power of self-negation because he is centred and so his life represents all of existence.[470] He is centred because he is fully united with the ground of being.[471] Tillich's circle is complete, in reflecting on the Death-Resurrection event; the link with the Incarnation is confirmed.

2.4. Conclusion

This section consists of two parts. The first part summarises Chapter 2 in relation to Tillich's theology and Christology. The second part places Chapter 2 within the context of the study's thesis. In this context, Tillich's theology is construed as primarily oriented toward modernity. Now of itself, this is not a startling claim, considering Tillich's interests

467 Schelling, p. 202.
468 ST I, p. 132; ST II, p. 118 ff.; For Schelling, the second potency is the formal and efficient cause of being. It is both complete selflessness and the principle of love and it must overcome the first potency by the negation of universality; this leads to the existence of the manifold. Thus, Christ is the highest form of the second potency that surrenders to the wrath of the first potency.
469 ST I, p. 133.
470 ST II, p. 98.
471 ST I, p. 133.

and era. However, in Chapter 4, the argument is made that elements from Tillich's theology can be used to make a contribution to postmodern Christology.

2.4.1. Summary

In terms of Tillich's theology, the chapter consists of three sections, which evaluate successively his method, theology and Christology. First, Tillich's method is an intricate combination of philosophical concepts, theological themes and multiple sources. These elements are used to address an apologetic concern, where the underlying concern is the modern problem of the gap.[472] Second, though not always rigorous, Tillich's theology is a creative argument in favour of the presence of God in the world, where presence is the uniquely human awareness of its participation in Divine life. Tillich sees presence as part of human experience. He recognises, at least implicitly, the ambiguous nature of experience as consisting of absence as well as presence. Further, absence is a major though implicit theme in Tillich. For Tillich, absence is a symptom of estrangement, which is related to sin and entails the loss of essentiality. Subsequently, absence can evoke a yearning for the infinite. Paradoxically, God is still present in absence. Third, the concept of presence is related to the concept of self-transcendence. This means that an encounter with presence elicits the power of self-transcendence and self-transcendence is the means by which the gap is transcended. The gap is problematic for two reasons: human finitude and the nature of God (who cannot be part of the subject/object structure).[473] Tillich attempts to explain the paradox by means of self-transcendent realism. As an explanation it is persuasive and it makes sense of his view of presence, symbol and salvation, but it is based on speculative foundations.

In terms of his Christology, Tillich relies on the biblical picture of Christ but there are a number of problems with this concept. The problems revolve around the relationship between the Jesus of history and the Christ of faith. For Tillich, the Jesus evoked by the biblical *picture* of Christ, and not the Jesus *behind* the biblical text, is the Christ of faith.[474]

472 "Realism and faith", TPE, p. 86.
473 TCB, pp. 178-9.
474 ST II, pp. 114-5.

Only faith can say something about the reality, which is expressed through the biblical picture of Christ.[475] Above all, the biblical picture of Christ has the power to transform lives. Tillich explains this power by means of the concept of *analogia imaginis*.[476] It is not a convincing explanation.[477] Besides, even Tillich concedes that it is not a method of knowing but "a way (actually the only way) of speaking of God".[478] Nevertheless, in fairness to Tillich's theological agenda, he is trying to express in the biblical picture of Christ something of the ongoing soteriological significance of the presence of God in the world. In terms of soteriology, the themes of the Incarnation and the Death-Resurrection event are critical for Tillich. The importance of the Incarnation is found in the significance of Christ's participation in estrangement. The importance of the Death-Resurrection event is found in God's salvific victory over estrangement. Further, the interdependence of the symbols of death and resurrection is indispensable to his Christology. The concept of self-negation helps explain their interdependence in that the self-negation of Jesus in his death is the ground for the resurrection of Christ. Significantly, the resurrected Christ is the final revelation because of Jesus' power of self-negation. Jesus sacrifices himself completely and thus he fulfills his destiny.[479] His destiny is to be the final revelation; "Every new manifestation of the Spiritual Presence stands under the criterion of his manifestation in Jesus as the Christ".[480]

2.4.2. Tillich and Postmodernity

In this part, Tillich's theology is examined from the perspective of postmodernity, where the criteria for defining postmodernity relate to historiography, pluralism, language and intersubjectivity. On the basis of these criteria, this study argues that the theology of Tillich is primarily oriented toward modernity.

475 DF, p. 88.
476 ST II, pp. 114-115.
477 Heywood Thomas, *Tillich*, pp. 114-115, Macquarrie, *Jesus Christ*, p. 303.
478 ST II, p. 115.
479 ST I, p. 136.
480 ST III, p. 148.

Tillich is aware of the criticisms leveled against his work.[481] He acknowledges that he has not treated some matters adequately, for example "atonement, trinity, and particular sacraments".[482] He also prefigures elements of postmodernism.[483] Towards the end of his career, Tillich regrets not paying sufficient attention to the feminine.[484] He is uncomfortable with an overemphasis on "the male element in the symbolization of the divine".[485] In addition, references to the inorganic, organic and other worlds prefigure postmodern thinking, which is cognisant of ecological and cosmological horizons. For instance, he asserts that a theology of the inorganic is needed, "the genesis of stars and rocks, their growth as well as their decay, must be called a life process".[486] Here "growth" is used metaphorically to incorporate many things, "the dimension of the organic is so central for every philosophy of life that linguistically the basic meaning of 'life' is organic life".[487] With other worlds, Tillich is aware of the impact of cosmology on human living and thinking,[488] and he leaves open the possibility of "other singular incarnations for other unique worlds".[489] Indeed, his critique of theism has a postmodern ring,

> I well remember sitting in the woods in France reading Nietzsche's *Thus Spake Zarathustra*, as many other German soldiers did, in a continuous state of exaltation. This was the final liberation from heteronomy. European nihilism carried Nietzsche's prophetic word that "God is dead". Well, the traditional concept of God was dead.[490]

481 ST I, pp. 58-59.
482 ST III, p. 5.
483 IRCM, p. 10, we are entering (or have entered) "a post-Christian period".
484 UC, pp. 148-149.
485 ST III, p. 294.
486 *Ibid.* p. 12.
487 *Ibid.* pp. 19-20.
488 ST II, p. 95.
489 *Ibid.* p. 96.
490 *Time* 73, no. 11, (March 16, 1959), p. 47; cited by D.J. Hall in "The Great War and the German Theologians" in G. Baum ed., *The Twentieth Century: A Theological Overview*, (Maryknoll, New York: Orbis Books, 1999), p. 6.

Some studies depict Tillich as an uncritical child of the Enlightenment.[491] Certainly, Tillich is a *modern* theologian, but he is also a critic of modernity. For example, he consistently criticises modernity's emphasis on technical control. This is because modernity attributes a salvific function to technical control, which means the horizontal is attributed ultimate concern at the expense of the vertical.[492] Nevertheless, while he critiques modernity, he does this as a modern theologian. There are biographical and historical grounds that support this claim, "I am a product of the nineteenth century, which still taught me when I attended the university from 1904 to 1907".[493] In addition, a partial revival of modernism occurred in the period between the two World Wars.[494] The scholars Tillich esteems reflect his attachment to the Enlightenment and modernity (e.g. Kant, Schelling). Indeed, according to Tillich, modernity finds its classic expression in Kant.[495] Kant's *Critique of Pure Reason* was a prized possession of the young Tillich.[496] He purchased a copy as an adolescent and read it repeatedly.[497] Shortly before Tillich's death, Heywood Thomas, a personal friend and Tillich scholar, made this observation about Tillich, "he responded very positively to the suggestion that his theology bore the imprint of Kantian architectonic".[498] Similarly, Schelling is a major factor in his formation, "what I learned from Schelling became determinative of my own philosophical and theological development".[499] For Tillich, Schelling successfully synthesised "Kant's critical epistemology and Spinoza's mystical ontology".[500] None of this is meant to diminish the achievements of the Enlightenment, the use of reason and reliance on Kant or Schelling. The intention is to underline Tillich's primary intel-

491 K.J. VanHoozer, "Theology and the condition of postmodernity: a report on knowledge (of God)" in K.J. VanHoozer ed., *The Cambridge Companion to Postmodern Theology*, (Cambridge: Cambridge University Press, 2003), p. 19, "Paul Tillich's method of correlation … let modern culture and thought forms set the agenda by asking the questions which theology then explained".
492 IRCM, pp. 34-35.
493 *Ibid.* p. 37.
494 Toulmin, *Cosmopolis*, pp. 156-157.
495 PPT, p. 75.
496 OTB, p. 82.
497 Pauck and Pauck, p. 15.
498 Heywood Thomas, *Tillich*, p. 18.
499 PPT, p. 142.
500 *Ibid.* p. 143.

lectual orientation. Thus, while he attempts to explain how the gap between the finite and the infinite can be transcended, he accepts both the gap as a given and the modern construal of the gap. For example, his understanding of creation "emphasizes the infinite distance between the Creator and the creature. It places the created outside the creative ground. It denies any participation of the creature in the creative substance out of which it comes".[501] Tillich knows this is problematic, but he relies on it, as "The doctrine of creation is the one on which the doctrines of Christ, of salvation and fulfillment, depend. Without it, Christianity would have ceased to exist as an independent movement".[502]

Tillich can be identified as a modern on the basis of historiography and the three characteristics of pluralism, language and intersubjectivity. In terms of pluralism, Tillich's understanding of the world's religions appears to be in tune with postmodern pluralism.[503] Moreover, some scholars have argued that, near the end of his life, Tillich regretted his position on other religions and that this indicates a movement toward a more pluralist position.[504] However, Heywood Thomas is sceptical about this apparent change in Tillich. He says of Tillich that, "from his first publication to his last, he was able to defend a Christocentricity in theology".[505] Further, this study argues that Tillich's concept of the *latent Church* entails an implicit claim to a privileged metaphysical and epistemological position.[506] The study makes this claim on the grounds that Tillich's Christ is the final revelation.[507] In Tillich, Jesus as the Christ is the criterion of every religion and culture.[508] The other religions are still in the period of preparation.[509] Further, he makes claims for the uniqueness of Christ,[510] even in his later works.[511]

501 BRUR, p. 36.
502 *Ibid.* p. 35.
503 Pauck and Pauck, p. 260; Tillich showed interest in Buddhism.
504 Foster, ed. IRCM, p. xviii, suspects that had Tillich re-written ST, then Tillich would have been more appreciative of other religions.
505 Heywood Thomas, *Tillich*, p. 67.
506 Wildman, *Fidelity*, p. 322.
507 ST I, p. 132.
508 *Ibid.* p. 136.
509 *Ibid.* p. 144.
510 ST I, pp. 10, 46.
511 UC, pp. 142, 211.

In terms of language, Tillich's interest seems to sit well with postmodern conventions. Clearly, language is important for Tillich, as language "is fundamental for all cultural functions".[512] Both intellectual and spiritual life is embodied by language as language "grasps the encountered reality".[513] Language, consciousness and freedom set humankind apart.[514] Faith is dependent upon language and community.[515] However, by today's standards, Tillich's understanding of language is almost naïve (e.g. word studies). Moreover, "he had very little understanding of the developments in the philosophy of language".[516] He seemed ignorant of "the changes brought about by Anglo-Saxon philosophy in the period 1930-1950, the heyday of linguistic analysis".[517] Often, in situations where language and hermeneutics were involved, Tillich seemed to lose his way (e.g. biblical picture of Christ). More importantly, he did not anticipate some of the key postmodern language issues (e.g. problems of reference, representation). Moreover, his language was invariably premised on ontotheological assumptions (e.g. self-transcending realism, cf. 4.2.1).

In terms of intersubjectivity, Tillich's use of *persona* faintly resembles postmodern intersubjectivity,

> *Persona*, like the Greek *prosopon*, points to the individual and at the same time universally meaningful character of the actor on the stage. For person is more than individuality. "Person" is individuality on the human level, with self-relatedness and world relatedness and therefore with rationality, freedom, and responsibility. It is established in the encounter of an ego-self with another self, often called the "I-thou" relationship, and it exists only in community with other persons.[518]

The key phrase is "with self-relatedness and world relatedness". However, this is in marked contrast with the remainder of Tillich's work in which continually he depicts either a dynamic but isolated individual grappling with existence or a static, abstract and idealized individual, who represents the universal "man". On the whole, Tillich's work on the

512 ST III, p. 58.
513 ST III, p. 59.
514 ST I, p. 176.
515 DF, pp. 23-24.
516 Heywood Thomas, *Tillich*, p. 85.
517 *Ibid.* p. 62.
518 BRUR, p. 23.

self and the subject is reminiscent of a bygone era. For example, with humankind centredness is essentially a given but it is actualised in freedom through destiny by means of a moral act.[519] The key is freedom where freedom is realised in the context of destiny. In the process of realisation, the individual transcends biological necessity and social determinism,

> Being a self means being separated in some way from everything else, having everything else opposite one's self, being able to look at it and act upon it. At the same time, however, this self is aware that it belongs to that at which it looks. The self is 'in' it.[520]

Bearing in mind, that the postmodern debates about subjectivity, the decentred subject and intersubjectivity have not been settled, Tillich's anthropology lacks "the social, relational basis of either human or divine being" and he does not see the theological significance of "the material, embodied and economic grounds of human being".[521] While he is aware there are many *subjects*, he is only partially sensitive to the idea of *intersubjectivity*.[522] Moreover, he is inconsistent in how he defines the individual and the group and the relation between the two. On the one hand, Tillich argues there is a major difference between a person and a group, in that a group cannot be described as possessing a "natural, deciding center".[523] On the other hand, "History-bearing groups are characterized by their ability to act in a centered way".[524]

In summary, by today's standards Tillich's anthropology seems abstract and static (although less so in his sermons and radio broadcasts). Yet Tillich's faults seem unremarkable given he *is* a modern theologian. Clearly, he writes within the social, literary and theological conventions

519 ST III, p. 38.
520 ST I, p. 170.
521 Carter Heyward, "Being above", p. 31.
522 R.N. Brock *Journeys by Heart: A Christology of Erotic Power*, (New York: Crossroad, 1988), pp. 51, 67, Brock is critical of the focus of redemption being on Jesus as the heroic male individual. The Father, especially in classical trinitarian theologies, is good for some but not all women, as it fosters paternalism, individualism and dependency (pp. 53-57). Androgynous Christologies don't work (p. 61). In terms of presuppositions, Brock favours the particular over the universal (p. 63), where the particular is the network of relationships that link all people and creation.
523 ST II, p. 58.
524 ST III, p. 308.

of modernity. However, his theological system is persuasive. It is persuasive because he paints the big picture of life and death, the infinite and the finite, love and faith. It is persuasive because of his use of existential language, with its sense of urgency and immediacy. Moreover, what makes Tillich's modern theology particularly interesting for post-modernity is its understanding of experience as presence and absence. This will be explored more fully in Chapter 4.

Chapter 3: Rahner

The study's contribution to postmodern Christology depends in part on theological insights derived from Tillich and Rahner. This chapter is a critical analysis of Rahner's theology, which examines in order three major topics: his method, theology and Christology. This is followed by a critique of Rahner, which includes a comparison between his theology and postmodernity (3.4). An overview of the chapter will be presented now, before the three topics are outlined. To begin, the concept of the presence of God in the world permeates the theology of Rahner. To appreciate Rahner's understanding of presence, presence needs to be interpreted from the perspective of his theological vision. In short, Rahner's *God* is a God of grace and Rahner's *world* is a graced-world.[1] The experience of presence is characterised by an awareness of the nearness of the God of grace (i.e. God's "absolute proximity").[2] The experience of presence does not mean ownership or control of the divine, as presence is a gift that points beyond itself to God.[3] In all this, the concept of experience is critical for Rahner,

> The essential nature of genuine experience of the Spirit does not consist in particular objects of experience found in human awareness but occurs rather when a man experiences the radical re-ordering of his transcendent nature in knowledge and freedom towards the immediate reality of God through God's self-communication in grace.[4]

However, there is a fundamental difference between the divine and the human in Rahner; "experience of God and experience of self are not simply identical, still both of them exist within a unity of such a kind that apart from this unity it is quite impossible for there to be any such ex-

---

1 "Concerning the relationship between nature and grace", TI 1, "Nature and grace", TI 4.
2 "The concept of mystery in Catholic theology", TI 4, p. 61.
3 FCF, p. 119.
4 "Experience of the spirit and existential commitment", TI 16, pp. 27-28, cf. "Religious feeling inside and outside the Church", TI 17, pp. 234-235.

periences at all."[5] Thus, God is in the world, but God remains God and this is germane to Rahner's concept of absence, where absence is an encounter with the hiddenness of God.[6] This means that the experience of God as absent is real, but God is not absent in reality, as "Knowledge is primarily the experience of the overwhelming mystery of this 'deus absconditus'".[7]

In this chapter, the three main topics concern method, theology and Christology. In terms of method, that section begins with an examination of Rahner's Thomistic heritage and ends with an examination of his overall theological method. In terms of Rahner's use of Thomas, Thomas' understanding of the dynamism of the human mind informs Rahner's metaphysics of knowledge. In turn, Rahner's metaphysics of knowledge is a source of unity for his extensive theological vision. His theological method is designed to provide shape and content to his guiding theological vision. His method involves a complex interaction of factors.[8] The key factors are a Kantian construal of the problem of gap between the finite and infinite and a Thomistic construal of the dynamism of the mind that provides Rahner with a way of re-interpreting the problem of the gap.[9] However, for two reasons, this study is reluctant to label Rahner as strictly Thomist, Kantian or Heideggerian. First, Rahner uses many sources and adapts them for his own theological agenda. Second, in the process of adaption, Rahner adds his own touch so that while he uses various sources, there is sufficient originality to describe the guiding theological vision as very much Rahner's vision.

In terms of theology, Rahner's concept of presence is related to his metaphysics of knowledge, where the act of knowing is simultaneously dependent on sense intuition and the fact that sense intuition is grounded in God,

> We call this basic makeup of the human person, affirmed in every act of knowledge and of freedom, our spiritual nature [*Geistigkeit*]. To be human is to be spirit [*Der*

---

5   "Experience of self and experience of God", TI 13, p. 125.

6   "The hiddenness of God", TI 16, p. 238.

7   *Ibid.*

8   G. A. McCool, *A Rahner Reader*, (London: Darton, Longman and Todd, 1975), p. xxv.

9   W. Dych, *Karl Rahner*, (London and New York: Continuum, 1992, 2000), p. 2, to a lesser extent than Thomas or Kant, Heidegger was an important influence.

134

Mensch ist Geist], i.e., to live life while reaching ceaselessly for the absolute, in openness toward God.[10]

This is the metaphysical precursor of his supernatural existential. Further, a key element in Rahner's vision is his theological anthropology, i.e. it is God's nature to give and God gives God's self to humankind. The gift of God's self is posited intrinsically in humankind and the process of positing is an ontological process.[11] The early Rahner uses the concept of intrinsic causality – in particular the variant quasi-formal causality – to explain the supernatural existential and the hypostatic union. In both cases, Rahner uses quasi-formal causality to affirm God's involvement and preserve God's transcendence.[12] This reveals the influence of his metaphysics of knowledge. The later Rahner emphasises a broader vision of transcendence than strict adherence to his original metaphysics of knowledge.

In terms of Christology, for Rahner the Incarnation means that the grace of God is in the world in a decisive way.[13] Christ is part of the history of the world and the history of the world is different because of Christ's participation. Moreover, there is divine purpose in the Incarnation, which is fulfilled in the death and resurrection of Christ, in which Christ became the absolute saviour of the world. Christ is an exemplar, but he is more than that, as "Christ in his historical existence is both reality and sign, *sacramentum* and *res sacramenti*, of the redemptive grace of God".[14] Thus, Rahner interprets the significance of the life, death and resurrection of Jesus symbolically. Christ is the reality and sign of God, and "in this causality what is signified, in this case God's salvific will, posits the sign, in this case the death of Jesus along with his resurrection, and in and through the sign it causes what is signified".[15] Consequently, Christ is the definitive expression of the presence of God in the world.

---

10   HW, p. 53, cf. p. 122, *Vorgriff* is "the transcendence of the spirit" toward pure being. It is not *a priori* knowledge; rather it is the *a priori* manner of knowing the appearances of objects *a posteriori*.

11   FCF, p. 116.

12   "Incarnation", TI 4, p. 113, cf. J. Donceel, *The Searching Mind: An Introduction to a Philosophy of God*, (London: University of Notre Dame Press, 1979), p. 188.

13   CS, p. 15.

14   *Ibid.* cf. "What does it mean today to believe in Jesus Christ?" TI 18, p. 147.

15   FCF, p. 284.

3.1. Theological Method

Rahner's method provides a clue to his understanding of the nature of the presence of God. The heart of his method is the skilful combination of Kant and Thomas. This combination undergirds his attempt to affirm the presence of God in the modern world. Thus, Rahner responded to modernity by intentionally bringing together key elements of tradition and modernism. The purpose of this section is to outline Rahner's theological method in order to appreciate his vision in a way that does justice to its complexity. The immediate interest is how Rahner interpreted the significance of neo-Scholasticism and how it informed his theological vision. To begin, it is difficult to make categorical assessments of a complex social and historical phenomenon like neo-Scholasticism, as it is not a seamless whole; rather it is a convergence of strands each employing their interpretation of Thomas in response to modernity.[16] In the language of this study, the Church in the nineteenth century was grappling with the threat of the marginalisation of God.[17]

3.1.1. Transcendental Thomism

To appreciate the concept of presence in Rahner it is necessary to look at his metaphysics of knowledge, which derives in part from Thomas.[18] Theoretically, Rahner can be described as a transcendental Thomist who uses aspects of Aquinas to address the challenge of modernity.[19] During

16   G. McCool, *From Unity to Pluralism: The Internal Revolution of Thomism*, (New York: Fordham University Press, 1989), p. 225, the new theology debate was "the culmination of the development within Thomism itself which gradually led to its decease as a single organized movement. The emergence of pluralism in its epistemology and metaphysics challenged its internal coherence as a unitary speculative system".

17   R.R. Reno, *The Ordinary Transformed: Karl Rahner and The Christian Vision of Transcendence*, (Grand Rapids, Michigan, Cambridge, UK: Eerdmans, 1995), p. 79.

18   Dych, p. 42, "one can also recognize the influence of Pierre Rousselot and Joseph Maréchal in Rahner's interpretation of Thomas Aquinas".

19   T.F. O'Meara, "transcendental Thomism", in R.P. McBrien ed., *The HarperColllins Encyclopedia of Catholicism*, (San Francisco: HarperCollins, 1995), hereafter EC,

136

his career, Rahner remained faithful to the work of Thomas as he aimed "to place Thomas in conversation with modern thought".[20] This is unexceptional given that,

> The Roman Catholic mind is inevitably Thomist in some of its viewpoints. The impact of Aquinas' synthesis and of neo-Thomist revivals from the sixteenth to the twentieth centuries explains why Catholics, consciously or unconsciously, perceive human nature as good, society as built upon the political common good, grace as ordinary and suited to individual men and women, the psychological analysis of the person and the sacraments as having their own reality, and the dynamic of incarnation continuing after Jesus Christ.[21]

However, there are specific reasons for Rahner's indebtedness to Thomas. This is evident in *Spirit in the World*. In particular, Rahner embraces Thomas' *conversio* (3.2.2). Later, Rahner builds on this as he develops his own theological anthropology (e.g. HW) and version of transcendence (e.g. FCF). In the introduction of *Spirit in the World*, Rahner provides an insight into the place Thomas holds in his theology,

> If it is absolutely necessary, then, to begin with the starting point given by Thomas and to abandon one's self again and again to the dynamism of the matter itself so that the historically accessible fragments of his philosophy can really become philosophy, it is naturally inevitable that such starting points given by Thomas will be pushed further by one's own thought.[22]

Thomas is more than another important philosophical and theological source for Rahner. According to Rahner, Thomas is an exemplar, a mentor and a mystic who adores the incomprehensible mystery.[23] Rahner's

---

p. 1263, while there are variations on a theme (cf. Rahner, Lonergan), transcendental Thomism combines Thomas with the transcendental philosophy of Kant, from the perspective of the human subject.

20 J.A. Bonsor, *Athens and Jerusalem: The Role of Philosophy in Theology*, (New York: Paulist Press, 1993), p. 62.

21 T.F. O'Meara, "Thomas Aquinas and Today's Theology", *Theology Today* 55 (1998), pp. 16-28, for O'Meara, there are four periods in Thomism: the age of defenses (13th to 15th century), the age of commentaries (mid 14th to early 16th century), the age of controversies, encyclopedias (mid 15th to early 17th century) and the neo-Thomist revival (1840-1960).

22 SW, p. l.

23 "Thomas Aquinas: patron of theological studies", TGCY, p. 317.

reverence for Thomas is omnipresent.[24] They shared similar interests.[25] Lastly, Rahner's description of Thomas applies equally to Rahner's work,

> He shows almost no preference for certain themes of theology rather than others. The whole is important to him and therefore every detail. As a further consequence, he is not dazzled by detail; he always thinks on the basis of the whole and in relation to the whole ... He is a systematic thinker who always considers the individual in the light of clearly grasped first principles. But because he is objective, the individual never becomes a mere occasion for declaiming about principles.[26]

To discern where Rahner sits in relation to Thomas, it is important to clarify the meaning of key terms. Even then the process of clarification needs to be performed with caution because of the complexity of the issues involved. Neo-Thomism has been characterised as a negative reaction toward modernity and the philosophies and theologies that embraced it.[27] The term neo-Thomism is often used synonymously with neo-Scholasticism.[28] In this study, the term neo-Scholasticism is used, though not exclusively, because it is the term Rahner favours, but also because it suggests a broader scope than neo-Thomism. That is, there is more to this reaction to modernity than a rediscovery of Thomism. However, the distinction between the two terms is not absolute. Further, over the centuries there have been several revivals of interest in Thomas, which come under the broad heading of Thomism. In this study, neo-Thomism is used to describe a specific revival of interest in Thomas that

24   *Ibid.* p. 315, Rahner argues for the continuing life and the relevance of the saints by using a similar argument to the one he uses for advocating the continuing validity of the person of the resurrected Christ, cf. p. 318, "Thomas is alive. He is living *his* life with God. In God it has become wholly pure and established in its utter purity. It has remained his own and yet open into God's infinity and into the incalculable range of other vocations. And therefore each can say with genuine faith: St. Thomas, pray for me".

25   O'Meara, *Thomas Aquinas*, p. 23, "For Aquinas, God is first grasped as an infinite and wise knower whose choices are fired by love. Not an arbitrary will nor a startling impresario of power, God has set up on earth two intricate patterns, one of nature and one of grace".

26   "Thomas Aquinas", TGCY, p. 316.

27   Küng, *Christianity*, p. 517.

28   B.M. Ashley, "neo-Scholasticism", EC, p. 911, "a term used for the revival, from 1860 to 1960, of the philosophical tradition of the medieval and baroque universities".

occurred in the nineteenth and twentieth centuries, which forms the main strand within neo-Scholasticism. Furthermore, the term neo-Scholasticism is difficult to define concisely. Like many complex social and historical phenomena, neo-Scholasticism is more a syndrome or constellation of ideas and events than a single identifiable historical movement.[29] Moreover, "we cannot underestimate the intellectual appeal of the neo-scholastic revival of the Thomistic synthesis. This appeal can be broken down into two basic elements: (1) the philosophical power of Thomism, and (2) the capacity of neo-Scholasticism to secure the supernatural status of the institutional church".[30] Arguably, neo-Scholasticism ended as an intellectual force with the conclusion of Vatican II (1962-5) and Rahner himself asserts that Vatican II, "brought to an end, or so I believe, a neoscholastic period of theology".[31] Likewise McCool states, "The history of the modern Neo-Thomist movement, whose *magna charta* was *Aeterni Patris*, reached its end at the Second Vatican Council".[32]

Neo-Scholasticism influenced Rahner from the time of his priestly formation to the middle stages of his career and beyond. At the very least, it influenced Rahner's theological teachers. Rahner's description of the historical period is compelling,

> After the Pius popes, from Pius IX to Pius XII. A kind of defensive mentality, a certain defensive turning of the Church in on itself against the world, characterized this era in which the Church certainly had great missionary success, but in fact only by exporting Western European Christianity to all the world. It was also an era of typical Latin neoscholasticism.[33]

Rahner describes Neo-Scholastic theology elsewhere as "anxious and defensive theology".[34] Rahner is aware of neo-Scholasticism's shortcomings.[35] However, in all this there is a risk of making a caricature out of

---

29   W.J. Courtenay, "Neoscholasticism", NDCT, pp. 396-397.

30   Reno, *Ordinary*, p. 74.

31   Rahner, *I Remember: An Autobiographical Interview with Meinhold Krauss*, H.D. Egan trans. (London: SCM Press, 1984, 1985), p.89.

32   McCool, *Unity to Pluralism*, p. 230.

33   Rahner, *IR*, p. 87.

34   "The present situation of Catholic theology", TI 21, p. 71.

35   "Dogmatics", ET, p. 369, in praise of Vatican II, Rahner reflects on "the too exclusively analytic dogmatics of later Scholasticism and neo-Scholasticism, in which

neo-Scholasticism. Significantly, Rahner is also aware of neo-Scholasticism's merits.[36] Moreover, it is misleading to label blithely neo-Scholasticism as anti-modern.[37] Consequently, some scholars have argued for more historical research on neo-Scholasticism.[38] Indeed, a neutral case can be made that the most important feature of neo-Scholasticism is the revival of interest in Thomas in which Thomas, or an interpretation of Thomas, is set up as a significant theological standard by which the soundness of other philosophies and theologies is tested. The inference is that the establishment of Thomas as a theological standard is not of itself a problem; the problem is the inflexible or exclusive application of the standard. Nonetheless, while it is appropriate to exercise caution in defining neo-Scholasticism, there are influential events. These include the *Syllabus Errorum* (1864),[39] the founding of *Accademia di San Tommaso* (1874),[40] *Aeterni Patris* (1879),[41] *Lamentabili* (1907),[42] *Sacrorum Antistitum* (1910)[43] and *Humani Generis* (1950).[44] For example, *Aeterni Patris* was partly intended for seminarians, for the purpose of establishing Thomas not as *a* significant, but as *the* theological standard.[45]

---

the 'positive sources' were consulted too one-sidedly simply in support of certain traditionally prescribed theses".

36   "Theology", ET, p. 1699.

37   Reno, *Ordinary*, p. 70

38   T.F. O'Meara, *Church and Culture: German Catholic Theology, 1860-1914*, (Notre Dame, London: University of Notre Dame Press, 1991), p. 33; cf. Reno, *Ordinary*, p. 78, "In this respect, the legacy of Pius IX may be far more positive than 'progressive' historians are willing to admit".

39   "Syllabus Errorum", ODCC, p. 1565; R.R. Gaillardetz, "Syllabus of Errors", EC, p. 1233, it addresses various concerns: pantheism and naturalism, faith and reason, and political liberalism.

40   Courtenay, "Neoscholasticism", pp. 396-397.

41   "*Aeterni Patris*", EC, p. 19, "deprecated post-Cartesian philosophy and modern science as tainted with skepticism and so incapable of attaining truth or entering into a fruitful relationship with theology".

42   "*Lamentabili*", EC, p. 748.

43   M.R. O'Connell, "oath against Modernism", EC, p. 926.

44   "Humani Generis", EC, p. 642, it attempted "to show errors in contemporary philosophy and science ... and again to propose Thomism as the true Christian philosophy".

45   R.P. Phillips, *Modern Thomistic Philosophy: An Explanation For Students*, Vol. 1 (London: Burns, Oates and Washbourne, 1934), p. vii, Phillips presents Thomas as

Among the Scholastic Doctors, the chief and master of all, towers Thomas Aquinas, who, as Cajetan observes, because "he most venerated the ancient doctors of the Church, in a certain way seems to have inherited the intellect of all." The doctrines of those illustrious men, like the scattered members of a body, Thomas collected together and cemented, distributed in wonderful order, and so increased with important additions that he is rightly and deservedly esteemed the special bulwark and glory of the Catholic faith.[46]

Likewise, in the next century with Pius XII,

As the experience of several centuries has clearly shown, St Thomas's method is remarkable for its outstanding superiority both in training pupils and in searching for the truth; then, too, his doctrine is in harmony with divine revelation and is very efficacious in protecting the foundations of the faith and also in gathering usefully and safely the fruits of wholesome progress.[47]

According to Reno, there was a *grassroots* reaction toward modernity within Catholicism, which paralleled and in some cases reinforced the impact of these defining historical events. This seems a reasonable assertion on Reno's part. For example, the doctrines of papal primacy and infallibility received support at Vatican I (1869-70) from the Ultramontane movement.[48] Reno, who tries to recontextualise neo-Scholasticism, argues that this support represented a grassroots movement going back to the mid-nineteenth century and the establishment of Pius associations that "became bastions of lay support for ultramontanism".[49] Further, Reno argues that the single-minded focus on Thomas is not the identifying mark of neo-Scholasticism, "what identifies neo-scholasticism is the application of Aristotelian metaphysics to the question of nature and

------

developed by modern Thomists as the object of his two volume work; cf. "Aeterni Patris" ODCC, p. 23.

46   Cited by J. Maritain, *St Thomas Aquinas*, (New York: Meridian Books, 1931, 1958), p. 199.

47   Pius XII, "Erroneous Trends in Modern Theology", pp. 252-270, M. Chinigo ed., *The Teachings of Pope Pius XII*, (London: Methuen, 1958), p. 265.

48   H.J. Pottmeyer, "Ultramontanism", EC, p. 1278. Ultramontanism was a nineteenth century movement in France, Germany, Spain and England that promoted the papacy in defense "against political liberalism and modern philosophical and scientific trends".

49   Reno, *Ordinary*, p. 73.

grace".[50] Likewise, Owens argues "A Neoscholastic could be strongly Aristotelian without being Thomistic".[51]

If the present overview is to illuminate Rahner's theology then there are specific nuances which need to be drawn out. In relation to twentieth century Thomism, McDermott asserts that there was a methodological shift from conceptualist to transcendental thought. In this shift, old problems were addressed but new problems emerged. In particular, McDermott is critical of both the conceptualist Thomism that dominated the pre-Vatican II era and transcendentalist Thomism that dominated the post-Vatican II era. For McDermott, the central issue concerns "philosophical presuppositions".[52] With the conceptualist position, knowledge is bound to concepts, and knowledge that exceeds concepts is supernatural knowledge. In this view, theology is a true science, though it is subservient to "the higher science possessed by God".[53] While understanding requires concepts, there are problems.[54] For McDermott, conceptualist theology fails to account for history,

> The fundamental methodological dilemma regarding the relation of faith and reason manifests itself in the problem of historicity. Conceptualist theology collapsed because its absolute, abstract dogmas did not allow adequately for historical pluralism and development; transcendental thought has so relativized all thought to subjective experience that past history contains nothing binding on the Christian conscience. Hence both proved insufficient for a religion that glories in its historical truth. Doubtless there is need of a new theology that does not concentrate primarily on the permanent, necessary structures of objective natures or subjective dynamisms.[55]

According to McDermott, transcendental Thomists "located man's access to reality in an intuition or judgement, of which the concept is only

50   *Ibid.* p. 97, n. 14.

51   J. Owens, "Aristotle and Aquinas" in Kretzmann, N. and E. Stump eds., *The Cambridge Companion to Aquinas*, (Cambridge: Cambridge University Press, 1993), p. 39.

52   J.M. McDermott, "The methodological shift in twentieth century Thomism", *Seminarium* 31 (1991), p. 245.

53   *Ibid.* p. 247.

54   *Ibid.* p. 251, "It must seem strange that the clarity of the concept which provided homogeneity from revelation to theology should collapse into pluralism. The conceptualist system had difficulty in fully reconciling faith and reason; that tension reappeared in its doctrine of analogy, dogmatic development, and hermeneutics".

55   *Ibid.* p. 265.

a part".[56] McDermott argues that this raises other difficulties, as it makes judgement dependent on subjectivity.[57] He claims that, while transcendental theology accounts for subjectivity, it is "in danger of adaptation to the relativistic modern culture with its loss of truth".[58] According to McDermott, the means and mode of interpreting nature in Transcendental Thomism are not clear; the inference is that this represents an unavoidable risk in an approach that is excessively subjective. Inevitably, revelation is reduced to personal encounter.[59] In terms of truth statements, McDermott sees this as the source of relativism.[60] Certainly, McDermott's concern about Transcendental Thomism's emphasis on subjectivity is warranted. Rahner grants subjectivity a privileged position in his theological anthropology. But there are other aspects in Rahner's theology that need to be mentioned, such as the purpose behind his emphasis on subjectivity (3.2.2). In particular, Rahner's anthropology is the way he attempts to overcome the problem of extrinsicism.[61] Further, the subjective in Rahner is held in tension by the transcendental and the historical. With the transcendental, human subjectivity is the recipient (i.e. hearer), but God remains the constitutive principle of anthropology. With history, Rahner interprets subjectivity in the context of history because history is the place of God's revelation. Significantly, the issue at stake is not just subjectivity, but the kind of subjectivity that Rahner is promoting (3.4).

In summary, in the period circumscribed by the term neo-Scholasticism, there was a high degree of uncertainty as to how to respond to modernity. Thomism played a significant but not exclusive role in that response. In some instances, the type of response could be described positively as *apologetic*, in other instances as *defensive*. In the defensive cases, neo-Scholasticism elevates a particular interpretation of Thomas at the expense of alternative interpretations. In the process it presumes it is possible to arrive at a uniform interpretation of Thomas,

---

56   *Ibid.* pp. 253-254.
57   *Ibid.* p. 260.
58   *Ibid.* p. 264.
59   *Ibid.* p. 257.
60   Not everyone sees this risk as inevitable, cf. McCool, *Unity to Pluralism*, pp. 228-229.
61   Metaphorically, Rahner's God works *from the inside out*; extrinsicism is about God working *from the outside in*.

that is, "a single perennial system of theology".[62] By contemporary hermeneutical standards the presumption that the philosophical and theological significance of Thomas could be reduced to a single reading lacks credibility.[63] Further, it is difficult to make categorical assessments of a complex social and historical phenomenon like neo-Scholasticism; "Catholic truth therefore expressed itself through several essentially different speculative systems".[64] Thus, neo-Scholasticism is neither a seamless whole nor an uninterrupted movement. It is a confluence of various strands of thought, with exponents employing their interpretation of Thomas in response to modernity.[65] The interest here is in how Rahner interpreted the significance of neo-Scholasticism and how that informed his theological vision. In the end, Rahner chose to respond to modernity creatively by intentionally bringing together diverse elements of tradition (e.g. Thomism, immutability of God, hypostatic union) and modernism (e.g. Kant, Hegel, Heidegger).

3.1.2. Theological Method

If Rahner's theology of presence is to be appreciated, then it needs to be interpreted in the light of his theological method. The key to understanding Rahner's method is his consistent application of his theological vision to a plethora of theological, ecclesial and pastoral issues. It is the systemic application of this vision which lends weight to the claim that he is a systematic theologian. Admittedly, Rahner has not produced one substantial work (i.e. *summa*), which focuses systemically on a series of fundamental theological issues in accord with clearly enunciated theological and philosophical principles.[66] In this regard, *Foundations of Christian Faith* is not the same as the systematic theologies of others

---

62 McCool, *Unity to Pluralism*, p. 228.

63 This is similar to asserting that there is only one possible reading of the Gospels.

64 McCool, *Unity to Pluralism*, p. 228.

65 *Ibid.* p. 225.

66 Cf. S.W. Sykes, "Systematic Theology", NDCT, pp. 560-562; J. Macquarrie, "Systematic Theology", Musser and Price, pp. 469-474; A.E. McGrath, *Christian Theology: An Introduction*, 3rd ed., (Oxford: Blackwell Publishers, 2001), pp. 143-144.

(e.g. Pannenberg).[67] However, Rahner did not feel obliged to follow traditional forms of systematic theology. Moreover, he argues that theology is always changing.[68] In addition, and in fairness to Rahner, there is no universal agreement in theology about a single, uniform definition of what constitutes a systematic theology. Further, the scope of Rahner's interests is vast, but he consistently applies his vision to those interests.[69] Thus, as Burke concludes, "Rahner's theology is rightly recognized as a theological system because of the fundamental unity that runs throughout his writings".[70] In this sense, Rahner is a *systematic* theologian.[71] Subsequently, this part will look at the following issues: Rahner in relation to philosophy, Rahner's commitment to the immutability of God and most importantly the modern construal of the problem of the gap which Rahner adopts and critiques. This part will conclude by enumerating key factors in Rahner's complex method.

Philosophy plays an important role in Rahner's theology. He makes extensive and effective use of philosophical sources and concepts. For Rahner, philosophy is a pre-condition of theological reflection; "Theology is based on the grace of revealed faith and regards the revealed mysteries of God, while philosophy proceeds from natural reason and is concerned with the objects accessible to this".[72] However, the relationship between philosophy and theology in Rahner is complex and he admits that it is not easy to determine the nature of this relationship.[73] Moreover, Rahner considers philosophical analysis of his work unwarranted,

> I myself aim to be a theologian and really nothing else; simply because I am just not a philosopher, and am under no illusions that I could ever be one. Not that this

67   W. Pannenberg, *Systematic Theology* Vol. 1-3, G.W. Bromiley trans., (Grand Rapids, Michigan and Edinburgh: Eerdmans, T and T, Clark, 1991, 1994, 1998).

68   "Theology", ET, p. 1700.

69   *Ibid.* on the future of theology, "Transcendental theology, as an element in every theology which understands what it is doing, will again cut across these perhaps foreseeable theologies".

70   P. Burke, *Reinterpreting Rahner: A Critical Study of His Major Themes*, (New York: Fordham University Press, 2002), p. vii.

71   Dulles, *Craft*, p. 52.

72   "Theology", ET, p. 1692; "Transcendental theology", ET, pp. 1748-1749, the distinction between grace and nature is not absolute, in anthropological terms, human nature is "radicalized by grace".

73   "Theology", ET, p. 1692.

means that I despise philosophy, or consider it unimportant. On the contrary, I have a dreadful respect for it.[74]

Rahner claims his work represents a peculiar genre, which tries to address existential concerns that cannot be confirmed by the "philosophy of expert, specialized scholarship".[75] However, although Rahner does not regard his work as philosophical, he recognises that every theologian brings a certain "self-understanding" (i.e. a philosophy) to bear on his/her theology,[76] "Living dogmatic theology is also a 'philosophical' work, for any particular conception of man and the world is expressed principally in the prevailing philosophy of the age".[77] Conversely, Rahner argues that a philosopher brings a certain theology (i.e. "ultimate mental horizons") to bear on his/her philosophy.[78] By his own admission,[79] Rahner never resolves the tension between the two disciplines of theology and philosophy. However, he uses the tension purposefully and creatively. The tension between the immutability of God and a neo-Kantian understanding of the mind/world relationship is a crucial example of the interplay of theology and philosophy in Rahner.

The tension between the concept of the immutability of God and the claim that God is in the world plays a major role in Rahner's theological system.[80] This reflects a number of influences. On the one hand, the influence of Ignatius of Loyolla is a feature of Rahner's vision.[81] *Indifferençia* is a theme in Ignatius' spiritual exercises, the object of which is the discernment of the will of God.[82] *Indifferençia* presumes God can be found in all things and yet God is distinct, thus, "we must make our-

74 "Some clarifying remarks about my own work", TI 17, pp. 243-248.
75 *Ibid.* p. 244.
76 "Theology", ET, p. 1692.
77 "Dogmatics", ET, p. 369.
78 "Clarifying remarks", TI 17, p. 243.
79 "Theology", ET, p. 1692.
80 Burke, *Reinterpreting*, p. 1, is right to highlight the formative significance of both *Spirit in the World* and *Hearer of the Word* in Rahner's vision. However, Burke has probably overemphasised its significance. Other factors, like finding God in all things, are part of the Rahner vision, cf. H.D. Egan, *Karl Rahner: Mystic of Everyday Life*, (New York: Crossroad Publishing, 1998), pp. 28-54.
81 Dych, *Rahner*, p. 29; Egan, *Rahner*, p. 41.
82 E. Niermann, "indifference", ET, pp. 699-700.

146

selves indifferent to all created things",[83] and "I must be indifferent, without any inordinate attachment".[84]

> Whoever possesses an ultimately Ignatian indifference even toward all those realities in the church and in the world that, although good, are still distinct from God; and whoever in this indifference of love encounters God himself in the immediacy of his gracious self-communication – such a person becomes homeless in the true sense.[85]

On the other hand, the sense of the *other* is important for Rahner, in particular, he sees the immutability of God as indispensable to the Church's tradition. The incorporation of the immutability of God into the tradition can be traced back to the Church Fathers. This understanding of God led to the emergence of a pronounced dualism between divine and human in the early Christian tradition.[86] The dualism is partly the consequence of the adoption of static middle and Neo-Platonic conceptions of God.[87] Subsequently, Rahner uses Kant, Thomas and other sources to address this tension. The tension surfaces profoundly in the theme of the Incarnation.

Overall, Rahner adopts a Kantian world-view.[88] In tandem with a Thomistic nuance, Rahner addresses the Kantian problem of the gap between the finite and the infinite. The modern version of the problem of the gap stems from Descartes (2.2.2).[89] Descartes' quest for certainty

83   *The Spiritual Exercises of St Ignatius*, L.J. Puhl trans., (New York: Random House, 1951, 2000), p. 12 [par. 23].

84   *Ibid.* p. 58 [par. 179]

85   Rahner, "Ignatius of Loyola", TGCY, p. 339.

86   Küng, *Christianity*, p. 166.

87   Küng, *The Incarnation of God: An Introduction to Hegel's Theological Thought as Prolegomena to a Future Christology*, J.R. Stephenson trans., (New York: Crossroad, 1970, 1987), p. 530, "the notion of God's immutability, taken over from Greek metaphysics, served the apologists and the later Fathers (especially Origen and Augustine) well in the struggle against Stoic pantheism and Gnostic and Manichaean dualism and for stressing the eternity and constancy of God, in the middle ages it was an important aid in resisting any kind of pantheism … the idea created a variety of difficulties for the apologists and the later Fathers in their Christology and it was the same with the scholastics when they came to reflect on the christological question".

88   G. Vass, *A Theologian in Search of a Philosophy: Understanding Karl Rahner* Vol. 1, (Westminster and London: Christian Classics, Sheed and Ward, 1985), p. 24.

89   Toulmin, *Cosmopolis*, pp. 13, 152-160.

elevated the status of the subject over the world. In his view, knowledge of the world is unreliable. In contrast, Kant reclaims the external world by means of the mind. For Kant, the link between the mind and the phenomenal is indispensable and access to the phenomenal is predetermined by *a priori* categories of the mind. Kant's attempt to link the empirical and the rational influenced Rahner. Rahner acknowledges that while transcendental theology is not a replication of transcendental philosophy, "transcendental philosophy in particular easily passes over in the concrete to transcendental theology".[90] Rahner uses Kant's transcendental subject and re-interprets it in the light of Thomas.[91] In particular, Rahner sees a connection between the supersensible and the sensible in the dynamism of the human mind, where the mind can grasp the object, because God first grasped humankind. Based on Thomas, Rahner asserts that God is not the topic (*subjectum*) but the principle of the topic (*principium subjecti*),

> The thesis that God is incomprehensible was always present in Catholic theology. For Thomas Aquinas, something like that was self-evident. For Thomas Aquinas, it was also self-evident that God, even in the so-called immediate vision of God in eternity, still remains the incomprehensible, unfathomable mystery. But a contemporary theology could place such a thesis much more radically, I might add, at the center of the theological enterprise. And from this center, all other theological statements receive yet another color and shading. Therefore, there is something like a controlling center for theology.[92]

Therefore, the fusion of horizons, Kantian and Thomistic, allows Rahner to develop a theology of presence that speaks to modernity on its own terms (i.e. the turn to the subject).[93]

In conclusion, Rahner's method provides a clue to his understanding of the presence of God in the world. The philosophical heart of Rahner's method is his adroit use of Kant and Thomas. This combination undergirds his attempt to affirm that God is in the world (i.e. *Geist in Welt*).

90 "Theology", ET, p. 1692.
91 "Maréchal, Joseph", EC, p. 813, Maréchal "asserted that Kant's critical philosophy could be reconciled with Thomism if the intellect was conceived as a dynamic, rather than static, faculty". This is a formative influence on Rahner.
92 Rahner, IR, p. 58.
93 R.C. Solomon, "subjectivity", OCP, p. 857. The term *the turn to the subject* refers to the shift in the locus of the philosophical debate toward human subjectivity, instigated and exemplified by Descartes, Kant and others.

Further, while the influence of Thomas is formative (cf. Burke) it is not final (cf. Kilby). That is, Rahner's theology evolves. Rahner's vision, while grounded in his early work, is not bound to it. On this note, Kilby makes an important distinction; "It is important to be clear that what is at issue is the *logical* independence, and not the chronological independence, of Rahner's theology from his philosophy".[94] This study has some sympathy for Kilby's position, hence the use of the general term vision, rather than a more specific term like model. However, Kilby, in an effort to establish the credibility of a non-foundationalist reading of Rahner, runs the risk of underemphasising the degree of unity in Rahner. In this study the contention is that while there is not necessarily a strict "logical" dependence between Rahner's philosophy and his theology, his philosophy has had a formative role in shaping his vision; especially in the way Rahner construes humankind, the world and the relationship between humankind and the world. It is this *vision* and this *world*, which provide the context for understanding Rahner's concept of presence. Furthermore, Rahner's theology has been influenced by many factors.[95] It is worth noting then that in *Reinterpreting Rahner*, an exacting study, Burke barely makes a reference to Kant or Hegel and only one to Heidegger.[96] Burke correctly claims that while Rahner's system has a certain internal coherence it has problems with its metaphysical foundations,[97] but Kant, Hegel and Heidegger play a role in shaping Rahner's foundations. Moreover Rahner's system, in spite of its flaws, is directed toward addressing a modern world and it seems an omission on Burke's part not to have made more here of Rahner's philosophical sources and the world that Rahner addressed. In particular, Rahner's vision of the *world* is significantly, but not exclusively, a Kantian construal.

Undoubtedly, Rahner's method involves a complex interaction of factors and it is not easy to unravel them, especially as he does not always identify his sources. Some of the factors are listed below. The order of

---

94   K. Kilby, *Karl Rahner: Philosophy and Theology*, (London, New York: Routledge, 2004), p. 70.

95   H. Vorgrimler, *Understanding Karl Rahner: An Introduction To His Life And Thought*, (London: SCM Press, 1985, 1986), p. 61, "in the steps of Thomas, in conversation with Kant, German Idealism, Heidegger, but also guided by Ignatius and the significance which human senses have for him in relationship with God".

96   Burke, *Reinterpreting*, p. 3.

97   *Ibid.* p. 298.

presentation is not intended to suggest Rahner uses them in a fixed or step-by-step manner. Indeed, Rahner has a seemingly circular style of writing, which is the product of the interplay of these factors as well as Rahner's tendency to re-visit themes and concepts from new angles. However, his style does lead to some inadequacies of argument and the logical dependence between the factors is not always clear.

– Rahner uses Kant's understanding of the problem of gap between the finite and infinite, in which the locus of the problem is found in the relationship between the mind of the subject and the external world. While he is indebted to Thomas for his metaphysics of knowledge, Rahner's focus is fixed on the modern problem of the gap as enunciated by Kant. In addition, as Rahner becomes less dependent on his earlier metaphysics of knowledge, his notion of transcendence becomes more Kantian in its scope.

– Rahner embraces Thomas' understanding of the dynamism of the human mind as the basis of his metaphysics of knowledge, where simultaneously God is the source of the mind's capacity to render the world in a meaningful way and the perception of the world evokes awareness of God. This helps Rahner explain how "the gap is possible at all".[98] It offers hope that the gap might be transcended.[99] In due course, Rahner's metaphysics of knowledge recedes into the background; nonetheless, it is implicitly present.[100]

– In conjunction with his interpretation of quasi-formal causality, the early Rahner finds in Hegel a means of explaining of how the divine and human can be one, while the divine is not one with the human (i.e. unity-in-difference).

– In addition to certain terms and concepts, Rahner learnt from Heidegger how to read texts, question the tradition and incorporate modern philosophy into theology.[101]

98   SW, p. 75.
99   FCF, p. 133.
100 Rahner, "Christology today" in K. Rahner and W. Thüsing, *A New Christology*, (London: Burns and Oates, 1972, 1980), p. 7; FCF, pp. 121, 284.
101 IR, pp. 45-46. HW, p. 67, "Human existence, which permeates in this way the insight into an ultimate necessity, is a purely factual existence. It is contingence, thrownness [*Geworfenheit*], to use Heidegger's term".

150

3.2. The Presence of God in the World

Rahner's theological vision can be summed up in this way: theological anthropology is *the* context for a discussion about the presence of God in the world. This means that it is God's nature to give and God gives God's self to humankind.[102] The aim of this section is to survey Rahner's use of presence and place this in the context of his understanding of the relationship between God and the world in general and God and humankind in particular. For Rahner, God is in the world (i.e. *Geist in Welt*) and presence is the awareness of the nearness of God in the world. This awareness is elicited by the world and in the perception of the world humankind experiences the presence of God. Moreover, the capacity to experience the presence of God is not a human virtue, achievement or construction. On the contrary, the capacity to experience the presence of God is itself a divine, gratuitous and innate gift:

> Even when he does not 'know' it and does not believe it, that is, even when he cannot make it an individual object of knowledge by merely inward reflexion, man always lives consciously in the presence of the triune God of eternal life. God is the unexpressed but real 'Whither' of the dynamism of all spiritual and moral life in the realm of spiritual existence which is in fact founded, that is, supernaturally elevated by God. It is a 'purely *a priori*'.[103]

Anthropology is critical for Rahner, but this does not mean God is bound to human experience, only that experience is the way humankind encounters God. Therefore, in Rahner's guiding theological vision, subjectivity is not a problem; it is the place for an encounter with the presence of God in the world.

3.2.1. Presence

The aim of this part of the study is to survey Rahner's use of the concept of presence. For Rahner, the gratuitous initiative of God is decisive in the experience of presence.[104] The capacity to experience presence is

---

102 FCF, p. 116.
103 "Nature and grace", TI 4, pp. 180-181.
104 "The specific character of the Christian concept of God", TI 21, p. 189.

God-given; even the concept of God is received as gift and cannot be achieved by means of human effort.[105] So, all *God-talk* is *a posteriori* knowledge; but there is prior experience and this is the mystery of God.[106] In fact, to understand presence fully, presence needs to be seen from within the context of mystery,[107]

> In this unnamed and unsignposted expanse of our consciousness there dwells that which we call God. The mystery pure and simple that we call God is not a special, particularly unusual piece of objective reality, something to be added to and included in the other realities of our naming and classifying experience. God is the comprehensive though never comprehended ground and presupposition of our experience and of the objects of that experience.[108]

God would not be God, if God ceased to be this holy mystery.[109] Mystery is not the unknown but the unfathomable.[110] Mystery is not a problem to be solved, it is the answer graciously posited by God in humankind.[111] Therefore, the incomprehensible mystery cannot be treated as though it was a categorical reality,[112] as "Christianity is not a religion which brings 'God' into the equation of human existence, using him as a known integer as one totals up the results".[113] Humankind is innately oriented toward mystery and the orientation is a "constitutive element" of what it means to be human.[114] The constitutive element is what Rahner means by the notion of transcendental.[115] In the disclosure of mystery, humankind receives a new revelation of the incomprehensible God (i.e. "unknown God").[116] Therefore, revelation does not mean the reception of a

105 FCF, p. 54.

106 *Ibid.* p. 52.

107 *Ibid.* p. 119, "the presence of God as the absolute mystery".

108 Rahner, "Experiencing the spirit" in G.B. Kelly ed., *Karl Rahner: Theologian of the Graced Search for Meaning*, (Edinburgh: T and T, Clark: 1992), p. 227.

109 "Concept of Mystery", TI 4, p. 54.

110 FCF, p. 217.

111 "Concept of Mystery", TI 4, p. 41.

112 FCF, p. 66.

113 *Being and Time*, p. 111.

114 "Concept of Mystery", TI 4, p. 49.

115 FCF, p. 57, mystery is the whither of transcendence.

116 HW, pp. 8, 23; cf. p. 64, "Humanity stands before God as before one who is at least for a time unknown. For God is the Infinite, whom we can know as infinite only by denying the finite and referring to that which lies beyond any finiteness. This referring is the condition of the objective knowledge of finite realities".

152

set of *facts*; it is a different kind of knowledge.[117] It is self-evident knowledge;[118] "What is made intelligible is grounded ultimately in the one thing that is self-evident, in mystery".[119]

In Rahner, there are three prominent expressions for presence. They are the Word of God, the Spirit and Christ. However, before proceeding to look at these expressions, there are five points relating to grace that need to be mentioned. First and foremost, the focus in this study is on the experience of God as presence and absence in relation to the two Christological themes of the Incarnation and the Death-Resurrection event. Second, in Rahner, presence is a gracious encounter with God's self, the Holy Mystery, the ineffable, the incomprehensible one. For Rahner, presence is always gracious presence. Third, there are other manifestations of presence as well as Word, Spirit and Christ. Fourth, the boundaries between these three are not fixed. This is partly a weakness in Rahner, but it is linked to his understanding of grace. For example, Rahner's description of the experience of mystics: "they experience grace, the direct presence of God, and union with God in the Spirit, in the sacred night".[120] In terms of grace, the divine act of instilling an orientation in humankind toward God is an act of ("uncreated") grace.[121] Fifth, Rahner explicitly relates the Word, Spirit and Christ to grace. For instance, the capacity to hear the word is grace-given. The grace of God is expressed in and through the Spirit in the world. The Spirit is a spirit of grace. Rahner's description of grace is similar to how others describe the work of the Spirit (e.g. Tillich). This part will now focus on the Word of God, the Spirit and Christ.

Rahner links presence with the Word of God. He claims an immediate encounter with God's self is not possible because of the nature of God (i.e. God's hiddenness) and human nature (i.e. finitude). Therefore, humankind must wait for a word (i.e. "a *conceptual* sign").[122] By Word, Rahner means more than a human utterance, as the Word is a revelatory event. From the divine perspective, the Word of God occurs once in a

---

117 "Mystery", ET, p. 1002.
118 "Concept of mystery", TI 4, pp. 58-59.
119 FCF, p. 22; cf. "Nature and grace", TI 4, p. 183.
120 "Experiencing", Kelly ed., p. 223.
121 "Grace", ET, p. 591; cf. p. 592, where Rahner acknowledges that the distinction between uncreated and created grace has not been resolved.
122 HW, pp. 132 and 93, previously Rahner described it as a vicarious sign.

person's life as the unique and defining element that constitutes a person's identity (i.e. "a constitutive element").[123] From a human perspective, words are needed to sustain the memory of the impact of the revelatory event; such revelation takes place in history, as revelation "is essentially a historical process".[124] Further, Rahner links the Word with the Spirit. Specifically, he links revelation with human subjectivity and the Spirit, "through this *a priori* subjectivity which is constituted by God himself that the Word of God (spoken by the prophets, for example) acquires its specifically theo-logical quality – it is spoken and heard 'in the Holy Spirit'".[125] There are two points that need to be made. First, in terms of human subjectivity, "the word is the place of a possible encounter with and revelation of the free God".[126] The Word of God is an encounter and the encounter is made possible by God, because God is "the inner precondition constituting the possibility of hearing what is said".[127] Second, in terms of the Spirit, the revelation of the Word of God is the free self-manifestation of the absolute to the finite spirit.[128] Indeed, the experience of salvation and the Word of salvation "form a unity with the 'Spirit'".[129]

The Spirit is a key term in Rahner for presence; "any meditation on the Holy Spirit must think of the Spirit as the gift in which God bestows God's self on human beings".[130] The Spirit has an active role in galvanising the created order so that it may be caught up in the movement toward God,

> The Holy Spirit in particular must not be understood as one side of a dialectic, the other being made up of the letter, the law, the institution, rational calculation. Rather is he the one who constantly blasts open all such empirical, dialectical unities of opposites (although these have their justification) and sweeps them into the movement directed toward the incomprehensible God.[131]

123 "Concept of mystery", TI 4, p. 49.
124 HW, p. 7; cf. pp. 94-95, 135.
125 Rahner, "Word of God and theology", ET, p. 1828.
126 HW, p. 133.
127 "Word of God and theology", ET, p. 1827.
128 HW, pp. 40, 73.
129 "Word of God and theology", ET, p. 1828.
130 Rahner, "Experiencing", Kelly ed., p. 220.
131 Rahner, "Pentecost: fear of the spirit", TGCY, p. 219.

154

In terms of experience, spiritual experience is different from other experiences.[132] There are mystical experiences.[133] All people have the potential for this kind of experience.[134] In fact, to be human is to be spirit.[135] In this context, presence is the awareness of the Spirit and the human orientation toward God. The experience of presence is possible because of what Rahner refers to as "mediated immediacy."[136] This means that the experience of presence as Spirit is possible because of the innate divine orientation, "God's most immediate self-bestowed presence is the vocation of the spiritual creature".[137] This experience is immediate because it is intrinsic to human nature and it is mediated in and through humanity; hence the term "mediated immediacy". Further, every action of the Spirit is oriented towards God as absolute being.[138] Absolute being is the "incomprehensible ground" and "innermost center" of the Spirit.[139] Here is the universal ground of human vocation, "we can conquer the depths of our own nature and thereby realize ourselves to the fullest, only by an adoring belief and acceptance of this Divine Presence".[140]

Mystery was experienced prior to the arrival of Jesus of Nazareth, but Christ represents for Rahner the definitive expression of presence, that is, the mystery of God's self in the world. In places, Rahner implies that the ambiguity of experience as presence and absence is virtually a precondition for comprehending the meaning of Christ,

> In this life the chalice of the Holy Spirit is identical with the chalice of Jesus Christ. It is drunk only by those who have slowly and with difficulty learnt to discern the fullness that is in emptiness, the sunrise in sunset, the life in death, the self-discovery in self-renunciation. They who learn to do this experience the working of the spirit, the real spirit, the Holy Spirit of grace. For this freeing of the spirit from

132 "Experiencing", Kelly ed., p. 221.
133 *Ibid.* p. 223.
134 *Ibid.* p. 224.
135 HW, pp. 53-54.
136 FCF, p. 83.
137 "Mystery", ET, p. 1003.
138 SW, p. 283.
139 "Pentecost", TGCY, p. 216.
140 OP, p. 31.

its earthly fetters can be fully and finally accomplished only through the grace of Christ working upon faith.[141]

Rahner describes absence as an existential experience; it is the universal experience of the hiddenness of God in history.[142] The hidden God is nameless and is experienced as "distant aloofness" or "distant and aloof".[143] The whither of transcendence itself is "there in its own proper way of aloofness and absence. It bestows itself upon us by refusing itself, by keeping silence, by staying afar … It can never be approached directly or experienced immediately".[144] In the hiddenness of God, humankind encounters the reality of God's silence.[145] The name of *this* God is "holy mystery" and the mystery *is* the incomprehensibleness of God.[146] Thus, God can be experienced but not fully known, as "no amount of questioning will ever fathom Your depths – You will still be the Incomprehensible".[147] In the end, God cannot be known because God is beyond categorisation, "the whither of transcendental experience is always there as the nameless, the indefinable, the unattainable … absolutely beyond determination".[148] Significantly, all this means is that the incomprehensibleness of God is experienced as absence as well as presence. In short, the experience of presence and absence is grounded in the very nature of the incomprehensible God.[149] This part has outlined issues relating to the concept of presence in Rahner. The next part places Rahner's understanding of presence in the framework of his understanding of the relationship between God and the world.

141 BT, pp. 42-43.
142 "The hiddenness of God", TI 16, cf. J. Macquarrie, "Deus Absconditus", NDCT, p. 155.
143 "Concept of mystery", TI 4, pp. 52-56, 67.
144 *Ibid.* p. 52.
145 HW, pp. 64, 151. Reno, *Ordinary* p. 222, "the more clearly we grasp the 'surface', the more extensive becomes the depth; the more clearly we see God, the more hidden he becomes".
146 "Concept of mystery", TI 4, p. 61.
147 ES, p. 7; cf. FCF, p. 120.
148 "Concept of mystery", TI 4, pp. 50-51.
149 FCF, p. 119; Pekarske, D.T. *Abstracts of Karl Rahner's Theological Investigations 1-23*, (Milwaukee: Marquette University Press, 2002), p. 453, "treating God's abiding hiddenness … as a central theological concern leads Rahner to reappraise radically the traditional notions of revelation, revelation history, and human knowledge".

3.2.2. God and the World

To understand Rahner's view of presence, it needs to be assessed from
the broad theological perspective of the relationship between God and
world. This part will explore the God-world relationship in relation to a
number of key concepts in Rahner, namely: grace, metaphysics of
knowledge, pre-anticipation, quasi-formal causality and symbol.

A World of Grace

Grace is a fundamental theme in Rahner and whatever is said of presence
is said in the context of grace, this is because Rahner's God is a God of
grace and Rahner's world is a graced-world, "Grace is God himself, the
communication in which he gives himself to man as the divinizing favour which he is himself".[150] God's self-communication is "God's free,
personal, uncovenanted favour".[151] The capacity to receive the gift of
God's self is God-given; even the concept of God is received as a gift
and cannot be achieved by human effort.[152] Further, God's gracious self-
communication is God's expression of God's self in the world, it derives
from the life of God and is effective within the life of humankind.[153] This
gift of grace brings with it primal knowledge of what it means to be human, namely, being human is bound to humanity's relationship with
God, "to this extent the differentiation between this ineffable term and
the finite is obviously not only a distinction which has to be made, but
this differentiation is the *one and original* distinction which is experienced".[154] All told, the presence of God in the world is the experience of
the awareness of the nearness of God's self; in that context, grace is a
description of both the experience itself and the source of the experience.
In the early Rahner, the question of how this is worked out in anthropological terms is partly the question of the metaphysics of knowledge.

150 "Nature and grace", TI 4, p. 177.
151 "Grace", ET, p. 589.
152 FCF, p. 54.
153 "Grace", ET, pp. 589-590.
154 FCF, p. 63, cf. pp. 77-79, a sense of creaturehood is part of what it means to be
     human; this includes an element of freedom because humankind is independent as
     well as dependent, cf. "Nature and Grace", TI 4, p. 177.

Rahner's metaphysics of knowledge has a formative role in his theological vision. *Spirit in the World* is an important starting point. As such, the work is a formative but not final influence on Rahner's vision. In *Spirit in the World*, Rahner addresses Kant's problem concerning the possibility of attaining knowledge of God by means of pure reason.[155] For Kant, the problem stems from the relationship between human knowing and sensible objects, because only sensible objects as they appear (i.e. the phenomenal) are accessible to human knowing. Further, the mind has dual but interrelated capacities known as sensibility and understanding, this means that the mind has the capacity to give content to the appearance of an object through forms of sensibility (i.e. time, space), where the form of the object is imposed by the mind through the categories of understanding. Kant considers the categories of understanding as *a priori* categories. Furthermore, Kant maintains that in order to engage the categories of understanding, the mind depends on sensible objects. In this context, a problem arises concerning the knowledge of God: if knowledge depends upon sensible objects and God is not a sensible object, then knowledge of God is unattainable (i.e. on the basis of pure reason). In contrast, Rahner argues that there is a way to attain knowledge of God, based on his metaphysics of knowledge, which still depends on sense knowledge.[156] In relation to his metaphysics of knowledge, judgement is the central issue. A judgement can only be made because of the

155 Kilby, *Rahner*, p. 14, "one might say that in *Spirit in the World* Rahner is developing, under the general influence of Maréchal and with a few particular borrowings from Heidegger, a reading of Aquinas through the lens of Kant and the post-Kantians".

156 McCool, *Rahner Reader*, p. xvi, "Kant and Thomas both agree that man is a receptive knower. Human knowledge must begin with sensation and man's conceptual knowledge depends upon the senses for its objective content. Consequently the unity of sense and intellect in the single act of the receptive knower's existential affirmation demands as the condition of its possibility that both the receptive knower and the sensible objects of his knowledge be composed of matter, form, and existence. How else would the synthesis of intelligible form, sensible subject, and existential affirmation in the judgment be possible? Maréchal was content, however, to indicate the possibility of such a transcendental metaphysics in *Le Point de départ de la métaphysique*. He left the task of working it out to his successors in the movement which has since become known as Transcendental Thomism".

158

power of transcendence. The major features of judgement are sensibility
and abstraction, sensible and intelligible species, and *Vorgriff* (i.e. pre-
anticipation).

Rahner's metaphysics of knowledge can be described as a response to
the presence of a sensible object, in which there is a dynamic meeting of
images in the mind, and where *a priori* images throw light on and give
form to sense images. Rahner's metaphysics of knowledge is developed
in chapters 2, 3 and 4 of *Spirit in the World*. Chapter 2 deals with sensibility, chapter 3 with abstraction and chapter 4 with *Conversio*. Further,
Rahner claims the core of Thomas' metaphysics of knowledge is found
in questions 84, 85 and 86 of the *Summa Theologiae* I (ST). Question 84
relates to the issue of human knowledge of the world. In particular, Rahner uses article 7, question 84, as the touchstone of his metaphysics of
knowledge. The full title of the article is, "Can the intellect know anything through the intelligible species which it possesses, without turning
to the phantasms?"[157] The short answer is no. It is from the title of the
article that the shorthand term *Conversio* is derived, which will be used
to refer to the essential process of turning to the phantasms (i.e. conversion). Furthermore, Rahner is interested in the relationship between the
mind of a sentient being and a sensible object. He describes the mind in
terms of two interrelated capacities: sensibility and abstraction. They
represent the two sides of the one simultaneous process of reason. Sensibility is the passive capacity to receive the image of an object as a sensible species. The sensible species is known as the phantasm, "The
sensible species is an actuality of the thing itself".[158] Sensibility by itself
cannot discern that the sensible species corresponds to an object; to ac-
complish this sensibility needs abstraction. Abstraction is the active capacity to make the distinction between subject and object. It does this by
means of a process Rahner calls the *Vorgriff* (i.e. pre-anticipation). Abstraction enables sensibility to impart a specific form to matter, on the
basis of the universal forms that it has at its disposal, that is "Objective
knowledge is given only when a knower relates a universal, known intelligibility to a supposite existing in itself".[159] Thus, an object can be described as that which is constituted by form and matter. Alternatively,
the knower already knows the form of the object and in the act of know-

---

157 SW, p. 3.
158 *Ibid.* p. 87.
159 *Ibid.* p. 125.

ing the object is recognised as an object *per se*. Rahner claims that abstraction is grounded in God the absolute being, and the sentient being is linked to God and sensible objects by the dynamism of the human mind. For Rahner, the existential gap between subject and object is real but secondary to their ontological unity in God and this unity enables humankind to transcend the gap.

> The process of the judgment brings to light two irreducibly distinct forms of intellectual knowledge. The first is the objective, categorical knowledge expressed through the universal concepts of the judgment. The second is the human knower's unobjective grasp of himself and of Infinite Being which is the inseparable concomitant of every act of affirmation.[160]

Pre-anticipation

Transcendence is a key concept for Rahner. Its roots can be found in the notion of pre-anticipation. To begin, the intelligible species have a formal role in pre-anticipation. However, the intelligible species do not exist in themselves, as they are the ontological presuppositions of the intellect.[161] However, the concept of the intelligible species is difficult to grasp. To understand the concept, it needs to be placed in its anthropological context. Rahner's anthropology is a metaphysical anthropology; where the "senses" are metaphysical grounds.[162] In that context, "phantasia" refers to the imagination.[163] It creates the sensible species, which arise in response to the presence of a sensible object. The sensible species (i.e. phantasms) express the quiddity (i.e. whatness) of sensible objects. Metaphorically, they are like *objects* to the intellect. The intelligible species are images of a metaphysical kind; they are not the same as the sensible species.[164] The relationship between the intelligible and sensible species can be understood in material-formal terms. In principle, the sensible species can be described as a response to the presence of a sensible object; the intelligible species make this possible "The [in-

160 McCool, *Rahner Reader*, p. 2.
161 SW, p. 23.
162 *Ibid.* p. 45.
163 *Ibid.* p. 104.
164 *Ibid.* p. 141.

160

telligible] species is related to the phantasm as the formal to the material element".[165] This is not a sequential process; it is dialectical. That is, an object elicits a response from sensibility, but sensibility is only able to respond because of the *a priori* initiative of the intelligible species, which responds to the object. Thus, as a response to the presence of a sensible object, there is a dynamic meeting of images in the mind, in which *a priori* images give form to sense images.[166] That is, the intelligible species relate to the awareness of the known subject in order to bring form to the sensible species.[167] By inference, the intelligible species cannot respond directly to the sensible object; hence the need for conversion to the sensible species.

Rahner describes the function of the agent intellect in terms of pre-anticipation.[168] Pre-anticipation is "the dynamism of intentional consciousness",[169] or "the dialectic of self-differentiation".[170] The essence of intellect is found in its link with corporeality, but pre-anticipation represents another link,

> This transcending apprehension of further possibilities, through which the form possessed in a concretion in sensibility is apprehended as limited and so is abstracted, we call "pre-apprehension" *("Vorgriff")*. Although this term is not to be found literally in Thomas, yet its content is contained in what Thomas calls "*excessus*" (excess), using a similar image.[171]

Pre-anticipation opens up consciousness; it is "an *a priori* power given with human nature",[172] where the "a priori is general, universal, tran-

---

165 *Ibid.* p. 318.

166 Burke, *Reinterpreting*, p. 230, using McDermott's term "dialectical analogy", Burke describes the movement in this way, "this analogy consists in a *Schwebe* or an oscillation between the dynamic movement of the judgment, on the one hand, and the static moment of conceptualization, on the other".

167 SW, p. 310.

168 Tallon (ed.) HW, p. xiv, the meaning of *Vorgriff* is debatable. Essentially, it means to grasp before or pre-grasp. Tallon favours "anticipation" and warns against "pre-apprehension" and "pre-concept", because of cognitive connotations. Without attempting to resolve the debate, this study uses pre-anticipation as a working definition.

169 *Ibid.* p. xii.

170 W. Pannenberg, *Jesus – God and Man*, (London: SCM Press, 1964, 1968), pp. 317-318.

171 SW, p. 142.

172 HW, p. 47.

scendental revelation, identical with the presence of the divine Spirit in the world".[173] Pre-anticipation is not the infinite as the infinite is the whither of pre-anticipation and humankind can only know the infinite because of finite things.[174] Further, Rahner's pre-anticipation *(Vorgriff)* derives in part from Heidegger.[175] His use of *excessus* derives from Aquinas.[176] In Rahner, the meanings of the two concepts inevitably dovetail under the heading of transcendence.[177] Thus, pre-anticipation can be described in terms of transcendence. Transcendence is access to universal forms and by virtue of this access it is participation in universal being. In other words, transcendence is the capacity of the mind to grasp simultaneously the world and the divine. This means that grasping (i.e. anticipating) a single object is part of the same process as grasping God, though in the end God is never grasped. Mascall sums it up perfectly,

> Rahner appears to be telling us that God is grasped not in his character as the ground of the *objects* of our perception but in his character as the ground of us who are the *subjects* of perception.[178]

For Rahner, pre-anticipation's link to the universal is the basis of the human link to absolute being. This is possible because every sense object, delimited by form, is a bearer of *esse* (i.e. actual being), "the *affirmation* of the real limitation of an existent has as its condition the preapprehension of *esse*, which implicitly and simultaneously affirms an absolute *esse*".[179] Hence, knowledge of the agent intellect by its nature leads to thematic knowledge of God; "the agent intellect is the spontaneous pre-apprehension *(Vorgriff)* of *esse* absolutely, and thereby it is the faculty which apprehends the universal".[180] In summary, humankind as finite spirit is able to imagine the infinite. Thus, humankind can tran-

---

173 M.J. Scanlon "A Deconstruction of Religion: On Derrida and Rahner" in J.D. Caputo and M.J. Scanlon eds., *God, The Gift, And Postmodernism*, (Bloomington, Indianapolis: Indiana University Press, 1999), p. 226.

174 HW, p. 59.

175 Heidegger, *Being and Time*, p. 191, "In every case interpretation is grounded in *something we see in advance – in a fore-sight"*.

176 SW, p. 202 ff.

177 *Being and Time*, pp. 114-115; FCF, p. 34.

178 E.L. Mascall, *The Openness of Being: Natural Theology Today*, (London: Darton, Longman and Todd, 1971), p. 72.

179 SW, p. 182.

180 *Ibid.* p. 225.

162

scend the finite, through the power of the infinite, and by virtue of its awareness of the finite. The later Rahner's understanding of transcendence moves beyond this highly focused speculative position to a broader existential/anthropological approach (3.2.3).[181] But this early understanding informs and shapes Rahner's vision and is implicitly present in the later understanding.[182]

Quasi-formal Causality and Symbol

For Rahner, quasi-formal causality has a role in his method (3.3.2). In its simplest form, the issue is about how God causes things to happen, which presumes something about God's relationship to the world. That is, if God's distinction from humankind is not maintained, then the concept of the immutability of God is undermined. For Rahner, the sticking point then is to affirm both God's involvement and God's otherness. Further, with God's self-communication, God is cause and effect.[183] With efficient causality, the effect is different from the cause.[184] To this end, Rahner uses the notion of quasi-formal causality. Formal causality explains two things. First, it explains how two can be one, that is, how form and matter constitute an object (e.g. spirit and body constitute a person). This represents a unity (but not in a numerical sense).[185] Second, two can be one and both are needed, but one has priority over the other, that is, form has priority over matter (e.g. spirit over body). This allows for distinction. Thus, Rahner establishes a basis for unity-in-difference. Subsequently, from a human perspective, it is possible to refer to an embodied sentient being which lives in a sensible world and yearns for Absolute being, because the sentient being has access to Absolute being. From a divine perspective, it is possible to describe God's self as being in matter, but God is not matter as God gives form to matter through the intellect. This allows for the possibility of God changing *"in something*

181 "Transcendental theology", ET, p. 1748, cf. "Theology", ET, p. 1692, "transcendental philosophy in particular easily passes over in the concrete to transcendental theology".
182 Rahner, "Christology today", p. 7; FCF, pp. 121, 284.
183 FCF, p. 120.
184 *Ibid.* p. 121; cf. CS, pp. 34-40.
185 SW, p. 345.

else", but God's self does not change.[186] All through this, Rahner's view of causality has been influenced by his work on symbols.

In Rahner, the concept of symbol is another way of interpreting the relationship between God and the world. Moreover, Rahner's concept of symbol plays a role in explaining how presence is conferred, where Christ is the symbol of God, "Christ in his historical existence is both reality and sign, *sacramentum* and *res sacramenti*".[187] In particular, Rahner interprets the significance of the themes of the Incarnation and the Death-Resurrection event symbolically.

> If a theology of symbolic realities is to be written, Christology, the doctrine of the incarnation of the Word, will obviously form the central chapter. And this chapter need almost be no more than an exegesis of the saying: "He that sees me, sees the Father" (Jn 14:9) … the incarnate word is the absolute symbol of God in the world, filled as nothing else can be with what is symbolized. He is not merely the presence and revelation of what God is in himself. He is also the expressive presence of what – or rather, who – God wished to be, in free grace, to the world, in such a way that this divine attitude, once so expressed, can never be reversed, but is and remains final and unsurpassable..[188]

To appreciate Rahner's theology of symbol, it is necessary to put it in the context of Rahner's view of the world. Rahner is engaged with the modern world. He identifies matter/spirit unity as a growing conviction of the modern age, in which the world is being understood increasingly in terms of a process of *becoming*. Formerly, a static view of the world dominated (cf. *conservatio*).[189] Now a dynamic view of a changing, evolutionary world is surfacing.[190] This conviction enables the modern era to understand the Incarnation as the climax of the process of the acceptance of the world by God and the acceptance of God by the world.[191] Traditionally, the immanence of God has been understood in a *conservatio* sense as sustaining the world in being; any sense of *concursus* was seen

---

186　"On the theology of the Incarnation", TI 4, p. 113.
187　FCF, p. 15.
188　"The theology of the symbol", TI 4, p. 237. Pekarske, *Abstracts,* p. 112, 'the basic structure of Christian reality is symbol".
189　"Christology in the setting of modern man's understanding of himself and of his world", TI 11, p. 220.
190　*Ibid.* p. 221.
191　*Ibid.* pp. 226-227.

164

from this perspective.[192] But the process of self-transcendence reveals that *conservatio/concursus* was "the dynamic impulse towards precisely this self-transcendence present in all being in virtue of the immanence of God".[193] Self-transcendence explains becoming to the modern era as "the process of God's self-bestowal".[194]

The concept of expressiveness is a key to Rahner's understanding of symbol; in particular, the first basic principle of his ontology of symbolism is that "all beings are by their nature symbolic, because they necessarily 'express' themselves in order to attain their own nature".[195] Rahner is aware of the difficulties involved with the analysis of symbol, for example, "it is not easy to say where the function of being merely a sign and indicator so predominates over the 'function of expressiveness' that a symbol loses its 'overplus of meaning' … and sinks to the level of a sign with little symbolism".[196] Thus, Rahner's task is "to look for the highest and most primordial manner in which; one reality can represent another".[197] For Rahner, being is inherently symbolic because "it necessarily 'expresses' itself".[198] The symbol is the only way that *another* can attain knowledge of being.[199] To explain the dynamics of the symbol, Rahner returns to Aquinas and the notion of *causa formalis*, where "The 'form' gives itself away from itself by imparting itself to the material cause".[200] The symbol is the self-realisation of being in the *other*.[201] In God's salvific plan,

> God himself is the reality of salvation, because it is given to man and grasped by him in the symbol, which does not represent an absent and merely promised reality

192 *Ibid.* p. 223.

193 *Ibid.* p. 224.

194 *Ibid.* p. 225.

195 "Symbol", TI 4, p. 224.

196 *Ibid.* p. 225.

197 *Ibid.*

198 *Ibid.* p. 229.

199 *Ibid.* p. 231.

200 *Ibid.* cf. P.J. Mackie, "causality", OCP, pp. 126-128, in contemporary philosophy, causality is a complex thing and usually the focus is on events. Mackie describes here Aristotle's theory (material, formal, efficient and final) and by inference Aquinas' views of causation as explanations.

201 "Symbol", TI 4, p. 235, "the symbol shares this *'analogia entis'* with being which it symbolizes".

but exhibits this reality as something present, by means of the symbol formed by it.[202]

An example of Rahner's theology of symbol is found in his work on the sacraments. For Rahner, Christ instituted the sacraments of the Church. This is based on the assumption that Christ instituted the sacraments sacramentally, that is, through the body of Christ the Church.[203] The sacraments have power for two reasons: God is the principal cause and sacraments are intrinsic symbols. As principle cause, God is the foundation of Rahner's theory of sacramental causality. Rahner expresses this in terms of *opus operatum*, which means the bestowal of the grace of God is not dependent on the "subjective merit" of the priest or the recipient of a sacrament.[204] In contrast, Rahner's criticism of other theories of sacramental causality (i.e. physical, moral, intentional) has two aspects. The first is that these theories are based on a "pattern of transitive efficient causality".[205] With physical causality, it uses instrumental causality to explain the inherent limits of physical analogy. It does not explain how an instrumental cause causes and allows little room for symbolic interpretation. With moral causality, God responds to pleading, but "the sign is the cause of grace, not of God's decision physically to confer grace".[206] With intentional causality, it is based on a legal claim on God, where the impact of sign as signifier is not addressed. In these models, the sign dimension of the symbol is neglected. Subsequently, grace and sacrament have been compartmentalised as cause and sign have been separated. The second aspect of Rahner's criticism of these theories is "that the sacraments are signs plays no part in explaining their causality".[207] Thus, he introduces the concept of intrinsic symbol, where there is "an intrinsic and mutual causal relationship. What is manifesting itself posits its own identity and existence by manifesting itself in this manifestation which is distinct from itself".[208] This is based on Rahner's presumption of the existence of an "intrinsic connexion by virtue of the

202 *Ibid.* p. 245.
203 CS, p. 18.
204 *Ibid.* pp. 32-33, *ex opere operato*, from the work done.
205 *Ibid.* p. 37.
206 *Ibid.*
207 *Ibid.* p. 36.
208 *Ibid.* p. 38.

166

nature of things".[209] Consequently, symbols have the capacity to confer what they signify. Unlike the other theories of sacramental causality, cause and sign are united in symbol.

Rahner explains the difference between cause and sign in terms of formal causality; namely, cause and sign constitute a symbol as form and matter constitute an object. The sign and what is conferred are distinct but not separate. They are distinct in that the sign is not the same as what is bestowed. They form a unity in that what is bestowed is expressed by the sign; "the sign is therefore a cause of what it signifies by being the way in which what is signified effects itself".[210] Now, if a symbol is a sign, which confers what it signifies by virtue of its capacity for signification, then signification cannot take place in a vacuum. That is, Rahner links signification to human apprehension; this means that it is a human subject that attributes significance to a sign (e.g. a faith community). It is in and through human subjectivity that the reality of the sign is apprehended. It is in and through human subjectivity that the reality of the Christ is experienced. In other words, Rahner interprets the significance of Christ sacramentally.[211] Further, Rahner's understanding of symbol helps him address a major theological problem, which arises with the hypostatic union. The problem with the Incarnation is that God is involved but God is immutable. Subsequently, Rahner uses a special case of intrinsic causality to explain this (i.e. quasi-formal). For Rahner, there are other instances of intrinsic causality that threaten God's *otherness*.[212] With the Incarnation, Rahner asserts that he is dealing with a particular type of intrinsic causality. In order to make this difference apparent, he refers to it as quasi-formal causality. Quasi-formal causality is different from intrinsic causality *per se*, because unlike the other instances, it is God's self who is involved in the Incarnation.[213] In brief, Rahner uses

209 "Symbol", TI 4, p. 242.
210 CS, p. 38.
211 *Ibid.* p. 39.
212 FCF, p. 121.
213 SW, p. 272, unity-in-difference finds its locus in the cogitative sense, which is the "differentiated unity of individual and universal". The cogitative sense is the metaphysical *place* of connection; cf. SW, p. 299, "The cogitative sense has already been shown to be the manifestation of the free spirit in sensibility itself, as the unified center of spirit and sensibility, as the place of the illuminative, abstractive conversion to the phantasm, as the measure of the fact that the spirit can move and

quasi-formal causality both to affirm God's involvement and protect God's otherness; "God can become something, he who is unchangeable in himself can *himself* become subject to change *in something else*".[214] Thus, "God bears a quasi-formal relationship to the world".[215] In fact, "In a *quasi-formal* causality he really and in the strictest sense of the word bestows *himself*".[216]

Conclusion

In Rahner, the apprehension of the presence of God is related to the mind. For Rahner, Kant made a mistake in that "he failed to observe that the dynamism of the human mind is one of the *a priori* conditions of possibility for the *speculative intellect's* objective knowledge".[217] However, Rahner himself does not supply a detailed account of the metaphysics of his supernatural existential.[218] In particular, it is not entirely clear how the dynamism of the human mind works. Burke describes it in the following way; "Human knowing consists in a dynamic oscillation or *Schwebe* between the sensible singular and the preapprehended horizon of all being".[219] It has been described as "dialectical analogy".[220] This back-and-forth movement between the *a priori* and sense images is dialectical. Certainly, the concept of analogy is one way of explaining that though we have access to *a priori* images, which are of divine origin; we cannot possess them. Therefore, the concept of analogy simultaneously asserts divine and human identity (i.e. Burke's unifying role) and maintains divine and human difference (i.e. Burke's conceptualising role).[221]

---

inform sensibility and have it as the co-principle of its knowing because it actively lets it emanate from itself".

214 "Incarnation", TI 4, p. 113, cf. Donceel, *Searching Mind*, p. 188.
215 "Christology in the setting", TI 11, p. 225.
216 TT, p. 36.
217 McCool, *Rahner Reader*, p. xiii.
218 *Ibid.* p. xxvi.
219 Burke, *Reinterpreting*, p. 2.
220 P. Burke, "Conceptual Thought in Karl Rahner", *Gregorianum* 75 (1994), pp. 65-93; J.M. McDermott, "Dialectical Analogy: the Oscillating Center in Rahner's Thought", *Gregorianum* 75 (1994), pp. 675-703.
221 Burke, *Reinterpreting*, p. viii.

168

Significantly, Burke uses dialectical analogy to show Rahner's limitations,

> Notwithstanding its inner coherence and its compatibility with the truths of the Christian faith, Rahner's dialectical analogy, and with it his entire system, fails to ground itself fully. It is valid insofar as it reflects the tensions within the Catholic vision of reality, but as such it neither explains itself nor resolves the tensions it exposes. This problem, which is intrinsic to Rahner's theological system, has its origins in his foundational metaphysics.[222]

The use of the concept of analogy has helped Burke critique Rahner, but it does not solve the problem of understanding the God-humankind-world relationship. At the theological level, analogy is a useful form of explanation. Analogical predication involves the use of similarities and differences.[223] Similarities make it possible to speak about God. Moreover, that God-talk is analogous means God-talk is mediated. Implicitly, the analogous nature of God-talk is a reminder that God is different. Nevertheless, the use of the concept of analogy is problematic,[224]

> In LOGIC, reasoning by analogy is a form of non-demonstrative argument which, unlike INDUCTION proper, draws conclusions about the nature of a *single* unknown thing or things from information about a known thing or things which it to some extent resembles. It is a form of reasoning that is peculiarly liable to yield false conclusions from true premises.[225]

There is an inherent theological problem here. On the one hand, if God is God then we are restricted to the use of analogies (narratives, symbols) in our descriptions of God. On the other hand, assuming the premise that God is similar *and* different is true, the use of analogy explains how it works but it does not prove it. As a means of explanation, the concept of analogy has theological strengths but it has a philosophical weakness in that it shifts rather than solves the problem. In Burke's case, dialectical analogy does not fully explain the status of the concept in Rahner. This

---

222 *Ibid.* p. 298.
223 "Analogies", Baggini and Fosl, pp. 46-48.
224 "Analogy", ODP, p. 14, "Analogy butts upon literal meaning, but also upon metaphor, and thus forms a perplexing phenomenon in the philosophy of language".
225 A. Quinton, "Analogy" in A. Bullock and S. Trombley eds., *The New Fontana Dictionary Of Modern Thought*, 3rd ed., (London: Harper Collins Publishers, 1999, 2000), p. 27.

169

is why this study opts for the general term *the dynamism of the human mind,* instead of the more technical term dialectical analogy; the study's term is a shorthand way of describing the locus of Rahner's metaphysics of knowledge. The term *dynamism* picks up the vitality that Burke observes in Rahner's system as it is "this structure of dialectical analogy that enables him [Rahner] to maintain the unity of God and the world, spirit and matter, grace and nature, while simultaneously maintaining the distinctions between them".[226] In addition, the term *of the human mind* picks up the Kantian nuance, which is a vital aspect of Rahner's construal of the modern world and the gap between the finite and the infinite. It is also partly why this study considers it a reasonable option to explore a postmetaphysical use of elements of Rahner (4.2).[227]

3.2.3. Anthropology

In Rahner, anthropology is a crucial context for understanding presence. The key to his anthropology is the idea of a divinely instituted and constituted human capacity for openness to God. At the risk of oversimplification, God is in the world anthropologically. Therefore, the experience of the presence of God in the world is the innate awareness of the closeness of God's self, which in the process of self-reflection informs humankind about the innate capacity for God.[228] While this awareness is elicited extrinsically through the world by means of an act of perception, it is an *a priori* capacity, which means all people are able to hear the word.[229] For Rahner this intrinsic capacity is a transcendental condition of humankind. Subsequently, Rahner aims to develop an ontology of the human being,

> Our purpose is to explain the nature of the philosophy of religion by outlining it on the basis of Thomistic metaphysics in such a way that it may be seen as an ontology

226 Burke, *Reinterpreting*, p. 230.
227 Kilby, *Rahner*, p. 10, n. 22.
228 FCF, p. 119; "Grace", ET, p. 589.
229 HW, pp. 14, 41; cf. Donceel, *Philosophical Anthropology*, (New York: Sheed and Ward, 1967), p. 473, "traditional philosophy calls this potency *obediential*, to distinguish it from the ordinary natural potencies or possibilities, which may be actualized under natural influences. This potency can be actualized only by an extraordinary, supernatural, of its very nature unique, divine influence".

170

of the human person as the being who, in history, listens for an eventual revelation.[230]

For Rahner, ontology is the study of being. The starting point in the study of ontology is the notion of self-presence (i.e. luminosity).[231] In this setting, presence is self-presence, as divine presence is mediated intrinsically. Self-presence involves the idea of the return to the self, which is expressed in judgement (i.e. perception).[232] In brief, judgement is possible because of pre-anticipation and pre-anticipation opens up consciousness. The opening up of consciousness is a pre-condition for the experience of presence and subjectivity is *the place* for the simultaneous act of perception and experience of presence.

The movement from *Spirit in the World* to *Hearer of the Word* is indicative of a movement from his metaphysics of knowledge to the development of a broader, more theological anthropology. In *Hearer of the Word*, Rahner wants to establish a definition of the philosophy of religion that is found by making a comparison with theology. This is an epistemological problem,[233] where knowledge is found by discovering the metaphysical foundations of the disciplines of philosophy of religion and theology (i.e. "their common metaphysical ground").[234] This common ground is found in an analysis of the human person, in particular, the analysis of the openness of the person to revelation.[235] For Rahner, echoing Heidegger, the problem of the analysis of human nature has its ori-

230 HW, p. 55.
231 *Ibid.* p. 33, related expressions are luminosity of being (p. 28) and self-affirmation (p. 126).
232 *Ibid.* p. 43, linking here with the thrust of *The Spirit in the World* and his work on *Conversio*.
233 *Ibid.* p. 1.
234 *Ibid.* p. 3, cf. pp. 150, 153, philosophy of religion lays the foundation for theology.
235 *Ibid.* p. 16, Rahner contends that his metaphysical explanation of human nature demonstrates that history shows that "we are capable of listening to God's message". Rahner describes this capability as potency. It has an element of demand (*obedientia*) and "Thus we may speak of that part of fundamental theology that concerns us here as the ontology of our obediential potency for the free revelation of God", this has connections with "the problem of the possibility of a Christian philosophy". The Christian character of such a philosophy lies in openness. This becomes a crucial building block for Rahner's concept of anonymous Christianity. Within the parameters of Rahner's system, anonymous Christianity is the logical outcome of his analysis of human nature.

gins in human questioning as in "what is the being of beings?"[236] Rahner defines the problem ontologically,[237]

> In his second major work, *Hearers of the Word*, Rahner appropriated the thematics of speaking and hearing, claiming and being claimed, that Heidegger had begun to enunciate for the first time in the thirties in connection with his readings of the early Greeks. Rahner put Heidegger's reflections to theological use, which argued that the believer is ontologically disposed to revelation, that there is a kind of ontological structure in Dasein in virtue of which its very being is to be addressed by being itself.[238]

Humankind knows about being, and the unity of Being and knowing is revealed to humankind by means of human awareness. Being and knowing constitute an original unity (*unius generis*). This unity implies that an intelligibility and ordination to knowledge is characteristic of what it means to be human,

> We are facing the question of human being, as it is co-affirmed in the necessity of the general question of being. We wish to know whether and to what extent human being is open for a possible revelation of God ... Thus we come to the problem of human receptivity in knowledge".[239]

In summary, Rahner adopts an ontological approach in an attempt to explore the concept of openness to God. The existential awareness of being is his warrant for such an analysis.

Rahner makes a distinction between being and beings. Being is "the whence and the whither",[240] of all questions, that is, it is in the nature of beings to be directed towards being. Being cannot be categorised or objectified as being is an "analogous concept".[241] The specific *subject* for analysis then is *esse*, that is, *actual being*; where being means self-presence. Rahner then poses the following question: if being is self-presence then is an enquiry necessary? The degree of luminosity (i.e. self-presence) corresponds to the intensity of being.[242] Luminosity is not

---

236 *Ibid.* p. 25, cf. *Being and Time*, p. 21, in Heidegger it is "the question of the meaning of Being".
237 HW, pp. 7, 27.
238 Caputo, *Cambridge Companion*, p. 280.
239 HW, p. 45.
240 *Ibid.* p. 29.
241 *Ibid.* p. 37.
242 *Ibid.*

a passive characteristic as it involves a degree of intentionality, that is, a degree of will whereby everything strives for self-possession.[243] To enquire about self-presence is to will, to choose, to make our selves available to being. The experience of presence, as self-presence, leads us to God (absolute being).[244] From the ontological analysis, Rahner asserts that human existence is "a purely factual existence. It is contingence, thrownness".[245] Nevertheless, human will for Rahner points to God the Absolute. Therefore, humankind is able to live with contingency.

There is an important link between willing and knowing, arising as Rahner tries to reconcile contingency and transcendence.[246] The key is his contention that transcendence entails "voluntary self-affirmation ... it is a form of understanding".[247] Certainly existence is contingent, yet to describe the source of the knowledge of God as transcendence is also the focus of an act of will. In other words, in the face of contingency, humankind makes a choice on the basis of innate knowledge of God. In this, the concept of human freedom is implicit and the exercise of freedom is simultaneously a God-affirming and self-affirming act. Moreover, as Rahner's theology develops, freedom becomes more and more important for him, as he sees it is a transcendental aspect of what it means to be human. Further, the will is an effect of God; it is part of the self-disclosure of God in human existence.[248] The act of freedom is simultaneously divine and human; it is not an either/or but a both/and. This act of the will based on knowledge is a free act; as such it is "the fulfilment of one's own nature, a taking possession of oneself, of the reality of one's own creative power over oneself. Thus it is a coming to oneself, a self-presence in oneself".[249] Out of God's freedom humankind has been created and in the ongoing process of creation, God has given humankind the *a priori* capacity for freedom. Thus, in functional terms,

243 *Ibid.* p. 38.
244 Donceel, *Anthropology*, p. 284, n. 1.
245 HW, p. 67, "to use Heidegger's term".
246 *Ibid.* p. 78.
247 *Ibid.* p. 83.
248 *Ibid.* p. 70.
249 *Ibid.* p. 80, Rahner describes finite contingency in terms of God's love, which is interpreted epistemologically, "knowledge is but the luminous radiance of love" (p. 81).

the act of freedom is simultaneously divine and human, in ontological terms; God is the source of the human capacity for freedom.

Freedom in History

For Rahner, freedom is expressed in history. Revelation itself is an historical process.[250] It is the free self-manifestation of the absolute to the finite spirit.[251] Humankind cannot expect an immediate encounter with God's self because of the hiddenness of God and the finitude of human nature. Therefore, humankind waits for a word; "the place of a possible revelation is always and necessarily also our history".[252] While Rahner has been criticised for reducing revelation to a personal encounter,[253] his emphasis on history partly counters this (i.e. a personal encounter takes place in history). To appreciate this, it is important to return to one of Rahner's presuppositions, namely, human knowing is receptive knowing. This means humankind is present to itself when it is in the presence of an object; conversely, "returning into ourselves" is "stepping out into the world".[254] Therefore, history refers to both the context of the object that elicits presence and the medium through which awareness of presence is experienced. Further, Rahner's view of history is premised on the assumption that, "our being is that of matter ... we are material beings"[255] and humankind is only human in a sensible mode.[256] However, there is a danger of confusing Rahner's use of the term matter with the today's notion of the material world. He tends to use the term matter metaphysically (implying potential).[257] For Rahner, a material being is always open to change because of "the undetermined range of the possibilities of matter".[258] Furthermore, a material being is not an isolated being, on the contrary, "to be human is to be one among many ... we are actually hu-

250 *Ibid.* p. 7.
251 *Ibid.* pp. 40, 73.
252 *Ibid.* p. 94.
253 McDermott, "Methodological Shift", p. 260, cf. p. 257.
254 HW, p. 97.
255 *Ibid.* p. 111.
256 *Ibid.* p. 106.
257 *Ibid.* p. 101.
258 *Ibid.* p. 110.

174

man only in a humanity".[259] Significantly, *other* people elicit possibilities because knowledge is receptive knowledge. In this sense, *others* are the *objects* that elicit a response from the individual. All this says much about Rahner's understanding of human nature; "we go out toward God … only by entering into the world".[260]

The innate capacity is God's gift to us and it enables us to hear God, if we so choose. The gift is a transcendental condition; as such it entails knowledge and freedom.[261] Transcendence and freedom are two sides of the supernatural existential. Transcendence is the objective side: it is "a basic mode of being".[262] It is an *a priori* gift from God to humanity. Further, the later Rahner uses transcendence in two ways. First, it refers to the innate capacity of openness.[263] Second, it means, in the colloquial sense, an uplifting personal experience, as in faith involving a personal encounter with Christ.[264] Freedom is the subjective side of the supernatural existential: it means that we are able to respond to the gift. Thus, transcendental experience does not preclude human agency. On the contrary, freedom is a feature of Christian life and Christian life is "a life of freedom".[265] Freedom is "the power to decide about oneself and to actualize oneself".[266] Freedom is exercised by making a decision. Furthermore, for Rahner the decision making process has theological and ethical connotations. His understanding of the process is premised on the Thomist unity of knowing and being. For Rahner, knowledge and love are inseparable and they can only be understood in terms of each other.[267] The transcendental experience means the existence of the knowledge of God. The knowledge of God includes an experience of and an invitation to continue in the love of God and neighbour. Therefore, decisions represent more than passive acceptance of God; they have real impact on relationships with God and neighbour. Significantly, decisions

259 *Ibid.* p. 111.
260 *Ibid.* p. 120.
261 "Transcendental theology", ET, p. 1750.
262 FCF, p. 34.
263 *Ibid.* i.e. "a basic mode of being which is prior to and permeates every objective experience".
264 *Ibid.* p. 310.
265 *Ibid.* p. 402, freedom has eschatalogical significance (e.g. eternity interpreted as "a mode of the spiritual freedom", p. 437).
266 *Ibid.* p. 38, cf. pp. 230, 240.
267 HW, p. 83.

affect the life of the decision maker. That is, in exercising freedom, the person is shaped by the decisions that he/she makes, "a free decision about a single value is ultimately always a decision about and a molding of oneself as a person".[268] Consequently, human beings do not simply do good or bad things, they become good or bad people on the basis of the decisions they make.[269] Nevertheless, Rahner rejects the idea of unlimited freedom; likewise he rejects the alternative of rigid determinism. For him, the analysis of guilt and sin help to explain the true nature of freedom.[270] Guilt has a role in Rahner's theology as it points to freedom or at least its abuse and the need for redemption.[271] For him, guilt and sin are linked to the human agent's capacity to choose. In existential terms, freedom exists in relation to a choice between alternative categorical realities; in ontological terms, the ultimate choice is between saying yes or no to God.[272]

In summary, freedom is a transcendental reality and this means that even a *no* is an implicit *yes* to God, because it is made on the horizon of the transcendental. Moreover, a no to God is in reality a rejection of our own identity and as such it is an obstacle to the process of becoming our true selves. The universal, gratuitous, supernatural gift of self-communication, in grace, has to do with how humankind has been constituted by God. It has to do with essential being and whether the individual says yes or no to their essential being.[273]

3.2.4. Postscript: The Three-fold Experience of God

In Rahner's vision, anthropology is in the foreground. This is the main area of interest in this study of the presence of God in the world. However, his understanding of Trinitarian theology is also part of his theological vision.

268 *Ibid.* p. 85.
269 *Ibid.* p. 86.
270 FCF, p. 94.
271 "Salvation", *Sacramentum Mundi*, 5, hereafter SM, p. 425.
272 FCF, p. 97.
273 *Ibid.* p. 109, Rahner interprets original sin on the basis that we are influenced, whether we are aware of it or not, by the guilt of others (i.e. "co-determination").

The only really absolute mysteries are the self-communication of God in the depths of existence, called grace, and in history, called Jesus Christ, and this already includes the mystery of the Trinity in the economy of salvation and of the immanent Trinity. And this one mystery can be brought close to man if he understands himself as oriented towards the mystery which we call God.[274]

Rahner's God is a triune God; humankind however, cannot understand the nature of this triune God apart from human history in the world. This is the logic behind Rahner's *Grundaxiom*: "The 'economic' Trinity is the 'immanent' Trinity and the 'immanent' Trinity is the 'economic' Trinity".[275] The character of Rahner's economic Trinity is to be discerned from his theological anthropology and his soteriology. However, the issue here concerns what can be gleaned about the immanent Trinity, the inner life of God.

In Rahner, the Trinity is understood within the context of the God-world relationship, in which case Trinitarian theology is an exercise in describing how God is in but not of the world. Within history, God communicates "*himself* by grace *ad extra* to what is not divine".[276] But there is a tension here between Rahner's desire to affirm that God is in the world and God is different from the world. For Rahner, God is immutable; this means that there is a difference between God and the world. Equally, Rahner wants to affirm that God is in the world. The question is, what is to be made of the difference? According to Rahner, the difference between God and what is not God means there is separation from God but no division, because the difference has its origin in God. For Rahner, "God as God" is the formal object of theology.[277] This means God, by virtue of God's gracious nature (i.e. self-communication), is both the formal object of theology and the existential ground of the world. But as existential ground, God maintains distance from the created order. God created the difference but it is not the kind of difference as is found between categorical realities. Rahner describes

274 *Ibid.* p. 12.
275 TT, p. 22. D. Reid, *Energies of the Spirit: Trinitarian Models in Eastern Orthodox and Western Theology*, (Atlanta: Scholars Press, 1997), p. 31, "With the help of this so-called basic thesis or axiom (*Grundthese, Grundaxiom*) Rahner attempts both to overcome the division between the unity and the triunity of God, and thus to establish the doctrine of the trinity firmly on the basis of the history of salvation".
276 "Incarnation", ET, p. 690.
277 "Theology", ET, p. 1690.

both the *difference* and the *nearness* as asymptotic,[278] "the concept 'God' is not a grasp of God by which a person masters the mystery, but it is letting oneself be grasped by the mystery which is present and yet ever distant".[279] Dallavalle claims that this is a consequence of Rahner's commitment to a theology (and a Christology) from below,

> Rahner's axiom reorients the landscape of trinitarian theology from the descending order of *De Deo Uno – De Deo Trino* to the ascending perspective that asserts (however problematically this assertion is grounded) that God's life with us is a genuine self-gift of God's life.[280]

According to Dallavalle, the problem stems from Rahner's location between "the pre-modern ontotheological presuppositions of neo-scholasticism and the epistemological commitments of modernity".[281] While the Trinity is fundamental to his system, Rahner does not conduct an exhaustive analysis of the Trinity. In particular, he does not articulate the inner relations of the immanent Trinity. He is in fact consistent in maintaining that it is not possible to know the essence of the incomprehensible God: in fact, he is reluctant to speculate about "the inner life of God" apart from human existence in the world,[282] as though the immanent Trinity was something extra to or distinct from the economic Trinity.[283]

To conclude, for Rahner talk of God outside the context of the world is speculative. For Rahner, the Trinity is a formal summary statement, which has no material content of its own. It refers to humanity's experience of God in Christ and the Spirit as three-fold. The experience of the three-fold (economic Trinity) is the experience of God's self (immanent Trinity). In all there is an underlying unity which means neither the economic Trinity nor the immanent Trinity can be understood without the other, "the goal of our efforts is rather to bring out a prior and original identity of the two realities, in relation to which the immanent and eco-

278 FCF, p. 119.
279 *Ibid.* p. 54.
280 N.A. Dallaville, "Revisiting Rahner: on the theological status of Trinitarian Theology", *Irish Theological Quarterly* 63 (1998), pp. 147-148.
281 *Ibid.* p. 135.
282 FCF, p. 135.
283 "Symbol", TI 4, p. 227.

178

nomic Trinity offer developments, clarifications and aspects of this underlying unity".[284]

3.3. Christology

In Rahner, the decisive expression of the presence of God in the world is found in Christ. Subsequently, the aim of this section is to examine Rahner's Christology. This will include an overview of his Christology, but the focus will be on key theological factors and how they relate to the Christological themes of the Incarnation and the Death-Resurrection event. In particular, Rahner attempts to hold in tension two commitments. First, there is his commitment to addressing the challenge posed by modernity. Second, there is his commitment to what he considers to be non-negotiable aspects of the Church's tradition (e.g. the immutability of God). In this, Rahner is determined to show that in Christ, God is intimately involved in the world and yet remains the transcendent, holy, ineffable, incomprehensible one. Further, his Christology can be looked at historically. His early work emphasises Christology from above and his later work emphasises more a Christology from below. However, even this distinction is too neat. For Rahner, a contemporary Christology holds in tension through the hypostatic union: the ontological and the functional, the essential and the existential, the vertical and the horizontal, the descending and the ascending.[285] These pairs represent the two basic types of Christology, namely, a Christology from above and a Christology from below.[286] Rahner tries to address the problems presented by these types, "After emphasizing for more than 10 years the ascending Christology, Rahner's last major work, *Grundkurs des Glaubens*, tried to synthesize his descending and ascending Christolo-

---

284 "The mystery of the Holy Trinity", TI 16, p. 259.
285 "Christology today?" TI 17, pp. 34-36.
286 Others followed Rahner's lead, e.g. J. Dupuis, *Who do you say that I am? Introduction to Christology*, (New York: Orbis Books, 1994), Dupuis, using language like from above/from below and ascending/descending, tries to maintain the tension between functional and ontological approaches.

gies".[287] All in all, Rahner's Christology is multifaceted and it is not easy to classify. However, there are some major themes, which help to shape and give content to Rahner's theological vision.

Rahner's Christology is soteriological, anthropological, transcendental, evolutionary and an inquiring Christology. First of all, Rahner's Christology has a soteriological framework, "From the outset Christology must be soteriology".[288] In Rahner's soteriology, Christ confers the saving power of God and the Incarnation is *the* access point into the mystery of the Trinity and the fulfilment of the promise of participation in the divine.[289] Access is found in faith in the Jesus who died and rose. He is God's answer to humankind because he is "the definitive and irrevocable Word of God to us".[290] Thus, Jesus is the irrevocable Word, because he expresses God's self in history.

Second, Rahner's Christology is an anthropological Christology, "Christology is the end and beginning of anthropology".[291] For Rahner, there is one Gospel and the Gospel makes a claim on everyone (e.g. Gal 1: 8-9). However, the nature and impact of the Gospel extends beyond the limits of Scripture and dogma to embrace all people by virtue of their humanity (i.e. supernatural existential). Clearly, Rahner's anthropological premise stands behind his search for a contemporary Christology. It is a key to understanding his theology. It can be summed up as: humankind is the mystery.[292] The mystery concerns the innate capacity to be open to mystery. This *a priori* capacity makes transcendental experience possible.[293] Subsequently, the Incarnation is "the unique, supreme, case of the total actualization of human reality, which consists of the fact that man *is* in so far as he gives himself up".[294]

Third, Rahner's Christology is an evolutionary Christology. This is a later development which encompasses earlier themes. In this, Rahner posits that the structure of the cosmos is derived from the spirit, that is,

---

287 J.M. McDermott, "The Christologies of Karl Rahner", *Gregorianum* 67 (1986), p. 89.
288 "Brief observations on systematic Christology today", TI 21, p. 234.
289 FCF, p. 213.
290 "Christology today?" TI, 17, p. 33.
291 "Incarnation", TI 4 p. 117.
292 *Ibid.* pp. 108, 119; FCF, p. 216.
293 FCF, p. 20.
294 "Incarnation", TI 4, p. 110.

all things have their origin in God because God's presence is the world's "innermost life".[295] Thus, there is within creation an "inner similarity and community".[296] This raises the issue of the relationship between matter and spirit. This is a complex relationship and it is related to but not identical with the complex relationship between nature and grace,

> If man is thus the self-transcendence of living matter, then the history of Nature and spirit forms an inner, graded unity in which natural history develops towards man, continues in him as *his* history, is conserved and surpassed in him and hence reaches its proper goal with and in the history of the human spirit.[297]

Thus, Rahner's Christology is the inevitable outworking of an evolutionary process, the climax of which is the Incarnation.

Fourth, Rahner's Christology is an inquiring (or searching) Christology. This is related to the issue of human limits (i.e. the finite), whereby the awareness of limits invites humankind to seek the limitless (i.e. the infinite).[298] For example, the topic of death figures prominently in Rahner. He is aware of the biological realities surrounding death, but the way an individual faces death is crucial for Rahner as the prospect of death can evoke an act of human freedom and divine consummation. Following Heidegger, Rahner regards humankind as a finite spirit,[299] who is able to imagine and experience the infinite by virtue of the awareness of the finite. Death is the ultimate limit and the defining moment of human finitude. Thus, readiness for death allows an individual, who accepts the limits, to exercise freedom and seek the hope of final consummation in the Death-Resurrection event in which God validates the significance of life and death for humankind.[300]

---

295 "Christology within an evolutionary view of the world", TI 5, p. 172.

296 *Ibid.* p. 161; FCF, p. 182.

297 "Evolutionary view", TI 5, p. 168.

298 "Jesus Christ: history of dogma and theology" ET, p. 753, Rahner considers that there are three arguments for inquiring Christology, which appeal to "present-day conceptions of human reality". They are the love of neighbour, readiness for death and hope in the future; "These three arguments are all based on the principle that if man resolutely accepts his own existence, he in fact acts upon what may be called an 'inquiring Christology'".

299 Heidegger, *Being and Time*, p. 305 and "Being-towards-death".

300 "The quest for approaches leading to an understanding of the mystery of the God-man Jesus", TI 13, p. 199.

3.3.1. Absolute Saviour

For Rahner, Christ is the decisive manifestation of the presence of God
in the world. This claim is based on the premise that Christ's identity is
unique and this is because Christ is the absolute saviour. To establish
this, Rahner wants to ground the theological identity of Christ in the
historical reality of Jesus. In particular, he is concerned about the relationship between the Christ of dogma and the pre-Easter Jesus. He accepts that there is a difference between the two and that the difference is
evident in the New Testament.[301] Rahner admits, with modesty, that he is
no exegete.[302] Moreover, Küng observes, "A fundamental defect of Rahner's theology suddenly dawns on me: a manifest lack of consistent historical thinking ... a second fundamental defect in Rahner's theology
also becomes evident: the lack of historical-critical exegesis".[303] Nonetheless, Rahner accepts the general findings of modern exegesis concerning what can be known historically about the life of Jesus.[304] He accepts
the claim that Jesus saw his own identity as linked to his message and
that the early church embellished the portrait of pre-Easter Jesus.[305]
However, he contends that the post-Easter elaboration is congruent with
the pre-Easter Jesus. Subsequently, Rahner argues that the pre-Easter
Jesus had a developing sense of awareness about his identity as absolute
saviour. This self-awareness can be used to establish the existence of
continuity between the pre-Easter Jesus and the Christ of dogma. Certainly, Rahner is consistent with his theological anthropology. That is, in
transcendental terms, Rahner asserts that Jesus saw himself as absolute
saviour on the basis of his own subjectivity. However, in historical
terms, Rahner does not establish satisfactorily that Jesus did see himself
that way. Nonetheless, and in fairness to Rahner, it is not necessarily the
case that Jesus had to see himself as saviour to be the saviour.[306] That is,

---

301   "The position of Christology in the Church between exegesis and dogmatics", TI
     11, p. 194.

302   "Brief observations", TI 21, p. 232.

303   Küng, *My Struggle For Freedom* J. Bowden trans., (Michigan, Cambridge: Eerd-
     mans, 2003), pp. 251-252.

304   FCF, pp. 247-249.

305   *Ibid.* pp. 252-254.

306   P. Fredriksen, "What does Jesus have to do with Christ? What does knowledge
     have to do with faith? What does history have to do with theology?" in A.M. Clif-
     ford and A.J. Godzieba eds., *Christology: Memory, Inquiry, Practice* CTS 48

continuity between the pre-Easter Jesus and the Christ of dogma does not necessarily depend on Jesus' self-awareness.

Rahner makes four claims in relation to the identity of Jesus. First, he accepts that the self-awareness of Jesus underwent historical development. Second, he asserts that the limits of exegesis are determined by dogmatics, interpreting exegetical findings from within the dogmatic setting of salvation history.[307] For Rahner, dogmatics and exegesis work at different levels (i.e. *existentielle*, historical);[308] dogmatics includes the *a priori* (transcendental) level of analysis, whereas exegesis concentrates on the *a posteriori* (categorical) level.[309] According to Rahner, both are needed. This distinction, however, does not mean historical data are inconsequential as faith "in saving history has an historical content".[310] Humankind receives a revelation through subjectivity, which is the place for revelation but the revelation begins with the historical Jesus as the object of faith. Third, on the basis of human subjectivity, Rahner makes a claim for Jesus' awareness of his own unique identity. Jesus knew he was unique by means of his subjectivity. From the outset, Rahner assumes that Jesus had a direct vision of God and that this was an intrinsic, unformed, unreflective, unsystematic, *a priori* part of the hypostatic union. For Rahner, the Chalcedonian hypostatic union presumes "a subjective centre of action"; this is the humanity of Jesus.[311] Fourth, Rahner uses his metaphysics of knowledge to explain how Christ's vision of God was given and awareness of his identity developed (i.e. self-presence).[312] The development does not refer to Christ's *unique* identity, so much as to his growing *awareness* of his identity.[313] In this context, the resurrection is the dogma that supports the claim of continuity between the pre-Easter Jesus and post-Easter Christ. Furthermore, Rahner

---

(Maryknoll, New York: Orbis Books, 2003), p. 11. Fredriksen calls this type of assertion a "fallacy of intention", namely, "If Jesus himself did not think a thought, then the thought – usually, a theological thought – seems less than legitimate for the tradition".

307 "Remarks on the importance of the history of Jesus for Catholic dogmatics", TI 13, p. 208.
308 "Between exegesis", TI 11, p. 189.
309 *Ibid.* p. 194.
310 *Ibid.* p. 191.
311 *Ibid.* p. 198, Jesus' awareness of the *visio immediata* developed over time.
312 HW, p. 33.
313 "Between exegesis", TI 11, p. 211.

presumes that knowledge has a multi-layered structure.[314] The dynamics of the mind mean that consciousness has the capacity to know in different ways,

> There is among these forms of knowledge an *a-priori*, unobjectified knowledge about oneself, and this is a basic condition of the spiritual subject in which it is present to itself and in which it has at the same time its transcendental ordination to the totality of possible objects of knowledge and of free choice.[315]

The spiritual subject is present to itself in direct proportion to the degree it possesses being.[316] For Rahner, Jesus has the highest degree of being possible and was present to himself to the highest degree possible. Hence, the *visio immediata* makes sense in the light of the transcendental ordination of Jesus; it is an existential of the hypostatic union, "consciousness of sonship and of direct presence to God ... is therefore situated at the subjective pole of our Lord's consciousness".[317]

In conclusion, Rahner claims Christ is the decisive expression of presence. This is partly based on the premise that Christ's identity is unique because he is the absolute saviour. Subsequently, Rahner is concerned that the absolute saviour of Christian dogma is grounded in the life of the pre-Easter Jesus. The Jesus of history is not one thing and the Incarnation another,

> A transcendental theology as such cannot undertake to prove that Jesus of Nazareth is the Lord, the absolute bringer of salvation, the incarnation of the Word of God. This experience comes in history itself, not in an *a priori* theology of history. And a transcendental Christology need not proceed as if it had formed the Christian notion of the God-man independently of the historical experience of this God-man in the concrete figure of Jesus.[318]

For Rahner, the developing self-awareness provides him with an important link between the pre-Easter Jesus and the Christ of dogma; without the link Christ as absolute saviour appears as an invention of the early Church. In all this, the concept of subjectivity plays a role. For Rahner, a text, event or person can only be seen in a revelatory light by means of

---

314 "Dogmatic reflections", TI 5, p. 199.
315 *Ibid.* pp. 200-201.
316 HW, p. 28.
317 "Dogmatic reflections", TI 5, p. 208.
318 "Transcendental theology", ET, p. 1750.

184

subjectivity. Similarly, the subjectivity of Jesus was the means by which he received the *visio immediata*. The problem is how is Jesus' consciousness different from others,

> It is debatable whether his [Rahner's] increased emphasis on the human reality of Jesus really encompasses the traditional Christology of the church. If Jesus' self-consciousness consists in openness to transcendence (through an unthematized *visio immediata*) and in simultaneous orientation to the historical/categorical, then it is difficult to establish how his consciousness was different from any other human being's.[319]

Ultimately, Rahner's claim about the identity of Jesus is worked out in relation to the Incarnation and Death-Resurrection event. For Rahner, Jesus is unique because it is God's self who has been expressed in history, "Jesus himself is what comes to be if God wills to express and communicate himself 'externally'. God's self-utterance (as content) is the man Jesus, and the self-utterance (as process) is the hypostatic union".[320]

3.3.2. The Incarnation

The Incarnation is a major theme in Rahner. For the sake of convenience, the Incarnation and the Death-Resurrection event are being treated separately. However, the Incarnation and the Death-Resurrection event form a unity in Rahner.[321] Specifically, this part of the study will explore: the Incarnation as central mystery, Rahner's appreciation of classical Christology and the hypostatic union.

For Rahner, the Incarnation is the central mystery of the Christian faith. Certainly, God's self-communication is a mystery and mystery is the essence of human nature. The Incarnation, however, is the climax of the evolutionary process of God's self-communication, "from this point, the Incarnation appears as the necessary and permanent beginning of the divinization of the world as a whole".[322] Further, Rahner was wary of reductionist and functionalist approaches. He contends that, "the field,

---

319 Burke, *Reinterpreting*, p. 274.
320 "Jesus Christ", ET, p. 770.
321 FCF, 266.
322 "Evolutionary view", TI 5, pp. 160-161.

the whole as such, cannot be determined by the same means used for the determination of the parts".[323] Moreover, he discerned within modernity the emergence of an evolutionary world-view of "one homogeneous history of matter, life and man"[324]. Subsequently, he posited that all things have their origin in God because God's presence is the world's "innermost life".[325] If the life of God and the existence of the world are intimately related, then the critical issue is the nature of the unity of spirit and matter. However, there is only one Incarnation. Rahner bases this claim on the assertion that while God is involved in humankind in a general (universal) way, God is involved in Christ in a unique (particular) way.

> The Incarnation is a mystery of faith and therefore involves all that a mystery implies: the impossibility of compelling the free assent of faith, the "paradox" involved in any formulation of such a mystery, the character of being a stumbling-block to the pride of a rationalism autonomously accepting only what is fully comprehended. But a mystery is not a myth or a miracle ... That means that the mystery must possess for man a genuine intelligibility and desirability.[326]

Rahner uses classical Christology to confirm God's involvement in the world and preserve God's immutability.[327] This tension is pronounced in the Incarnation. In this context, he wants to assert the priority of the Chalcedonian formulation (i.e. one person in two natures).[328] This formulation is an important part of Rahner's theological vision, "Young theologians who study theology today without learning in Christology what the Council of Chalcedon says, what person, nature, hypostatic

---

323 *Ibid.* p. 162.

324 *Ibid.* p. 166.

325 *Ibid.* p. 172.

326 "Incarnation", ET, p. 695.

327 "Christology today", TI 21, p. 220, if it is Catholic Christology, then it is grounded in the Orthodox christological formulations, classical Christology is an indispensable part of the ecclesial and theological tradition and must be included in contemporary christological projects as normative, cf. "Brief observations", TI 21, p. 237-238.

328 J. Moltmann, *The Crucified God: The Cross of Christ as the Foundation and Criticism of Christian Theology*, (London: SCM Press, 1973, 1974), p. 231, "The doctrine of two natures in christology attempted not only to make a neat separation between the natures of Godhead and manhood, but also to assert their unity in the person of Christ and reflect upon it".

186

union, and communication of properties mean, would be deprived of the obvious and requisite tools of Catholic Christology".[329] In Rahner, classical Christology sets the parameters for modern Christology,

> The legitimacy and the permanent validity of the classical Christology lies, first of all negatively, in the fact that when it is presupposed it prevents Jesus unambiguously from being reduced merely to someone in a line of prophets, religious geniuses and reformers, and from being incorporated within the course of an ongoing history of religion; and positively, it clarifies that fact that in Jesus God has turned to us in such a unique and unsurpassable way that in him he has given himself absolutely.[330]

For Rahner, classical Christology runs the risk of idealising the person of Jesus (cf. deification); it is a descending Christology that does not make clear the relationship between Christ as Incarnate *Logos* and Christ's function as mediator of salvation.[331] That is, it does not spell out the distinction between the ontological and functional Christ. Furthermore, as far as Rahner is concerned, the preservation of the Chalcedonian formulation (i.e. one person in two natures) is non-negotiable. His non-negotiable concepts also include the immutability of God, the unsurpassability of Jesus as absolute saviour and the nature of hypostatic union. They are non-negotiable because they are grounded in mystery and they can only be experienced by means of revelation. They cannot be deduced. However, while Rahner does not always adequately justify these non-negotiable aspects, he recognises that their significance has to be reinterpreted for modernity. In the process, he tries to distinguish between non-negotiable and negotiable aspects. The non-negotiable elements set the limits of his system.

For Rahner, the Chalcedonian formulation is a non-negotiable. He recognises that, while the formulation is problematic, it acts as a safeguard against the danger of mythological readings of the Incarnation.[332] He warns "the ordinary consumer",[333] about the danger of Monophysite

---

329 "Brief observations", TI 21, p. 228.
330 FCF, pp. 288-289.
331 "Christology today?" TI 17, p. 29.
332 "Incarnation", ET, pp. 690-699; cf. Pekarske, *Abstracts*, p. 105, "Rahner rejects as heretical any christology which leaves the impression that Jesus merely dons the guise of humanity to signal his presence".
333 "Between exegesis", TI 11, p. 198.

"distortions and misunderstandings".[334] This concern lies behind his critique of Bultmann's demythologisation.[335] Significantly, Rahner is not an unthinking critic of Bultmann. Even so, he sees demythologisation as a negative by-product of modernity. For instance, Rahner wants to re-claim the doctrine of resurrection of the body from demythologisation.[336] However, the issue here is how Rahner's re-interpretation of classical Christology is any different from a program of demythologisation. For instance, Rahner looks at the concepts of image and reality (representation/object).[337]

> When someone undertakes in this sense a critique of the representation-schemata of the religious concepts which are used for a Dogma, and does so cautiously and slowly, in the constant endeavour (under the control of the *magisterium* of the Church) of not losing anything of the content of faith in the process, then he does not 'demythologize', but does something which theology has always done and must always do.[338]

Rahner admits that the difference between image and reality is not always clear and that there are "certain dangers of mythology" in traditional formulations.[339] But he is concerned that the removal of the so-called mythological layers would leave behind a docetic Christ. The driving force is Rahner's desire to preserve the Chalcedonian formulation, "Jesus is the irrevocable, unsurpassable, and definitive self-promise of God to us. And he can only be this as the consubstantial Son".[340] Moreover, he claims that the historic formulas of the Church, "are not end but beginning, not goal but means, truths which open the way to the – ever greater – Truth ... This holds good for the Chalcedonian formulation of the mystery of Jesus too. For this formula is – a formula".[341] Thus, Rahner explores different ways of conceiving the Chalcedonian formulation.

Rahner's attempt to re-interpret the Chalcedonian formulation involves the concept of the *communicatio idiomatum* (i.e. exchange of

334 *Ibid.* p. 197.
335 "Jesus Christ", ET, p. 763.
336 "The resurrection of the body", TI 2, pp. 204-205, 208-209.
337 *Ibid.* pp. 208-209.
338 *Ibid.* p. 209.
339 "Brief observations", TI 21, p. 231.
340 "Jesus Christ – the meaning of life", TI 21 p. 218.
341 "Current problems in Christology", TI 1, pp. 149-150.

188

properties). *Communicatio idiomatum* is a traditional means of making the hypostatic union comprehensible.[342] *Communicatio idiomatum* is a method of attribution used to explain that, while the two natures are distinct, the attributes of one nature can be predicated of the other by virtue of their union in Christ.[343] However, Rahner is not convinced that *communicatio idiomatum* can overcome the problems because it does not address the issue of identification.[344] If without separation *(adiairetos)* is overemphasised, and one of the natures is allowed to dominate the union, then the idea of *two distinct natures* has little meaning. Alternatively, if without mixture *(asunchutos)* is overemphasised, then the idea of a *union* has little meaning. Consequently, Rahner sees an urgent apologetic task to address the problem of identification by reformulating the Chalcedonian formula in a non-mythological way.[345] Furthermore, Rahner asserts that the problem of identification arises in relation to the copula *is*. For him, the copula *is* in the classical formula does not refer to the function of identification (e.g. Karl *is* a man). Rahner argues that in classical formulations the copula *is* presumes two distinct realities: divine and human. Hence, the importance of the boundaries set by Chalcedon, meaning that the Incarnation is divine and human without separation *(adiairetos)* and without mixture *(asunchutos)*,

> The conciliar "unmixed and undivided" will always remain a fundamental (dialectical) formula not only of Christology but of the Christian conception of the relation between God and world generally.[346]

Moreover, Rahner recognises that "the purely *formal* (abstract) schema *nature-person* is inadequate".[347] So he aims to establish a different kind of unity, "the unity must itself be the ground of the diversity".[348] Based on his theology of symbol, he uses quasi-formal causality to find a new basis for union (i.e. a unity-in-difference).

In Rahner there are two prominent approaches to the problem of the hypostatic union. First, there is a general and later approach that shall be

---

342 "Christology Today?" TI 17, p. 37.
343 "communicatio idiomatum", ODCC, p. 386.
344 "Current problems", TI 1 pp. 179-180.
345 "Jesus Christ", ET, pp. 755-756.
346 *Ibid.* p. 762.
347 "Current problems", TI 1, p. 162.
348 *Ibid.* p. 181.

referred to simply as his (later) evolutionary approach. Second, there is a specific and earlier approach that shall be referred to as his (earlier) symbolic approach. There are similarities between the two (e.g. formal causality); the difference however between the two is partly a matter of emphasis. The evolutionary approach has a cosmic-evolutionary horizon and finds its locus of meaning in the concept of self-transcendence. In terms of this horizon, Christ is the "peak and conclusion" of the evolutionary process through which God's redemptive plan is operative.[349] Rahner contends that the evolutionary process is a redemptive process and the impetus for the process is God's "efficacious salvific will".[350] The redemptive process means God, who has created and now sustains the world, will bring the world to its consummation by means of God's self-emptying activity in the Incarnation. Rahner notes a problem as redemption "objectively presupposes a need of redemption and subjectively the admission (the acceptance) by man of his need".[351] He addresses the problem by distinguishing between two dimensions of redemption: the objective and subjective. Redemption as an objective event is, in metaphorical terms, *the God-side* of redemption. It is objective in the sense that it is not contingent upon human initiative and that the initiative is with God. The assumption is that redemption begins and proceeds prior to our subjective response.[352] Moreover, the Incarnation is not a divine afterthought. In contrast, redemption as subjective response is *the human-side* of redemption and it entails the acceptance of createdness.[353] For Rahner, createdness includes the experience of guilt. Humankind needs to be delivered from guilt, because it cannot be achieved by human effort, and it is God's action alone that brings about redemption. The issue of guilt presumes a dialogue in that God communicates, humankind rejects it and God offers forgiveness.[354] This dialogue between God and humanity is part of the evolutionary history of the world.[355]

349 *Ibid.* p. 164.
350 "Salvation", SM 5, p. 406.
351 *Ibid.* p. 425.
352 *Ibid.* p. 427.
353 *Ibid.* p. 405.
354 *Ibid.* p. 427.
355 "Evolutionary view", TI 5, p. 175.

190

In terms of focus, the evolutionary approach to the hypostatic union focuses on the concept of self-transcendence in relation to spirit and matter. With spirit and matter, there is unity-in-difference in which spirit and matter form a unity, but spirit has priority over matter. Self-transcendence refers to the dynamic nature of this unity. Thus, matter develops toward spirit.[356] This development involves a becoming, where becoming is understood as a fullness of being, "a real self-transcendence, a surpassing of self or active filling up of the empty".[357] The self-transcending movement is from the lower to higher order of being by virtue of the power of being-itself. The higher order emerges from and contains the lower order and the higher order emerges when the lower order reaches a limit situation and transcends it.[358] In this movement, being is both inherent and transcendent.[359] Further, humanity entails for Rahner a particular type of self-transcendence; "the self-transcendence of living matter".[360] Humankind represents a breakthrough in the world's self-transcendence, which finds its ground in the hypostatic union.[361] He explains humanity's self-transcendence in terms of consciousness, where it should be understood in terms of a "process of being lifted out of one-self and being drawn into the infinite mystery".[362] This process is not divorced from the material world. In Rahner, matter is not a problem for the human spirit as it makes the experience of the *other* possible.[363]

Indeed, humankind is "the self-transcendence of living matter".[364] Without matter, there can be no experience of the presence of God. Moreover, Rahner argues that the self-transcendence reveals the incarnational structure of humanity. This becomes the basis for Rahner's claim that the Incarnation of Christ is unique because human self-

356 *Ibid.* pp. 164-166; FCF p. 184.
357 "Evolutionary view", TI 5, p. 164.
358 *Ibid.* pp. 167, 178.
359 *Ibid.* pp. 165, 168.
360 *Ibid.* p. 168; FCF, p. 187.
361 FCF, p. 181.
362 "Evolutionary view", TI 5, p. 163.
363 *Ibid.* p. 163, cf. p. 167, non-human life and inanimate objects have no sense of the other.
364 *Ibid.* p. 168, where, "the history of Nature and spirit forms an inner, graded unity in which natural history develops towards man, continues in him as *his* history, is conserved and surpassed in him and hence reaches its proper goal with and in the history of the human spirit".

transcendence in Jesus reaches a new level; it "is the unique and *highest* instance of the actualization of the essence of human reality".[365] The Incarnation of Christ is more than God disclosing *something* of God's self as it is *God's self* who is disclosed. But there are objections,

> Rahner's reversal of incarnation christology into a christology of self-transcendence is in line with the new interpretation of metaphysical christology by way of anthropological categories which we find in Kant and Schleiermacher. Rahner too ends up with Jesus, the perfect image of God, because he equates 'the idea of Christ' with fulfilled human existence. But did tradition really mean no more by the redeeming God-human being than the prototypical 'man of God'? Is Jesus' relationship to God his Father really identical with the creature's relationship to his Creator?[366]

From the perspective of the cosmic, evolutionary, transcendental horizon, Moltmann is partly right in that Christ appears different from humankind only by degree. That is, the difference is relative. However, Rahner himself is aware of the problems.[367] His earlier approach, based on symbol, is a persuasive attempt to explain simultaneously the human identity of Jesus and the otherness of God,

> It is possible to point to a visible, historically manifest fact, located in space and time, and say, Because that is there, God is reconciled to the world. There the grace of God appears in our world of time and space. There is the spatio-temporal sign that effects what it points to. Christ in his historical existence is both reality and sign, *sacramentum* and *res sacramenti*, of the redemptive grace of God.[368]

While the later evolutionary approach captures something of the *modern* existential and scientific mood, the older symbolic approach is worthy of consideration.

To appreciate Rahner's (earlier) symbolic approach, it needs to be kept in mind that symbol is fundamental to Rahner's theological vision. Rahner uses the theology of symbol to explain the meaning of the Incarnation.[369] To achieve this, he has to re-cast a version of formal causality

365 FCF, p. 218.
366 J. Moltmann, *The Way of Jesus Christ: Christology in Messianic Dimensions*, (London: SCM Press, 1989, 1990), p. 62.
367 FCF, p. 292, NB. Rahner's discussion on the choice between the terms hypostatic union and person, and the problem of the indeterminacy of "the point of unity in the hypostatic union".
368 CS, p. 15.
369 "Symbol", TI 4, p. 237.

192

(i.e. intrinsic causality) into quasi-formal causality. Formal causality has a role in Rahner's supernatural existential.[370] With efficient causality, and within the limits of categorical experience, the effect is different from the cause.[371] However, with God's self-communication, God is cause and effect (i.e. giver and gift).[372] If God is not delineated from humankind, then the concept of the immutability of God could be undermined.

> We learn from the incarnation that immutability (which is not eliminated) is not simply and uniquely a characteristic of God, but that in and in spite of his immutability *he* can truly *become* something. He himself, he, in time. And this possibility is not a sign of deficiency, but the height of his perfection, which would be less in addition to being infinite, he could not become less than he (always) is.[373]

Subsequently, Rahner uses quasi-formal causality to explain this process. To reiterate, in the case of a symbol and what it signifies there is "an intrinsic and mutual causal relationship".[374] Rahner draws out from this the idea of an intrinsic symbol and by inference the idea of intrinsic causality.[375] He uses intrinsic causality to explain the hypostatic union, that is, God is involved but God is immutable. However, according to Rahner there are other instances of intrinsic causality which may jeopardise the concept God's immutability. In the case of the hypostatic union, "this intrinsic, formal causality is to be understood in such a way that the intrinsic, constitutive cause retains in itself its own essence absolutely intact and in absolute freedom".[376] So Rahner establishes quasi-formal causality as a special case of intrinsic causality as it is God's self who is involved in this quasi-formal causality.[377] Thus, he uses quasi-formal

370 *Ibid.* p. 245, n. 21; "Trinity, divine", ET, p. 1760.
371 CS p. 36; FCF, p. 121.
372 FCF, p. 120.
373 "Incarnation", TI 4, p. 113, n. 3.
374 CS, p. 38.
375 *Ibid.* p. 39.
376 FCF, p. 121.
377 SW, p. 272, in terms of Rahner's metaphysics of knowledge, unity-in-difference finds its locus in the cogitative sense, which is the "differentiated unity of individual and universal". The cogitative sense is the metaphysical *place* of connection (p. 299; cf. TT, p. 36 n. 34).

causality to affirm God's involvement and to protect God's otherness.[378] Though persuasive, Rahner's argument is problematic.

Rahner uses Hegel's dialectic in an attempt to overcome the logical problems in his argument, ("the immutability of God is a dialectical truth like the unity of God").[379] Thus, Rahner asserts that, "God can become something, he who is unchangeable in himself can *himself* become subject to change *in something else*".[380] Historically, theology has tried to resolve the tension between the Incarnation and the laws of philosophy. That is, according to the law of non-contradiction the divine and the human cannot be one, but the tradition asserts that they are one in the Incarnation.[381] Now traditional logic accepts the principles of identity and non-contradiction.[382] Hegel also accepted the principle of correlativity, namely, whatever *is* is both identical with itself and not identical with itself. For Hegel, this was the superior principle of the three.[383] While it is persuasive, it is difficult to justify Hegel's principle of correlativity and even if Hegel's principle is accepted, Rahner's use of Hegel's metaphysics has been a target of criticism.[384] The problem is that:

> Theological and metaphysical doctrines of unity require more than the abstract identity and abstract difference of the understanding. They require a type of identity or unity that differentiates itself into plurality, or a type of identity that enables us to say not simply that God is flatly identical with the world or flatly distinct from it, but that he is related to it by a self-developing identity-in-difference.[385]

---

378 McDermott, "Christologies", p. 100, McDermott observes, "thus 'quasi-formal' is the least inept term to describe the intimate union while preserving the diversity of God and the soul."

379 "Incarnation", TI 4, p. 113, n. 3.

380 *Ibid.* p. 113.

381 N. Everitt and A. Fisher, *Modern Epistemology: A New Introduction*, (New York: McGraw – Hill, 1995), p. 120 "a proposition and its negation cannot both be true".

382 Donceel, *Searching Mind*, p. 185.

383 Hegel, "Christianity: The consummate religion" in P.C. Hodgson ed., *G.W.F. Hegel: Theologian of the Spirit*, (Edinburgh: T and T Clark, 1997), pp. 205-259, this is an example of Hegel's principle of correlativity expressed in theological terms.

384 McCool, *Rahner Reader,* p. xxvii.

385 M. Inwood, *A Hegel Dictionary*, (Oxford: Blackwell, 1992), p. 133.

194

In Rahner, the particular relationship of *Son* to *Father* and *Son* to *world* is essential. In terms of mood and style they are Hegelian as they follow "the Hegelian metaphysics of the spirit which, abiding changelessly 'in itself', changes 'in the other', into which it 'goes over' in order to return to itself".[386] This is problematic, as "the law of noncontradiction is a nonoptional part of our future intellectual equipment and hence is something that *no* possible future empirical discoveries could give us reason to abandon".[387]

Rahner's use of the *quasi* qualification of formal causality does not of itself explain how the Incarnation is a unique instance of intrinsic causality; it only asserts that it is a special case.[388] It is not clear in Rahner how the Incarnation is logically different from the incarnational structure of humanity. However, for Rahner, there is more to this than questions of logic. It is a question of revelation. He argues that even the classical understanding of the Incarnation does not adequately highlight the soteriological significance of "the Christ event".[389] According to Rahner, the salvific significance of Jesus is not found in the idea of God sharing the fate of Jesus (i.e. identification) but in the hypostatic union.[390] Significantly, the history of Jesus reveals that, "the hypostatic union is not a mystery *beside* the mystery of the absolute proximity of God as holy mystery: it is this mystery itself in an unsurpassable form".[391] In Jesus, humankind discovers the salvific mystery of God. Rahner describes the soteriological affirmation of Christianity in terms of two types: Chalcedonian and neo-Chalcedonian. Neo-Chalcedonian equated the fate of God with the fate of Jesus and yet "pure Chalcedonism was always suspicious that the other soteriology would covertly evolve from a communication of properties (of the two natures) into an identity of properties

386 McCool, *Rahner Reader*, p. xxii.
387 Everitt and Fisher, p. 121.
388 McCool, *Rahner Reader*, pp. xxvi-xxvii, this gives credence to McCool's critique that Rahner does not supply an adequate metaphysics for his supernatural existential. McCool asserts that the best that can be done is to look back at Rahner's metaphysics of knowledge, where unity-in-difference finds its (metaphysical) locus in the cogitative sense (SW p. 272). Cf. Reno, *Ordinary*, pp. 120-121, Reno claims that Rahner's so-called *grammatical* response does not solve the logical problem
389 FCF, pp. 292-3.
390 "Meaning of life", TI 21, p. 215.
391 "Concept of mystery", TI 4, p. 69.

(of both)".[392] Thus, the importance of Rahner's unity-in-difference approach as a means of explaining the two natures: without mixture and without separation,

> And this is precisely what is meant by hypostatic union. It means this and, properly speaking, nothing else: in the human reality of Jesus, God's absolute saving purpose (the absolute event of God's self-communication to us) is simply, absolutely and irrevocably present; in it is present both the declaration made to us and its acceptance – something effected by God himself, a reality of God himself, unmixed and yet inseparable and hence irrevocable. This declaration, however, is the pledge of grace to us.[393]

Finally, Rahner has been criticised for not explaining clearly "how Jesus's humanity actually mediates salvation".[394] His theology of symbol offers a possible explanation. In Rahner, the symbol is the only way that *another* can attain knowledge of being, "The being is known in this symbol, without which it cannot be known at all".[395] Equally, the Incarnation is the only way that humankind can attain knowledge of Absolute Being, that is, God is only known in and through the symbol of Christ.[396] Concerning Christ,

> He is not merely the presence and revelation of what God is in himself. He is also the expressive presence of what – or rather, who – God wished to be, in free grace, to the world, in such a way that this divine attitude, once so expressed, can never be reversed, but is and remains final and unsurpassable.[397]

Thus, the humanity of Christ as symbol is the sign that signifies and confers the presence of God as "the symbol renders present what is revealed".[398] However, while Rahner's theology of symbol is persuasive it is based on unsubstantiated metaphysical assumptions about God, causality and the world (e.g. distinction between intrinsic and quasi-formality). In the end, Rahner relies on his broader understanding (and experience) of revelation for support.

392 "Meaning of life", TI 21, p. 214.
393 "Evolutionary view", TI 5, pp. 183-184.
394 McDermott, "Christologies", p. 108.
395 "Symbol", TI 4, p. 231.
396 *Ibid.* pp. 235-237.
397 *Ibid.* p. 237
398 *Ibid.* p. 239.

196

3.3.3. Death and Resurrection

This part explores a number of key issues: the death of Jesus as the closure of revelation, the death of Jesus transforming death and the resurrection as a consequence of his death. The importance for Rahner of the connection between the Christ of dogma and the pre-Easter Jesus comes into view again, partly to underline the distinctiveness of Christ, but also to counter idealist interpretations of the Death-Resurrection event.

Rahner claims that the revelation of God came to an end with the death of Jesus, but the impact of the death continued into the future.[399] In the process, death had been transformed. Consequently, the death of Jesus has the power to effect transformation for those who identify with him. Thus, Rahner argues that the death of Jesus meant the closure of revelation. This argument hinges upon a two-fold assumption: Jesus is the unsurpassable revelation and the cross is essential to the claim of unsurpassability. For Rahner, the full significance of the death of Jesus can only be seen in the light of the Incarnation. The Incarnation is "the absolute self-promise of God" manifested through the *Logos* in the hypostatic union.[400] The cross represents the complete acceptance of the absolute promise, through the death of the body, by the God-man. The idea of the acceptance of the promise can be understood more easily by returning to the concept of the developing self-awareness of Jesus. In essence, the concept implies that Jesus gradually became more aware of his identity and purpose. That is, Jesus realised through his subjectivity that he had not come simply to proclaim the promise like John the Baptist; on the contrary, Jesus realised he was the fulfilment of the promise. This realisation compelled Jesus to say yes or no to the promise. He said yes in the most emphatic and compelling way possible by the open way he faced the prospect of his death. Consequently, the cross in Rahner represents the complete acceptance by Jesus of the gift of God's promise. Therefore, the death of Jesus is an unsurpassable revelation for two reasons. First, it was God's self who accepted the gift. Second, the acceptance was total and without reserve.

399 "The death of Jesus and the closure of revelation", TI 18, p. 142.
400 *Ibid.* p. 136.

An existentially oriented understanding of limits has shaped Rahner's view of the death of Jesus. In Rahner, limits function in various ways to define, complete and inform:

–   The limit defines – the life of Jesus represents God's gift of the absolute promise and the death of Jesus means it is the definitive gift.
–   The limit completes – the gift has been given and accepted.
–   The limit informs – the Incarnation means more than God is involved; it also has to do with God's salvific will. The death of Jesus informs humankind about the nature of God's salvific will as "the *death* of Jesus is an internal constitutive element of God's eschatological self-promise to the world".[401]

There is a dialectical relationship in Rahner between an individual's imminent death and the death of Jesus, meaning that the death of Jesus serves as a particular kind of example (i.e. a productive model). The insight is that openness to the prospect of death leads to new awareness of the significance of the death of Jesus. In turn, identification with the death of Jesus changes human orientation to death. In part, Rahner bases this on a theology of death, which "can link more closely the event of Jesus' death and the fundamental structure of human reality".[402] The key to Rahner's argument is a comparison between death from biological and existential perspectives: from a biological perspective we have no choice when it comes to death; from an existential perspective freedom lies in humankind's attitude to death.[403] Jesus, through his subjectivity, realised his true identity as the absolute promise of God. His identity could only be claimed by open acceptance of the prospect of his death and the death itself. Subsequently, as followers we choose to enter into our dying and this is the beginning of life.[404] Further, the death of Jesus is an example for Rahner, but it is also more than an example; it is a "productive model".[405] This is because the death of Jesus transforms the nature of death. The ground for transformation begins with the fact that as the

---

401   *Ibid.* p. 139.
402   "Jesus Christ", ET, p. 754.
403   "Death of Jesus", TI 18, p. 140.
404   "Following the crucified", TI 18, p. 160, an "imitative following" is developed, which means more than just an idea or a disposition.
405   *Ibid.* p. 166.

Logos assumed humanity, so to the *Logos* assumed death. Furthermore, Rahner explains the transforming nature of the death of Jesus by showing how it is bound to his resurrection; "Jesus died into his resurrection, his death is the event of gaining the finality of his human reality in the life of God himself".[406] Thus, Rahner speaks of an intrinsic unity between death and resurrection.[407] The key is the idea of a simultaneous event, where in death Jesus accepts completely the self-communication of God and in the resurrection God accepts completely human reality as redeemed.[408]

Rahner rejects interpreting the cross in terms of satisfaction theories because they implicitly undermine the priority of God's initiative in the plan of salvation.[409] For Rahner, God wills human redemption rather than demands satisfaction and Christ's death is an effect of God's will for redemption.[410] Thus, the saving will of God is the cause of the cross. Subsequently, if an individual seeks to work out his/her salvation, then they will seek out the divine-human one, who is,

> Another human being in whom, by God's free power of course, such salvation has really been achieved and as achieved becomes perceptible to him, in whom then, because of his solidarity with him, for himself, too, not only the abstract possibility of salvation, but salvation also as promise for his hope, becomes concretely apparent.[411]

The person sought is the *absolute* saviour, because the person is *the* symbol through which God has promised and expressed God's self.[412] Lastly, the death of the saviour is inevitable because "it is only there that history is completed, freedom becomes definitive, man surrenders himself freely and finally to the mystery of God and thus man's transcendence into God's incomprehensibility and his history reach their definitive unity".[413]

For Rahner, the resurrection is a consequence of the crucifixion,

---

406 *Ibid.*
407 *Ibid.* p. 167.
408 *Ibid.* p. 168.
409 "Salvation", SM 5, p. 430.
410 *Ibid.* p. 428.
411 "What does it mean today?" TI 18, p. 146.
412 *Ibid.* p. 147.
413 *Ibid.* pp. 146-147.

It is the consequence of his death itself as such, if it is seen at the same time as the death of him in whom the eternal God imparts his own life to the world as its gracious endowment and as the event in which this Jesus accepts finally and irrevocably this self-communication of God through death … In his resurrection the very thing that happened in his death is completed and made effective: the incomprehensible God finally accepted this human reality as redeemed, precisely because the latter was surrendered unsupported and unreservedly into the incomprehensibility of God himself. We can really say that (in the sense of an indissoluble essential connection) his death is his resurrection and vice versa, since he entered into definitive life precisely in death and in no other way.[414]

In particular, Rahner's theology of the resurrection can be understood in two basic ways: negative and positive. In negative terms, he asserts that the resurrection does not imply a body/spirit dualism; that is, the resurrection does not presume the existence of two separate "compartments".[415] For Rahner, the Old and New Testaments are clear, in that humankind learnt to take "existence in space and time and in the body really seriously".[416] As there is a unity of body and spirit, then the unity as such undergoes the same fate.[417] Therefore, the resurrection does not mean the spirit of Jesus was revived or his body was resuscitated. Nor does the resurrection presume a time of non-existence.[418] In positive terms, resurrection is critical for Rahner.[419] He argues that the resurrection establishes: the abiding validity of the person of Jesus, the vindication of Jesus as absolute saviour and the mediation of the full reality of the "God-man". Rahner admits that he can only hint at the nature of the abiding validity of Jesus, because resurrected existence is a different mode of existence. As part of human subjectivity, faith can intuit something of the reality of this non-historical mode of existence, but it cannot be defined in empirical terms. For Rahner, this does not mean the resurrected Jesus is less real. On the contrary Rahner asserts, in a metaphysical sense, that resurrected existence is more real; "the risen Christ is

414 "Following the crucified", TI 18, p. 167.
415 "Between exegesis", TI 11, p. 209.
416 "Jesus' resurrection", TI 17, p. 18.
417 "Between exegesis", TI 11, p. 207.
418 "Jesus' resurrection", TI 17, p. 17.
419 "The quest for approaches leading to an understanding of the mystery of the God-man Jesus", TI 13, pp. 199-200.

200

neither a resuscitated corpse or a spiritual idea but the fully transformed Jesus".[420]

Rahner's theology of the resurrection of Jesus is premised on his anthropology, in particular the concept of self-awareness. Self-awareness of the intrinsic capacity of openness to God carries with it the freedom to say yes or no to God. Hence, the history of freedom "already includes what we mean by the hope of the 'resurrection'".[421] That is, Rahner interprets the hope of the resurrection in terms of the human affirmation of God. For Rahner, hope is part of the transcendental condition. Using his metaphysics of knowledge, Rahner makes a deft connection between this hope as a transcendental condition and the New Testament resurrection appearance accounts. The appearance accounts have an important role in faith formation. With the act of knowing, an external object is required to elicit the *a priori* universal form. With the resurrection, an *a posteriori* experience as contained in the appearance accounts is required to elicit the *a priori* knowledge of Jesus. Thus, the early Church implicitly knew that Jesus was the transcendent one, but they could not come to that realisation without the aid of the appearance accounts. Further, faith is the result of the resurrection and "Jesus is risen into the faith of his disciples".[422] Indeed, the experience of the resurrection brings about the "objectification of the transcendental hope of resurrection".[423] In summary, the appearance accounts play an important role in Rahner's theology because they evoke faith in the resurrection and by so doing they bear witness to the resurrection and the continuing validity of Jesus. In all this, Rahner is not exegetically naïve as he recognises the non-historical character of the resurrection and the literary nature of the appearance accounts. He acknowledges that the appearance accounts are more like descriptions of a spiritual experience than an historical event.[424] Nevertheless, Rahner insists that the accounts presume that something *real* lies behind them.[425] They point to "the experience that Jesus is alive".[426]

420 Egan, *Rahner*, p. 136.
421 "Jesus' resurrection", TI 17, p. 16.
422 FCF, p. 268.
423 "Jesus' resurrection", TI 17, p. 18, hence, the importance of the apostolic witness (p. 19).
424 FCF, p. 276.
425 "Believe in Jesus Christ", TI 18, p. 152.
426 "Jesus' resurrection", TI 17, p. 19.

For Rahner, the link between death and resurrection is germane to explaining the mode of existence of the resurrected Christ. He asserts that the death and resurrection form a unity.[427] He explains this by focusing on life after death. Life after death is not the same as life as before death, it is not a continuation or something that is left over; it has to do with the validity of the person.[428] However, the precise meaning of the concept of the abiding validity of the person is not clear. Rahner interprets the appearance accounts in terms of human subjectivity, that is, faith as an expression of human subjectivity is a consequence of the resurrection and faith discerns the abiding validity of Jesus. The continuing validity of the person of Jesus means that the resurrected Jesus exists in a different mode, which is in a metaphysical sense *more* real. But this whole argument runs the risk of reducing the continuing validity of Jesus to human conviction. Rahner was aware of the limits of his argument and he accepts that there are "no conceptual models to explain to ourselves precisely *how* this comes to be".[429] In brief, Rahner's claim for the continuing validity of the person of Jesus is crucial to his theology, because if there is no continuity, then an idealist interpretation remains. The resurrection in Rahner means more than the successful continuation of an idea.

The nature of the resurrected mode of existence becomes a little clearer in Rahner's work on the doctrine of the general resurrection of the body. To protect the doctrine from the threat of demythologisation,[430] he looks at it in terms of the concepts of image and reality. The difference however between image and reality is not clear in Rahner.[431] Nevertheless, in relation to the resurrection of the body, Rahner claims he is looking for the reality behind the images (rather than demythologising). He admits this is neither a straightforward nor an unambiguous task. He claims, concerning this reality, that "'Body' (*Fleisch*) means the whole man in his proper embodied reality. 'Resurrection' means, therefore, the termination and perfection of the *whole* man before God, which gives

---

427 FCF, p. 266.
428 *Ibid.* p. 267; "Jesus' resurrection", TI 17, p. 21.
429 "Between exegesis", TI 11, p. 209.
430 "Resurrection of the body", TI 2, pp. 204-209.
431 *Ibid.* p. 209, this points to the importance of the Scriptures, tradition and "the proclamation of the Church".

202

him 'eternal life'".[432] Clearly, eternity is a different mode of existence in Rahner. Thus he is interpreting the resurrection of the body eschatologically, that is, in terms of the future consummation of the body, "this open, self-propagating history has a beginning and an end" and the end will be "the participation in the perfection of the spirit".[433] The end is the perfection of saving history.[434] Human beings come into perfection, into totality.[435] For Rahner, Paul's paradoxical "spiritual body" (I Cor 15: 44) is right and this will be the "pure form" (i.e. more real) of the body.[436] Therefore, on the basis of the general resurrection, Rahner argues that the continuing validity of the person of Jesus in his resurrection means his perfection, which takes place in a different (eschatological) mode.[437]

In conclusion, in contrast to Rahner, Carnley argues that the structure of resurrection belief is the proper starting point for Christology and not the Incarnation or the Christological titles.[438] For Carnley, "Genuine Christian faith is a post-Easter phenomenon".[439] In this context, Carnley is largely making an historical reading of the significance of the resurrection. In contrast, Rahner tends to make a theological reading of salvific events. For example, death and resurrection form a unity in Rahner (hence the term the Death-Resurrection event). He interprets this unity sacramentally (i.e. symbolically).[440] Moreover, Rahner is committed to making the Incarnation a priority because of his commitment to his theological anthropology, but the Incarnation includes the birth, life, death and resurrection of Christ.

> This climax of history, which does not bring history to a close, but makes known its meaning and the victorious finality of its goal *within* history itself, is the cross, the death, and the resurrection of Jesus in one.[441]

---

432 *Ibid.* pp. 210-211.
433 *Ibid.* p. 212.
434 *Ibid.* p. 213.
435 *Ibid.* p. 214.
436 *Ibid.*
437 "Current problems", TI 1, p. 167, Christ is the "prospective entelechy" of history.
438 P. Carnely, *The Structure of Resurrection Belief,* (Oxford: Clarendon Press, 1987), pp. 4-8.
439 *Ibid.* p. 6.
440 FCF, p. 284, "in this causality what is signified, in this case God's salvific will, posits the sign".
441 "The Cross", TGCY, p. 158.

Within Rahner's theological vision, there is something sweeping, unifying and symbolic about his Christology. His vision is grounded in an anthropology that encompasses the God-world relationship and finds its focus in Christ. This section has noted the complexity of his Christology. It has concentrated on theological factors that enhance the study's reading of the themes of the Incarnation and Death-Resurrection event. In the process, methodological and theological concerns have been highlighted. In terms of method, Rahner holds in tension two commitments: an apologetic concern to engage constructively with modernity and the concept of the immutability of God. In terms of theology, Rahner posits that the Incarnation means the grace of God is in the world in a new way.[442] In this context, presence is humankind's experience of the awareness of the proximity of God's self and Christ is the decisive expression of presence.[443] For Rahner, there is divine purpose in the Incarnation which finds its fulfilment in the Death-Resurrection event. In all this, Christ is an exemplar (e.g. prophet) but he is also more than that for Rahner. Rahner's Christ confers the saving power of God, because Christ "in his historical existence is both the reality and sign" of God.[444]

3.4. Conclusion

This section consists of two parts. The first part summarises Chapter 3. The second part places Chapter 3 within the context of the study's thesis and concludes that Rahner's theology is primarily oriented toward modernity. However, certain elements from the theology of Rahner can be used to make a contribution to postmodern Christology (Chapter 4). These elements relate to experience, presence, absence, the Incarnation and the Death-Resurrection event.

442 CS, p. 15.
443 "Grace", ET, p. 589, cf. FCF, p. 119.
444 CS, p. 15; "Believe in Jesus Christ", TI 18, p. 147.

3.4.1. Summary

This chapter has evaluated Rahner's theology. It has examined in sequence Rahner's method, theology and Christology. In general, Rahner's method consists of an elaborate interaction of factors.[445] Significantly, Rahner uses Thomas' understanding of the dynamism of the human mind to develop his own metaphysics of knowledge, which in turn informs his guiding theological vision. In the process, Rahner uses a Kantian construal of the modern problem of the gap between the finite and infinite, with his Thomistic construal, to find a new way of reinterpreting the problem of the gap. In particular, he uses the concept of quasi-formal causality to explain both the supernatural existential and the hypostatic union. In both cases, Rahner uses quasi-formal causality to affirm God's involvement and to protect God's otherness.[446] Further, the concept of presence pervades Rahner's theology. He sees presence in various ways. Above all, presence is the experience of the awareness of the nearness of God's self. It is a divine gift that points to God.[447] Therefore, human subjectivity is the place for the simultaneous act of judgement and experience of presence. However, even though God is in the world, God remains God (i.e. incomprehensible). From this, comes an insight into Rahner's concept of absence, namely, absence is an encounter with the hiddenness of God. Furthermore, the Incarnation means the grace of God is in the world in a new way.[448] There is a divine purpose in the Incarnation, which is fulfilled in the death and resurrection of Christ (i.e. Christ is more than a teacher).[449] He is the reality and sign of God.[450] All this is consistent with Rahner's earlier metaphysics of knowledge and his evolving theology of transcendence, that is, Christ as the object of faith in history elicits a faith response from humanity.

---

445 McCool, *Rahner Reader*, p. xxv.
446 "Incarnation", TI 4, p. 113.
447 FCF, p. 119.
448 CS, p. 15.
449 "Believe in Jesus Christ", TI 18, p. 147.
450 FCF, p. 284.

3.4.2. Rahner and Postmodernity

In this part, Rahner's theology is examined from the perspective of postmodernity, where the criteria for defining postmodernity are related to historiography, pluralism, language and intersubjectivity. On the basis of these criteria, the study argues Rahner's theology is primarily oriented toward modernity. Admittedly, Rahner was not captive to modernity, as he critiques modernity and prefigures elements of postmodernity. Nevertheless, in the end, Rahner's theology is grounded in the history and ideas of the era of modernity.

Rahner is aware of modernity's limitations, "For it is quite meaningless to want to be modern on purpose".[451] Moreover, Rahner uses exemplars of modernity like Kant and Hegel to address its deficiencies. Rahner's suspicion of positivism is a good example of his capacity to appraise modernity.[452] In general, logical positivism relates to the period between the two wars.[453] The horrors of the Great War and the Great Depression led scholars to seek Cartesian like universal and abstract truths, which they hoped might overcome the vicissitudes of post-war existence.[454] Consequently, the world has become "less divine, and, by the same token, less important".[455] Also, the world seems to humankind "a closed system, sealed off to a certain extent from God, a universe of unthinkable extent and variety, largely impenetrable and fully determined by its own laws".[456]

> As long as we measure the loftiness of knowledge by its perspicuity, and think that we know what clarity and insight are, though we do not really know them as they truly are; as long as we imagine that analytical, co-ordinating, deductive and masterful reasoning is more and not less than experience of the divine incomprehensibility; as long as we think that comprehension is greater than being overwhelmed by light inaccessible, which shows itself as inaccessible in the very moment of giving itself: we have understood nothing of the mystery and the true nature of grace and glory.[457]

---

451 "Current problems", TI 1, p. 153.
452 IR, p. 45.
453 Toulmin, *Cosmopolis*, p. 84.
454 Toulmin, *Cosmopolis*, p. 153, "a return to abstract fundamentals".
455 "Concept of mystery", TI 4, p. 36.
456 *Ibid.* cf. Charles Taylor, "Closed world structure", p. 47.
457 "Concept of mystery", TI 4, p. 56.

Rahner anticipated postmodern themes (e.g. religious pluralism, extraterrestrials).[458] Combined with his emphasis on mystery, Rahner anticipated something of postmodernism's anti-structuralist bent. On hearing Derrida in a discussion, M.J. Scanlon observes:

> As Derrida elaborated his reflections, I immediately jumped to what were to me intriguing connections between the great "postmodern" deconstructionist and the Roman Catholic "modernizer." In his own way Rahner had deconstructed religion and had developed from his own tradition a "religion without religion."[459]

For example, Rahner asserts that his own era is characterised by the experience of "frustration anxiety".[460] Frustration anxiety is the fear of missing out (cf. the desire to have everything). According to Rahner, people recognise the dangers of this anxiety and seek the ability to let these things go; but this is not an easy task.[461] Renunciation is hard. In contrast, Rahner posits another view of renunciation: what if letting go meant, rather than missing out, the attainment of "inconceivable fullness".[462] In other words, renounce all and "the whole, the fullness, 'God' will be received".[463]

Rahner has been immersed in modernity. Modernism plays a role in providing him with a theological agenda, critical tools and key concepts (e.g. transcendental philosophy). The formative part of Rahner's life and career occurred in the first half of the twentieth century. In that period, the people and institutions that fashioned Rahner's social, intellectual and religious milieu had previously been shaped by the nineteenth century. In the nineteenth century, Catholic orthodoxy wrestled with modernity and the church was, at least officially, suspicious of modernity.[464] As Rahner remarks, "My Jesuit teachers, who came from the old days, would probably have regarded Kant and Hegel and the whole mentality suggested by these names as adversaries".[465] In addition, J. Honner con-

458 “Natural Science and Reasonable Faith”, TI 21, pp. 16-55.
459 M.J. Scanlon, "Deconstruction of Religion", p. 223.
460 "Self-realisation and taking up one's cross", TI 9, p. 253, apparently, the basis for Rahner's notion of frustration anxiety is anecdotal.
461 *Ibid.* p. 254.
462 *Ibid.* p. 255.
463 *Ibid.*
464 Pius IX's promotion of *Syllabus of Errors* (1854), Leo XIII's *Aeterni Patris* (1879).
465 IR, p. 38.

tends that Rahner's theology of the last four years was not new.[466] In those years, Rahner was concerned with the unfinished work of Vatican II and he became more ardent in pursuing the practical and pastoral out-working of his earlier theology.[467] In summary, there are historical reasons for situating Rahner within the fold of modernity and this assessment is reinforced by the subsequent application of the criteria of pluralism, language and intersubjectivity (cf. Chapter 1).

Rahner was aware of pluralism and that the nature of pluralism had changed.[468] In Rahner's era, especially pre-Vatican II, his work on world religions was groundbreaking. However, this needs to be looked at in a wider theological context. He presupposes the "universal and supernatural salvific will of God".[469] For Rahner, the history of salvation and revelation are coextensive with world history.[470] Concerning revelation, he makes a distinction between the history of universal (transcendental) revelation and special (categorical) revelation.[471] For Rahner, universal revelation can only be accomplished in Christ.[472] This theology of revelation is linked to his anthropology, that is, the mind has an *a priori* structure and as such the mind anticipates an absolute saviour.[473] This is an important building block in Rahner's concept of anonymous Christianity, which is the logical outcome of his supernatural existential, "for Rahner, the a priori is general, universal, transcendental revelation, identical with the presence of the divine Spirit in the world. The world religions are the a posteriori historicizations of this transcendental revelation".[474] Undoubtedly, he recognised the need for a plurality of theologies. McCool, however, contends that Rahner's "changeless a priori structure of the human mind ... is the unrevisable revisor of all conceptual frameworks".[475] At worst, Rahner's anonymous Christianity

466 J. Honner, "Speaking in new tongues: Karl Rahner's writings from the grave", *Pacifica* 11 (1998), p. 66.
467 *Ibid.* reform of the teaching office, the future of Catholicism in a world church and the future of Christianity and world religions and new humanisms.
468 OH, pp. 42-43.
469 FCF, p. 313.
470 *Ibid.* p. 142.
471 *Ibid.* p. 153.
472 *Ibid.* pp. 157, 168, 175.
473 "Between exegesis", TI 11, pp. 200-201.
474 Scanlon, "Deconstruction of religion", p. 226.
475 McCool, *Rahner Reader*, p. xxviii.

208

can be construed as a colonising metanarrative or a form of totalisation in which religious differences are homogenised. However, this fails to acknowledge that Rahner's view is the logical outcome of his theological anthropology, which had been designed in and for another era. In addition, the later Rahner became more open to other religions; even if he was still bound to his transcendental model and his notion of universals.[476] For Rahner, God creates all people with the intrinsic capacity to hear the word, which is implicit (read anonymous) and universal, and only Christ can make it explicit.[477] As Wildman asserts, the sticking point in Rahner is the assumption of one central event of salvation,[478]

> The word of God as such, that guarantees God eschatologically as the actually victorious end of history, must then necessarily occur through an historical event, an event that can occur only in the factual and definitive acceptance of this offer by God of himself to the world by a person who of course must be seen as so constituted that *his* acceptance of this self-offering in obedient and increasingly definitive freedom guarantees the salvation of the world as a whole.[479]

Rahner's use of language also serves to locate him firmly in modernity. His view of language raises many problems: the problem of reference, pluralism, the establishment and the testing of truth statements. On the surface, Rahner is aware of some of the problems associated with language. For instance, in an effort to make a clear distinction between his re-interpretation of Christian orthodoxy and Bultmann's program of demythologisation, Rahner makes a distinction between representation and object (cf. idea and reality).[480] According to Rahner, the difference between representation and object is not always clear.[481] However, Rahner's approach differs from postmodern approaches (e.g. Derrida), in that he felt there was a *real* connection of sorts between representation and object. Though he does not resolve the issue, Rahner senses there are other issues at stake here:

---

476 "On the importance of the non-Christian religions for salvation", TI 18, p. 295.

477 "Anonymous and explicit faith", TI 16, pp. 58-59; P. Knitter, *Jesus and the Other Names: Christian Mission and Global Responsibility*, (New York: Orbis Books, 1996), p. 8.

478 Wildman, *Fidelity*, p. 327. By the same token, Wildman includes Tillich.

479 "Death of Jesus", TI 18, pp. 138-139.

480 "Resurrection of the body", TI 2, pp. 208-209.

481 *Ibid*, p. 209, If it is handled carefully, then the theologian will not be guilty of demythologisation.

Basically, Rahner has a metaphysical understanding of language. Subsequently, he asks a different set of questions to those deriving from post-modern perspectives.[483] This is not to say that there is a clear agreement about the meaning of language today, as there are a variety of approaches (cf. linguistic or philosophical; Wittgenstein or Derrida). Further, the issue of language is related to pluralism. Pluralism leads to the awareness of difference, relativism, problems associated with metanarratives (Lyotard), power associated with discourse (Foucault) and the problem of reference (Derrida).[484] For instance, the language of anonymous Christianity, which is premised on his transcendental anthropology, is a metanarrative that potentially leads to the homogenisation of the differences that exist between the religions, all in the name of Christ. All this raises questions about truth statements. For Rahner, the truth of faith has transcendental and historical dimensions.[485] It is unclear, however, how the transcendental dimension in Rahner can be analysed, let alone tested.

Subjectivity has an important role in Rahner's work (e.g. site of the experience of presence and the act of perception). It is largely a modern understanding of subjectivity (i.e. the turn to the subject):

> In the history of ideas the situation since the beginning of modern times has been
> characterized by a turning away from Greek cosmocentrism, with its thought based

---

482 "Word of God and Theology", ET, pp. 1828-1829.
483 HW, p. 133, "Every transcendent reality may in principle be represented to humanity not only in its most general determinations, but also according to its specific properties. It may be represented negatively through this historical appearance that we call word. This word itself is in its turn the synthesis of an intramundane, historical reality and of a negation. Thus we have established that the word is the place of a possible encounter with and revelation of the free God, before whom, because of our transcendence, we are always already standing".
484 "reference", ODP, p. 323, in short, reference is concerned about the relationship between language and reality, (e.g. relation between a name and an object or person).
485 "Dogma", ET, p. 352.

210

on things, objects, to modern anthropocentrism which in the question of being in general takes as the paradigm case the subject who knows and wills things.[486]

Hogan, however, claims that Rahner's view on the subject is still relevant.[487] In support, faith in Rahner takes place in the context of the Church and an authentic faith leads to love of neighbour.[488] The theme of contingency (i.e. Heidegger's thrownness) in Rahner hints at a postmodern notion of intersubjectivity, as it presents an opportunity to trust in Christ and Christians (i.e. limits enable people to discover limitlessness). Further, Rahner's understanding of trust includes the notion of a personal relationship with Christ and this dimension cannot be dismissed as "merely private subjectivity".[489] This is because it is part of God's immediacy.[490] Furthermore, hope for the resurrection, which is the confirmation and continuance of our own validity, invites us to believe in the resurrection of Jesus.[491] This is the basis of a personal relationship, based on trust, expressed in the Church and worked out in relation to our neighbour.[492] In brief, Rahner's understanding of the subject gently hints at postmodern intersubjectivity. However, by and large, his view of the subject is modern. Moreover, the precise nature of his metaphysically nuanced understanding of subjectivity is not clear. In particular, the site of subjectivity is opaque,[493] "the site of subjectivity has its own ambiguities, among which are its foundationalism, its conception of the self, its anthropocentrism, and its elitism".[494]

In conclusion, Rahner foreshadows some elements of postmodernism, but he is primarily oriented toward modernity. There are historical grounds for this assertion, which are supported by the use of the three characteristics of postmodernity (i.e. pluralism, language, intersubjectiv-

486 "Incarnation", ET, p. 696.
487 K. Hogan, "Entering into otherness: the postmodern critique of the subject and Karl Rahner's theological anthropology", *Horizons* 25 (1998), pp. 181-202.
488 "I believe in Jesus Christ", TI 9, p. 166.
489 *Ibid.* p. 165.
490 "What does it mean today?" TI 18, p. 155.
491 *Ibid.* p. 150.
492 FCF, p. 309.
493 *Ibid.* p. 292, he admits that it is difficult to distinguish between hypostasis and person and opts for the former.
494 F.S. Fiorenza, "Being, Subjectivity, Otherness", in J.D. Caputo, M. Dooley, M.J. Scanlon eds., *Questioning God*, (Bloomington and Indianapolis: Indiana University Press, 2001), p. 349.

ity). With the inception of postmodernity, the mood changes and new questions are being asked.

Chapter 4: The Presence of God in the World

The aim of Chapter 4 is to make a contribution to postmodern Christology. The key to understanding the nature of the study's contribution is the assertion that experience is ambiguous, consisting of presence and absence, and this ambiguity, which is *implicit* in Tillich and Rahner, is made *explicit* and then interpreted in postmetaphysical terms. Specifically, this entails developing a theology of presence and applying it to the themes of the Incarnation and the Death-Resurrection event. The completion of this task depends on two factors. First, Tillich and Rahner affirm the presence of God in part because of their understanding of experience, but the concept of experience, as a form of epistemological justification, needs to be examined before looking at their views on experience. Second, the credibility of the concept of presence needs to be established before developing a theology of presence, because presence has come under attack from precursors and proponents of postmodernism. Thus, section 1 develops a working definition of experience. Section 2 establishes the credibility of the concept of presence and develops a theology of presence. Section 3 looks at the Christologies of Tillich and Rahner in relation to contemporary Christological issues. Sections 4 and 5 make a contribution to postmodern Christology by applying the theology of presence to the themes of the Incarnation and the Death-Resurrection event, which have been distilled from the theological systems of Tillich and Rahner. In the process, major points of continuity and discontinuity between Tillich and Rahner and postmodernity are highlighted and similarities and differences between the two theologians are discussed.

In Tillich's work, ontology is critical. His method can be described as a metaphysical ontology and is this evident in his theology, hermeneutics and exegesis. Throughout, Tillich uses the language of being.[1] For example, Tillich's second formal criterion of theology is that ultimate con-

---

1   Lamm, "Revisited", p. 54, Lamm asserts that Tillich's emphasis is on both internal and essential relations.

cern determines *"our being or not-being"*.[2] For Tillich, presence is a matter of ultimate concern because presence is God's self. Consequently, presence is determinative of our being or not-being. According to Tillich, there are two ways of approaching the question of God, namely, the ontological and the cosmological. Subsequently, he makes three claims. First, he argues for the priority of the ontological over the cosmological. Second, he argues that the cosmological, without the aid of the ontological, creates a destructive gulf between philosophy and religion. Third, he contends that the ontological, when used with the cosmological, can lead to the reconciliation of religion and culture. The problem of the relationship between these two approaches has historical roots. This is the problem of the two absolutes, namely, the religious and philosophical. For Tillich, God and being cannot be seen as separate. Hence, he looks at two possible solutions: the Augustinian and the Thomistic. The Augustinian (ontological) solution hinges on the claim that *"God is the presupposition of the question of God"*.[3] Tillich claims that certain principles emerge from this approach and concludes that the Thomistic method of knowledge cannot attain the Absolute; inference alone cannot bridge the gap between the mind and God.[4] Consequently, he dismisses the Thomistic (cosmological) solution. For Tillich, ontological awareness is immediate and is not "mediated by inferential processes".[5]

Rahner's theological system is originally shaped by his metaphysics of knowledge, which owes its genesis to *Spirit in the World* and *Hearer of the Word*. However, his metaphysics of knowledge is formative but not final in the development of his guiding theological vision. At first glance, it seems to be based on circular reasoning. In his early work, Rahner develops his metaphysics of knowledge around the cognitive relationship between a sentient being and sensible objects. This is then used to argue simultaneously for the knowledge of God and the ontological unity of subject and object. However, the metaphysics of knowledge presumes God as its ground; that is, it presumes the ontological unity of subject and object. Rahner acknowledges the circular structure of faith knowledge.[6] This is in keeping with his use of Hegel's (and

---

2   ST I, p. 14.
3   "The two types of philosophy of religion", TOC, p. 13.
4   *Ibid.*
5   *Ibid.* p. 23.
6   FCF, p. 230.

Thomas') principle of correlativity.[7] Further, Rahner is consistent in his description of God and his reluctance to limit God. He expresses something here of the apophatic tradition of theology, describing God as an unknowable and equivocal cause, known only analogously. Rahner's later theology, with its emphasis on human experience and existential questioning, gives credence to these metaphysical presuppositions. He argues that experience raises existential questions that both philosophy and theology need to engage. In fact, humankind is the starting point of metaphysics as humankind "questions necessarily".[8] It is our nature to question, to question being and to embody the questioning of being.[9] In other words, humankind is driven existentially towards the speculative. In terms of content, Rahner's argument is circular. In terms of argument, the circularity is part and parcel of the dialectical relationship between the speculative and the existential, as mystery cannot be analysed as though it was another categorical reality.[10]

The full extent of the similarities and differences between Tillich and Rahner cannot be compressed into a succinct summary. For example, Tillich and Rahner share similar assumptions (e.g. the gap) but they have different methods. They use similar philosophical sources (e.g. Kant, Hegel, Heidegger), but they have different attitudes to philosophy. This reflects Platonic and Aristotelian influence, via certain filters (e.g. Augustine, Aquinas), on Tillich and Rahner respectively.[11] Nevertheless, Christian revelation is decisive for Tillich and Rahner. On the surface, this may not seem to be the case as they both emphasise strongly the

---

7   Donceel, *Searching Mind*, Donceel claims that Maréchal (and followers like Rahner) use neither *a priori* or *a posteriori* arguments for God's existence but proffer *a simultaneo* vindication of God's existence. The problem, which Donceel recognises (p. 186), is how to explain the precise workings of this *a simultaneo*, "A basic principle is one that is a condition of the possibility of every affirmation, one which we affirm in the very act of denying it. It is easy to show that the principle of identity fulfills these conditions. I do not see how the principle of universal correlativity does".

8   SW, p. 57.

9   *Ibid.* pp. 58-59.

10   FCF, p. 66.

11   D.J. Keefe, *Thomism And The Ontological Theology Of Paul Tillich: A Comparison Of Systems*, (Leiden: E.J. Brill, 1971), p. 41, cf. p. 4, "For the Thomist, philosophy is, in the sense in which we are using the word, potential but not actual theology. For Tillich, philosophy is in dialectical tension with philosophy".

importance of being. In particular, Tillich emphasises the priority of being over knowing, where Rahner emphasises the unity of being and knowing. However, the differences between them are not so marked. Further, the priority of being has often been presented as the historical position of Aquinas, if only because he precedes Descartes and Kant by a long way. For this reason, it is the position adopted by more traditional twentieth century Neo-Thomists, like Maritain and Gilson. After all, it is a question of method and what the starting point should be. In the present case, it is not that Rahner questions the importance of being, on the contrary, "Being itself is the original, *unifying* unity of being and knowing in their *unification* in being-known".[12]

In many ways, Tillich and Rahner finish at the same place. For example, Tillich asserts that there can be an immediate awareness of God without inference. Indeed, he presumes Thomistic inference is not linked to God. Further, his reference to "sense perception and abstraction" implies he had some knowledge of Aquinas' *excessus*. For Rahner, *excessus* is about how God is connected with the process of inference. Ironically, Tillich blurs the very distinction he is trying to promote "Truth, therefore, is the essence of things as well as the cognitive act in which their essence is grasped".[13] In short, being is fundamental to their theological systems. While it is tempting to describe the role of being in their theologies as complementary, complementarity implies a degree of dependence, as though revelation requires a philosophical explanation in order to be complete. Certainly, they use the concept of being to explain the mystery of revelation, but they are adamant that mystery cannot be explained. Moreover, while there is strong speculative interest in the nature of being in both Tillich and Rahner, this is balanced in both by an equally strong interest in existentialist issues. In this light, the following comment of Donceel's about Rahner, also applies to Tillich,

This does not imply that we take over the starting point of Descartes, "I think, therefore I am." This is not the real starting point of human knowledge. We start by knowing people or things "out there." "There is Mother, here is a box." Gradually we become aware of the fact that *we know* these realities. Finally, as philosophers, we discover that *we are aware of being aware*, that *we know that we know*. This

12   SW, p. 69.
13   ST I, p. 102.

216

brings us into the core of our being, which is basically an "active identification with itself."[14]

However, the place of being in their theological systems is complicated. In particular, they both rely on being as a form of epistemological justification (i.e. ontotheology) and so an assessment of this form of justification, in relation to presence, becomes critical to this study (4.3).

In this study, the major difference between Tillich and Rahner is attributed in the main to their different understandings of human existence. According to Macquarrie,

> Fundamental to Rahner's thinking is his anthropology ... whereas the existentialists had stressed human finitude, Rahner saw the human being as a finite centre which reaches out toward the Infinite. The essence of man is spirit, and spirit is to be understood not as some thing or substance but as the capacity for going out ... a human being, therefore, is not a static entity with a fixed nature, but is a 'transcending' being, that is to say, is always passing across into new phases of existence.[15]

Macquarrie is reflecting on the theological impact of Rahner on Vatican II. His comparison between Rahner and the existentialists could equally apply to the present comparison between Rahner and Tillich. Rahner is aware of the impact of human finitude.[16] However, he is not bound to the *effects* of original sin in the same way as Tillich. Conversely, Rahner emphasises human freedom to a greater degree than Tillich. Further, Rahner's supernatural existential means it is difficult to construe the gap between the finite and the infinite in the same way as Tillich. It may not have been Tillich's intention, but his account of the human being has something of what Macquarrie describes as "a fixed nature".[17] Thatcher describes it as Tillich's "negative doctrine of existence".[18] The differences then between Tillich and Rahner largely emanate from Tillich's understanding of the fragmented nature of existence in contrast to Rah-

14   Donceel, *Anthropology*, p. 284, n. 1.
15   J. Macquarrie, *On Being A Theologian*, J.H. Morgan ed., (London: SCM Press, 1999), p. 137.
16   FCF, p. 115.
17   Macquarrie, *On Being*, p. 137.
18   Thatcher, *Ontology*, p. 152.

ner's understanding of the unified nature of existence.[19] Tillich depicts faith in a heroic light, but there is an underlying pessimism about human nature. It is no coincidence that he places theological, psychological and mythological weight on the symbol of the Fall. This may reflect a personal predilection on Tillich's part, in the light of his experience in World War I and his angst-ridden relationship with his second wife Hannah.[20] In contrast, Rahner is aware of the impact of sin, but there is also in his work an overwhelming optimism about humankind living in and by means of the grace of God. In brief, experience is critical in both Tillich and Rahner. On the basis of experience, each theologian affirms the presence of God in the world. Moreover, they both recognise the ambiguous nature of experience. They do however construe ambiguity differently and this reflects their different construals of absence. Having broached their understandings of presence and absence, it is important now to develop a working definition of experience.

4.1. Experience

4.1.1. Experience and the Epistemological Strategy

The aim of this section is to develop a working definition of experience.[21] This statement needs to be put in context. In this study, the pri-

---

19 Tillich, DF, pp. 108, 110; Rahner "Evolutionary view", TI 5, p. 161, "inner similarity and community", FCF, p. 141, "in the origin, unfolding and goal of its history mankind forms a unity".

20 Pauck and Pauck, p. 86, "The marriage was unhappy from the beginning".

21 There are alternative theological approaches to experience. For example, Lindbeck's *The Nature of Doctrine* (1984). Lindbeck is an advocate of the "cultural linguistic" model of religion. According to Lindbeck, a religion is learnt like a language by participating in it. At one level, this study has sympathy with Lindbeck's approach and this is why the study is focused on a Western Christian tradition, rather than attempting to speak for other cultures and religions. At another level, Lindbeck's approach is postliberal rather than postmodern. For instance, his epistemology reserves a place for ontology (pp. 51, 64-68, 101). Likewise, he is dependent on Wittgenstein over Derrida. Compare the references to Wittgenstein (pp. 13, 20, 27-28, 33, 38-39, 43-44, 107, 111, 130) and Derrida (p. 136). In summary,

218

mary focus is on the ambiguous experience of God as presence and absence; it presumes theology is provisional and existence is contingent. Contingency is used in two ways here. First, it is used in a broad theological and metaphorical sense suggesting that the quest for certainty is fraught with difficulties and that there is always an element of doubt. Second, it is used in a philosophical sense to say that the truth claims in this study are not made in absolute terms; they are expressed in terms of probability.[22] In addition, the study's understanding of experience recognises that there is a place in epistemology for social and public factors (4.1).[23] In short, the task of developing a working definition of experience has important theological implications. Namely, faith incorporates doubt, lives with contingency and, most importantly, learns this in its encounter with the experience of God in the world as presence and absence.[24]

Experience has a major role in the theologies of Tillich and Rahner. Their interpretation of experience plays a role in their critique of modernity. Ironically, there is a postmodern nuance in the way they challenge the epistemology of modernity. For example, the way Tillich refers to the *objectifying* effects of modernity is reminiscent of postmodernism's use of the term totalisation.[25] That is, Tillich's problem with the activity of *defining* is the danger of *objectifying* the infinite and making the infinite finite. For both Tillich and Rahner, modernity marginalises God and the tendency to marginalise God stems from modernity's defining characteristics. Modernity accepts implicitly the assertion that there is an unambiguous division between the *material* and *spiritual*. Modernity presumes a mechanistic view of the material world. Modernity employs a particular type of reason to study the world (e.g. technical reason). In all, modernity accords privileged epistemological status to the outcomes of this type of reason over the benefits of other types of reason (e.g. Til-

---

like Tillich and Rahner, Lindbeck considers experience as important. For Lindbeck, different religions indicate different experiences. In Lindbeck, experience is "derivative", whereas with Tillich and Rahner experience is "primordial" (pp. 41, 35).

22 Baggini and Fosl, p. 155; Everitt and Fisher, pp. 205-206, the distinction between necessary and contingent truths is helpful but not absolute.

23 Everitt and Fisher, pp. 202-203, 207-208.

24 Caputo, "Experience of God", p. 128, "*The* experience of God always comes down to *our* experience, and our experience is of a God of *experience*, a God who lends himself to experience".

25 IRCM, pp. 34-35.

lich's ontological reason; Rahner's judgement).[26] In response, Tillich and Rahner challenge the presumption of a clear division between the material and the spiritual. They reject the mechanistic world-views of modernity. However, in keeping with modernity, they assert that it is possible to conduct an *objective* study of God and religion from which truth statements, of a different order, can be derived. In brief, there are two reasons why experience has been chosen as a starting point in this chapter. First, experience is a major theme in Tillich and Rahner. Second, this study assumes that humankind *experiences* the presence of God.

In this study, experience has a role in contributing to Christological knowledge. Of course, the nature and extent of that role is debatable. What is more, the meaning of the concept of knowledge is problematic, especially given that philosophers cannot agree about the nature and importance of epistemology in general. All this makes for a note of caution about pronouncing anything more than a working definition of knowledge.[27] Nonetheless, this does not mean that epistemological considerations are treated lightly here. In this study, the epistemological strategy is to limit the aim of the study to achieving an *incremental* contribution to Christological knowledge, where knowledge is understood in *cumulative* terms as part of an ongoing *conversation* and is expressed in terms of *probability* statements.[28] The term *incremental* is used in a postmetaphysical sense of not seeking to make new or revert to old universal claims. The term *cumulative* is used in the sense of seeing the acquisition of knowledge as an incremental process, played out over time and in conversation with other voices, that is, this is a "method of successive approximation".[29] This represents a shift in expectations from the more ambitious expectation of establishing a comprehensive epistemo-

---

26   Toulmin, *Cosmopolis*, p. 75.

27   Everitt and Fisher, p. 50, "Does knowledge have a definition or not? Our conclusion here must be provisional, but at the moment the state of current research does not justify the belief that there is a definition to be found".

28   P. van Inwagen, "Quam Dilecta", p. 46, van Inwagen states, "All that I have said so far in this section amounts to a polemic against what I perceive as a widespread double standard in writings about the relation of religious belief to evidence and argument. This double standard consists in setting religious belief a test it could not possibly pass, and in studiously ignoring the fact that almost none of our beliefs on any subject could possibly pass this test". In the end, most fields of inquiry, including theology, cannot go beyond reasoned probability statements.

29   S. Haack, *Evidence and Inquiry*, p. 73.

logical *system* (i.e. grand narrative) to a cumulative *process* that canvasses incremental and collaborative increases in knowledge. In this context, knowledge is understood in terms of justified belief rather than some kind of abstract, objective entity, which is some how completely separate from the process of interpretation. Concerning the accumulation of knowledge, C.S. Peirce posits the metaphor of a cable, where the strength of the cable is based on the number of fibres and their interconnections.[30] Similarly, J. Armstrong describes the accumulation of knowledge this way,

> This might be called Venetian Justification. There is no solid ground upon which the city is built. But by way of millions of piers driven into the lagoon it does actually (still) stand, although no pier on its own can be thought of as uniquely supporting it.[31]

Similarly, Susan Haack,

> My approach will be informed by the analogy of a crossword puzzle – where there is undeniably pervasive mutual support among entries but, equally undeniably, no vicious circle. The clues are the analog of experiential evidence, already-completed intersecting entries the analog of reasons. As how reasonable a crossword entry is depends both on the clues and on other intersecting entries, the idea is, so how justified an empirical belief is depends on experiential evidence and reasons working together.[32]

In all three images (i.e. cable, Venice, crossword puzzle), knowledge is cumulative and dependent on a degree of coherence between various beliefs (i.e. fibres, piers, clues). This presumes that individual beliefs (i.e. fibre, pier, clue) do not have their own "distinctive, simple bit of direct experiential evidence".[33] The term *conversation* presumes that this process of accumulation of knowledge will take place by means of a

---

30   Peirce, "Some consequences", p. 157 [265].
31   *Looking at Pictures*, p. 151. Cowdell, *Unique*, pp. 283, 289, Cowdell describes these as cumulative approaches.
32   S. Haack "A foundherentist theory of empirical justification" in L.P. Pojman *The Theory Of Knowledge: Classical and Contemporary Readings*, (Belmont: Wadsworth, 2003), p. 242.
33   Haack, *Evidence and Inquiry*, p. 226, n. 6; cf. p. 15, Haack means by empirical, "roughly equivalent to 'factual', not as necessarily restricted to beliefs about the external world". It may include religious experience, but that is not the focus of her study (p. 214).

dialogue with other *voices*, ecclesial and societal voices as well as theological and philosophical. In other words, "justification is essentially public and social".[34] From a different philosophical perspective, Rorty claims that "justification is not a matter of a special relation between ideas (or words) and objects, but of conversation, of social practice".[35] The epistemology of this study includes a place for conversation as well as other factors (unlike Rorty, who sees the concept of conversation as undermining epistemology).[36] In other words, conversation by itself does not ensure justified true belief. But the concept of conversation militates against the simplistic correlation between a belief and a "simple bit of direct experiential evidence".[37] Further, all epistemological claims in this study are expressed in *probability* statements. This does not mean probability statements of a mathematical kind, but it does mean that an element of doubt is acceptable and unavoidable, "knowledge may entail belief and the truth of what is believed, but, whatever else it entails, it is not evident that it is that such a truth must be indubitable".[38]

In general, the meaning of the word *experience* includes *putting to the test, proof by trial*, an *interior state of being* and *personal knowledge.*[39] The word experience connotes subject, subjects and a world. There is also a technical nuance, where experience has to do with observation, knowledge and sense experience. Philosophically, experience is associated with empiricism. In its naïve form, empiricism reduces experience to sense experience and presumes that there is a simple correlation between object, sense experience and human perceptions. But there is more to the concept of experience than is conveyed by the term *sense experience.*

---

34   Everitt and Fisher, p. 208.

35   Rorty, *Philosophy And The Mirror Of Nature*, p. 170. Dancy, "epistemology, problems of", OCP, p. 245, where epistemology "is explicitly *normative*; it is concerned with whether we have acted well or badly (responsibly or irresponsibly) in forming the beliefs we have"; cf. Alston, "Realism", p. 50.

36   Haack, *Evidence and Inquiry*, p. 194, concerning Rorty, "since his argument for abandoning epistemology rests, at bottom, on nothing more that a manifestly false dichotomy of extreme realism versus extreme irrealism about truth, the legitimacy of epistemology seems pretty secure".

37   *Ibid.* p. 226, n. 6.

38   W.D. Hamlyn "epistemology, history of", OCP, p. 245.

39   New SOED

The term "experience" here covers all the sensory impressions associated with the five senses. It covers what the internal senses, such as pain and kinesthesia, tell us. It covers anything we come to know by introspection. So beliefs both about the external world and about your own mind will count as empirical.[40]

Broadly defined, the term experience can include the internal senses and introspection. Specifically, experience is used in this study in two senses. The first sense of experience is described here as the objective sense, for example, sociological information about the *jewishness* of Jesus.[41] The second sense of experience is described here as the subjective sense.[42] In other words, historical evidence is scarce for major Christological themes (e.g. resurrection); on the other hand, there is the experience of the early church as presented in scripture and tradition. Thus, for example, Tillich and Rahner argue that Jesus has risen into the faith of the disciples, that is, the experience of the disciples is a significant instance of justification for Tillich and Rahner. Further, this study does not use this subjective sense of experience alone to justify theological beliefs without qualification and support. Experience alone may not be true or justifiable. Its validity depends on its coherence with theological themes (i.e. Incarnation, Death-Resurrection) and the concepts of presence and absence.[43] Furthermore, the distinction between the objective and subjective understandings of experience is not absolute.

40 Everitt and Fisher, p. 72.
41 J.D. Crossan, *The Historical Jesus: The Life of a Mediterranean Jewish Peasant*, (San Francisco: Harper Collins, 1991), p. 421, "The historical Jesus was, then, a *peasant Jewish cynic*".
42 W.P. Alston, "The autonomy of religious experience", *International Journal Of Religious Experience* 31 (1992), p. 67, "In this paper, I want to make a start at defending the idea that the experience of God, or, as I shall say, the *perception* of God plays an epistemic role with respect to beliefs about God importantly analogous to that played by sense perception with respect to beliefs about the physical world". Alston is not ignoring the differences between sense perception and the perception of God (cf. p. 86). He is arguing that, on the basis of similarities between sense perception and the perception of God, there is a case for considering the idea of the perception of God as innocent until proven guilty. In contrast, Rahner ("The experience of God today", TI 11, p. 153) has a problem with this type of approach. For Rahner, sense objects and sense perception have a place, but the experience of God is *ontologically* prior to sense experience, even if sense experience has an important *functional* role in evoking in the subject an awareness of God.
43 J.F. Keating, "Epistemology and the theological application of Jesus research", A.M. Clifford and A.J. Godzieba eds., *Christology: Memory, Inquiry, Practice,*

The issues of experience and knowledge raise the issue of truth. So, if experience is to make a contribution to Christological knowledge, then it is important to demonstrate that knowledge can be justified. In demonstrating that knowledge can be justified, the inference is that the knowledge is true. However, the concept of truth and its relationship to justification and knowledge is complex. To begin, justification needs to be based on some form of evidence. Justification includes experience, because a closed system of conceptual analysis is incapable of providing adequate justification in a theological setting.[44] Justification includes interpretation, which is made by an inquirer who has a social context as inquirers are immersed in a world.[45] Further, the concept of truth itself is complicated. For Nietzsche, truth is far from fixed or certain,

> What, then, is truth? A mobile army of metaphors, metonyms, and anthropomorphisms – in short, a sum of human relations, which have been enhanced, transposed, and embellished poetically and rhetorically, and which after long use seem firm, canonical, and obligatory to a people: truths are illusions about which one has forgotten that this is what they are; metaphors which are worn out and without sensuous power; coins which have lost pictures and now matter as only metal, no longer as coins.[46]

For Rorty, truth cannot be clinically separated from the inquirer; this is by virtue of the fact that truth is always presented in the form of a description (e.g. a physicist interprets results and writes reports). Therefore,

> Truth cannot be out there – cannot exist independently of the human mind – because sentences cannot so exist, or be out there. The world is out there, but descriptions of the world are not. Only descriptions of the world can be true or false. The world on its own – unaided by the describing activities of human beings – cannot.[47]

(New York: Orbis Books, 2003), pp. 34-35, "Experience, however, does not settle the matter because the justification of any proposition involves the support of other beliefs as well".

44　E.A. Johnson, *She Who Is: The Mystery of God in Feminist Theological Discourse*, (New York: Crossroad, 1992), p. 61, the credibility of feminist Christology is often measured on the basis of how it reflects "the lived experience of women".

45　R. Kane, "The ends of metaphysics", *International Philosophical Quarterly*, 33 (1993), p. 414; Everitt and Fisher, p. 208.

46　Nietzsche, *On Truth and Lie in an Extra Moral Sense* in *Vision of Nietzsche*, p. 42.

47　Rorty, *Contingency*, p. 5.

The search for an adequate definition of truth is an expression of the quest for certainty and there is an element of futility in this search for "absolutely secure foundations for knowledge".[48] Thus, for example, Kane argues that any mode of inquiry has its limitations (below). In particular, he claims that there is something over and above the language game which is not necessarily being as such but rather a different view of the way things are. Accordingly, there is the way that the world is and "This does not mean that our procedures for warranting assertions cannot attain truth. But it does mean that we cannot be *absolutely certain* they do because reality always outstrips our modes of inquiry".[49] Hence, in this study there is a preference for a form of coherence; that is, coherence with other beliefs, justified by the use of reason and social and public grounds.[50] Reminiscent of Toulmin, Everitt and Fisher assert that,

> There is no "purely conceptual" discipline, which deals only in timeless, a priori knowledge. However, if we are right that beliefs are justified by their coherence with other beliefs and that justification is essentially public and social, then there is still a great deal to be understood and explained.[51]

In summary, this study incorporates a concept of experience in its objective (i.e. empirical) and subjective (i.e. non-empirical as in introspection) senses, as it coheres with other beliefs in social and public contexts. This concept of experience and the study's epistemological strategy both depend upon the concept of coherence, in particular, the coherence between experience, other beliefs and the use of reason. Clearly, experience is difficult to define. Certainly, it can be expressed in and shaped by language.[52] It is belief-like in character. It can be expressed in the form of

---

48   Everitt and Fisher, p. 207.

49   Kane, "The ends", p. 420.

50   Everitt and Fisher, pp. 202-203, this is based a broad understanding of coherence in relation to belief structure, rather than a narrow understanding of coherence in relation to truth theory.

51   Everitt and Fisher, p. 208; cf. Toulmin, *Cosmopolis*, p. 75.

52   D. Lane, *The Experience of God: An Invitation to Do Theology*, (New York, Ramsey: Paulist Press, 1981), p. 5; E. Schillebeeckx, *Church: The Human Story of God*, (New York: Crossroad, 1989, 1990), p. 17. The concept of external world is difficult to define. It can include an object like a house or another person, but it can include the subject's body, hand or brain. The difficulty is the categories of external and internal worlds do not necessarily do justice to reason or experience.

propositions.[53] Nonetheless, an epistemology-in-the-world is more than a series of propositions as justification "depends on experiential evidence and reasons working together".[54] Experience by itself does not necessarily justify belief.[55] Experience can yield a new belief, but its justification depends upon how it resonates with other beliefs.[56] This resonance is in part a rational process of judging the way beliefs cohere. For example, an individual could claim, "I began to believe in God when I experienced an inner power". In this example, the interpretation of the significance of the experience is achieved partly by means of introspection, that is, personal reflection on the precipitating event. However, new knowledge is justified on the basis of its perceived fit with other beliefs, for instance, "the experience of God as an inner power made sense because I had always trusted my instincts".[57] Hence, this study uses the term knowledge in the sense of justified true belief.[58] In conclusion, experience has a role in epistemic justification, providing it is interpreted in conjunction with reason, public and social grounds and coherence with other beliefs. This view is intersubjective partly because the study has adopted a particular postmodern approach, which includes the importance of public and social grounds in epistemic justification, but also because experience is always interpreted experience. In this study, experience as interpreted experience includes the reflections of faith communities as well as theologians.[59] In particular, the ambiguity of the experience of God as presence and absence rings true with faith communities.

53   F. Dretske, "experience", OCP, p. 261.

54   S. Haack "A foundherentist theory", p. 242.

55   Everitt and Fisher, p. 84.

56   Haack, *Evidence and Inquiry*, p. 187, the cause of an experience is not necessarily a form of justification.

57   M.J. Scanlon, "The Humiliated Self as the rhetorical self" in J.D Caputo, M.D. Dooley and M.J. Scanlon eds., *Questioning God*, (Bloomington; Indianapolis: Indiana University Press, 2001), p. 267, "Our only cognitive access to reality is through interpreted experience".

58   Everitt and Fisher, p. 7; cf. Caputo, *On Religion*, pp. 111, 115-116.

59   Alston, "Autonomy", p. 86 n. 7, ultimately, this study has sympathy for Alston's aside, "Let me emphasize that I do not by any means suppose that the main significance of the perception of God lies in its provision of epistemic justification for beliefs, any more than the main significance of human interpersonal perception lies in its epistemic role. In both case[s] the main value of the experience is found in the way it is crucial for interpersonal relations and for leading a truly fulfilling life".

226

4.1.2. Experience in Tillich and Rahner

The concept of experience is fundamental to the theological visions of Tillich and Rahner. For both of them, experience simultaneously incorporates the interior, transcendental, subjective, and the exterior, categorical, and objective. Significantly, they differ over their understanding of the nature of human existence and this manifests itself in their respective views of experience. For Tillich, experience is crucial on two counts.[60] First of all, the concept of experience has an important role in his systematic theology. For Tillich, the theologian only has access to the sources of theology by means of experience.[61] Thus, experience is the medium through which the sources are "existentially received".[62] Tillich describes this use of the concept of experience as "the principle of experience".[63] Second, the concept of experience has a role in his anthropology; in particular, experience encompasses *awareness* of self, the self and the other, and the self-world relationship. As a rule, experience in Tillich is *human* experience; this is because of the link that Tillich makes between experience and self-awareness. For Tillich, humankind is "the highest being within the realm of our experience"[64] because, unlike other beings, humankind has a *world* as well as an environment.[65] Further, experience has a role in revelation.[66] In terms of the dynamics of revelation, Tillich makes a distinction between original and dependent revelation.[67] The coming of the New Being in Christ is the original revelation and everything else is dependent revelation given to a group through an individual in a concrete situation by means of experience. Revelation offers truth in existentially oriented truth statements, but it is first of all "the experience in which an ultimate concern grasps the human mind and creates a community in which this concern expresses itself in symbols of action, imagination and thought".[68] Experience is the means by which

60   ST I, pp. 40, 46, he is not consistent in the way he defines the concept.
61   *Ibid.* p. 40.
62   *Ibid.* p. 42.
63   *Ibid.* p. 40.
64   ST III, p. 17.
65   *Ibid.* pp. 36-38.
66   ST I, pp. 45, 110.
67   *Ibid.* p. 126.
68   DF, p. 78.

revelation is received, that is, the "mystical element is the inward participation in and experience of the presence of the divine".[69] Further, the mystical element forms the common ground between rationalism and piety.[70] The inference is that the rational and the mystical co-exist within subjectivity. The idea of coherence between the mystical and the rational, between experiential and existentially oriented truth statements is implicit in Tillich's epistemology. In brief, the concept of experience in Tillich refers specifically to a medium in theology and more generally an anthropological perspective (e.g. experience of estrangement). Moreover, Tillich recognises the ambiguous nature of experience,

> It is my intention to discuss the particular functions of life, not in their essential nature, separate from their existential distortion, but in the way they appear within the ambiguities of their actualization, for life is neither essential nor existential but ambiguous.[71]

Experience is crucial for Rahner,[72] as experience "always already knows and has known" the ineffable mystery.[73] It involves reflection, but experience is prior to the process of reflection.[74]

> Now this transcendental experience, which is always mediated by a categorical experience of the concrete and individual data of our experience in the world and in time and space (all of our experience, including so-called "secular" experience), may not be understood as a neutral power by which, among other things, God can be known. It is rather the basic and original way of knowing God, so much so that the knowledge of God we are referring to here simply constitutes the very essence of this transcendence.[75]

In Rahner, experience is integrally related to his anthropology that grounded the speculation of neo-Scholasticism while retaining the breadth of his Thomistic heritage. For Rahner, "God is the comprehensive though never comprehended ground and presupposition of our ex-

69 PPT, p. 22.
70 *Ibid.* p. 19.
71 ST III, p. 32.
72 FCF, pp. 26-30, 37.
73 HW, p. 21, cf. drawing on Thomas, pp. 25-46, 113-114. FCF, p. 53.
74 "The experience of God today", TI 11, p. 152, "Experience always involves at least a certain incipient process of reflection. But at the same time the two are never identical. Reflection never totally includes the original experience".
75 FCF, pp. 57-58.

perience and of the objects of that experience".[76] In *Hearer of the Word*, knowledge is discovered in the common metaphysical foundation of theology and philosophy of religion[77] by means of an analysis of the human person, in particular, the analysis of the openness of the person to revelation.[78] Rahner defines the problem by recalling the metaphysics of knowledge of *Spirit in the World*. He is especially interested in the *a priori* capacity of the human mind, which links the mundane and extra-mundane.[79] In *Spirit in the World*, he uses the concept of pre-anticipation *(Vorgriff)* to describe this orientation. In *Hearer of the Word*, Rahner builds on this description in existential terms. For Rahner, the problem of the analysis of human nature has its origins in human questioning as in "what is the being of beings?"[80] Rahner defines the problem ontologically.[81] However, his approach does not make experience redundant, because human experience "always already knows and has known" about being.[82] The unity of being and knowing is revealed to humankind by means of human awareness. Being and knowing together constitute an original unity *(unius generis)*. This unity implies that intelligibility and an ordination to knowledge is characteristic of what it means to be human, (i.e. "the problem of human receptivity in knowledge").[83]

In Rahner, the concept of experience is tied to his anthropological premise (2.2.3),

> The essential nature of genuine experience of the Spirit does not consist in particular objects of experience found in human awareness but occurs rather when a man experiences the radical re-ordering of his transcendent nature in knowledge and freedom towards the immediate reality of God through God's self-communication in grace.[84]

The anthropological premise is grounded in mystery.[85] The mystery has to do with the innate human capacity to experience and to grasp the mys-

76 "Experiencing the spirit", Kelly ed., p. 227.
77 HW, p. 3, cf. p. 150.
78 *Ibid.* p. 16.
79 FCF, pp. 51-55.
80 HW, p. 25, cf. Heidegger, *Being and Time*, p. 20.
81 HW, p. 27.
82 *Ibid.* p. 21.
83 *Ibid.* p. 45.
84 "Spirit and existential commitment", TI 16, pp. 27-28.
85 "Incarnation", TI 4, pp. 119-120. FCF, p. 216.

tery. This *a priori* capacity makes transcendental experience possible.[86] Transcendence is not one experience along side others; it is "a basic mode of being which is prior to and permeates every objective experience".[87] This capacity for transcendent experience is part of the human constitution.[88] It is achieved through the idea of mediated immediacy.[89] Transcendence and transcendentality are historically mediated on the basis of his metaphysical anthropology; "This place is our transcendence in its specifically *human* peculiarity".[90] Thus, in Rahner, subjectivity is the *place* of experience. The place of subjectivity can be opaque, therefore, "experience of God and experience of self are not simply identical, still both of them exist within a unity of such a kind that apart from this unity it is quite impossible for there to be any such experiences at all".[91] In brief, the human and the rational are essential components in Rahner's guiding theological vision for two reasons. First, Rahner is concerned about *actual* human experience and this is apparent from his vast body of work (e.g. prayers, sermons). Second, Rahner speculates about the nature of experience (e.g. transcendence). Above all, he recognises the epistemic significance of experience[92],

> This experience of God should not be discredited as a mere mood carrying no conviction, or as an unverifiable feeling. Nor is it merely a factor in our private interior lives. On the contrary it has a fully social and public significance. This experience is no mere mood, no matter of mere feeling and poetry carrying no conviction. It is of course different from that knowledge which the individual achieves at the conceptual level, and *within* the sphere of knowledge. In fact it bears upon the totality of knowledge and freedom as such.[93]

86   FCF, p. 20.
87   *Ibid.* p. 34.
88   *Ibid.* p. 21.
89   *Ibid.* p. 83.
90   HW, p. 98.
91   "Experience of self", TI 13, p. 125.
92   P. Endean ed., *Karl Rahner: Spiritual Writings*, (Maryknoll: Orbis Books, 2004), p. 180, *"'Postmodern' critics of Rahner, both within and beyond Catholicism, have failed to see how much he shares their concern. He may still believe, literally and without complication, in an all-knowing God, but he is well aware that human knowledge is always partial, always shaped by its own situation, inevitably pluralist."*
93   "Experience of God", TI 11, p. 159.

For Tillich, then, experience is interpreted on the basis of human fallenness, that is, the fragmented nature of existence forms the hermeneutical backdrop for the way he interprets the meaning of experience.[94] In terms of Tillich's epistemology, awareness of estrangement highlights essential nature and essential nature bestows upon humankind an insight into the depth of the knowledge of being-itself. For Rahner however, humankind has an innate capacity for knowledge of the divine by virtue of the supernatural existential. In terms of Rahner's epistemology, to know something is to know God. The existential outworking of the fracture between the finite and the infinite in Tillich does not have a direct equivalent in Rahner who, without denying the reality of sin, presumes a fundamental union between the infinite and the finite. While sharing much in common, Tillich and Rahner are moving in different directions. Rahner is part of a general (neo-Thomistic) movement away from essentialism, whereas Tillich embraces existentialism without necessarily shifting away from essentialism.

In conclusion, this study uses a concept of experience, which includes social and public, objective (i.e. empirical) and subjective (i.e. non-empirical) dimensions, and coheres with other beliefs. Other theologies appeal to experience (e.g. Asian, feminist, liberation), but not all explicitly establish their epistemologies. This is not necessarily an oversight, but often a choice of a particular reading or style of theology. However, the epistemological value of experience is often presumed and not philosophically justified.[95] In the process experience is valued more highly than the use of reason or the timeless abstract truths of rational philosophy.[96] In keeping with Tillich and Rahner this study affirms the value of *both* reason and experience. Moreover, the study's concept of experience makes the truth-value explicit, without privileging abstract reason over experience or experience over reason. However, and this is critical, the

94   S. Kierkegaard, *Concluding Unscientific Postscript*, D.F. Swenson and W. Lowrie, trans., (Princeton: Princeton University Press, 1941), p. 350, "Existence is a synthesis of the infinite and the finite, and the existing individual is both infinite and finite". Tillich was influenced by Kierkegaard's notion of separated finitude.

95   R.R. Ruether, *Sexism and God-Talk: Towards a Feminist Theology*, (London: SCM Press, 1983), p. 18. Besides philosophy, there are other forms of justification. In feminist theology, justification can range from personal experience to sociological evidence of inequity.

96   Toulmin, *Cosmopolis*, p. 75; Brock, *Journeys*, p. 51, "Hence abstract, philosophical concepts have political and psychological roots".

point is not that the sole or even primary value of experience is its contribution to epistemic justification, but that the human experience of God as presence and absence has a role in the epistemological conversation.[97] Further, the study's concept of experience does not rely on the modern understanding of the subject *per se*, but rather the postmodern notion of intersubjectivity (1.4.3), although the distinction between the two is not regarded as absolute.

Experience is understood in postmetaphysical terms. In other words, the study employs an epistemological strategy that accounts for experience without explicitly resorting to ontotheological grounds. For example, this means that references to transcendence do not depend upon the concept of being. If the concept of experience is used, then transcendence takes place through experience in the world; it is not an out of body experience even if it feels like it, and it does not come to experience from "out there". Self-transcendence is linked with what it means to be human and what it means to be human is evoked by the experience of the presence of God in the world,

> Experience, therefore, is not primarily a screen or a veil that separates the human subject from knowledge of the world. Rather, experience is precisely the openness of the human subject to the objective world, the very process of interchange by which the world is presented to and known by the knowing subject.[98]

But there is an assumption in all this about human nature, which Rorty addresses,

> Only if one thinks that religious yearnings are somehow pre-cultural and "basic to human nature" will one be reluctant to leave the matter at that – reluctant to privatize religion completely by letting it swing free of the demand for universality. But if one gives up the idea that either the quest for truth or the quest for God is hard-

---

97   Alston, "Autonomy", p. 86, n. 7, Alston offers a timely warning about the danger of trying to establish the "reliability" of the perception of God. Nevertheless, while it needs to be treated differently from sense experience, it ought to be part of the epistemological strategy. In other words, at some level, the experience of God needs to be part of the conversation.

98   Haight, *Jesus Symbol of God*, p. 190.

232

wired into all human organisms, and allows that both are matters of cultural formation, then such privatization will seem natural and proper.[99]

For Tillich and Rahner, transcendence, while emanating from God, is "basic to human nature". Rorty is right to challenge this assumption (cf. Lindbeck). However, the study's focus is on the experience of presence and absence within a Western Christian context. Within that context, the experience of presence can be understood in part by means of the concept of transcendence. However, transcendence per se will not be the primary focus. Much of what has been discussed so far is premised on a concept of presence and so the credibility of presence will now be tested.

4.2. Presence

4.2.1. The Credibility of Presence

Tillich and Rahner grapple with many of the theological and philosophical issues of their day: matter and spirit, time and eternity, the finite and the infinite, the universal and the particular. In terms of Christology, they each claim that the significance of Christ is illustrative (i.e. Christ as exemplar) and constitutive (i.e. Christ as saviour). For them, Christ is the quintessential expression of the presence of God in the world. Tillich and Rahner share similar interests (e.g. experience). They use similar sources (e.g. Kant, Hegel, Heidegger). They address the modern dilemma, that is, the gap between the finite and the infinite. Moreover, experience is imperative for them as it is the medium through which humankind encounters presence. Significantly, absence as well as presence is an essential part of their understanding of experience. Above all, the relationship between presence and absence reflects something of the nature of experience and the character of God. Nevertheless, the theological systems and premises of Tillich and Rahner pose difficulties for postmodern sensibilities. In particular, presence is a problem. This section addresses the issue

99   R. Rorty, "Anti-clericalism and atheism" in M.A. Wrathall ed., *Religion After Metaphysics*, (Cambridge: Cambridge University Press, 2003), p. 44.

of the credibility of the concept of presence and develops a theology of presence.

In recent years, presence has been critiqued as part of a movement away from metaphysics. This movement can be detected in a constellation of signs ranging from ontotheology and logocentrism to Archimedean points outside the text. Language is important here,

> The fetishization of the literal, the unacknowledged presupposition that language refers to things that are pre-linguistic, that words correspond to objects, that discourse is primarily concerned with reference, with responding to and describing the objective nature of the world outside its system – this ideology of language has constructed, borne, and affirmed the project of modernity.[100]

In terms of presence, ontotheology is particularly important. The concept of ontotheology harks back to the metaphysical tradition of platonic Christianity. The term itself stems from Kant,

> Transcendental theology aims either at inferring the existence of a Supreme Being from a general experience – without any closer reference to the world to which this experience belongs, and in this case it is called *cosmotheology*; or it endeavours to know the existence of such a being, through mere concepts, without the aid of experience, and is then termed *ontotheology*.[101]

In short, ontotheology means to go beyond the text, the argument or the sensible world in order to rely on being, as an *external* source of authority, for the purpose of justifying a belief or set of beliefs. It is part of the quest for the ground of certainty, where ontotheology "progresses as the thinking subject's attempt to circumscribe and guard itself: to trace its own boundaries, to gather itself together, and to tie itself securely with a stable, knowable super-object".[102] For instance, Tillich and Rahner develop their respective understandings of the presence of God on the assumption that they too have located an objective foundation in being (e.g. Tillich's ground of being; Rahner's Absolute being). In the light of this, it is important to know something of the significance of the concept of ontotheology.

---

100 Ward, "Introduction", p. xxi.
101 I. Kant, *Critique of Pure Reason*, V. Politis ed., (London: Everyman, 1993), p. 428.
102 M. Rubenstein, "Unknow thyself: apophaticism, deconstruction, and theology after ontotheology", *Modern Theology*, 19 (2003), p. 410.

For Kant, ontotheology is an attempt to infer the existence of a "Supreme Being" through "mere concepts". For Nietzsche, the Supreme Being is dead, but ontotheological thinking alive and has a vice-like grip on "seekers after knowledge",

> It is still a *metaphysical faith* upon which our faith in science rests – that even we seekers after knowledge today, we godless anti-metaphysicians still take our fire, too, from the flame lit by a faith that is thousands of years old, that Christian faith which was also the faith of Plato, that God is the truth, that truth is divine.[103]

Heidegger builds on Nietzsche's insights,

> Nietzsche's statement "God is dead" means that the transcendent world is without effective power. It is not life-giving. Metaphysics, by which Nietzsche means occidental philosophy understood as Platonism, has come to an end. If God as ground of the transcendent and end of all that is real is dead; if the transcendent world of ideas has lost its binding and, above all, its evocative and constructive force, then there remains nothing to which man can turn for support and guidance.[104]

Heidegger interprets ontotheology as encompassing various attempts to solve theological and philosophical problems by resorting to being.[105] For Heidegger, the problem with these attempts is that they do not consider sufficiently the problematic nature of being.[106] To put it another way, ontotheology operates on the presumption that there is something akin to a metaphysical chain of command, with being in charge (i.e. Being-God-presence-world-humankind). However, problems are not solved but simply deferred along the chain of command. Subsequently, the idea

---

103 Nietzsche, *The Gay Science* [1887, p. 344] in *Vision of Nietzsche*, p. 49.

104 M. Heidegger, "Nietzsche's statement God is dead", (*"Nietzsche's Wort 'Gott ist Tot'"*, Holzwege. Frankfurt am Main: Vittorio Klostermann, 1950, p. 199), in M. Friedman ed. E. Kern trans. *The Worlds Of Existentialism: A Critical Reader*, (New Jersey: Humanities Press, 1964, 1991), p. 264.

105 M. Westphal, "Divine Excess: the God who comes after", in J.D. Caputo ed., *The Religious*, (Oxford: Blackwell, 2002), p. 259, "Heidegger derives his term from the move by which Aristotle's metaphysics becomes theology. First philosophy starts out as ontology, as the theory of being qua being, but finds that in order to complete itself it needs to posit a highest being, the Unmoved Mover. This ontology that becomes theology Heidegger calls onto-theology. Its fundamental assertion is that there is a Highest Being which is the key to the meaning of the whole of being".

106 Heidegger, *Hegel's Concept of Experience*, (New York: Harper and Row, 1970), p. 135; cf. Rubenstein, *"Apophaticism"*, p. 389.

of the presence of God in the world flies in the face of both the death of God and the end of platonic-based metaphysics. As a result, presence is under scrutiny because of its associations with ontotheology. Thus, it is important to establish the credibility of a theology of presence. Therefore, the study's intention is to use presence in a postmetaphysical manner, but this however is more a question of emphasis, than of making metaphysics redundant. This study is interested in exploring a postmetaphysical approach, although, it presumes that the fate of metaphysics in general and ontology in particular has not been fully resolved. The aim is to avoid the totalising effects of platonic metaphysics, but there is an element of caution concerning the presumption that theology can work without an element of ontology.

Today, the challenge for theology is to speak meaningfully about the presence of God in the world.[107] However, speaking meaningfully about God is difficult enough, let alone speaking about the presence of God.[108] The issues are related. For instance, a discussion about the attributes of God will impinge upon a discussion about how God is in or not in the world. It is partly the difference between the God of the philosophers and the God of the theologians.[109] From a philosophical perspective, there are many issues at stake ranging from the attributes of God to the agency of God. Assuming that things can be predicated of God, a discussion on the attributes of God does not of itself constitute a theology of presence. In addition, the issue of the agency of God is important because, if God cannot be spoken about in terms of agency, then it is difficult to describe God's involvement in the world. Further, the laws of logic complicate the question of God's agency.[110] In addition, the problem of free will also can limit what God can do or know.[111]

From a theological perspective, the concerns about the nature of God-talk have changed rapidly since World War 2 and the 1960's in particular.[112] Most of all, the metaphysical basis of God-talk has been chal-

---

107   Hodgson, "Winds of the Spirit", p. 65.
108   L. Gilkey, "God" in W.D. Musser and J.L. Price eds., *A New Handbook of Christian Theology*, (London: SCM Press, 1992), pp. 198-209.
109   Hart, *Trespass*, p. 29.
110   R.G. Swinburne, "God", OCP, pp. 314-315.
111   *Ibid.* p. 315.
112   J. Macquarrie, *God-Talk: An Examination of the Language and Logic of Theology*, (London: SCM Press Limited, 1967), p. 11, "IF WE SUBSTITUTE Anglo-Saxon

236

lenged.[113] In addition, there is wide a range of theological opinions as to the meaning of the presence of God in the world. The range includes biblical, patristic, Augustinian, Thomistic, Reformation, liberal, neo-orthodox, process, death of God, feminist, womanist, Asian, African and African-American perspectives. The presence of God has also been addressed under headings like the Kingdom of God, the Trinity, the Holy Spirit and the attributes of God. In many ways, all of the above issues represent a challenge to traditional theism. Theism itself has been subjected to intense critical analysis by philosophers, "Can God change the rules of logic – can he make $2 + 2 = 5$, or make a thing exist or not exist at the same time, or change the past?"[114] Theologians have challenged the idea of the presence of God in the world. For example, the so-called *death of God* theologians protested against theism.[115] They were not so much challenging the existence of God as responding to the apparent failure of theism; "It is God himself who is the transcendent enemy of the fullness and the passion of man's life in the world, and only through God's death can humanity be liberated from that oppression which is the real ruler of history".[116] In Altizer's case, this type of theology is an argument in favour of radical presence.[117] For him, the Incarnation is critical. He argues that in the Incarnation God is fully in Christ by means of a kenotic process. How the process works is not entirely clear. Others have raised similar concerns about classical theism but from different perspectives. With Moltmann, human suffering and the apparent absence of God, compels the theologian to re-interpret the nature of God.[118] For

---

roots for Greek ones, the word 'theology' would seem to be equivalent to 'God-talk". It is a form of discourse professing to speak about God … theology is rather a strange kind of language. It is a special form of God-talk, and God-talk itself seems to be different from our everyday discoursing about what is going on in the world". In this study, the term God-talk is a short hand term for theological discourse about the nature of God.

113 Gilkey, "God", p. 204.

114 Swinburne, "God", OCP, pp. 314-315.

115 The term *so-called* is used to make the point that this is not a homogenous group.

116 Altizer, *The Gospel of Christian Atheism*, (Philadelphia: Westminster Press, 1966), p. 22.

117 Altizer, *Genesis and Apocalypse: A Theological Voyage Toward Authentic Christianity*, (Louisville, Kentucky: Westminster/John Knox Press, 1990), p. 115.

118 Moltmann, *Crucified God*, p. 278.

Moltmann, "The murder of the Jews was an attempt to murder God".[119] Others have embraced postmodern perspectives. M.C. Taylor adopts some of Altizer's insights via a deconstructionist reading. Taylor has notion of a presence but its domain is restricted to the world of the text,

> Within the economy of speculative theology, death does not discredit God but is actually the climax of divine self-realization. Through a kenotic process, God's transcendence becomes an immanence in which the divine is *totally* present here and now. The death of the transcendent signified effectively divinizes the web of images and simulacra that constitute postmodern culture. When there is nothing beyond the sign, image is all.[120]

The critique of presence is often linked with deconstructionism. Deconstruction is but one postmodern perspective (cf. Lyotard, Foucault). Moreover, not all theologians and philosophers embrace deconstruction theory with equanimity.[121] Indeed, deconstructionism has its critics.[122] In particular, it has been accused of neglecting major philosophical figures and issues,

> When Jacques Derrida turned his attention to the problem of reference … he went back to the linguist Ferdinand de Saussure. Derrida struggled with him (in *De la grammatologie*) apparently in blissful ignorance of the fact that many of the problems which concerned him, and the (very slippery) position he himself came to, had, in the opinion of many in the philosophical community (even in France), been far better stated and more rigorously analysed by Ludwig Wittgenstein. But Derrida does not mention Wittgenstein in his early work. Many Derridean literary theorists were therefore seriously ignorant of the history of philosophical problems, and were unaware of some of the standard solutions to them in the Anglo-American philosophical tradition.[123]

However, there is a danger of equating postmodernism solely with deconstructionism. Postmodernism means more than deconstruction. Postmodernism incorporates a number of disciplines, styles and values.

---

119 Moltmann, *God for a Secular Society*, p. 171, cf. p. 185, perhaps, God can only be understood (i.e. justified) from an eschatological perspective.

120 Taylor, *About Religion*, p. 26.

121 C. Butler, *Postmodernism: A Very Short Introduction*, (Oxford: Oxford University Press, 2002), p. 10.

122 G. Ward, "Deconstructive Theology" in K.J. Vanhoozer ed., *Postmodern Theology*, (Cambridge: Cambridge University Press, 2003), p. 89.

123 Butler, *Postmodernism*, p. 8.

238

Moreover, some exponents of postmodernism have themselves been accused of creating new metanarratives or producing new forms of totalisation. In an attempt to surpass the limits of modernity, postmodernism runs the risk of setting in concrete its own standards (e.g. "there is nothing outside of the text").[124] There is a danger that exponents of postmodernism are at risk of becoming the new "legislators" (Lyotard) who establish with impunity the text, the narrative or their expertise as the privileged critical vantage point. Ironically, in the process they are forced to use modernism's methods.[125] Nevertheless, the issue in this section is the critique of presence and its apparent dependence on onto-theology. Despite the fact that no single postmodern perspective is perfect, the collective critique of presence cannot be lightly dismissed.

> If we understand by modernity the completed and therefore terminal figure of metaphysics, such as it develops from Descartes to Nietzsche, then "postmodernity" begins when, among other things, the metaphysical determination of God is called into question.[126]

In this section, a brief survey of the critique of presence will begin with Heidegger as he prefigured many of the challenges to presence. Heidegger had problems with equating being with presence because such an equation ran the risk of treating being as *a* being.[127] More recently, Derrida challenged the metaphysics of presence.[128] He ranked writing over speech and focused on text, "there is nothing outside of the text".[129] Moreover, "our reading must be intrinsic and remain within the text".[130] He drew attention to the relationship between signifier and signified and the problem of slippage, which can only be detected in writing.[131] All

124   J. Derrida, *Of Grammatology*, corrected edition, G. Chakravorty trans., (Baltimore and London: John Hopkins University Press, 1967, 1974, 1976, 1997), p. 158.

125   G. Steiner, *Real Presences*, p. 129.

126   J. Marion, *God Without Being*, T.A. Carlson trans., (London: University of Chicago Press, 1982, 1991), pp. xx-xxi.

127   Heidegger, *Being and Time*, p. 22.

128   N. Lucy, "presence" in *A Derrida Dictionary*, (Oxford: Blackwell Publishing, 2004), pp. 101-104, presence in Derrida is bound to metaphysics.

129   Derrida, *Of Grammatology*, p. 158.

130   *Ibid*, p. 159.

131   Lucy, *Derrida Dictionary*, pp. 144-145, "The dyadic structure of the sign constitutes it as a unity, the unity of the sensible and the intelligible, signifier and signified … *On the basis of the trace*: there is something, then, that comes 'before' the

that is left is a trace; as with a footprint, the one who made the impression is no longer present.

> All dualism, all theories of the immortality of the soul or of the spirit, as well as all monisms, spiritualist or materialist, dialectical or vulgar, are the unique theme of a metaphysics whose entire history was compelled to strive toward the reduction of the trace. The subordination of the trace to the full presence summed up in the logos, the humbling of writing beneath a speech dreaming its plenitude, such are the gestures required by an onto-theology determining the archeological and eschatological meaning of being as presence, as parousia, as life without differance: another name for death, historical metonymy where God's name holds death in check. That is why, if this movement begins in the form of Platonism, it ends in infinitist metaphysics.[132]

Subsequently, an argument could be made that language about the presence of God in the world is a trace and ought not to be confused with any notion of the so-called *actual* presence of God. In this light, it can be argued that deconstruction is not necessarily a critique of God but a critique of both the language about God and the relationship between language and God. According to Kevin Hart, deconstruction critiques theism in particular and theology in general but not God *per se*.[133] Further, following Kant and modernity, there is no access to a supersensible God because minds can only perceive sensible objects. Following Derrida and postmodernity, there is no access to God via language because we are confined to a sign system. Furthermore, postmodernism's reading of presence and absence is more than a new form of negative theology. With negative theology, "created categories" are inadequate means of referring to an unknowable God.[134] The inadequacy of these categories does not necessarily mean God is absent. It may mean God is present but hidden or God is present but beyond human comprehension. However, with the death of God theology and its successors, absence is not just hiddenness or incomprehensibility; "the theology of the death of God is grounded on an experience of an absence".[135] While the theme of ab-

---

sign. *The trace within it*: there is something, then, that remains 'after' the sign is constituted, which both effects that constitution and is inseparable from it".

132 Derrida, *Of Grammatology*, p. 71.
133 Hart, *Trespass*, p. 27.
134 R.C. Bondi, "apophatic theology", NDCT, p. 32.
135 W. Hamilton, *A Quest for the Post-Historical Jesus*, (London: SCM Press, 1993), p. 13.

sence is not new, it is understood differently now from preceding eras; "a new total presence is dawning in our midst, but it is a total absence of everything we once knew as either world or humanity".[136] Interestingly, the outcome is similar to Moltmann's understanding of the cross, but he approaches absence from a different perspective.[137]

Moltmann specifically addresses the question of suffering and the nature of God, and by inference the question of absence is raised. For Moltmann, the absence of God compels the theologian to re-interpret the nature of God.[138] Thus, Altizer and Moltmann react in different ways to the theism of the victors, but they do not represent a strictly postmodern position. In spite of its critique of theism, Altizer's concept of "total presence" is modern in its construction. In contrast, M.C. Taylor approaches absence from a postmodern perspective. With Taylor, only absence is present.[139] Ironically, absence is like a *constitutive* element in postmodern existence. In an existential sense, absence in Taylor means *sheer* absence as opposed to either God's vacuum (Tillich) or God's hiddenness (Rahner). Taylor summarises the difficulties associated with the search for presence and implicitly underlines the ambiguous nature of experience; "The very *search* for presence, through which the historical actor attempts to deny absence and embrace plenitude, testifies to the absence of presence and the 'presence' of absence".[140] Ironically, some postmodern critics use the *experience* of absence in their critique and rejection of presence, for example, "Contrary to expectation, the repressive quest for presence ends by disclosing the irreducibility of absence and the inevitability of death. Absolute plenitude and total presence are nowhere to be found".[141] In conclusion, this study aims to take the experience of absence seriously and, at the same time, affirm the experience of presence. It does not pretend the dilemmas can be easily resolved; rather it makes a case for the *ambiguity* of experience. Specifically, presence and absence represent two distinct meanings of the ex-

<hr>

136 T.J.J. Altizer, *The Contemporary Jesus*, (London: SCM Press, 1997), p. 204.
137 Moltmann, *Crucified God*, p. 36.
138 *Ibid.* p. 278.
139 C. Raschke, "Mark C Taylor" in D.W. Musser and J.L. Price eds., *A New Handbook of Christian Theologians*, (London: SCM Press, 1996), pp. 434-439.
140 M.C. Taylor, *Erring: A Postmodern A/theology*, (Chicago, London: Chicago University Press, 1984, 1987), p. 72.
141 Taylor, *Erring*, p. 71.

perience of God in the world and presence and absence cannot be separated from each other as though they are distinct phenomena.[142]

4.2.2. Alternative Views

In the face of the challenge to presence, there are a number of views that can be put forward as alternative views. Two contrasting examples will be examined. In the first, G. Steiner claims that presence is a reasonable option and certainly no less reasonable than absence. In the second, R. Kane attempts to rehabilitate metaphysics.

Steiner thinks it is worth making a "wager" on presence, just as absence is a wager.[143] He proposes, "that any coherent understanding of what language is and how language performs, that any coherent account of the capacity of human speech to communicate meaning and feeling is, in the final analysis, underwritten by the assumption of God's presence".[144] Steiner is passionate about language. In particular, Steiner claims that the speech-act involves an integral relationship with presence and this is underwritten by a profound trust in the divine.[145] He calls this "the deed of semantic trust".[146] He locates the origin of the loss of this trust to the period between the 1870's and 1930's.[147] This is the loss of trust between word *(logos)* and world *(cosmos)*, which is "one of the few genuine revolutions of spirit in Western history and which defines mod-

---

142 M. Pearson, "Where is he now? A Christology of absence and presence" in C. Pearson ed. with a sub-version by J. Havea, *Faith in a Hyphen: Cross-Cultural Theologies Down Under*, (Adelaide: Openbook Publishers, 2004), p. 125, "The feeling of the absence of Christ calls for a new way of seeing that might enable us indeed to discover Christ's presence". On general biblical, theological and experiential grounds, Pearson sees the need for a Christology of presence and absence. Her brief article does not develop these ideas in detail, but it points to the need for studies like the present one.

143 Steiner, *Real Presences*, Steiner talks about the experience of the other (i.e. transcendence), primarily as it relates to aesthetics.

144 *Ibid.* pp. 3-4.

145 *Ibid.* p. 89.

146 *Ibid.* p. 91.

147 *Ibid.* p. 93, the end of Steiner's *period*, which coincides with the period in Toulmin (*Cosmopolis*, p. 84), is the era that propagates a positivist notion of truth, knowledge and the world.

242

ernity itself".[148] Before the 1870's, there existed a fundamental trust in the word and the word referred to something; this is the time of the *logos*, "the saying of being".[149] He describes the period after the 1870's as *after-word* (i.e. epi-logue). From the 1870's on, the problems of meaning and the meaning of meaning became paramount. Consequently, doubt is cast upon key relationships like word/world, world/God, word/God and the related notions of *theos*, *cosmos* and *logos*. For Steiner, deconstruction dismisses the link between word and world as ontotheological. In response, Steiner wants to make a wager on presence.

> This essay argues a wager on transcendence. It argues that there is in the art-act and its reception, that there is in the experience of meaningful form, a presumption of presence … It is, I have argued, the irreducible autonomy of presence, of 'otherness', in art and text which denies either adequate paraphrase or unanimity of finding.[150]

Without doubt, Steiner's critique of deconstructionism is compelling, "The deconstructive discourse is *itself* rhetorical, referential and altogether generated and governed by normal modes of causality, of logic and of sequence. The deconstructive denial of 'logocentrism' is expounded in wholly logocentric terms."[151] However, Steiner makes a number of metaphysical leaps and unsubstantiated assumptions.[152] First, he highlights the problems associated with deconstructionism's critique of metaphysics. Even so deconstructionism's critique of metaphysics is worth taking seriously (cf. Derrida) and it has a pedigree (e.g. Heidegger). In addition, Steiner never really tackles deconstructionism's critique of metaphysics head on, partly because his interests are primarily literary and not philosophical. That is, he attacks deconstructionism's method rather than its critique of being *per se*. Second, Steiner's wager on presence appears to be an unsubstantiated ontotheological claim.[153]

---

148 *Real Presences*, p. 93.
149 *Ibid.*
150 *Ibid.* p. 214.
151 *Ibid.* p. 129.
152 *Ibid.* pp. 148, 152, e.g. his assumption about the nature and reliability of common sense.
153 Steiner, *Grammars of Creation*, (London: Faber and Faber, 2001), p. 104, "Being is axiomatically twinned with non-being: to be is ' not not to be'".

R. Kane, while not attempting to address the issue of presence, tries to re-interpret metaphysics in a way that it could be used to support the use of the concept of presence. Specifically, Kane attempts to re-orient metaphysics by making a claim for "a metaphysical culture".[154] He is responding to the postmodern dismissal of metaphysics. He argues *provisionally* that the credibility of metaphysics depends upon how the *ends* of metaphysics are understood. He defines the ends in terms of objective explanation (i.e. truth) and objective worth (i.e. good). Based on Aristotle, Kane defines *objective explanation* "as understanding what is *reasonable to believe* about the nature of things and why".[155] For Kane, this end must be transformed. He defines *objective worth* as "what is objectively *reasonable to strive for* in the nature of things".[156] Kane argues that there is a place for a metaphysics that aspires to these ends. His argument hinges on the word aspiration, which is "a good word for this idea of radically contingent seeking".[157] For Kane, "Truth transcends texts. That is why it can be aspired to, and even possessed, but not known with certainty".[158] He recognises that there are many possible responses to metaphysics and that what lies behind all of them is "the idea that all knowing and understanding involve interpretation in terms of some conceptual scheme or linguistic framework, some language game or form of life, which is local and particular to the knower or inquirer".[159] He agrees with the postmodern caution against asserting that things can be known with absolute certainty, but he does not see this as an argument against "the attainability in principle of objective truth and hence objective explanation".[160] On the contrary, it is an argument for the radical contingency of any such attainment. According to Kane, if modernity meant the elevation of objective explanation over and above objective worth, postmodernity challenges both of these metaphysical ends. In particular, in terms of objective explanation, Kane challenges Kant's idea of the noumenal. Traditionally, the objective is understood

---

154 R. Kane, "The ends", p. 427.
155 *Ibid.* p. 415.
156 *Ibid.*
157 *Ibid.* p. 421.
158 *Ibid.* p. 422.
159 *Ibid.* p. 414.
160 *Ibid.* p. 421.

"as it is in itself, and not merely as it is known or as it appears to us".[161] In contrast, the postmodern critique is "if all understanding is dependent on a conceptual scheme or linguistic framework, how can we grasp an objective Reality in the sense of the way things are in themselves, rather than merely as they appear to us?"[162] Given that the world can only be described by means of a language game, Kane asserts that objective explanation and objective truth may be "the logical sum of truths from different perspectives, not their logical product" (cf. Peirce, Armstrong, Haack).[163]

The aim of this study is to contribute to Christological knowledge, without expecting to establish absolute certainty and without attempting to re-configure metaphysics. However, this study is not convinced that Kane has arrived at his "metaphysical culture" or that metaphysics can be rehabilitated, although by Kane's own admission his argument is provisional. In other areas, Kane's essay points in the right direction: awareness of contingency, attention to language games and the distinction between the world of language and the world itself. Kane offers the possibility of a different understanding of knowledge to the external, timeless, decontextualised facts of modernity, as well as captivity to the text-world of deconstructionism and the postmodern legislators who rule out metaphysical conceptions.[164]

4.2.3. A Theology of Presence and the Ambiguity of Experience

In this part, the aim is to re-define the meaning of presence on the basis of the ambiguity of experience, that is, experience consisting of presence and absence. To begin with, there are three main reasons for redefining presence.

- The capacity to re-define a concept is in the nature of language
- There is room for doubt about the absolute claims of the postmodern critique of metaphysics and presence

---

161 *Ibid.* pp. 417-418.
162 *Ibid.* p. 418.
163 *Ibid.* p. 419.
164 Toulmin, *Cosmopolis*, pp. 44, 87.

-   There is experience; humankind vouches for the experience of presence

First, this study acknowledges that historically the concept of presence has had ontotheological associations. Consequently, the aim is to redefine presence without explicit ontotheological associations. Nevertheless, a counter-argument could be made that it is not possible to do this because of the metaphysical associations. In other words, the inference is that presence cannot be re-defined because it is metaphysically surcharged. However, this counter-argument runs the risk of imposing a totalising view on language, when it assumes that the meaning of words like presence is fixed,

> Whether it's unequivocally here or unequivocally never here, presence remains presence: disallowing presence completely only re-reifies it as such. Presence, in other words, returns to disrupt the now-repressive post-structuralist counter-order.[165]

Of all eras, surely the meaning of a concept can be re-defined in the postmodern era. Re-defining a concept is not a perfect process, because we read language differently, but there seems a reasonable postmodern argument for re-defining a concept, even if it is presence.

Second, the postmodern critique of presence is inconclusive; this is due to the inherent limitations of the critique itself and certain unresolved metaphysical issues. While there is a justifiable measure of reserve about the use of metaphysics in theology, the question of whether or not theology can be conducted without any metaphysical assumptions whatsoever has not been resolved (i.e. the jury is out on the question of metaphysics). Moreover, the so-called binary opposition of presence and absence has been critiqued on the basis that absence has been defined on the basis of presence and presence is defined at the expense of absence, in other words, presence has been privileged over and above absence. In this study, absence is equally valued along with presence as being part and parcel of the human experience of God in the world (4.2.4). Moreover, the debate about metaphysics itself has been stifled by the implicit imposition of the binary opposition of metaphysical or non-metaphysical approaches. Certainly, a distinction can be made between the two approaches, but it seems unreasonable to argue that the distinction is abso-

---

165 Rubenstein, *Apophaticism*, p. 411.

246

lute. Ironically, Rorty discerns what could be described here as a quasi-dependent relation between the two approaches, "no constructors, no deconstructors. No norms, no perversions".[166] Thus, doubt about the absolute claims of postmodernity represents an opportunity to re-think the concept of presence and to claim some critical space for it without necessarily or explicitly adopting an ontotheological approach.[167] As Breisach suggests:

> In the case of the Enlightenment, there had been a peculiar ontological reduction … It aimed to reduce to one the two levels of beings affirmed by the Christian view of history that had been dominant during the medieval and early modern periods. The one remaining level has been that of the experiential-empirical world. Yet as many postmodernists have pointed out relentlessly, the Enlightenment's antimetaphysical ardor had been restricted to the rejection of religious explanations of the world and history. Reason's presence … had been condoned in order to give legitimacy to progress as well as to the authoritative truth derived from it. Indeed, the postmodernist quest has often been linked to the twentieth-century attempts to purge metaphysics … completely from Western culture – a quest that made plausible the view of postmodernism as advocating a radically new view of life rather than as a call for technical adjustments in epistemology.[168]

Admittedly, the anti-metaphysical postmodern literature has an inquisitorial tone. This study is not inherently anti-metaphysical in its approach or tone, however, it is using a postmetaphysical approach, in conjunction with "technical adjustments in epistemology" (e.g. experience), as a means of engagement with postmodernism and postmodernity.

Third, there are pastoral and cultural grounds for reclaiming presence. These grounds are not conclusive by themselves, but they have a legitimate place in the process of epistemic justification, namely, there are social and public grounds in favour of using and re-defining the concept presence.[169] In pastoral terms, the language of presence is a major part of

166 R. Rorty, "Philosophy as a kind of writing: An essay on Derrida", *Consequences of Pragmatism (Essays, 1972-1980)*, (Sussex: The Harvester Press, 1982), p. 108.

167 Caputo, *On Religion*, p. 57, "Now in my efforts to reinstate a dialogue with pre-modern thinkers, I do not think that we can get the old metaphysical style of arguing that the medievals cherished back on its feet. I have not given up on philosophy, but I take philosophy to be a phenomenological, not a metaphysical or speculative enterprise, that is, I steer its nose close to the earth of concrete description".

168 E. Breisach, *On The Future Of History: The Postmodernist Challenge And Its Aftermath*, (Chicago and London: University of Chicago Press, 2003), p. 13.

169 Everitt and Fisher, pp. 202-203, 207-208.

the communal, sacramental and spiritual experience of the Church. In cultural terms, the language of presence figures prominently in everyday experience. All this assumes that, justification has public and social dimensions.[170]

In this study, presence is re-defined in relation to absence and in the context of experience.[171] It presumes theology is provisional; this does not rule out the possibility of the existence of theological constants, but it does presume that constants have to be re-interpreted in new settings and re-appropriated by new faith communities. Thus, presence needs to be re-appropriated for postmodernity. In postmodernity, absence is presumed and the onus of proof is on presence.[172] However, at this stage, it would be helpful to look at absence in more detail before returning to presence. There are many reasons in favour of the absence of God in the world. First, the God-metanarrative, which usually refers to a traditional theistic view of God, has been undermined theologically and philosophically. Second, the God-metanarrative does not hold in the light of the experience of suffering (e.g. Auschwitz). Third, the ontotheological foundations of the language of presence have been challenged. Furthermore, the concept of absence is common to both modernity and postmodernity, but it is construed differently in each period. In modernity, God is absent partly because God is construed as supersensible, that is, non-factual or not real in the sense that God is not conceived of as a thing or an object. Generally, this means that there is no apparent evidence (empirical, rational or factual) that can be used to support the claim that God is present in the world. God is absent because there is no *objective* proof to say that God is present. God is absent by default. In postmodernity, the issue of what constitutes evidence – sensible, rational, factual or otherwise – is debatable. In modernity, God is absent because God is defined as spiritual and the world as material and the spiritual and material are different and separate. In postmodernity, there are a number of possibilities. For example, God is absent because writing has been given a privileged epistemological status, "since the sign does not re-present the real but is always a signifier of another signifier, there

---

170 *Ibid.* p. 208.

171 Pearson, "Where is he now?" p. 121, "The reality is that there is never presence without absence".

172 Caputo (e.g. *On Religion*) and Hart (e.g. *Trespass*) make claims for a new understanding of religion, but without necessarily honing in on presence.

248

appears to be nothing outside the play of signs".[173] Alternatively, God is absent because the metaphysical foundations of theism have been discredited. Alternatively, God may be present but there are many gods. In this study, the contention is that the experience of God is ambiguous. There is no explicit commitment to theism in general or to a particular model of theism. This is not to say that this study refutes theism, but only to argue that a certain kind of theism is problematic. Moreover, the binary opposition of theism/atheism is also an obstacle to discussion. If God is mystery, then all theological models inevitably fall short of the mark (e.g. theism, deism, Thomism, process theology).

In this study, the thesis is based on the ambiguous experience of God in the world, where ambiguity cannot be resolved.[174] The ambiguity is understood in terms of presence and absence.[175] This is not a new approach, but the way it is applied here is different.[176] This will become clear by way of comparison with two parallel approaches to experience in general and presence and absence in particular. First, the distinctive tradition of American empirical theology has placed a premium on experience.[177] While there are parallels, this study is not located in the American empirical and/or pragmatic theological tradition.[178] Indeed, the study incorporates a wide range of philosophical and theological sources; besides it is not attempting to establish an ontology of ambiguity. In its place, the study is committed to a postmetaphysical approach; which means it does not intend to rely on being as a form of epistemic justification (4.2). Moreover, instead of *experience* in general, the study is focused on *the experience of God* in particular where ambiguity is defined specifically in terms of presence and absence. This is not a repudiation of

---

173   M.C. Taylor, *About Religion*, p. 21

174   Metaphorically, the ambiguous encounter between God and Moses comes close to the mark of a postmodern faith "the bush was blazing, yet it was not consumed" (Exod 3:2, NRSV). God is simultaneously present and absent (Exod 24:15-18).

175   Caputo, *Radical Hermeneutics*, p. 280.

176   Rubenstein, *Apophaticism*, p. 396, "If, however, apophaticism is understood always to be itself *and* cataphaticism, it becomes clear that negative theology aims neither to negate negation nor to affirm it, but to move constantly between the two poles in such a way that one becomes the other and their polarity collapses".

177   W. Dean, "Empiricism and God" in R.C. Miller ed. *Empirical Theology: A Handbook*, (Birmingham, Alabama: Religious Education Press, 1992), pp. 107-128.

178   American empirical theology tradition and Rorty are grounded in pragmatism (cf. Peirce).

empirical theology, but a different approach. Second, studies have used presence and absence; for example, in the context of sacramental theology, Ries asserts,

> The presence of God is neither a secure anchor nor an overwhelming power, but an *absent* presence calling one ever-deeper into one's bottomless freedom, to what might be termed the occasion/moment of grace.[179]

Similarly de Certeau claims,

> The process of the death (the absence) and the survival (the presence) of Jesus continues in each Christian experience: What the event makes possible is different each time, as a new remoteness from the event and a new way of erasing it.[180]

Ruth Page looks at the issues of ambiguity in relation to the presence of God.[181] She defines ambiguity in general terms.[182] For Page, ambiguity incorporates three concepts: change, diversity and polyvalence.[183] This is a postmodern approach in the sense that it takes into account religious and cultural pluralism. However, Page is committed to a metaphysical approach.[184] From a philosophical perspective, her definition of ambiguity resembles the idea of vagueness rather than the philosophical concept of ambiguity as distinct and different meanings.[185] Moreover, Page does not address the issue of absence, whereas absence is fundamental to this

---

179 J.C. Ries, "The concept of 'sacramental anxiety': A Kierkegaardian locus of transcendence?" in L. Boeve and L. Leijssen eds., *Sacramental Presence in a Postmodern Context*, (Leuven: Leuven University Press, 1997), p. 323.

180 M. de Certeau, "How Christianity is thinkable today?" in G. Ward ed., *The Postmodern God*, (Oxford: Blackwell Publishers, 1997), p. 145.

181 R. Page, *Ambiguity And The Presence Of God*, (London: SCM Press, 1985).

182 R. Page, "Ambiguity" in D.W. Musser and J.L. Price ed., *A New Handbook Of Christian Theology*, (Nashville: Abingdon Press, 1992), pp. 26-28.

183 Page, *Ambiguity*, p. 13.

184 R. Page, *The Incarnation Of Freedom And Love*, (London: SCM Press, 1991). Page begins to distance herself from a metaphysical approach. She rejects theism *per se*, because it is based on a dualistic ontology. While God is other, God is intimately related to the cosmos. This is not dualism but "concurrence" (p. 141). But how is concurrence different from the theism she rejects? For her, it is different because it is based on action and not ontology (p. 162). However, she uses *presence* as though it was *being* in said dualistic ontologies (p. 92).

185 Baggini and Fosl, p. 69; J. Cederblom and D.W. Paulsen, *Critical Reasoning*, 4th ed., (Belmont: Wadsworth, 1996), p. 194.

study. In summary, the use of presence and absence has been tried before; what is new is an explicit and sustained application of the ambiguity of the experience of God to Tillich and Rahner for the purposes of making a contribution to postmodern Christology.

In this study, the concept of ambiguity means more than one meaning: it is not to be confused with the idea of vagueness. The term ambiguity, for example, can be applied in a technical sense to language. With language there is lexical ambiguity as in a word like "can", as well as structural ambiguity, as in "all the nice girls love a sailor".[186] However, ambiguity has another application in relation to the concept of experience. In the perception of an object or in the experience of an event, different people interpret the meaning of the experience differently. In experience, an object or an event elicits multiple meanings. This in itself gives rise to the notion of contingency. In this study, ambiguity is defined in relation to the experience of God and as such ambiguity has two interrelated meanings: presence and absence. This does not mean that the meaning of the experience of God is exhausted by presence and absence. Further, the study asserts that presence and absence are integral parts of the experience of God in the world: presence alone leads to reification (i.e. Tillich's idolatry) and absence alone leads to nihilism. Both are needed to constitute the full meaning of the experience of God, as ambiguity is part and parcel of contingent human existence. All this is in keeping with "the postmodern awareness of no certain exit from uncertainty".[187] Indeed, "fear of the 'unfoundedness' of certainty was, arguably, the most formidable among modernity's many inner demons".[188] In everyday speech, presence and absence are construed as opposites. That is, presence or absence is understood in relation to the other. For example, presence means being there or existing as opposed to absence, which means not being there or not existing. This binary opposition can mean and has meant that presence has been esteemed over absence.[189] In this study, presence and absence are equally important. They are seen as

---

186 "Ambiguity", ODP, p. 13.
187 Z. Bauman, "Postmodernity, or living with ambivalence", in J. Natoli and L. Hutcheon eds., *A Postmodern Reader* (Albany: State University of New York, 1993), p. 15.
188 *Ibid.* p. 22.
189 Taylor, *Erring*, p. 9.

different from and in relation to each other as difference requires relation.[190]

> The dichotomies which determine the human condition, such as life and death, such as light and dark, can be understood as specialized, though pervasive, enactments of the welded duality of presence and absence: to be present is not to be absent. The seeming vacancy of absence entails ... the fullness of presence. This twinning is enunciated by each and every linguistic proposition, by each mental and articulate act of predication. A statement, a definition, a nomination are positive negations: 'this is not that'. The status of 'that which is not' will, first, imply the unpredicated, the unnamed incommensurability of alternatives. When I say, 'this is this and not that', I am also postulating that this 'not that' could, virtually without limit, be other.[191]

Presence and absence share a difference-in-identity; the origin of which is God.[192]

To sum up, this study intends to use a postmetaphysical approach to presence. The term postmetaphysical is used here as a heuristic device. The study is not convinced that the polemic surrounding metaphysics has been settled. Nevertheless, it intends to avoid the explicit use of universal or absolute statements. Further, the study has used elements from deconstructionism, but this study is not deconstructionist. In contrast to deconstructionism, it uses other sources (e.g. Lyotard) and concepts (e.g. history), which are not deconstructionist *per se*. In addition, the study does not agree that writing should be given privileged epistemological status. After all, someone writes (and reads) and writing is part of experience.[193] So while this study welcomes deconstructionism's concern about reference and representation, it affirms a connection between the concepts of presence and absence and the experience of God. Overall, there are four key features in the study's postmetaphysical approach. First, the study is aiming to avoid an ontotheological approach. This is a methodological intention; it is hard to make a theological statement

190 Rubenstein, *Apophaticism*, p. 406.
191 Steiner, *Grammars of Creation*, p. 104.
192 Rubenstein, *Apophaticism*, p. 407.
193 Taylor, *Erring*, p. 17, "insofar as others join with me in my undertaking, they will, I believe, gradually come to recognize themselves as both readers and writers. When this happens, the lines of the text not only stretch back to formative precursors but also extend beyond the pages of the book to entangle the readers-writers to whom it is addressed."

without a hint of an implicit ontotheology because of the nature of theological discourse. Words like *God, Jesus, Spirit, Church* and *sacrament* have a history saturated with metaphysical associations. Second, the study does not address the question of whether there is a God beneath or beyond presence or *out there* or *in here*.[194] There are alternative approaches.[195] However, the study is focused on the experience of God.[196] In the long term, the hope of this study is that the experience of Christian faith communities, which includes presence and absence, ought to be part of the wider Christological debate. Third, the study does not presume that presence and absence encompass the whole meaning of the human experience of God. It is tempting to make such a claim, but this would run the risk of homogenising the diverse and ambiguous experience of God. Fourth, this study's decision to set aside the ontotheological underpinnings of Tillich and Rahner is hardly problematic, if ontotheology has little credibility in postmodernism.

4.2.4. A Theology of Presence

Having established the credibility of a concept of presence, the aim in this part is to develop a theology of presence on the basis of Tillich and Rahner. This part of the study specifically asserts that the theologies of Tillich and Rahner can be interpreted from the perspective of the ambiguity of the experience of God as presence and absence. The differences between Tillich and Rahner, which are evident in their treatment of experience, derive in part from their different understandings of existence (i.e. fragmented; unified). However, the way they interpret absence often lacks the human edge that comes from addressing directly longstanding widespread issues of suffering, although this is less true of Tillich's ser-

194 Rorty, *Contingency*, p. 21.
195 Marion, *God Without Being*.
196 R. Gascoigne, "Looking beyond liberalism: Christianity and a civil society" *Colloquium* 33 (2001), p. 107, in an ethical setting, Gascoigne endorses an ongoing dialogue performed by Christians, between its own understanding of the Christian narrative and contemporary ethical challenges, "In this sense, participation in public normative debate is both a means of communicating the principled wisdom of Christian tradition and an opportunity to learn from the experience of all those whose needs, interests and aspirations motivate them to engage in such debate".

mons and radio broadcasts and Rahner's sermons and prayers. Nevertheless, both Tillich and Rahner, intuitively, implicitly and consistently recognise the ambiguity of the experience of God in terms of the interplay of presence and absence, in which absence is neither dismissed nor devalued (cf. God's space, God's hiddenness), but is seen as an integral part of the experience of God in the world.

Tillich

For Tillich, presence is the uniquely human awareness of its participation in Divine life; an experience of presence means the possibility of transcendence of the gap between the finite and the infinite. Further, there is no access to presence in modernity because of the gap and the problem of the gap cannot be resolved by strictly rational means.[197] In this context, absence is the outcome of designating the presence of God as inaccessible, that is, if presence is excluded by the prevailing definition of the world then absence remains by default. In contrast, Tillich's theology is directed toward making a positive theological statement about presence in modernity. Subsequently, the idea of the presence of God in the world permeates the work of Tillich. He uses many terms for presence. He expresses it implicitly with love,[198] holiness,[199] word of God,[200] and mysticism.[201] He expresses it explicitly with omnipresence,[202] sacramental presence,[203] Spirit,[204] Divine Spirit[205] and Spiritual Presence.[206] However, Tillich does not always define his terms clearly. Terminological ambiguity is a feature of his work.[207] In some instances, the ambiguity is incidental. In other instances, the ambiguity is intended as he sees theological possibilities in ambiguity. For instance, there is a theological

197 "Realism and faith", TPE, p. 76.
198 ST III, p. 137.
199 ST I, p. 215.
200 BRUR, p.78.
201 PPT, p. 22.
202 ST I, pp. 276-278.
203 *Ibid.* p. 278.
204 *Ibid.* pp. 249-252; ST III, p. 139.
205 ST III, pp. 111-138; UC pp. 17, 79.
206 ST III, pp. 111-161.
207 Heywood Thomas, *Tillich*, pp. 35-36.

254

dimension to ambiguity which is consistent with his assumption that presence is pervasive and cannot be compartmentalised.[208] The ambiguity is the result of the fact that he sees experience as ambiguous. Further, life and the experience of life are ambiguous in Tillich,

> It is my intention to discuss the particular functions of life, not in their essential nature, separate from their existential distortion, but in the way they appear within the ambiguities of their actualization, for life is neither essential nor existential but ambiguous.[209]

Also, "Religion, like all life, is ambiguous".[210] In the end, for Tillich, the estrangement and the ambiguities of life can only be overcome by an encounter with the presence of God in the world.

The presence of God in the world is a way of describing the experience of participation in divine life, where the gap between the finite and the infinite is transcended. Presence evokes the capacity of transcendence. Tillich refers to this inherent capacity as the "power of infinite self-transcendence".[211] Tillich has been criticised for having a God that is inaccessibly distant (2.2.2), where all the good is on one side, "the infinite distance between God and man is never bridged; it is identical with man's finitude".[212] Subsequently, a critic like Van Beeck is partly right: Tillich does not have a sense of the created goodness of the world as it is because it is under the impact of existential estrangement.[213] However, Tillich's use of the presence of God could be interpreted in terms of the grace of God in the world. Further, it is Tillich's theology of transcendence that provides some shelter from the harsh light of estrangement and God's judgement. There is a subtle but significant distinction in Tillich between his claims that the gap between the finite and the infinite cannot be bridged and his claims that it can be transcended. A bridge is a human structure that makes it possible to transcend the gap. What Tillich means, and here he is congruent with Kant's understanding of the gap, is that the gap cannot be transcended by human means. What is required is

---

208 OTB, p. 18, his love of the sea and the metaphor of the sea reinforces the mystical in Tillich.
209 ST III, p. 32, cf. ST II, p. 4, "Life remains ambiguous as long as there is life".
210 ST II, p. 80.
211 ST I, p. 191.
212 ST III, p. 239.
213 Van Beeck, *Christ Proclaimed*, pp. 214-216.

the "power of infinite self-transcendence".[214] For Tillich, the presence of God in the world is the uniquely human awareness of its participation in Divine life. The presence of God is God's self present to humankind. Humankind cannot possess or control God's self, because God is not part of the subject-object structure of the world.[215] Moreover, God's participation in the world cannot be expressed in spatial or temporal terms; only in symbols.[216] In brief, if God is the God above the God of theism, then the problem is how to explain God's participation in the world. Tillich explains it by means of the idea of self-transcendence; this means humankind is able to participate in the divine.[217] There are limits to human participation in divine life, which are set in place by two factors: finitude and the character of God. In terms of finitude, "our existence is determined not only by the omnipresence of the divine but also by our separation from it".[218] The presumption behind self-transcendence is that "the finite world points beyond itself".[219] This means that metaphorically transcendence is more a leap over the gap than a bridge crossing. The capacity to leap is a God-given capacity, which is inherent in the created order, although only human nature is conscious of it and it is this consciousness that activates the inherent capacity. Presence elicits the capacity for transcendence.

Tillich's concept of self-transcendence has a major role in his theology as it provides an explanation of the cause of the experience of presence. It is premised on historical realism.[220] Historical realism becomes self-transcending realism when it points beyond itself to the ultimate ground.[221] The ultimate ground is "the really real" or "the power of reality".[222] Self-transcending realism is "a universal attitude toward reality … Self-transcending realism combines two elements, the emphasis on the real and the transcending power of faith".[223] Historical realism focuses on the present and it entails a personal investment in "a concrete

214 ST I, p. 191.
215 TCB, p. 180; ST I, p. 237.
216 ST I, p. 245.
217 ST II, p. 9.
218 "Nature and sacrament", TPE, p. 123.
219 ST II, p. 7.
220 "Realism and faith", TPE, p. 81.
221 *Ibid.* pp. 85, 87.
222 *Ibid.* pp. 77, 85.
223 *Ibid.* p. 75.

256

historical situation" and thus, the real is transcended.[224] For Tillich, faith and realism belong-together-in-tension.[225] Nonetheless, Tillich's striving for the unconditioned ground and his view of God as being-itself makes it hard to characterise his theology as realist.[226] Clearly, Tillich wants his theology to be seen as realist, but his tendency to draw out ontological implications from almost every major aspect of his theology creates the impression that his underlying view is idealist. It is hard to see how Tillich could establish a plausible non-speculative basis for making truth statements using his understanding of God. For Alston, Tillich has a nonrealist position, which is based on a form of conceptual transcendence.[227] The core idea in conceptual transcendence is otherness.[228] Alston asserts that the problem with extreme forms of conceptual transcendence is how to refer to God. This is the case with Tillich. Tillich claims God is not *a* being and so all references to God are of necessity symbolic. However, Tillich also claims that the statement that God is being-itself is a nonsymbolic statement (though it is not clear what Tillich means by this). Consequently, Tillich's God above the God of theism could be dismissed as an outmoded piece of metaphysical dualism, beyond conceptualisation (Alston), out there and out of touch with real experience (cf. Heyward, Moltmann).[229] In contrast, Tillich has been defended in recent years. Lamm contends that Tillich goes beyond Kant by repositioning Kant "in a non-dualistic world view."[230] Similarly, Morrison sees Tillich as putting forward a non-dualist position.[231]

Absence is an important theme in Tillich's work. For Tillich, there is no understanding of presence without an implicit understanding of absence, because presence and absence are in polar relation. Further, absence is an experience that can be understood from several standpoints: ontological, anthropological and sociological. From an ontological per-

224 *Ibid.* p. 87, the idea of concrete historical reality seems a permanent feature of modernity.

225 *Ibid.* p. 76, "Idealism relativizes, self-limiting realism denies, but self-transcending realism accepts the tension".

226 Alston, "Realism", p. 42, Tillich's God is beyond conceptualisation.

227 *Ibid.* p. 53.

228 *Ibid.* p. 51.

229 Heyward, "Being above", p. 31, Moltmann *Theology Today*, (London: SCM Press; Philadelphia: Trinity Press International, 1988), p. 86.

230 Lamm, "Revisited", p. 53.

231 Morrison, "Tillich, Einstein, and Kant", pp. 35-65.

spective, absence is a distorting effect of relative non-being.[232] From an anthropological perspective, absence is a symptom of existential estrangement in which "the Spirit of God hides God from our sight".[233] Thus, absence is symptomatic of finitude.[234] From a sociological perspective, absence is symptomatic of the secularisation associated with modernity.[235] In metaphorical terms, Tillich describes the absence of God as the space that evokes a longing for the presence of God.[236] This space is God's space because only God can fill the space. In this space, God is not absent because the Spirit is present, but the absence of God is experienced as emptiness by humankind, "we feel His absence as the empty space that is left by something or someone that once belonged to us and has now vanished from our view".[237]

The significance of absence in Tillich is clear in his work on estrangement "in the state of estrangement, the relation to the ultimate power of being is lost".[238] For Tillich, humankind has a world, which "is the structural whole which includes and transcends all environments".[239] Consequently, estrangement means the loss of the self and "with the loss of self, man loses his world".[240] The absence of God is a symptom of self-loss and a measure of finitude.[241] Tillich is not asserting that God is absent, only that humankind *experiences* absence in existential estrangement, because humankind is "never cut off from the ground of being, not even in the state of condemnation".[242] Moreover, the experience of the absence of God in the world entails a loss of essentiality (2.2.3). Consequently, the experience of absence can also evoke a yearning for the infinite. In summary, the experience of presence and absence reveals *something* about the nature of God.[243] In particular, presence and absence represent the experience of God as ground and abyss. They ex-

---

232 ST I, p. 113.
233 "Spiritual presence", EN, p. 88.
234 ST II, pp. 44-47.
235 UC, p. 5.
236 "Spiritual presence", EN, p. 88.
237 *Ibid.*
238 ST II, p. 68.
239 ST I, p. 170.
240 ST II, p. 61.
241 *Ibid.* p. 73, "the lack of a necessary place and a necessary presence".
242 *Ibid.* p. 78.
243 ST I, p. 113.

press the existential side of mystery: the human side. The terms ground and abyss represent Tillich's attempts to describe in metaphorical terms the essential side of mystery: the God side. However, the precise nature of the correlation between presence and absence on the one hand and God as ground and abyss on the other hand is unclear, because the nature of the relationship in Tillich between ground and abyss is obscure.[244] This may be because, while the experience of God may be reduced to presence and absence, the essential nature of God's self cannot be reduced to concepts or experiences. In a sense, Tillich wants it both ways. On the one hand, he wants to affirm the importance of this dialectical relation between ground and abyss. On the other hand, he asserts that in the end it is all a matter of mystery and all we have to appreciate mystery is myth and symbol. In short, from the existential side, the effects of God in the world, the meaning of presence and absence is clearer. Thus, absence is an experience of "the annihilating power of the divine presence",[245] and presence is an experience of "the elevating power of the divine presence".[246]

Rahner

Rahner's theological anthropology is the context for a discussion on his concept of presence. In Rahner, awareness of presence is humankind's awareness of an innate experience of God's self.[247] This experience is characterised by an awareness of the closeness of God.[248] This awareness is elicited by the world through an act of perception (i.e. judgement). In this setting, presence is self-presence because divine presence is mediated intrinsically. Self-presence involves the idea of the return to the self, which is expressed in judgement.[249] Judgement is possible because of pre-anticipation. Pre-anticipation opens up consciousness and the opening up of consciousness is a pre-condition for the experience of self-

---

244 *Ibid.* pp. 110, 113, 119.
245 *Ibid.* p. 113.
246 *Ibid.*
247 "Grace", ET, p. 589.
248 FCF, p. 119.
249 HW. pp. 35-43.

presence.[250] Thus, in Rahner, subjectivity is *the place* for the simultaneous act of perception and experience of presence. Further, the presence of God is in the world but God is not affected by the world. Later in Rahner, humankind participates in absolute being because everything resides in absolute being; but absolute being is not everything. Absolute being is present in matter, but it is not matter. For instance, in the case of spirit and matter, there is unity-in-difference (i.e. spirit and matter form a unity, but spirit has priority over matter). Self-transcendence refers to the dynamic within this unity, in which matter develops toward spirit.[251] The development involves a becoming, where becoming is understood in terms of "fullness of being".[252] The self-transcending movement is from the lower to higher order of being, by virtue of the power of being-itself. The higher order emerges from and contains the lower order and the higher order emerges when the lower order reaches the limit situation and transcends it.[253] In Rahner, matter makes the experience of the *other* possible.

Rahner's concept of transcendence can be explored further by means of the concept of quasi-formal causality. With God's self-communication, God is cause and effect (giver and gift)[254]. However, if God is not differentiated from humankind (i.e. giver from receiver), then the immutability of God is under threat. The point then is to affirm both God's involvement *and* God's otherness. Consequently, Rahner uses formal causality to account for this and establishes a basis for unity-in-difference. Thus, from the human perspective, it is possible to refer to an embodied sentient being which lives in a sensible world and yearns for Absolute being, because he/she has access to Absolute being. From the divine perspective, it is possible to describe God's self as being in matter (i.e. humankind) because God is not matter, but God gives form to matter. All this allows for the possibility that God causes and God changes *"in something else"*,[255] but that God does not change.[256] Rahner's view of formal causality is influenced by his work on symbols. In short, the

250   *Ibid.* p. 47.
251   FCF, p. 184, cf. "Evolutionary view", TI 5, pp. 163-164.
252   "Evolutionary view", TI 5, p. 164.
253   *Ibid.* pp. 167, 178.
254   FCF, p. 120.
255   "Incarnation", TI 4, p. 113.
256   FCF, pp. 120-121.

symbol has an intrinsic capacity to confer what it signifies.[257] He asserts that the supernatural existential is a form of intrinsic causality (i.e. *quasi-formal*).[258] Quasi-formal causality is different from other forms of intrinsic causality, because it is God's self who is involved and God's self cannot be diminished. Thus, Rahner uses the concept to both affirm God's involvement and protect God's otherness.[259] As an explanation of how God participates, without jeopardising God's immutability, it is an option but it does not solve the problem.[260]

For Rahner, the gift of grace brings with it primal knowledge of what it means to be human. Being human is bound to humankind's relationship with God. This is a complex relationship,

> What we are really dealing with is a transcendental experience which gives evidence of itself in human existence and is operative in that existence. We can only appeal here to those individual experiences which a person has and can have of God's self-communication. They cannot indeed be recognized with *unambiguous* and reflexive certainty within an individual's experience, prescinding from possible exceptions, but they are nevertheless not simply and absolutely nonexistent for reflection.[261]

All God-talk is *a posteriori* knowledge. There is prior experience and this is the mystery of God;[262] "In this unnamed and unsignposted expanse of our consciousness there dwells that which we call God".[263] The concept of mystery is fundamental to Rahner's vision of presence and absence (3.2).[264] Mystery is not a question but the answer graciously posited by God in humankind.[265] Consequently, humankind is innately oriented toward mystery and the divine orientation is a "constitutive element" of what it means to be human.[266] In the disclosure of mystery, humankind receives a revelation of the incomprehensible God; "What is made intelligible is grounded ultimately in the one thing that is

257 CS, pp. 38-39.
258 TT, p. 36.
259 "Incarnation", TI 4, p. 113.
260 Reno, *Ordinary*, p. 120, n. 58 and p. 123.
261 FCF, pp. 130-131.
262 *Ibid.* p. 52.
263 "Experiencing the spirit", Kelly ed., p. 227.
264 FCF, p. 119.
265 "Concept of Mystery", TI 4, p. 41.
266 *Ibid.* p. 49.

self-evident, in mystery".[267] In Rahner, absence is part of human experience of the mystery of God in the world. In particular, it is the description of the universal experience of the hiddenness of God in history.[268] This hidden God is nameless and is experienced as "distant and aloof",[269]

> So the Whither of transcendence is there in its own proper way of aloofness and absence. It bestows itself upon us by refusing itself, by keeping silence, by staying afar ... It can never be approached directly or experienced immediately.[270]

In the hiddenness of God, humankind encounters the reality of the silence of God.[271] In short, the absence of God is a real experience, but God is not absent in reality.[272] The name of this God is "the holy mystery" and the mystery is the incomprehensibleness of God.[273] When God is not hidden, God is still incomprehensible and so God can be experienced but God cannot be fully known.[274]

Rahner has been criticised for reducing revelation to personal encounter[275] but for him the personal encounter takes place in relation to others in the midst of history. Thus, he places his understanding of the experience of mystery into the context of intersubjectivity. To appreciate this, it is important to return to one of Rahner's presuppositions, namely, human knowing is receptive knowing. This means humankind is present to itself, when it is in the presence of an object.[276] Thus, history refers to both the context of the object that elicits self-presence and the medium through which the awareness of self-presence is expressed. Rahner contends that in the context of history, humankind is human in a sensible mode.[277] A material being is not an isolated being, on the contrary, "To be human is to be one among many ... We are actually human only in a

267 FCF, p. 22.
268 "Hiddeness", TI 16, p. 237.
269 "Concept of Mystery", TI 4, pp. 52-56.
270 *Ibid.* p. 52.
271 HW, pp. 64, 88, 151; cf. Reno, *Ordinary*, p. 222.
272 "Concept of Mystery", TI 4, p. 55.
273 *Ibid.* p. 61.
274 ES, p. 7.
275 McDermott, "Methodological Shift", pp. 257-260, cf. Moltmann, *Theology Today*, p. 86.
276 HW, p. 96.
277 *Ibid.* p. 106.

humanity".[278] Here, therefore, is an insight into Rahner's incipient understanding of intersubjectivity: others are the human *objects* that elicit a response from within an individual.[279] To sum up, presence and absence have their origin in God. Presence is experienced by virtue of the innate gift of divine orientation and hence is always self-presence. This does not mean that the human self is regarded as the source of presence, only that presence is mediated intrinsically. In addition, this does not mean that God's self is captive to experience. The experience of presence is vital, but the initiative is with God.[280] The relationship between presence and absence is dialectical and this reflects the incomprehensible character of God. At the least, dialectical implies a notion of dialogue with the *other*.[281] So, if presence is the "absolute proximity" of God,[282] then absence is the other, the "distant aloofness" of God.[283]

Conclusion

In this study the ambiguity of experience is interpreted in terms of presence and absence. Subsequently, a postmetaphysical view of presence has been developed. The theologies of Tillich and Rahner have then been interpreted from the perspective of the ambiguity of the experience of God. Overall, their theological approaches to absence lack the specificity of today (cf. feminist, liberation theologies). Both Tillich and Rahner however, intuitively, implicitly and consistently recognise the ambiguity of the experience of God in terms of an interplay between presence and absence in which absence is not dismissed or devalued (cf. God's space, God's hiddenness) but is seen as an integral part of the experience of God in the world. The task now is to apply explicitly this understanding of experience as presence and absence to the two Christological themes of the Incarnation and the Death-Resurrection event.

278   *Ibid.* p. 111.
279   *Ibid.* pp. 120-121.
280   "Concept of God", TI 21, p. 189.
281   Baggini and Fosl, p. 44.
282   "Concept of Mystery", TI 4, p. 61.
283   *Ibid.* pp. 52, 55, 56, 67.

4.3. Christology

4.3.1. Tillich, Rahner and Christology

Theism and Other Approaches

In this part, the aim is to show something of where Tillich and Rahner fit in relation to today's spectrum of approaches to Christology. As a preliminary step, it is noted that there are a number of obvious differences to consider between their Christologies and contemporary perspectives. The Christologies of Tillich and Rahner were premised largely on a particular version of theism. Moreover, they relied on metaphysical accounts to explain the universal significance of Christ. Within postmodernity, there are Christologies that are not based on theism *per se*.[284] There is also now a willingness to focus attention on the particular without supplying metaphysical justification.[285] The differences between the two periods are significant on these counts alone.

The Real Jesus

The next step is to look at the issues Tillich and Rahner wrestled with. In their era, history, historical consciousness and historical reductionism were seen as symptoms of the Enlightenment and the development of modernity. They were interested in history in general terms, but Tillich and Rahner saw themselves primarily as theologians and presumed that theology had a different set of objectives to history. Moreover, they were actively reacting to the historical positivism of their day. Today, there has been a revival of interest in the relationship between history and Christology. The so-called *third quest* for the historical Jesus has captured the public imagination.[286] This reflects something of modernity's

---

284 Page, *Incarnation*, pp. 141, 162.
285 Brock, *Journeys*, pp. 51, 67.
286 St Peter's Cathedral, Adelaide, normally has two hundred people at its main Sunday Eucharist. When Bishop John Spong preached there in 2003, six hundred people attended. They were mainly traditional Anglicans who were grateful that at last they were being presented with the *facts*; cf. L.T. Johnson, *The Real Jesus: The Mis-*

quest for certainty. Correspondingly, there is a renewed sense of confidence that history, in conjunction with sociological insights, will provide the facts and once the facts are known then the dogmatic interpretations of the Church can be revised or even dispensed with.[287] For example, Mack asserts that the importance of Jesus "as a thinker and teacher can certainly be granted and even greatly enhanced once we allow the thought that Jesus was not a god incarnate but a real historical person".[288] Luke Johnson represents the other side of the debate.[289] His main criticism of the third quest and the Jesus Seminar concerns historical reductionism.[290] For Johnson, members of the Jesus Seminar are in danger of granting history foundational status.[291] However, historiography has its problems.[292] In addition, it is important to understand the historian and the historian's social context.[293] The irony is that in many ways these issues are similar to those Tillich and Rahner addressed.

---

guided Quest for the Historical Jesus and the Truth of the Traditional Gospels, (San Francisco: Harper Collins, 1996), p. 32, Johnson describes Spong as an amateur, who is representative of the popular face of the third quest. E.S. Fiorenza has a useful description of the third quest in "Jesus of Nazareth in historical research", T. Wiley ed., *Thinking of Christ: Proclamation, Explanation, Meaning*, (New York and London: Continuum, 2003), pp. 34-37.

287 Keating, "Epistemology", p. 27. he asserts "no sharp separation between the historical Jesus and the object of Christian faith is possible without denying the capacity of the historian to attain any truth about Jesus whatsoever. Short of this extreme step, theologians must seek greater clarity on the precise place of the quest in their enterprise".

288 B.L. Mack, *Who Wrote the New Testament? The Making of the Christian Myth*, (San Francisco: Harper Collins, 1995), p. 47.

289 Johnson, *The Real Jesus*, pp. 2, 5, according to Johnson, the New Testament offers the *real* Jesus and this is also what the Church experiences. However, he does not adequately define the real Jesus.

290 *Ibid.* p. 112, Johnson argues that they do not adequately treat the narrative framework of the Gospels, as a framework can in fact be established using lines of convergence. Similarly, Fiorenza, *Jesus of Nazareth*, p. 33.

291 Keating, "Epistemology", p. 28.

292 Carr, "What is history?" p. 3.

293 *Ibid.* pp. 34, 38, cf. Scott, "After history?" p. 1.

The formative period for the personal and intellectual development of Tillich and Rahner took place between "the first and the second quest, which began with the work of Martin Kähler in 1896 and ended with Ernst Käsemann's revival of historical-Jesus research in 1953".[294] While Tillich and Rahner were influenced by philosophy, they were also part of a broader theological movement which was comparatively sceptical about the promised outcomes of the quest for the historical Jesus. Specifically, they were critics of historical reductionism, and at this level, this makes them precursors of postmodernity. Moreover, they respected the achievements that had been made by means of historical-critical method, but for them the focus was on the contemporary meaning of Christ. Indeed, Tillich argues that research into the historical Jesus had failed.[295] For him, the reality of the Christ-event is actualised by faith through human participation and not by means of historical evidence.[296] Human participation means it is not possible to get behind biblical texts via historical criticism to the historical Jesus, because Jesus in the texts is the Christ of human faith.[297] Anticipating Johnson, Tillich claims,

> Faith can say that the reality which is manifest in the New Testament picture of Jesus as the Christ has saving power for those who are grasped by it, no matter how much or how little can be traced to the historical figure who is called Jesus of Nazareth.[298]

Likewise, Rahner accepts the general findings of modern scientific exegesis about the life of Jesus.[299] However, Rahner asserts that the limits of exegesis are determined by dogmatics, this meant that he interpreted exegetical findings from within the dogmatic setting of salvation history.[300] For Rahner, dogmatics includes the *a priori* (transcendental) level of analysis, whereas exegesis concentrates on the *a posteriori*

294 Fiorenza, "Jesus of Nazareth", p. 33.
295 ST II, p. 105.
296 *Ibid.* p. 114.
297 *Ibid.* pp. 114-115.
298 DF, p. 88. As noted, Tillich later opts for the term image over picture (e.g. UC, p. 154).
299 FCF, p. 247.
300 "Remarks", TI 13, p. 208.

(categorical) level.[301] For Rahner, the significance of Christ can only be appreciated by means of human experience.

Overriding Theological Concerns

The issues raised by the quest for historical Jesus are complex. They pertain to the nature of history, the use of history in exegesis, the relationship between history and narrative and the relationship between narrative and theology (as outlined in the previous paragraph). Tillich and Rahner had a commitment to the importance of history and considered the results of New Testament exegesis as important. This raises something of an anomaly, in that while they thought it was important for Christology to be grounded in the results of New Testament exegesis, they did not feel bound to them. Neither of them resolved this grey area. In fairness to them, the relationship between historical figure, text and salvific figure is complex. History is not the same as narrative.[302] Theology may use insights from history, but in many ways it is arguably more like philosophy than history.[303] Furthermore, while historical and sociological techniques have improved over the last hundred years, there are limits as to what can be gained from socio-historical reconstructions. One of the limits is the influence of personal bias on any reconstruction, as Schweitzer argued in relation to the first quest.

> The Jesus of Nazareth who came forward publicly as the Messiah, who preached the ethic of the kingdom of God, who founded the kingdom of heaven on earth, and died to give his work its final consecration, never existed. He is a figure designed by rationalism, endowed with the life by liberalism, and clothed by modern theology in a historical garb.[304]

In the end, because their work was governed by broad theological concerns, Tillich and Rahner were not interested in exploring comprehen-

---

301 "Between exegesis", TI 11, p. 194.
302 Fredriksen, "What does Jesus have to do with Christ?" p. 6; J. McEvoy, "Narrative or history? – A false dilemma: The theological significance of the historical Jesus", *Pacifica* 14 (2001), pp. 279-280.
303 Fredriksen, "What does Jesus have to do with Christ?" p. 5.
304 A. Schweitzer, *The Quest of the Historical Jesus*, first complete edition J. Bowden ed., (London: SCM Press, 1906, 1913, 2000), p. 478.

sively the impact of exegetical insights about the historical Jesus on the meaning of the Christ of faith.

4.3.2. A Symbolic Reading of Christological Themes

Both Tillich and Rahner make a distinction between signs and symbols: the distinction depends in part on social context and who it is that imbues a symbol with significance. The strength of this approach is that it is consistent with their emphasis on experience (cf. perception) and that it overcomes some of the problems associated with extrinsic approaches (e.g. causality). The weakness, however, is that the distinction seems relative to context and individual perception. It begs the question of whether or not it is a distinction. Certainly, the distinction is not always clear. Nevertheless, symbols are of fundamental importance to the theological systems of Tillich and Rahner. In particular, their understanding of symbol shapes their view of the significance of Christ, the Incarnation and the Death-Resurrection event.

Their approach to symbol is conducive to this study's interest in the ambiguity of the experience of God. For example, in Tillich and Rahner, a symbol and the perception of the significance of a symbol are inherently ambiguous.[305] This is because the significance of a symbol is dependent upon the perception (i.e. experience) of the individual or the group that attributes significance to the symbol. Further, for Tillich signs and symbols point beyond them selves.[306] However, unlike the sign, "The symbol participates in the reality which is symbolized".[307] Admittedly, Tillich has been criticised for failing to distinguish clearly between "symbolic or metaphorical and analogical speaking of God"[308] and confusing symbolic modes.[309] The distinction between symbols and religious symbols is not clear in Tillich. It seems that what makes a symbol specifically a religious symbol for Tillich has to do with the consciousness and intention of the individual.

305 Cooke, *Distancing of God*, p. 259.
306 DF, p. 41.
307 ST II, p. 9.
308 Gamwell, "Speaking of God after Aquinas", p. 201, n. 13.
309 Weisbaker, "Aesthetic elements", p. 253; cf. Macquarrie, *Principles*, p. 135, n. 10.

At this stage, it is important to signal another criticism of Tillich and Rahner, that is, why distinguish symbols as a special category of sign in the first place? Surely, depending on the perception (i.e. experience) of an individual or a group any sign could be a symbol? Rahner is aware that the distinction between sign and symbol is not straightforward.[310] Therefore, on the basis of a particular understanding of revelation, this study contends that the distinction between symbols and signs is relative and is based on the fact that an individual or a group attributes to a sign the status of symbol. For instance, the Eucharist is a meaningful symbol for many Christian traditions but not for the Society of Friends or the Salvation Army.

In the case of Christ, the concept of symbol helps Tillich and Rahner mine the theological significance of Christ from history and Scripture to apply it to the present. Christ is the meaning imputed, discovered and discerned through the experience of the disciples of the Jesus of history and, ultimately, the Jesus of the biblical text and the Jesus of history is the tangible aspect of the symbol,

> But although the historical Jesus of Nazareth is not the sufficient ground for an affirmation of his resurrection, he is its necessary ground. One cannot affirm a resurrection of Jesus without reference to Jesus of Nazareth. Moreover, one must account in some way for the resurrection of *Jesus*. The one affirmed to be risen was Jesus, and such an affirmation necessarily presupposes a memory of him.[311]

The description of Christ as the symbol of God provides them with a means of understanding the ongoing experience of God in the world. In Tillich and Rahner, their understanding of symbol forms the background for how they interpret the meaning of the Incarnation and the Death-Resurrection event (4.4; 4.5). Moreover, no matter how good the historical reconstruction, the historical Jesus is still a reconstruction. While Tillich and Rahner had a place for the historical Jesus in their systems, the emphasis in both Tillich and Rahner is on the contemporary meaning of Christ and not the historical Jesus. For them, meaning is discovered in experience and expressed in and through symbols. Hence, the notion of Christ as symbol explains how they interpret the contemporary (modern) meaning of Christ. In short, what they say about the contemporary mean-

310 "Symbol", TI 4, p. 225.
311 Haight, *Jesus Symbol of God*, p. 142.

ing of Christ hinges on two key themes: the Incarnation and the Death/Resurrection event. While the importance of these themes in Tillich and Rahner cannot be restricted to their appreciation of symbol, their appreciation of symbol has a significant impact on how they read these themes.

4.4. The Incarnation

The aim of this section is to examine the theme of the Incarnation in Tillich and Rahner in relation to the study's theme of the presence of God in the world. For both, the Incarnation is a crucial Christological theme, implicitly for Tillich and explicitly for Rahner. The contention here is that this theme is illuminated by an understanding of the experience of God as presence and absence. Initially, and for the sake of practical convenience, the Incarnation and the Death-Resurrection event are treated separately. In Tillich and Rahner however, the Incarnation and the Death-Resurrection form one salvific event. In Tillich, they are "interdependent symbols".[312] In Rahner, they form a unity.[313]

Tillich

The Incarnation is an important but implicit part of Tillich's Christology. For him, the sticking point is the problem of maintaining Christ's full participation in the Divine along with the full humanity of the Christ. To begin, in Tillich the original and final revelation of the presence of God is manifested in Christ the incarnate *Logos*.[314] According to Tillich, the idea of the incarnate *Logos* makes sense only in relation to the universal *Logos*.[315] They are the same.[316] However, Christ as the *Logos* raises two issues. First, Christ as the *Logos* produces a Trinitarian problem (i.e. the

312 ST II, p.153.
313 FCF, 266.
314 ST I, pp. 126-127.
315 BRUR, p. 75.
316 *Ibid.*

270

problem of explaining how the universal is manifested in the concrete).[317] Second, Christ as the *Logos* provides an answer to the Trinitarian problem (i.e. self-transcendence). Self-transcendence is Tillich's attempt to explain how human life participates in divine life. For Tillich, this participation is possible because one particular personal life participates fully in divine life.[318] And Christ is the decisive expression of the presence of God in the world because of this full participation in the divine. In addition, Tillich is concerned about "the monophysitic distortion of the picture of Jesus as the Christ".[319] Therefore, he wants to affirm the full humanity of Christ in conjunction with Christ's full participation in the divine.[320] Thus, Christ experiences finitude and, although the New Testament portrays Jesus in mythical terms (e.g. temptation stories), "A real, individual life shines through".[321] Hence, the presence of God is manifested in the full humanity of Christ.

Tillich interprets the overall theological significance of the Incarnation in terms of the theme of salvation. For Tillich, the Incarnation represents the decisive breakthrough of the presence of God in human history.[322] A new reality has been inaugurated in Christ,[323] which enables humankind to transcend the limits of existence (2.3.1).[324] It is possible to transcend the limits of existence because Christ overcame the fractured nature of human existence and inaugurated a new salvific era.[325] While salvation has a cosmic sweep, it is grounded in a personal life.[326] It is grounded in the experience of Jesus. In particular, the outworking of salvation hinges on this notion of one personal life; "the Logos is not metamorphosis but his total manifestation in a personal life".[327] But there are problems. On the basis of an unclear premise Tillich asserts that, unlike a group, only a personal life has a centre. This partly reflects an

317 ST I, p. 17.
318 ST II, pp. 120-121, 149.
319 *Ibid.* p. 128.
320 UC, p. 137.
321 ST II, p. 151.
322 TPE, p. 53, a kairos moment; OTB, p. 28, the idea of *breakthrough* in relation to revelation.
323 ST I, pp. 49-50.
324 ST II, p. vii.
325 *Ibid.* p. 97.
326 *Ibid.* pp. 166-168.
327 *Ibid.* p. 149.

understanding that is grounded in the tradition of the subject, going back to Descartes and Kant (1.2.3). That is, the individual subject is defined as having a centre or being the centre. This also reflects Tillich's conviction about what has been revealed in Christ. On the basis of Tillich's theology of revelation, he asserts that only this one particular personal life, that is, this Jesus is capable of the requisite act of self-negation, because Jesus is characterised by a unique connection i.e. "the undisrupted unity of the center of his being with God".[328] This unity is maintained in the midst of estrangement. To sum up, Tillich asserts that Christ is the definitive expression of the presence of God in the world. However, his argument is tautological in that Christ is the definitive expression of the presence of God because Christ participates fully in the presence of God. In defense, Tillich would argue that this is part of what it means to receive the original revelation, upon which subsequent revelation is dependent, but at this stage, it is not a convincing justification for treating Christ as the definitive expression of presence. This study is not exploring the issue of whether there was more than one incarnation. What is important here is that Tillich's argument for the Incarnation is not convincing. In contrast, his argument that the Incarnation means Christ experiences estrangement is more convincing for and pertinent to this study.

In Tillich's theology, absence is a symptom of the experience of estrangement (4.2.4) and Christ, who is the definitive expression of presence, experienced the absence of God by virtue of the experience of estrangement. In this context, the concept of paradox is important. It explains how Christ simultaneously experienced absence and maintained his unique, uninterrupted, ontological connection with God.[329] For Tillich, Jesus the Christ as a theological designation is a paradox.[330] Paradox is *de facto* an article of faith in Tillich, because those who profess Jesus as the Christ must assert the paradox that he who overcame estrangement participated in it.[331] The acceptance of the paradox is the state of being grasped by a power that bursts into experience. Thus, it is a new reality, which does not defy the laws of formal logic.[332] Further,

328 *Ibid.* p. 138.
329 *Ibid.*
330 *Ibid.* p. 92, cf. ST I, pp. 135-136.
331 ST II, p. 97.
332 *Ibid.* p. 92.

Tillich's concept of paradox can be interpreted by means of this study's conception of experience. Absence as well as presence is part of the experience of God and there is no permanent boundary between the two; rather a recurring interplay between the difference and identity they share. This is consistent with Tillich's preference for "dynamic-relational concepts" (e.g. polarities).[333]

In summary, the Incarnation is an important but understated premise of Tillich's Christology. It makes human self-transcendence possible. In the Incarnation, God in Christ participates fully in the ambiguities of the fragmented human predicament. The negativities of experience, absence as well as presence, are incorporated into the "eternal God-man-unity".[334] Conversely, humankind participates in God through an encounter with the presence of God in the world in Christ ("The Christ is God-for-us!").[335] The experience of the absence of God, entails a loss of essentiality (2.2.3), and evokes a longing for the presence of God in the world. However, there are limits to human participation in divine life (i.e. the gap), which are set in place by two factors: existential finitude and the transcendent character of God. Tillich however, recognises the danger of reinforcing the Kantian gap and failing to explain participation in the Divine, hence, the importance of self-transcendence.[336] The presumption behind self-transcendence is that "the finite world points beyond itself".[337]

Rahner

For Rahner, Christ is the decisive mode of presence of God in the world. Human self-transcendence reveals the incarnational structure of humanity, which explains the salvific import of Christ. For Rahner, the Incarnation is the central mystery of the Christian faith,[338] and the climax of the evolutionary process of God's self-communication.[339] This is based on

333 *Ibid.* p. 148.
334 *Ibid.*
335 *Ibid.* p. 100.
336 *Ibid.* p. 9.
337 *Ibid.* p. 7.
338 "Incarnation", TI 4, p. 105.
339 "Evolutionary view", TI 5, pp. 160-161.

his observation of an emerging evolutionary scientific world-view.[340] Subsequently, Rahner posits that all things have their origin in God.[341] In his view, there is only one Incarnation because God is present in Christ in a unique way. Moreover, Rahner declares that mystery must have for humankind, "a genuine intelligibility and desirability".[342] So he explores classical Christology to bring to modernity a theology of the Incarnation that has these features as Classical Christology is a descending Christology; it does not clarify the link between Christ as Incarnate *Logos* and Christ as saviour.[343] For Rahner, however, Christology has two sides: ascending and descending, and it is the ascending side that is coupled to saving history.[344] The link between the two sides can be explained by Rahner's early metaphysics of knowledge; namely, the *a priori* (transcendental) condition explains the *a posteriori* (historical) experience.[345] Thus, humankind has a transcendental orientation toward a saving event in history by virtue of the supernatural existential. This transcendental orientation is elicited by an encounter with Christ who is the definitive expression of the presence of God in the world.

That Christ is the decisive mode of presence raises a complicated theological issue for Rahner. He is determined to affirm the presence of God in Christ in the world without threatening his commitment to a theology of the immutability of God. This tension is a major concern in Rahner's theological system, surfacing in his work on sacramental causality in particular and the supernatural existential in general. In a christological context the tension is worked out in relation to the hypostatic union. Rahner sees the validity of the Incarnation as dependent on the hypostatic union. Subsequently, he uses the concept of *communicatio idiomatum* (3.3.2). If *without separation* is overemphasised, then one of the two natures presides over the union and the concept of distinct natures is undermined. If *without mixture* is overemphasised, then the union is undermined.[346] Nevertheless, *communicatio idiomatum* explains

340 *Ibid.* pp. 166-167.
341 *Ibid.* p. 161.
342 "Incarnation", ET, p. 695.
343 "Christology Today?" TI 17, p. 29.
344 "Two basic types", TI 13, pp. 213-214.
345 "Brief observations", TI 21, p. 235.
346 "Jesus Christ", ET, p. 762, for Rahner the problem of identification occurs in relation to the copula *is*. In classical formulations, the copula presumes two separate re-

but does not resolve the problem of one person in two natures.[347] Further, Rahner is able to address more convincingly the one person in two natures on the basis of the concept of unity-in-difference. In general, spirit and matter form a unity but spirit has priority over matter. Matter develops toward spirit.[348] The development involves a becoming.[349] This self-transcending movement is from the lower to the higher order of being by virtue of the power of being-itself.[350] Humanity expresses a type of transcendence.[351] Humankind constitutes a breakthrough in the world's self-transcendence.[352] Rahner explains humankind's self-transcendence in terms of consciousness.[353] In this context, matter is not a problem to be overcome because it makes the experience of the *other* possible.[354] In other words, there is no experience of the presence of God in the world apart from matter.

Self-transcendence reveals the incarnational structure of experience and this structure is the basis for Rahner's claim that the Incarnation of Christ is unique.[355] The Incarnation is a special case of self-transcendence because God is not just disclosing *something* of God's self, God is disclosing *God's self*. Moreover, Rahner sees the Incarnation of Christ in the context of the history of salvation, where the Incarnation is the climax of the salvific process in which the presence of God is realised in the world. Hence, the hypostatic union is "this mystery itself in an unsurpassable form".[356] Rahner's theology of symbol helps explain the nature of the hypostatic union, which is the heart of his theology of Incarnation. From his theology of symbol, it is clear that Christ is more than an exemplar for Rahner. The Incarnation means that the presence of God is in the world in a new and decisive way.[357] Jesus the Christ was a

---

alities: divine and human, hence, the importance of the boundaries set by Chalcedon (i.e. without separation/without mixture).

347 "Current problems", TI 1, pp. 179-180.
348 "Evolutionary view", TI 5, p. 164. FCF, p. 184.
349 "Evolutionary view", TI 5, p. 164.
350 *Ibid.* pp. 167-168.
351 FCF, p. 187.
352 *Ibid.* p. 181.
353 "Evolutionary view", TI 5, p. 163.
354 *Ibid.* pp. 164-167.
355 FCF, p. 218.
356 "Concept of Mystery", TI 4, p. 69.
357 CS, p. 15.

prophet and a saviour, but he was more.[358] Therefore, he is the *absolute* saviour. Consequently, as the symbol of God, Christ confers the saving power of God. It is true that Christ is an exemplar, but Christ as exemplar is able to cause something in a sacramental (symbolic) way. Later in his career, Rahner locates his understanding of the Incarnation within a broader, historical, evolutionary movement of becoming; arguing that the evolutionary process is a redemptive process and the impetus for the redemptive process is the "efficacious salvific will" of God.[359] This redemptive process means God creates and sustains the world and God will bring the world to its consummation by means of God's self-emptying activity in the Incarnation (i.e. God's self-communication). This is the climax of the redemptive process. This is the gift of divine presence. Thus, the Incarnation is the definitive and decisive expression of the presence of God in the world.

Conclusion

There are three points to be made here concerning the Incarnation in Tillich and Rahner. First, for both, the Incarnation is the decisive expression of the presence of God in the world. Compared with Rahner, Tillich has an under-developed theology of the Incarnation, in that it is neither explicit nor expansive. However, while his interest in the Incarnation is implicit, it is important and pervasive. Overall, Tillich is more concerned about the existential impact of the New Being than the theological constitution of the Incarnation. Nevertheless, in Tillich the Incarnation is a given. Compared with Tillich, Rahner's interest in the Incarnation is considerable, all embracing and explicit. For him, the Incarnation is the major focus of his Christological vision. For Rahner, unlike Tillich, nothing can be taken for granted with the Incarnation.

Second, for both Tillich and Rahner, absence is part of the experience of the Incarnation. For Tillich, absence has an explicit role in his theology of the Incarnation. The Incarnation means Christ, the definitive expression of presence, experiences the absence of God because he participates in existential estrangement. For Rahner, absence has an im-

358 "To believe in Jesus Christ?" TI 18, p. 147, i.e. reality and sign.
359 "Salvation", SM 5, p. 406.

276

plicit role in his theology of the Incarnation, which becomes more explicit in conjunction with the Death-Resurrection event. For Rahner, it is critical that Jesus Christ was fully human, "He has a true body capable (before his resurrection) of suffering".[360] Prior to the resurrection, Christ was capable of experiencing suffering.[361] Therefore, if Christ was fully human, then Christ had the capacity to experience absence, which is an experience of suffering. After all, absence in Rahner is the *universal* experience of the hiddenness of God in *human* history (3.2.1).[362]

Third, in the face of modernity, the Incarnation in Tillich and Rahner represents a vigorous affirmation of the presence of God in the world. However, their claim that God is uniquely present in the Incarnation does not resonate with postmodernism.[363] Tillich and Rahner were aware that there was a tension between the Incarnation of Christ, as the decisive expression of presence, and their respect for the world religions. However, their attempts to create a theology (e.g. latent church; anonymous Christian), which accounts for other religions, submerged the very tension they sought to redress. For example, Tillich, towards the end of his career, expressed a desire to re-visit his theology in relation to the world religions.[364] Nonetheless, it seems that the one personal life of Christ is still the implicit basis of his salvific metanarrative, or at the least, it still functions implicitly as *the* measure of the validity of other religions.[365] The problem is that Tillich's Christology is bound to his metaphysical foundations. All this betrays the complex and unsolved philosophical

---

360 "Incarnation" ET, p. 694.

361 *Ibid.*

362 "Concept of Mystery", TI 4, p. 52.

363 Macquarrie *(Jesus Christ)* develops a Christology based on a principle of transcendence in which Jesus is the archetype of humankind. The key issue in the book is the identity/difference dilemma. For Macquarrie, Jesus is different from us by the degree to which he embodies the capacity for transcendence (p. 359). However, his use of the concept *Christ-event* illustrates the problems with the book. He acknowledges the analogical nature of theological language (pp. 9, 13). The Christ-event is the central analogy and the Christ-event stands for the interpretation of the significance of Christ in the life of early Christian communities. For Macquarrie, this interpretation is not the opinion of an individual but the experience of the group; it is a social phenomenon (pp. 83, 163, 315). The Christ-event embodies the key moments in the life of the group (pp. 346, 398). He modifies this view in more traditional terms in *Christology Revisited* (London: SCM Press, 1998).

364 CEWR, p. 76.

365 *Ibid.* p. 73.

problem of universality and particularity. In Tillich and Rahner this problem is a corollary of their ontotheological perspectives.[366] Each of them is committed to universal being, which they used to justify their systems, so that they cannot address the tension without the risk of surrendering their foundations. While the resolution of the tension is beyond the scope of this study, it needs to be noted because it reveals the limits of their ontotheological perspectives.[367]

4.5. The Death-Resurrection Event

In this section, the contention is that the theme of the Death-Resurrection event in Tillich and Rahner's theology is illuminated by an understanding of the experience of God as presence and absence.

Tillich

This study has shown that Tillich's view of estrangement can be interpreted in terms of the experience of absence (2.2). If the death of Christ is the definitive expression of estrangement, then it follows that the death of the Christ is the definitive expression of absence.[368] Further, absence

---

366 As well as Rahner's commitment to the concept of the immutability of God.

367 Knitter, *Jesus*, this begins with a description of his experience of religious pluralism. He argues that while Jesus is *truly* God's saving word, Jesus is not the *only* saving word (e.g. Acts 4:12; p. xvii). For him, there is no contradiction between the "message and mission of Jesus and valuing and taking seriously the religious vision and mission of other persons" (p. 1). He develops a "globally responsible, correlational dialogue of religions" model of mission (p. 17). The model assumes: the importance of dialogue, the existence of true religions and the world's need for such a model in the face of injustice (p. 35). So Knitter has to revise the notion of the uniqueness of Jesus, because of this correlational dimension (p. 35). He examines objections, which can be made of his model. The main objection concerns the contention that Jesus is the *only* saviour. Knitter describes the *one and only* language as "performative language" (p. 68); the NT language is more like the language of lovers than philosophers.

368 DF, pp. 97-98.

278

represents for him the experience of a vacuum rather than the actual absence of God. This is also true of the cross. For Tillich, while the cross is the definitive symbol of absence, God is still present. This is because the unity with God cannot be destroyed,

> The acceptance of the cross, both during his life and at the end of it, is the decisive test of his unity with God, of his complete transparency to the ground of being. Only in view of the crucifixion can the Fourth Gospel have him say that "he who believes in me does not believe in *me*" (John 12:44).[369]

For Tillich, the symbol of the cross functions as a safeguard for personal faith and ecclesial life. Faith can embrace the idolatrous component but "in the picture of the Christ itself the criterion against its idolatrous abuse is given – the cross".[370] The cross guards against the risk of attributing ultimacy to symbolic expressions of ultimate concern. The cross, as a symbol and expression of absence, is an encounter with non-being, which militates against the reification of all Christian symbols.

The importance of absence in Tillich is evident in his discussions on estrangement. In this context, he refers to the basic ontological structure of self-world polarity. For Tillich, estrangement means the loss of self and loss of a world.[371] Without a world, there is no presence because presence is mediated presence. Thus, the absence of God is a symptom of self-loss and as such it is a measure of finitude.[372] However, Tillich is not intending to say that God is absent in reality, only that humankind experiences absence in estrangement.[373] Specifically, the experience of absence can be explained in terms of the ontological shock.[374] Thus, absence is an experience and expression of the ontological shock. Tillich describes the experience of the ontological shock as simultaneously "preserved in the annihilating power of the divine presence (*mysterium tremendum*)" and "overcome in the elevating power of the divine presence (*mysterium fascinosum*)".[375] The "annihilating power of the divine presence" is the negative side of mystery. The negative side is experi-

369 ST I, p. 136.
370 DF, p. 104.
371 ST II, pp. 59-62.
372 *Ibid.* p. 73.
373 *Ibid.* p. 78.
374 *Ibid.* pp. 67-68.
375 ST I, p. 113.

enced as the awareness of finitude and confrontation with the abyss.[376] The abyss is "the depth of the divine life, its inexhaustible and ineffable character"[377] and "the abyss of possible nonbeing".[378] The "elevating power of the divine presence" is the positive side. The positive side is experienced in revelation where "the mystery appears as ground and not only as abyss".[379] The negative and positive sides do not form a binary opposition,[380] as "the ground of being is at the same time the abyss of any definite being".[381] In ontological terms, this means "Non-being is the negation of being within being itself".[382] So just as being and non-being have their unity in being, presence and absence have their unity in the experience of God in the world, "The God above God of theism is present, although hidden, in every divine-human encounter".[383] For Tillich, this is a mystery that has been hidden; the paradox of religion is that the mystery has now been revealed.

The importance of absence in Tillich is illustrated by his concept of atonement. Comparatively, the doctrine of atonement has a secondary role in his Christology. This is because it has been subsumed under his soteriology, which focuses on the healing effects of the presence of God.[384] Nonetheless, Tillich interprets atonement as "the effect of the New Being in Jesus as the Christ on those who are grasped by it in their state of estrangement".[385] In his system, the atoning processes come from God.[386] For Tillich, God's removal of guilt and punishment does not mean the impact of estrangement is minimised, on the contrary, God's atoning processes mean God-in-Christ participates in estrangement. That is, Christ experiences the absence of God.

This study re-interprets Tillich's view of the resurrection of Christ as the symbol of the abiding presence of God in the world. Tillich claims

---

376 *Ibid.*
377 *Ibid.* p. 156.
378 *Ibid.* p. 164.
379 *Ibid.* p. 110.
380 ST I, p. 60, negative and positive, absence and presence, form a correlation that is "the logical interdependence of concepts, as in polar relations".
381 "Symbol and knowledge", *Mainworks* IV, p. 273.
382 LPJ, p. 38.
383 TCB, p. 180.
384 ST II, pp. 170-176.
385 *Ibid.* p. 170.
386 *Ibid.* pp. 173-176.

the resurrected Christ has "the character of spiritual presence".[387] Moreover, he links spiritual presence with the experience of disciples.[388] Tillich acknowledges that his reflections on the resurrection seem theoretical.[389] But he asserts that "a real experience" lies behind the biblical accounts, in that the disciples found this experience of spiritual presence commensurate with the post-exilic Jewish symbol of resurrection.[390] The familiar symbol of the resurrection made sense of their new experience of presence. For Tillich, this is more than a coincidence of spiritual presence on the one hand and the experience of the disciples on the other hand, because the reception and naming of presence as the resurrection of Christ, by the disciples, is part of the resurrection. Therefore, the resurrection, which is initiated by God, is conceived within the experience of the disciples.[391] Tillich admits that there is a danger here of reducing the resurrection to solely a psychological explanation. Consequently, it is important for Tillich to clarify the nature of the relationship between the meaning of the spiritual presence and the role of the disciples within the resurrection experience. Tillich's clarification consists of two elements: the resurrection is not an *ordinary* experience of presence and the event is made up of fact and reception. First of all, the resurrection, like the Incarnation, forms an integral part of Tillich's understanding of the salvific process of the presence of God in the world.[392] In the salvific process, the central event in history is the advent of Christ the New Being,[393] such that the death and resurrection is the decisive revelation of God in human history.[394] Therefore, because the resurrected

387 *Ibid.* p. 157.
388 *Ibid.* p. 154.
389 *Ibid.* p. 158.
390 *Ibid.* p. 154.
391 ST III, p. 308, the disciples represent a "history-bearing group".
392 Schelling, p. 202, this reflects something of Schelling's view of history as a dynamic evolving historical process, which he explains in terms of higher causes "the content of revelation is nothing but a higher history which goes back to the beginning of things and on to the end".
393 ST III, p. 364.
394 "The New Being", TNB, p. 24, "resurrection means the victory of the New state of things, the New Being born out of the death of the Old. Resurrection is not an event that might happen in some remote future, but it is the power of the New Being to create life out of death, here and now, today and tomorrow … Resurrection happens *now*, or it does not happen at all. It happens in us and around us, in soul and history, in nature and universe".

Christ inaugurates a new reality, which takes root in and grows out of the experience of the disciples, the disciples' experience is an *extraordinary* experience of presence.[395] However, this cannot be tested in an empirical sense as it is only received as revelation. Second, an event consists of two parts: the fact and the reception of the fact by a group of followers.[396] In this instance, the fact is the personal life of Christ and the reception is the salvific significance bestowed by the disciples on this experience of spiritual presence. All told, Tillich has been criticised for presenting a modern, individualistic picture of humankind; "He does not question the social conditions and the political conditions of this modern experience of subjectivity".[397] Certainly, Tillich's version of subjectivity is abstract by today's standards. However, Tillich's linking of resurrection and experience prefigures something of postmodernity's understanding of intersubjectivity (1.4.3). Intersubjectivity acknowledges that human identity, ideas and values are all shaped by social interaction and cultural factors (1.2.3). In Tillich, the resurrection is conceived within intersubjectivity. It has social and cultural dimensions. Thus, the resurrection simultaneously takes place in and gives rise to early Christian communities, as it is "a restitution which is rooted in the personal unity between Jesus and God and in the impact of this unity on the minds of the apostles".[398] Hence, the resurrection is both the definitive expression of presence and the confirmation of the indestructibility of presence.

For Tillich, death and resurrection signify two sides of the one salvific event. The salvific effect of the event means it is possible for humankind to transcend the gap between the finite and the infinite. In this context, the presence of God in Tillich is the human awareness of its participation in Divine life. However, God is not part of the subject-object structure.[399] Here is the importance of self-transcendence, where "the finite world points beyond itself".[400] In metaphorical terms, this means transcendence is more a leap over the gap than a bridge crossing. The capacity to leap is God-given; it is inherent in the world and is evoked by an experience of presence and works through human con-

---

395 ST III, p. 308.
396 IRCM, p. 46.
397 Moltmann, *Theology Today*, p. 86.
398 ST II, p. 157.
399 ST I, p. 237.
400 ST II, p. 7.

282

sciousness. However, there are limits to human participation in Divine life, which are set in place by human finitude and the character of God, hence, the need for the death-resurrection event. The Death-Resurrection event surpasses these limits and allows for full but not perfect participation in Divine life. The Death-Resurrection event in Jesus mirrors the absence and presence of God in its most radical form. Specifically, the cross is a symbol that expresses Christ's subjection to existence and the resurrection is a symbol that expresses Christ's conquest of existence.[401] In addition, the absence of God is symptomatic of the experience of estrangement, which in turn is a consequence of sin.[402] Thus, for Tillich, the resurrection as an expression of presence represents the overcoming of the impact of sin.

In summary, a personal act of self-negation is central to the meaning of the cross for Tillich.[403] He interprets the Death-Resurrection event as the final revelation, which occurs in the personal life of Jesus because of Jesus' unique power of self-negation.[404] This act of self-negation means Jesus of Nazareth sacrifices himself completely to Jesus the Christ.[405] Jesus is able to achieve this because he is fully united with "the ground of his being and meaning".[406] Thus, the cross in Tillich is the definitive symbol of self-negation and self-negation the ground of the resurrection. Further, on the basis of the self-negation of Jesus, the resurrection is conceived within the experience of the disciples. Self-transcendence is critical here, in that the resurrection is the definitive instance of self-transcendence. This self-transcendence is evoked by means of an encounter between Divine presence and human consciousness, which takes place within the experience of the disciples. In other words, presence is the catalyst that initiates the resurrection of Christ within the experience of the disciples as the definitive experience of self-transcendence. Thus, on the side of the cross, there is an act of self-negation in a personal life that embraces estrangement. On the side of the resurrection, there is an

---

401 *Ibid.* pp. 152-153.
402 *Ibid.* pp. 46, 49, 56.
403 *Ibid.* p. 134.
404 ST I, p. 133, "a revelation is final if it has the power of negating itself without losing itself".
405 *Ibid.* p. 136.
406 *Ibid.* p. 133.

experience of transcendence in the life of the disciples that overcomes the distance between the humankind and God.

Rahner

This study re-interprets Rahner's notion of the hiddenness of God in terms of the absence of God, arguing that the symbol of the cross is an invitation to embrace absence as the beginning of a redemptive process of transformation. To begin, the death of Jesus in Rahner means the closure of revelation. This argument hinges on a dual assumption that Jesus is the unsurpassable revelation and that the cross is essential to the claim of unsurpassability. Further, the significance of the death of Jesus needs to be seen in the light of the Incarnation, which is "the absolute self-promise of God" expressed through the *Logos* in the hypostatic union.[407] The cross represents Jesus' complete acceptance of the absolute promise. Jesus realised that through his own subjectivity he was the fulfilment of the promise. This realisation forced Jesus to say yes or no to the absolute promise. He said yes in the most emphatic way possible and that was by the way he faced the prospect of his death. For Rahner, the cross represents Jesus' complete acceptance of the gift of God's self-promise. Thus, the death of Jesus is an unsurpassable revelation for two reasons: it is God's self who accepts the gift and the acceptance is without reserve. Further, an existentially oriented understanding of limits shapes Rahner's view of the death of Jesus. The life of Jesus is God's gift of the absolute promise. The death of Jesus means his life is the definitive gift. Indeed, his death is the measure of the value of the gift. Moreover, God accepts the gift. In addition, there is a dialectical relationship between our imminent death and the death of Jesus, which means the death of Jesus serves as a particular kind of example. The inference is that openness to the prospect of our own death leads to new awareness about the significance of the death of Jesus. In turn, identification with the death of Jesus changes our orientation to death.[408]

For Rahner, the death of Jesus is both an example and a "productive model".[409] This is because the death of Jesus transforms the nature of

407 "The death of Jesus", TI 18, p. 136.
408 "Jesus Christ", ET, p. 754-755.
409 "Following the crucified", TI 18, p. 166.

284

death. Rahner explains the transforming nature of the death of Jesus by demonstrating how it is bound to the resurrection, "Jesus died into his resurrection".[410] Subsequently, Rahner refers to "the intrinsic unity of the death and resurrection".[411] The key to Rahner's argument is his conviction that the death and resurrection constitute one event. In death, Jesus accepts completely the self-communication of God. In the resurrection, God accepts completely human reality through the "God-man". In all this, the initiative is with God. God, rather than demanding satisfaction, wills our redemption.[412] All the same, Rahner takes the problem of human sinfulness seriously. For Rahner, humankind needs to be delivered from guilt because it cannot be achieved by human effort alone; it is God's action alone that brings redemption by means of forgiveness.[413] There is an ongoing dialogue here between God and humanity, in that God's offer of redemption requires a human response (a yes or a no). If yes is the answer, Rahner explains the transformation of humanity in terms of sacramental causality.[414] For Rahner, the cross is "the *signum efficax*".[415] The cross is able to function as a symbol because of Jesus' identification with human existence.[416]

In Rahner, the "indissoluble essential connection" between death and resurrection is related to the validity of the connection between the pre-Easter Jesus and the post-Easter Christ. Rahner's theology of the resurrection can be understood in two ways. In negative terms, Rahner asserts that there is a unity of body and spirit, and that this unity undergoes the same fate.[417] The resurrection does not mean that the spirit of Jesus was revived or his body was resuscitated or that the resurrection is an extrinsic event.[418] In positive terms, resurrection means the abiding validity of the person of Jesus, that is, Jesus has been vindicated as absolute saviour and the full reality of the "God-man" has been mediated to the world. This is part of the basis for the "indissoluble essential connection". By

410 *Ibid.*
411 *Ibid.* p. 167.
412 "Salvation", SM 5, p. 430.
413 *Ibid.* p. 427.
414 FCF, p. 284, "God's salvific will, posits the sign".
415 "The Christian understanding of redemption", TI 21, p. 250.
416 "What does it mean today?" TI 18, p. 146.
417 "Between exegesis", TI 11, p. 207.
418 "Jesus Christ", ET, p. 752.

his own admission, Rahner can only provide informed clues concerning the nature of the abiding validity of Jesus; this is because resurrected existence is a different mode of existence. Further, Rahner's theology of the resurrection is premised on his anthropology and the intrinsic capacity for openness, so that the history of freedom "already includes what we mean by the hope of the 'resurrection'".[419] Furthermore, he uses Thomistic metaphysics of knowledge to make a connection between hope as a transcendental condition and the New Testament resurrection appearance accounts. With the act of knowing, an external object is required to elicit the *a priori* universal form. Likewise, with the resurrection, an *a posteriori* experience, as portrayed in the appearance accounts, is required to elicit the *a priori* knowledge of Jesus. That is, the appearance accounts depict the birth of the resurrection faith in the life of the early Church, "Jesus is risen into the faith of the disciples".[420] Like Tillich, Rahner prefigures his interpretation of the Death-Resurrection event with a sense of postmodern intersubjectivity, in that the experience of the disciples is a constitutive part of the resurrection. Indeed, God's self-communication is not restricted to "an isolated and individualized subjectivity".[421] In particular, the experience of the resurrection brings about "the secure objectification of the transcendental hope of resurrection".[422] Rahner is aware of the limits of his own argument.[423] He recognises the non-historical character of the resurrection.[424] All the same, he insists that something *real* lies behind the appearance accounts.[425] The accounts point to "the experience that Jesus is alive".[426]

To sum up, in the death of Jesus, humankind receives an invitation to enter into the experience of absence (i.e. hiddenness). In the resurrection, the disciples experience the presence of the risen Jesus in that the incomprehensible mystery of God emerges from within the depths of their experience by means of self-transcendence. In Rahner, the experience of absence and presence stems from God. Concerning absence, it can be

---

419 "Jesus' resurrection", TI 17, p. 16.
420 FCF, p. 268.
421 *Ibid.* p. 193.
422 "Jesus' resurrection", TI 17, p. 18.
423 "Between exegesis", TI 11, p. 209.
424 FCF, p. 276.
425 "What does it mean today?" TI 18, pp. 152-153.
426 "Jesus' resurrection", TI 17, p. 19.

described as the universal experience of the hiddenness of God in human history.[427] The hidden God is experienced as "distant and aloof".[428] The whither of transcendence is there "in its own proper way of aloofness and absence. It bestows itself upon us by refusing itself, by keeping silence, by staying afar".[429] God is not absent in reality, but the absence of God is a real experience.[430] Concerning presence, it is God's-self. The name of this God is "holy mystery" and the mystery *is* the incomprehensibleness of God.[431] In the disclosure of mystery, humankind receives a new revelation of the incomprehensible God.[432] Therefore, God can be experienced in reality, but God cannot be fully known.[433] Further, the experience of presence helps to explain the disciples' experience of the risen Jesus in particular. Self-transcendence is the common denominator. In Rahner, absolute being is present in matter, but it is not matter. Similarly, absolute being as the *Logos* is present in Jesus of Nazareth as one person in two natures but it is not a simple amalgam of *Logos* and matter. With spirit and matter, there is unity-in-difference, where spirit and matter form a unity but spirit has priority over matter. This unity is not static. To re-iterate, self-transcendence refers to the dynamic within this unity (i.e. matter develops toward spirit).[434] The self-transcending movement is from the lower to the higher order of being by virtue of the power of being-itself.[435] Matter makes the experience of the *other* possible.[436] Likewise, the presence of the disciples makes the experience of the resurrection a possibility. This does not reduce the resurrection to human consciousness. On the contrary, human consciousness is activated by means of an experience of presence.

427 "Hiddenness", TI 16, p. 237.
428 "Concept of Mystery", TI 4, p. 53.
429 *Ibid.* p. 52.
430 *Ibid.* p. 55.
431 *Ibid.* p. 61.
432 "Experiencing the spirit", Kelly ed. p. 227, "God is the comprehensive though never comprehended ground and presupposition of our experience and of the objects of that experience".
433 FCF, p. 120.
434 *Ibid.* 184.
435 "Evolutionary view", p. 165.
436 *Ibid.* p.163.

Conclusion

In this section the Death-Resurrection event in Tillich and Rahner's theology has been examined from the perspective of the ambiguous experience of God as presence and absence. With Rahner, death and resurrection form a unity.[437] In death, Jesus accepts completely the self-communication of God. In the resurrection, God accepts completely human reality as redeemed.[438] In this setting, the symbol of the cross is an invitation to embrace absence as the beginning of a redemptive process of transformation, where the resurrection is the culmination of the redemptive process. The resurrection is realised in the disciples' experience as presence, which evokes self-transcendence and as such, it is an encounter with the incomprehensible God. With Tillich, the Death-Resurrection event overcomes both the limits of existence and that God is not part of the subject-object structure; in the process it allows for full but not perfect participation in Divine life. The Death-Resurrection event consists of interdependent symbols.[439] Specifically, the cross is a symbol that expresses Christ's subjection to existence and the resurrection is a symbol that expresses Christ's conquest of existence.[440]

437 FCF, 266.
438 "Following the crucified", TI 18, p. 167-168.
439 ST I, p. 60.
440 ST II, pp. 152-153.

Chapter 5: Conclusion

The aim of this chapter is to articulate the study's contribution, which is outlined in detail in the foremost section of the chapter (section 3). The key to understanding the contribution is the assertion that the experience of the presence of God in the world is ambiguous, consisting of presence and absence. Consequently, the ambiguity, which is *implicit* in both Tillich and Rahner, is made *explicit* and then re-interpreted in postmetaphysical terms. Specifically, this entails developing a theology of presence and applying it to the themes of the Incarnation and the Death-Resurrection event. The study has also argued that it is artificial to separate presence and absence or to grant privileged epistemic status to one over the other. In particular, a Christology without presence has little to offer living faith communities and a Christology without absence is unconvincing in the face of widespread, unrelenting suffering. Thus, the application of the study's construal of the experience of God evokes power and poignancy from the themes of the Incarnation and the Death-Resurrection event. As a preliminary step, it is important to summarise the study and outline its limitations, in order to clarify the full extent of the study's contribution.

5.1. Summary

The study addresses the problem of the presence of God in the world. Its thesis is that the presence of God in the world can be affirmed, if presence is understood in relation to absence and in the context of experience. Subsequently, the study claims that experience of God in the world is ambiguous and it consists of presence and absence. While interpreting experience from the perspective of presence and absence is not new, new insights can be gleaned by the application of this interpretation to the theological systems of Tillich and Rahner. However, the theologies of Tillich and Rahner are primarily oriented toward modernity and so their theologies are interpreted from the perspective of postmodernity. Further, the nature of the marginalisation of God has changed with the emergence of postmodernity. In modernity, God is displaced from the world. In postmodernity, God is displaced from other realms as well (e.g. text) and there are other gods (cf. pluralism). In modernity, the problem is the unbridgeable gap between the material and the spiritual. Tillich and Rahner accept the gap as a given, it is part of the modern worldview, but they assert that the problem can be overcome by means of an inherent God-given capacity in humankind. For them, an encounter with the presence of God in the world elicits the God-given capacity in humankind to transcend the problem of the gap. Even so, presence is problematic for contemporary scholarship because of its metaphysical associations. Thus, the study re-defines presence. Furthermore, it is a theological study, which concentrates on the theologies of Tillich and Rahner published from 1933 on. Tillich and Rahner have been selected because they engage modernity constructively and say something positive about Christology. In addition, little has been done in the way of comparing the two theologians. The study's overall aim is to contribute to postmodern Christology. Its epistemological strategy limits this aim to an incremental contribution to Christological knowledge. To that end, the themes of the Incarnation and the Death-Resurrection event in Tillich and Rahner, when viewed from the perspective of presence and absence, form the basis of the study's contribution to Christology. In Tillich, presence is humankind's experience of the awareness of its participation in Divine life. In Rahner, presence is humankind's experience of the awareness of the closeness of God's self. However, there are limitations to this study that need to be addressed before the extent of its contribution can be fully appreciated.

5.2. Limitations

The purpose of this section is to articulate the limitations of the study. The articulation of the limitations serves a dual purpose. First, it highlights unresolved issues and in so doing it indicates areas for future research. Second, it gives greater clarity to the critical issues in this study.

Now the study's main concepts are experience, presence and absence. In terms of limitations, the full import of these concepts will be addressed in the next section (5.3). Suffice it to say that the philosophical debate about the meaning and status of experience has not finished. Moreover, there is an ongoing debate about the meaning of presence and absence and the relationship between the two. No doubt, new insights will emerge in the future in relation to these issues. In the interim, the study has taken a careful approach along the following four lines. First, while open for debate, the concept of experience used in this study has philosophical credibility (4.1.1). Second, the study has taken a postmetaphysical approach to presence and bracketed out being (4.2). The bracketing out is a methodological intention; it does not mean that the issue of the place of metaphysics in theological discourse has been resolved. Further, the study does not address the question of the nature of God *per se* as its focus is fixed on the experience of God in the world.[1] Hence, the study does not assume that presence and absence encompass the whole meaning of the experience of God. Third, the relationship between theology and other disciplines is complex. This study responds to this complexity by designating specific secondary roles to philosophy and history. The primary concerns, method and substance of the study are theological. Fourth, the study's understanding of experience as the interplay of presence and absence does not attempt to homogenise the inherent ambiguity of human experience. This is important to remember, as there is always a danger of reifying the concept of experience in the interests of developing a critical account of experience. However, experience is not neat. With the probable exception of fundamentalism, faith communities experience ambiguity, that is, absence as well as presence.[2] Further, the interplay between presence and absence is implicitly dialectical in character and is a reflection of humankind's experience of God in the world. The interplay says something about God in the world, that is, as God is experienced, perceived and interpreted. Moreover, the study suspects that is not useful to expect that we can know more about

---

1   Future research could pursue work on the relation between the ambiguous experience of God, as presence and absence, and the issue of contingency.

2   It would be interesting to explore in the future the place of the ambiguity of the experience of God, as presence and absence, in Christian fundamentalism. Presumably, fundamentalism asserts there is no absence and so the question is how they maintain this position in the face of absence.

the nature of God, that is, God in God's self. Lastly, this study has established the credibility of seeing God in terms of the ambiguity of experience as interplay between presence and absence, it focused on the interplay in relation to humankind, future research would do well to investigate the nature of the interplay in relation to God, the nature of God and the issue of contingency. Not that we can presume to know God's perspective, but the ambiguity of experience may be informative on that note.

In this study there are general historical and hermeneutical limitations. In historical terms, Tillich and Rahner witnessed similar events. They shared similar philosophical and theological interests, in part because they emerged from a similar European intellectual *environment*. However, there are problems. Tillich was eighteen years older than Rahner; the difference is nearly a generation. The difference is potentially significant for a number of reasons. For example, the difference between their anthropologies (cf. fragmented, unified) may reflect biographical and historical factors as well as theological and philosophical differences. Tillich, unlike Rahner, witnessed the horror of the Great War. Hypothetically, this experience may have contributed to Tillich's comparatively pessimistic anthropology. In the future, this issue could be pursued within the context of a study dedicated to comparing Tillich and Rahner. In this study, which is focused on comparing the two theologians and posmodernity in a christological context, there are ample grounds for situating them in the same broad historical period of modernity (1.1; 1.3). Further, there are hermeneutical problems associated with defining the theological systems of Tillich and Rahner. Each of their theological systems is a complex amalgam of philosophical, theological, ethical, spiritual, homiletical and pastoral material and insights. This complexity raises the issue of determining an appropriate way of characterising their work. Moreover, their work evolves, not smoothly but abruptly. This raises the hermeneutical issue of whether later material is *truer* than earlier material. All in all, this means that a note of caution needs to be exercised in the way their work is re-presented in this study. This helps explain the use of the term vision or guiding theological vision, which has been a means of circumscribing the inherent unity of their work, without circumventing the complexities. In brief, in terms of limitations, there are general historical and hermeneutical issues, but the main issues relate to historical periodisation and the meaning of modernity and postmodernity.

There are problems associated with defining the appropriate historical period of study. In terms of Tillich and Rahner, 1933-1984 has been selected as the period of study. This period has been selected for sound reasons (e.g. Tillich migrates to America, 1933). However, the period of study, the range of works consulted, the number of historical and biographical *facts* that have been assembled, could all have been expanded. It is partly a question of the scope of the study, but it also is a question of the reliable determination of criteria for defining a particular historical period. Further, there is the more general issue of the relationship between history and theology. Specifically, the use of history in theology does not automatically solve theological problems. For example, chronologically *Foundations* is much later than *Hearer*, but this does not mean that *Foundations* is better or truer than the earlier text. Moreover, there are debates in historiography about the meaning and use of history and historical facts. To sum up, historical periodisation can be described metaphorically as the question of how and where to draw the line. The key is that periodisation is a provisional process, which will disclose somethings and conceal others. Moreover, the problem of periodisation surfaces in another form in relation to the task of defining modernity and postmodernity and distinguishing between them.

The study's definitions of modernity and postmodernity are working definitions. The use of the term *working definition* implies that there is something provisional about the definition of both the historical *period* (i.e. modernity, postmodernity) and the cultural *movement* (i.e. modernism, postmodernism). Provisionality does not necessarily mean that the working definitions are at fault, only that they should be applied with care. For example, the issue of whether modernity and postmodernity represent *distinct* historical periods is debatable (1.2.2). Certainly, there are good grounds for considering modernity and postmodernity as distinct historical periods (e.g. historical events, pluralism, language, intersubjectivity). However, the debate has not been settled. In addition, there is the related problem of whose version of postmodernity is accepted as the benchmark (e.g. Derrida, Foucault, Lyotard). Besides, postmodern exponents are forced to use many of modernity's tools. Moreover, others refute the concept of postmodernity altogether. Further, the question of the difference between postmodernity as an historical period and postmodernism, as a cultural movement is part of the debate. For the benefit of comparative analysis (1.3.), the study has made a distinction between historical period and cultural movement, but one informs the other and the distinction is not absolute. Therefore, this study uses working definitions, but recognises there are other ways of bracketing history and culture. Furthermore, these qualifications help explain why the study adopts its particular epistemological strategy. To aspire to anything more than an incremental addition to Christological knowledge, runs the risk of falling into *old* modernist traps (e.g. homogenising difference). All told, the use of the working definitions of modernity and postmodernity is a means of comparative analysis. The purpose of these working definitions is to provide a means of comparing Tillich and Rahner with the present. In short, there are limitations in relation to periodisation and definitions, but they make critical comparisons possible.

5.3. Contribution and Implications

The aim of this section is to draw out the study's contributions, explain their significance and show how they advance theological research. The main contribution concerns the themes of experience, presence and absence. The study also makes a contribution in terms of general insights into Tillich and Rahner's theology and offers a plausible account of the differences between them.

Insights

The study distills some insights about the respective work of Tillich and Rahner.[3] First, in relation to Tillich, the study argues that he is more critical of modernity than has been attributed. For example, Tillich's criticism of the undue emphasis on the horizontal dimension in modernity is an incisive critique of modernity (2.1.3). This example serves to underline the fact that the classification of Tillich and his work cannot be

---

3   The order in which these insights are presented here is not significant.

oversimplified. Second, in relation to Rahner, the issue of the unity of his works is not an either/or issue. For example, this study contends that the influence of Thomas and Kant is formative (cf. Kilby) but not final (cf. Burke) in determining Rahner's guiding theological vision. Clearly, there are jumps and detours in the evolution of his theological vision, such that a degree of caution is warranted in too readily classifying his theological system. Nonetheless, while not captive, Rahner's vision is grounded in his early work. Third, the complexity of Rahner's theology makes it challenging reading, but it is also part of its appeal. There is a constant tension in reading Rahner between the parts and the whole. For example, a Rahner article or essay can be read in its own right, but in the process, the reader is constantly drawn to the horizon of Rahner's guiding theological vision.

Difference

There are similarities between Tillich and Rahner (e.g. Kant, symbol), which have been noted, but there are differences too. They are different people (cf. war experience), from different traditions (i.e. Protestant; Catholic) with different methods (cf. correlation; transcendental). Moreover, this study asserts that the nature of human existence is the main source of difference between Tillich and Rahner. That is, many of the differences stem from Tillich's understanding of the fragmented nature of existence in contrast to Rahner's understanding of the unified nature of existence.[4] Further, there is in Tillich an underlying mood of pessimism regarding human nature. Tillich's humankind has something of what Macquarrie describes as "a fixed nature".[5] It is no coincidence that Tillich places much theological, psychological and mythological weight on the symbol of the Fall. In contrast, in Rahner, who is aware of the impact of sin, there is a pervasive optimism about humankind living in and by the grace of God. Furthermore, the way they construe absence is another expression of difference between Tillich and Rahner. Tillich's construal of absence is largely governed by his understanding of human

---

4 Tillich, DF, pp. 108, 110; Rahner, "Evolutionary view", TI 5, p. 161, "inner similarity and community"; FCF, p. 141, "in the origin, unfolding and goal of its history mankind forms a unity".

5 Macquarrie, *On Being*, p. 137.

existence, where Rahner's construal of absence is largely governed by his understanding of God as experienced by humankind. The difference is partly a question of emphasis, but the difference is pronounced. In detail, Tillich's concept of absence is like a static quality of existence (i.e. God's vacuum). Humankind is burdened with absence because of the apparent withdrawal of God. As a symptom of estrangement, absence is something to be endured or accepted with a sense of resignation. Onto-logically, absence is a response to the shock of non-being and non-being has its origin in God as being-itself.[6] In this sense, absence has its onto-logical origin in the very nature of God (i.e. the abyss). Nonetheless, absence in Tillich says more about the existential reality of human exis-tence under the weight of estrangement. In contrast, Rahner's concept of absence is like a dynamic quality of God (i.e. God's hiddenness). Hu-mankind is faced with the experience of absence because this is the na-ture of God. As a symptom of finitude, humankind endures absence, but this absence is also a source of mystery. For Rahner, absence has its ontological origin in God, but it is to be accepted like a gift, as part of the mystery of existence. Absence in Rahner, in comparison with Tillich, says more about God than human existence. All told, the differences between Tillich and Rahner reveal personal and theological differences. They bear witness to their different understandings of existence (i.e. fragmented; unified). The study's construal of presence, and in particular absence, has helped crystallise the differences. Finally, these differences are manifested in their Christologies. For Tillich, existence is fragmented because of the reality of finitude. Thus, Tillich's *fallen* anthropology is the existential and theological warrant for the New Being. For Rahner, while he acknowledges the impact of finitude, existence is unified be-cause of the very presence of God in the world (cf. supernatural existen-tial, transcendental nature). Consequently, Rahner's *graced* anthropology is the existential and theological ground for the Absolute Saviour.

This study argues that the main source of difference between Tillich and Rahner is due to their different understandings of human existence. This is especially evident in their treatment of the Atonement. For Tillich and Rahner, the initiative in the Atonement is with God. With Tillich, in contrast to substitutional theories, the atoning processes stem from God's salvific process in human history. For Tillich, there is no conflict be-

6   LPJ, p. 38.

tween God's love and justice.[7] With Rahner, in contrast to satisfaction theories, the priority of God's initiative in the plan of salvation is critical.[8] For Rahner, God wills our redemption rather than demands satisfaction. Certainly, Rahner takes the problem of human sinfulness seriously. For example, Rahner's analysis of sin and guilt helps him explain the meaning of freedom, as guilt points to freedom, its abuse and the need for redemption.[9] In Rahner, there is a creative tension between guilt and freedom. Implicitly, Rahner sees a link between guilt (and sin) and human agency.[10] Like Rahner, Tillich values freedom and in true existential style, Tillich acknowledges the importance of the human capacity to make decisions. However, the Fall means freedom is at odds with sin and guilt. It is not a theologically creative tension because sin and guilt threaten to consume freedom. Thus, sin and guilt in Rahner are the means by which humankind actualises its God-given capacity for freedom. In contrast, Tillich constantly wrestles with the effects of estrangement. Tillich's interpretation of humankind reads like a victim who is constantly labouring under the weight of sin and guilt. Subsequently, humankind carries the burden of finitude more heavily in Tillich than Rahner.

Experience, Presence, Absence

This study has developed a concept of experience that is epistemologically credible. It is a critical concept of experience that incorporates public and social grounds and coheres with other beliefs (it makes sense in terms of everyday experience). Not all theologies choose to explain their view of experience in philosophical terms. This is often by choice, though the epistemic value of experience is often presumed.[11] This study affirms the value of reason, experience and coherence with other beliefs. For example, if the subjective (i.e. non-empirical) understanding of experience is involved, then the subject is understood in terms of the postmodern concept of intersubjectivity. In other words, the study's concept

7   ST II, pp. 173-176.
8   "Salvation", SM 5, p. 430.
9   *Ibid.* p. 425.
10   FCF, p. 94.
11   Ruether, *Sexism and God-Talk*, p. 18.

of experience attempts to overcome some of the problems associated with the modern understanding of the subject. The importance of inter-subjectivity in particular and experience in general becomes more apparent when the theological and pastoral significance of experience is explored below.

In this study, one of the aims has been to simultaneously re-claim the concepts of experience, presence and absence and address the critical problems they raise. In order to illustrate the significance of these concepts, the study will broach some potential research issues. While there is an element of conjecture here, it sits well within the constraints of the study. To begin, the study presumes the ambiguous nature of experience. In particular, it presumes that theology is provisional and theological constants have to be re-appropriated by new faith communities (1.1). In this study, faith communities represent part of the public and social grounds for justifying belief.[12] It is reasonable to speculate that faith communities, as well as individual Christians, have helped to shape and sustain the tradition and theology of the Church throughout its history. The inference is that the tradition and theology of the Church are partly a reflection of the shared experience (i.e. meanings) of faith communities (i.e. intersubjectivity). It is reasonable to speculate that, as gleaned from everyday speech, faith communities intuitively appreciate the importance of the three concepts (i.e. non-empirical experience). In pastoral terms, faith communities know first hand the impact of absence (e.g. suffering, secularisation) and the longing for presence (e.g. prayer, meditation, introspection). While there are objections to the use of the concepts of experience, presence and absence, many of which have been addressed in this study, the concepts are constitutive of the spiritual and ecclesial life of many of the Church's faith communities. In practice, it is hard to imagine a discussion about prayer or the Eucharist that does not use the language of experience, presence and absence or at least look for alternative ways of expressing what these three concepts embody. Therefore, one of the study's contributions is to make a strong case for experience. In particular, experience as part of the process of epistemic justification can be used to speak meaningfully about the presence and absence of

12   Everritt and Fisher, p. 208; Scanlon, "The humiliated self", p. 267, and the importance of interpreted experience.

298

God in the world (4.1.1). It also argues that there is a place in theology for a credible concept of presence.

Admittedly, the place of presence in theology has been challenged because of presence's dependency on the concept of being as a means of epistemic justification. In response, this study's view of presence is not explicitly dependent on the concept of being or the resolution of outstanding metaphysical issues (4.2.3). Further, the study's understanding of experience as the interplay of presence and absence honours the complexity and diversity of real human experience. Faith communities experience ambiguity; that is, absence as well as presence. Furthermore, the interplay between presence and absence says something about God in the world, that is, God as experienced, perceived and interpreted. In terms of implications, the study is probably not conducive to traditional theism's approach to the God and the world (i.e. Tillich's supernaturalism). Nevertheless, it does not make easy concessions to secular accounts of the world, which separate the material and the spiritual (i.e. Tillich's naturalism). Presumably, the nature of God and God's involvement is complex and cannot be reduced to concise theological maxims or theoretical models. However, this study, by developing an epistemological place for experience, which includes religious experience, is implicitly a critique of both secular culture's compartmentalism and empirical foundationalism. In everyday speech, religion is dismissed as not factual in contrast to history and science. The study's use of justified true belief (i.e. experience, reason, coherence, public and social grounds) overcomes some of the problems associated with an extreme empirical or positivistic approach, without reverting to religious formulae which seek to bypass reason and coherence for the sake of experience alone.

The Incarnation And The Death-Resurrection Event

The study's construal of the ambiguity of experience as presence and absence grounds the meaning the Incarnation and the Death-Resurrection event pastorally, epistemologically and theologically. First, a Christology that overemphasises presence runs the risk of failing to speak to faith communities who know the experience of absence, in other words, absence as well as presence rings true with experience. For example, the season of Lent and Holy Week seems banal without the acknowledgment of the presence of absence. Thus, this is partly an argument for a pastorally relevant Christology, but it is also an argument for the recognition of the public and social grounds of epistemic justification as well as the complex nature of human experience.[13] In short, the study grounds its Christology in experience.

Second, if experience has a role in epistemic justification, then there is a danger of Christology becoming confined to a particular individual's or faith community's experience (cf. tribalism). However, experience is not privileged over reason or coherence with other beliefs. In other words, the study's concept of experience, which includes reason, coherence with other beliefs as well as public and social grounds, means Christology, is not captive to a particular faith community's experience. In short, the study grounds its Christology in an epistemologically plausible understanding of experience.

Third, the application of the construal to the Christologies of Tillich and Rahner helps identify a line of continuity between their period and postmodernity; expressly, Tillich's emphasis on estrangement and Rahner's on finitude are amenable to an interpretation based on absence (4.4 and 5). Further, in Tillich's work presence is humankind's experience of the awareness of its participation in Divine life. In Rahner's work, presence is humankind's experience of the awareness of the closeness of God's self. Concerning presence, the difference between Tillich and Rahner is an issue of nuance as well as method. Concerning absence, there are parallels between Tillich and Rahner, in terms of the relation between the concept of absence and the nature of God. For Tillich, absence is the human side of an encounter with God as abyss, in which there is a link between absence and the nature of God (i.e. abyss). For Rahner, absence is an encounter with the hiddenness of God, in which there is also a link between absence and the nature of God (i.e. incomprehensibleness). The difference between Tillich and Rahner can be seen in terms of the experience of absence in the world and it reflects different conceptions of humankind and humankind's relationship with God. One of the contributions of this study is to make explicit the concept of absence which is implicitly present throughout their work.

Finally, Tillich and Rahner partly depend upon the concept of being as a form of epistemic justification. A Christology that relies on being

13   Everitt and Fisher, pp. 202-203, 207-208.

300

for justification runs the risk of failing to speak to significant intellectual communities who question the validity of ontotheological approaches. While the postmodern critique of ontotheology is not itself above criticism, serious concerns have been raised about the link between presence and being (e.g. Heidegger, Derrida). Consequently, this study has chosen to re-interpret presence, partly for apologetic reasons. In short, the study's construal grounds its Christology in a postmetaphysical approach. Having placed this study's construal in its broader Christological context, it is important to re-visit its incremental contribution to Christology.

The themes of the Incarnation and Death-Resurrection event have been interpreted from the perspective of the ambiguity of experience as presence and absence. Initially, the themes were treated separately for practical reasons (4.4; 4.5). In Tillich and Rahner's theology, the two themes are part of the one divine work of salvation. The Incarnation and the Death-Resurrection event, as a unity, constitute the definitive expression of the presence of God in the world. In terms of the Incarnation, Tillich has an implicit theology of the Incarnation, as he is generally more concerned about the existential impact of the New Being than the theological structure and justification of the Incarnation. Nonetheless, the Incarnation is a given in Tillich. By comparison, Rahner has an explicit and extensive theology of the Incarnation. For him, the Incarnation is paramount and the theological structure and justification of the Incarnation is critical because of its profound connections with tradition (e.g. Chalcedonian formulation) and doctrine (e.g. immutability of God). Further, for Tillich and Rahner, absence is implicitly part of the experience of the Incarnation. In Tillich, the Incarnation means if Christ is fully human, then he experiences the absence of God. In Rahner, if Christ is fully human, then he experiences finitude (i.e. absence).[14]

In Tillich, the Death-Resurrection event overcomes the limits of existence and that God is not part of the subject-object structure; in the process it promises to humankind full but not perfect participation in Divine life. The Death-Resurrection event consists of interdependent symbols.[15] Specifically, the cross is a symbol that expresses Christ's subjection to existence and the resurrection is a symbol that expresses Christ's con-

14 "Incarnation", ET, p. 694.
15 ST I, p. 60.

quest of existence.[16] In other words, the cross in Tillich is the definitive symbol of both the power of absence and the indomitability of presence, such that presence overcomes the power of absence in and through the resurrection. Thus, Tillich's understanding of the Death-Resurrection event honours the ambiguous experience of faith communities. In Rahner, death and resurrection also form a unity.[17] In Rahner, the Incarnation means Christ had the capacity to experience suffering, this includes the experience of absence. For Rahner, the symbol of the cross is an invitation to embrace absence as the beginning of a redemptive process, where the resurrection is the culmination of the process. In death, Jesus accepts completely the self-communication of God. In the resurrection, God accepts completely human reality as redeemed.[18] In this setting, the symbol of the cross is an invitation to embrace absence as the beginning of a redemptive process of transformation, where the resurrection is the culmination of the redemptive process. Moreover, the resurrection is realised in the disciples' experience as presence, which evokes self-transcendence and as such is an encounter with the incomprehensible God.[19] Rahner's understanding of the Death-Resurrection event also honours the ambiguous experience of faith communities and gives them hope. In short, the hermeneutical key to this study is the application of the construal of the experience of God as presence and absence to the Christological themes in Tillich and Rahner, without their metaphysical foundations.

5.4. The Presence of God in the World

The study's thesis is that the presence of God in the world can be affirmed, if presence is understood in relation to absence and within the context of experience. Tillich and Rahner understand presence primarily in metaphysical terms; so the study redefines presence in postmetaphysical terms in order to address a contemporary situation. Thus, it is able to

16   ST II, pp. 152-153.
17   FCF, 266.
18   "Following the crucified", TI 18, pp. 167-168.
19   *Ibid.* p. 160.

make an incremental contribution to Christology. A cursory reading of this study could give the impression that it is concerned with new definitions (e.g. experience, presence, absence), which it is, but ultimately what is at stake is the nature of existence, how is it perceived and how it is lived in the context of living faith communities. Generally, modernism defines existence in such a way that there is no place for the presence of God in the world (i.e. the gap), whereas strands within postmodernism define existence in such a way that the concept of the presence of God in the world is meaningless. In contrast, this study argues that there is a place in the world for the presence of God. Moreover, the study argues that there is a place in the world for a Christ who discloses something of God in terms of the experience of presence and absence. Its argument is based on two key assumptions. First, the study advocates an epistemology in which experience, in conjunction with reason, coherence with other beliefs, public and social grounds, has a significant place. Second, the study argues that if experience is construed this way then presence, as part of experience, can be defined so that it does not rely on the concept of being for epistemic justification.

The study presumes that a theology, which speaks meaningfully about the presence of God in the world in terms of experience, is relevant to faith communities in the Western Christian tradition. More significantly, it argues that the experience of faith communities is a part of the epistemic justification of the belief of the presence of God in the world. Subsequently, the study has developed a concept of experience that is epistemologically credible. However, it is not possible or advisable to try and resolve the ambiguity of human experience. In fact, the ambiguity of experience as presence and absence makes sense of the experience of faith communities (i.e. it rings true). Moreover, the use of presence and absence helps make Christology relevant. Without absence, the Incarnation and the Death-Resurrection event are empty symbols or pious signs, which do not speak to actual faith communities or the real world. Without presence, Christology is at best historical remembrance of Jesus of Nazareth. In other words, a Christology that does not address experience is irrelevant. A Christology that does not incorporate absence is unreal. A Christology that does not augur presence offers no hope.

References

Adams, J.L. *Paul Tillich's Philosophy of Culture, Science and Religion*, (New York: Harper and Row, 1965).

Allen, D. *Christian Belief in a Postmodern World: The Full Wealth of Conviction*, (Louisville, Kentucky: Westminster/John Knox Press, 1989).

Alston, W.P. "God's action in the world" in W.P. Alston ed., *Divine Nature and Human Language*, (Ithaca and London: Cornell University Press, 1989), pp. 197-222.

Alston, W.P. "The autonomy of religious experience", *International Journal of Religious Experience*, 31 (1992), pp. 67-87.

Alston, W.P. "Realism and the Christian faith", *International Journal of Philosophy of Religion*, 38 (1995), pp. 37-60.

Altizer, T.J.J. *The Gospel of Christian Atheism*, (Philadelphia: Westminster Press, 1966).

Altizer, T.J.J. *Genesis and Apocalypse: A Theological Voyage Toward Authentic Christianity*, (Louisville, Kentucky: Westminster/John Knox Press, 1990).

Altizer, T.J.J. *The Contemporary Jesus*, (London: SCM Press, 1997).

Ankersmit, F.R. "Historicism: An attempt at synthesis", *History and Theory*, 34 (1995), pp. 143-161.

Armstrong, D.M. "universals" in J. Kim and E. Sosa eds., *A Companion to Metaphysics*, (Oxford: Blackwell Publishers, 1995), pp. 502-506.

Armstrong, J. *Looking at Pictures: An Introduction to the Appreciation of Art*, (London: Duckworth, 1996).

Ashley, B.M. "neo-Scholasticism", EC, p. 911.

Baggini, J. and Fosl, P.S. *The Philosopher's Toolkit: A Compendium of Philosophical Concepts and Methods*, (Oxford: Blackwell Publishing, 2003).

Bauman, Z. "Postmodernity, or living with ambivalence", in J. Natoli and L. Hutcheon eds., *A Postmodern Reader*, (Albany: State University of New York, 1993), pp. 9-24.

Benavides, G. "Modernity" in M.C. Taylor ed., *Critical Terms for Religious Studies*, (Chicago: University of Chicago Press, 1998), pp. 186-204.

Berger, P.L. *A Rumor of Angels: Modern Society and the Rediscovery of the Supernatural*, (Garden City, New York: Anchor Books, 1969).

Berger, P.L. *The Sacred Canopy: Elements of a Sociological Theory of Religion*, (Garden City, New York: Anchor Books, 1969).

Berger, P.L. "The Desecularization of the world: A Global Overview" in P.L. Berger ed., *The Desecularization of the World: Resurgent Religion and World Politics*, (Grand Rapids, Michigan: Eerdmans, 1999), pp. 1-18.

Blackburn, S. *Oxford Dictionary of Philosophy*, (Oxford: Oxford University Press, 1996).

Bondi, R.C. "apophatic theology", NDCT, p. 32.

Bonsor, J.A. *Athens and Jerusalem: The Role of Philosophy in Theology*, (New York: Paulist Press, 1993).

Breisach, E. *On the Future of History: The Postmodernist Challenge and its Aftermath*, (Chicago and London: University of Chicago Press, 2003).

Breuilly, J. "What is social history...?" in J Gardiner ed., *What is History Today...?* (Houndmills, Basingstoke, Hampshire: MacMillan Press, 1988), pp. 48-51.

Brock, R.N. *Journeys by Heart: A Christology of Erotic Power*, (New York: Crossroad, 1988).

Bryant, R.H. "An Evaluation of the Christological dimensions of Tillich's theology of culture" in J.J. Carey ed., *Kairos and Logos: Studies in the Roots and Implications of Tillich's Theology*, (Mercer: Mercer University Press, 1978, 1984), pp. 261-269.

Bullock, A. and S. Trombley, S. ed. *The New Fontana Dictionary of Modern Thought*, (London: HarperCollins Publishers, 1977, 1988, 1999, 2000).

Bulman, R.F. and Parella, F.J. *Paul Tillich: A New Catholic Assessment*, (Collegeville, Minnesota: The Liturgical Press, 1994).

Bulman, R.F. and Parella, F.J. "Introduction" in R.F. Bulman and F.J. Parella eds., *Paul Tillich: A New Catholic Assessment*, (Collegeville, Minnesota: The Liturgical Press, 1994), pp. 1-8.

Bulman, R.F. and Parella, F.J. eds. *Religion in the New Millennium: Theology in the Spirit of Paul Tillich*, (Mercer: Mercer University Press, 2001).

Burke, P. "Overture: the new history, its past and its future" in P. Burke ed., *New Perspectives on Historical Writing*, (Cambridge: Polity Press, 1991), pp. 1-23.

Burke, P. "Conceptual thought in Karl Rahner", *Gregorianum*, 75 (1994), pp. 65-93.

Burke, P. *Reinterpreting Rahner: A Critical Study of His Major Themes*, (New York: Fordham University Press, 2002).

Butler, C. *Postmodernism: A Very Short Introduction*, (Oxford: Oxford University Press, 2002).

Caputo, J.D. *Radical Hermeneutics: Repetition, Deconstruction, and the Hermeneutic Project*, (Bloomington and Indianapolis: Indiana University Press, 1987).

Caputo, J.D. "Heidegger and theology" in C. Guignon ed., *The Cambridge Companion to Heidegger*, (Cambridge: Cambridge University Press, 1993), pp. 270-288.

Caputo, J.D. *On Religion*, (London and New York: Routledge, 2001).

Caputo, J.D. "The experience of God and the axiology of the impossible" in M.A. Wrathall ed., *Religion After Metaphysics*, (Cambridge: Cambridge University Press, 2003), pp. 123-145.

Carey, J.J. ed. *Kairos and Logos: Studies in the Roots and Implications of Tillich's Theology*, (Mercer: Mercer University Press, 1978, 1984).

Carey, J.J. ed. *Theonomy and Autonomy: Studies in Paul Tillich's Engagement with Modern Culture*, (Mercer: Mercer University Press, 1984).

Carnley, P. *The Structure of Resurrection Belief*, (Oxford: Clarendon Press, 1987).

Carr, E.H. *What is History?* (Hampshire: Palgrave, 1961, 1986, 2001).

Carse, H. "Simple water, consuming flame: nature, sacrament and person in Paul Tillich", *Theology*, 99 (1996), pp. 22-27.

Caygill, H. *A Kant Dictionary*, (Oxford: Blackwell Publishers, 1995).

Cederblom, J. and Paulsen, D.W. *Critical Reasoning*, 4th ed., (Belmont: Wadsworth, 1996).

Clayton, J.P. "Is Jesus necessary for christology?" in S.W. Sykes and J.P. Clayton eds., *Christ Faith and History: Cambridge Studies in*

Christology, (Cambridge: Cambridge University Press, 1972), pp. 147-163.

Cooke, B.J. *The Distancing Of God: The Ambiguity of Symbol in History and Theology*, (Minneapolis: Fortress Press, 1990).

Courtenay, W.J. "Neoscholasticism" in A. Richardson and J. Bowden eds., *A New Dictionary of Christian Theology*, (London: SCM Press, 1983), pp. 396-397.

Cowdell, S. *Is Jesus Unique? A Recent Study in Christology*, (New York: Paulist Press, 1996).

Cross, F.L. and Livingstone, E.A. *The Oxford Dictionary of the Christian Church*, 3rd ed., (Oxford, New York: Oxford University Press, 1997).

Crossan, J.D. *The Historical Jesus: The Life of a Mediterranean Jewish Peasant*, (San Francisco: Harper Collins, 1991).

Dallaville, N.A. "Revisiting Rahner: on the theological status of trinitarian theology", *Irish Theological Quarterly*, 63 (1998), pp. 133-150.

Dancy, J. "Epistemology, problems of", OCP, pp. 245-248

Dean, W. "Empiricism and God", in R.C. Miller ed., *Empirical Theology: A Handbook*, (Birmingham, Alabama: Religious Education Press, 1992), pp 107-128.

De Certeau, M. "How Christianity is thinkable today?" G. Ward ed., *The Postmodern God*, (Oxford: Blackwell Publishers, 1997), pp 142-155.

De Schrijver, G. "Postmodernity and the withdrawal of the divine: A challenge for theology", in L. Boeve and L. Leijssen eds., *Sacramental Presence in a Postmodern Context*, (Leuven: Leuven University Press, 1997), pp. 39-64.

Derrida, J. *Of Grammatology*, corrected edition, G.C. Spivak trans., (Baltimore and London: John Hopkins University Press, 1967, 1974, 1976, 1997).

Descartes, R. Second meditation from "Meditations on the first philosophy in which the existence of God and the distinction between mind and body are demonstrated" in E. Chávez-Arvizo ed., and E.S. Haldane and G.R.T. Ross trans., *Descartes: Key Philosophical Writings*, (Hertfordshire: Wordsworth Editions Limited, 1997), pp. 139-147.

Dillistone, F.W. *The Power Of Symbols*, (London: SCM Press, 1986).

Donceel, J.F. *Philosophical Anthropology*, (New York: Sheed and Ward, 1967).

Donceel, J.F. *The Searching Mind: An Introduction to a Philosophy of God*, (London: University of Notre Dame Press, 1979).

Dretske, F. "experience", OCP, p. 261.

Dulles, A. *The Craft Of Theology: From Symbol To System*, (New York: Crossroad, 1992).

Dupuis, J. *Who do you say that I am? Introduction to Christology,* (New York: Orbis Books, 1994).

Dych, W. *Karl Rahner*, (London and New York: Continuum, 1992, 2000).

Edwards, D.L. "secularization" in A. Bullock and S. Trombley eds., *The New Fontana Dictionary Of Modern Thought*, 3rd ed., (London: Harper Collins, 1977, 1988, 1999), pp. 778-779.

Egan, H.D. *Karl Rahner: Mystic of Everyday Life*, (New York: Crossroad Publishing, 1998).

Everitt, N. and Fisher, A. *Modern Epistemology: A New Introduction*, (London: McGraw-Hill, 1995).

Fiorenza, E.S. "Jesus of Nazareth in historical research", in T. Wiley ed., *Thinking of Christ: Proclamation, Explanation, Meaning*, (New York and London: Continuum, 2003), pp. 29-48.

Fiorenza, F.S. "Being, subjectivity, otherness" in J.D Caputo, M.D. Dooley and M.J. Scanlon eds., *Questioning God*, (Bloomington and Indianapolis: Indiana University Press, 2001), pp. 341-369.

Fredriksen, P. "What does Jesus have to do with Christ?" in A.M. Clifford and A.J. Godzieba eds., *Christology: Memory, Inquiry, Practice*, 48 (New York: Orbis Books, 2003), pp. 3-17.

Gaillardetz, R.R. "Syllabus of errors", EC, p. 1233.

Gamwell, F.I. "Speaking of God after Aquinas", *The Journal of Religion*, 81 (2001), pp. 185-210.

Gascoigne, R. "Looking beyond liberalism: Christianity and a civil society" *Colloquium*, 33 (2001), pp. 95-108.

Gilkey, L. "God" in Musser, D.W. and Price, J.L. eds., *A New Handbook of Christian Theology*, (London: SCM Press, 1992), pp. 198-209.

Gunton, C. *The Actuality of Atonement: A Study of Metaphor, Rationality and the Christian Tradition*, (Edinburgh: T and T Clark, 1988).

Gunton, C. *The One, The Three And The Many: God, Creation And The Culture Of Modernity*, (Cambridge: Cambridge University Press, 1997).

Haack, S. *Evidence and Inquiry: Towards Reconstruction in Epistemology*, (Oxford: Blackwell Publishers, 1993, 1995).

Haack, S. "A foundherentist theory of empirical justification" in L.P. Pojman ed., *The Theory of Knowledge: Classical and Contemporary Readings*, (Belmont: Wadsworth, 2003), pp. 237-247.

Haight, R. *Dynamics Of Theology*, (Mahwah: Paulist Press, 1990).

Haight, R. *Jesus Symbol of God*, (New York: Orbis Books, 1999).

Hall, D.J. "The Great War and the German theologians" in G. Baum ed., *The Twentieth Century: A Theological Overview*, (New York: Orbis Books, 1999), pp. 3-13.

Hamilton, W. "Death of God Theology" in D.W. Musser and J.L. Price eds., *A New Handbook of Christian Theology*, (Nashville: Abingdon Press, 1992), pp. 120-122.

Hamilton, W. *A Quest for the Post-Historical Jesus*, (London: SCM Press, 1993).

Hamlyn, D.W. "Epistemology, history of", OCP, pp. 245-248.

Hart, K. *The Trespass of the Sign: Deconstruction, Theology and Philosophy*, (New York: Fordham University Press, 1989, 2000).

Hart, K. "The experience of God" in J.D. Caputo ed., *The Religious*, (Oxford: Blackwell, 2002), pp. 159-174.

Hegel, G.W.F. "Christianity: The consummate religion" in P.C. Hodgson ed., *G.W.F. Hegel: Theologian of the Spirit*, (Edinburgh: T and T Clark, 1997), pp. 205-259.

Heidegger, M. "Nietzsche's statement God is dead" (*"Nietzsche's Wort 'Gott ist Tot,'"* Holzwege. Frankfurt am Main: Vittorio Klostermann, 1950, p. 199, ff), in M. Friedman ed., E. Kern trans. *The Worlds Of Existentialism: A Critical Reader*, (New Jersey: Humanities Press, 1964, 1991), pp. 264-265.

Heidegger, M. *An Introduction to Metaphysics*, R. Mannheim trans., (New York: Anchor Books, 1961).

Heidegger, M. *Being And Time*, J. Macquarrie and E. Robinson trans., (Oxford and Cambridge: Blackwell Publishers, 1962).

Heidegger, M. "The way back into the ground of metaphysics" in W. Kaufman ed. and trans., *Existentialism: From Dostoevsky to Sartre,* revised and expanded, (New York: New American Library, 1965, 1975), pp. 265-279.

Heidegger, M. *Hegel's Concept of Experience*, J.G. Gray trans., (New York: Harper and Row, 1970).

Heidegger, M. "Building dwelling thinking," in A. Hofstadter trans. and introduction, *Poetry, Language, Thought*, (New York: Harper and Row, 1971), pp. 145-161.

Heyward, C. "Heterosexist theology: Being above it all", *Journal of Feminist Studies in Religion*, 3 (1987), pp. 29-38.

Heywood Thomas, J. *Tillich*, (London and New York: Continuum, 2000).

Hill, B.R., Knitter, P. and Madges, W. *Faith Religion and Theology: A Contemporary Introduction*, rev ed., (Mystic, CT: Twenty-Third Publications, 1990, 1997, 1998).

Hodgson, P.C. *Winds Of The Spirit: A Constructive Christian Theology*, (Louisville, Kentucky: Westminster John Knox Press, 1994).

Hogan, K. "Entering into otherness: the postmodern critique of the subject and Karl Rahner's theological anthropology", *Horizons*, 25 (1998), pp. 181-202.

Honderich, T. *The Oxford Companion to Philosophy*, (Oxford, New York: Oxford University Press, 1995).

Honner, J. "Speaking in new tongues: Karl Rahner's writings from the grave", *Pacifica*, 11 (1998), pp. 63-77.

Ignatius of Loyola. *The Spiritual Exercises of St Ignatius*, L.J. Puhl trans., (New York: Random House, 1951, 2000).

Inwood, M. *A Hegel Dictionary*, (Oxford: Blackwell Publishers, 1992).

Inwood, M. *A Heidegger Dictionary*, (Oxford: Blackwell Publishers, 1999).

Johnson, E.A. *She Who Is: The Mystery of God in Feminist Theological Discourse*, (New York: Crossroad, 1992).

Johnson, E.A. "The word was made flesh and dwelt among us: Jesus research and Christian faith", in D. Donelly ed., *Jesus: A Colloquium In The Holy Land*, (New York, London: Continuum, 2001), pp. 146-166.

Johnson, L.T. *The Real Jesus: The Misguided Quest for the Historical Jesus and the Truth of the Traditional Gospels*, (San Francisco: Harper Collins, 1996).

Kane, R. "The ends of metaphysics", *International Philosophical Quarterly*, 33 (1993), pp. 413-428.

Kant, I. *Critique of Pure Reason*, rev. and expanded translation based on Meiklejohn, V Politis ed., (London: Everyman, 1993).

Kant, I. "What is Enlightenment?" in C J Friedrich ed. and trans., *The Philosophy of Kant: Immanuel Kant's Moral and Political Writings*, (New York: Random House, 1949).

Kaufman, G.D. *An Essay on Theological Method*, rev. ed., (Montana: Scholars Press, 1975, 1979).

Kaufman, G.D. "Religious diversity, historical consciousness and Christian theology" in J.H. Hick and P.F. Knitter eds., *The Myth of Christian Uniqueness: Toward a Pluralist Theology of Religions*, (New York: Orbis Books, 1987), pp. 3-15.

Keating, J.F. "Epistemology and the theological application of Jesus research" in A.M. Clifford and A.J. Godzieba eds., *Christology: Memory, Inquiry, Practice*, (New York: Orbis Books, 2003), pp. 18-43.

Keefe, D.J. *Thomism and the Ontological Theology of Paul Tillich: A Comparison of Systems*, (Leiden: E.J. Brill, 1971).

Kierkegaard, S. *Concluding Unscientific Postscript*, D.F. Swenson and W. Lowrie, trans., (Princeton: Princeton University Press, 1941).

Knitter, P.F. *Jesus and the Other Names: Christian Mission and Global Responsibility*, (New York: Orbis Books, 1996).

Kilby, K. *Karl Rahner,* (London: HarperCollins, 1997).

Kilby, K. *Karl Rahner: Philosophy and Theology*, (New York: Routledge: 2004).

Kim, J. and Sosa, E. eds. *A Companion to Metaphysics*, (Oxford: Blackwell Publishers, 1995).

Küng, H. *The Incarnation of God: An Introduction to Hegel's Theological Thought as Prolegomena to a Future Christology*, J.R. Stephenson trans., (New York: Crossroad, 1970, 1987).

Küng, H. *Global Responsibility: In Search of a New World Ethic*, (London: SCM, Press, 1990, 1991).

Küng, H. *Christianity: The Religious Situation of Our Time*, J. Bowden trans., (London: SCM Press, 1994, 1995).

Küng, H. *My Struggle For Freedom*, J. Bowden trans., (Michigan, Cambridge: Eerdmans, 2003).

Lamm, J.A. "'Catholic substance' revisited: Reversals of expectations in Tillich's doctrine of God" in R.F. Bulman and F.J. Parella eds., *Paul Tillich: A New Catholic Assessment*, (Collegeville, Minnesota: The Liturgical Press, 1994), pp. 48-72.

Lane, D.A. *The Experience of God: An Invitation to Do Theology*, (New York: Paulist Press, 1981).

Lindbeck, G. *The Nature of Doctrine: Religion and Theology in a Post-liberal Age*, (Philadelphia: Westminster Press, 1984).

Lowe, E.J. "being", OCP, p. 82.

Lucy, N. *A Derrida Dictionary*, (Oxford: Blackwell Publishing, 2004).

Lyotard, J. *The Postmodern Condition: A Report on Knowledge*, G. Bennington and B. Massumi trans., (Minnesota: University of Minneapolis, 1979, 1984).

Lyotard, J. "Apostil on narratives" in J. Pefanis and M. Thomas trans. ed. and D. Barry, B. Maher, J Pefanis, V Spate and M Thomas trans., *The Postmodern Explained: Correspondence 1982-1985*, (Minneapolis and London: University of Minnesota Press, 1988, 1992), pp. 17-21.

McBrien, R.P. ed. *The HarperCollins Encyclopedia of Catholicism*, (San Francisco: HarperCollins, 1995).

McCool, G.A. *A Rahner Reader*, (London: Darton, Longman and Todd, 1975).

McCool, G.A. *From Unity to Pluralism: The Internal Revolution of Thomism*, (New York: Fordham University Press, 1989).

McDermott, J.M. "The christologies of Karl Rahner", *Gregorianum*, 67 (1986), pp. 87-123.

McDermott, J.M. "The methodological shift in twentieth century Thomism", *Seminarium*, 31 (1991), pp. 245-266.

McDermott, J.M. "Dialectical Analogy: the oscillating center of Rahner's thought" *Gregorianum* 75 (1994), pp. 675-703.

McEvoy, J. "Narrative of history? – A false dilemma: the theological significance of the historical Jesus", *Pacifica*, 14 (2001), pp. 262-280.

McGrath, A.E. *Christian Theology: An Introduction*, 3rd ed., (Oxford: Blackwell Publishers, 2001), pp. 143-144.

Mack, B.L. *Who Wrote The New Testament? The Making Of The Christian Myth*, (San Francisco: Harper Collins, 1995).

Mackie, P.J. "causality", OCP, pp. 126-128.

Macquarrie, J. *God-Talk: An Examination of the Language and Logic of Theology*, (London: SCM Press, 1967).

Macquarrie, J. *Principles of Christian Theology*, rev. ed., (London: SCM Press, 1966, 1977).

Macquarrie, J. "Deus Absconditus", NDCT, p. 155.

Macquarrie, J. *Jesus Christ in Modern Thought*, (London, Philadelphia: SCM Press, Trinity Press International, 1990).

Macquarrie, J. "Systematic Theology" in D.W. Musser and J.L. Price eds., *A New Handbook of Christian Theology*, (Nashville: Abingdon Press, 1992), pp. 469-474.

Macquarrie, J. *On Being A Theologian*, J.H. Morgan ed., (London: SCM Press, 1999).

Macquarrie, J. "The continuing relevance of Kant" in *Stubborn Theological Questions*, (London: SCM Press, 2003), pp. 196-207.

Macquarrie, J. *Christology Revisited*, (London: SCM Press, 1998).

Macquarrie, J. "Moltmann on the suffering of God" in *Stubborn Theological Questions*, (London: SCM Press, 2003), pp. 49-63.

Marion, J. *God Without Being*, T.A. Carlson trans., (Chicago and London: Chicago University Press, 1991, 1995).

Maritain, J. *St Thomas Aquinas*, (New York: Meridian Books, 1931, 1958).

Mascall, E.L. *The Openness of Being: Natural Theology Today*, (London: Darton, Longman and Todd, 1971).

Miller, J.B. "The emerging postmodern world" in F.D. Burnham ed., *Postmodern Theology: Christian Faith in a Pluralist World*, (San Francisco: Harper Collins, 1989), pp. 1-19.

Modras, R. "Catholic Substance and the Catholic Church Today" in R.F. Bulman and F.J. Parrella eds., *Paul Tillich: A New Catholic Assessment*, (Minnesota: The Liturgical Press, 1994), pp. 33-47.

Moltmann, J. *The Crucified God: The Cross of Christ as the Foundation and Criticism of Christian Theology*, (London: SCM Press, 1973, 1974).

Moltmann, J. *Theology Today*, (London: SCM Press, Philadelphia: Trinity Press International, 1988).

Moltmann, J. *The Way Of Jesus Christ: Christology in Messianic Dimensions*, (London: SCM Press, 1989, 1990).

Moltmann, J. *God For A Secular Society*, (London: SCM Press, 1999).

Moltmann, J. *The Spirit of Life: A Universal Affirmation*, (Minneapolis: Fortress Press, 2001).

Morrison, R.D. "Tillich, Einstein, and Kant: Method, epistemology, and the personal God" in J.J. Carey ed., *Theonomy and Autonomy*, (Macon: Mercer University Press, 1984), pp. 35-65.

Muck, O. "Neo-scholasticism", SM 6, pp. 36-38.

Musser, D.W. and Price, J.L. eds. *A New Handbook of Christian Theology*, (Nashville: Abingdon Press, 1992).

Musser, D.W. and Price, J.L. eds. *A New Handbook of Christian Theologians*, (Nashville: Abingdon Press, 1996).

Newlands, G. "Monophysitism", NDCT, p. 381

Niermann, E. "indifference", ET, pp. 699-700.

Nietzsche, F. *On Truth and Lie in an Extra Moral Sense*, in P. Novak ed., *The Vision of Nietzsche*, (Rockport: Element, 1996), p. 42. Originally in W. Kaufman, *The Portable Nietzsche* (New York: Viking Press, 1954, 1968), pp. 42-47.

Nietzsche, F. *The Gay Science*, p. 344 (1887) in P Novak ed., *The Vision of Nietzsche*, (Rockport: Element, 1996) p. 49.

Oakeshott, M. "The activity of being an historian" in P. King ed., *The History of Ideas: An Introduction to Method*, (London: Croom Helm, 1983), pp. 69-95.

O'Connell, M.R. "oath against Modernism", EC, p. 926.

Ogden, S. *The Reality of God and Other Essays*, (London: SCM Press, 1963, 1965, 1967).

O'Meara, T.F. "transcendental Thomism", EC, p. 1263.

O'Meara, T.F. *Church and Culture: German Catholic Theology, 1860-1914*, (Notre Dame, London: University of Notre Dame Press, 1991).

O'Meara, T.F. "Paul Tillich in Catholic thought: the past and the future" in R.F. Bulman and F.J. Parrella eds., *Paul Tillich: A New Catholic Assessment* (Collegeville, Minnesota: The Liturgical Press, 1994), pp. 9-32.

O'Meara, T.F. *Thomas Aquinas Theologian*, (London: University of Notre Dame Press, 1997).

O'Meara, T.F. "Thomas Aquinas and today's theology", *Theology Today*, 55 (1998), pp. 16-28.

O'Meara, T.F. "Christian theology and extraterrestrial intelligent life", *Theological Studies*, 60 (1999), pp. 3-30.

O'Meara, T.F. *A Theologian's Journey*, (New York: Paulist Press, 2002).

O'Meara, T.F. and Weisser, C.D. (eds.). *Paul Tillich in Catholic Thought,* (London: Darton, Longman and Todd, 1964).

Osborne, K.B. *Christian Sacraments in a Postmodern World: A Theology for the Third Millennium*, (New York: Paulist Press, 1999).

Owens, J. "Aristotle and Aquinas" in N. Kretzmann and E. Stump eds., *The Cambridge Companion to Aquinas*, (Cambridge: Cambridge University Press, 1993), pp. 38-59.

Page, R. *Ambiguity and the Presence of God*, (London: SCM Press Limited, 1985).

Page, R. *The Incarnation of Freedom and Love*, (London: SCM Press, 1991).

Page, R. "Ambiguity" in D.W. Musser and J.L. Price ed., *A New Handbook of Christian Theology*, (Nashville: Abingdon Press, 1992), pp. 26-28.

Pannenberg, W. *Jesus – God and Man*, (London: SCM Press, 1968).

Pannenberg, W. *Systematic Theology*, Vol. 1-3, G.W. Bromiley trans., (Grand Rapids: Eerdmans; Edinburgh: T and T, Clark, 1991, 1994, 1998).

Pauck, W. and M. *Paul Tillich: His Life and Thought*, (San Francisco: Harper and Row, 1989).

Pearson, M. "Where is he now? A Christology of absence and presence" in C. Pearson ed., with a sub-version by J. Havea, *Faith in a Hyphen: Cross-Cultural Theologies Down Under*, (Adelaide: Openbook Publishers, 2004), pp. 118-126.

Peirce, C.S. "Some consequences of four incapacities" in C. Hartshorne and P. Weiss eds., *Collected Papers of Charles Sanders Peirce*, Vol. 5., (Cambridge: Harvard University Press, 1934, 1935, 1960), pp. 156-189.

Pekarske, D.T. *Abstracts of Karl Rahner's Theological Investigations 1-23*, (Milwaukee: Marquette University Press, 2002).

Peters, T. *God – the World's Future: Systematic Theology for a Postmodern Era*, (Minneapolis: Fortress Press, 1992).

Phillips, R.P. *Modern Thomistic Philosophy: An Explanation For Students*, Vol. 1 (London: Burns, Oates and Washbourne, 1934).

Pius XII. "Erroneous Trends in Modern Theology", in M. Chinigo ed., *The Teachings of Pope Pius XII*, (London: Methuen, 1958), pp. 252-270.

Poole, R. "Intersubjectivity" in A. Bullock and S. Trombley ed., *The New Fontana Dictionary of Modern Thought*, (London: Harper Collins Publishers, 1977, 1988, 1999, 2000), p. 442.

Pottmeyer, H.J. "Ultramontanism", EC, p. 1278

Quinton, A. "Philosophy", OCP, pp. 666-670.

Quinton, A. "Analogy" in A. Bullock and S. Trombley eds., *The New Fontana Dictionary Of Modern Thought*, 3rd ed., (London: Harper Collins Publishers, 1999, 2000), p. 27.

Rahner, K. *Encounters with Silence*, J.M. Demske trans., (Indiana: St Augusine's Press, 1938, 1999).

Rahner, K. *Hearer of the Word: Laying the Foundation for a Philosophy of Religion*, A. Tallon ed.; J. Donceel trans., (New York: Continuum, 1941, 1994).

Rahner, K. *Spirit in the World*, W.J. Dych trans., (New York: Continuum, 1957, 1968).

Rahner, K. *On Prayer*, (Collegeville, Minnesota: The Liturgical Press, 1958, 1953).

Rahner, K. *On the Theology of Death*, C. H. Henkey trans.; W.J. O'Hara rev., (New York: Herder and Herder; London: Burns and Oates, 1961, 1965).

Rahner, K. *Theological Investigations*, 23 Vols. trans., C. Ernst, K.H. Kruger, B. Kruger, K. Smith, D. Bourke, D. Morland, E. Quinn, H. Riley and J. Donceel.

TI 1 (London: Darton, Longman and Todd; New York: Seabury, 1961, 1965, 1974).
 – "Current problems in Christology", pp. 149-200.
 – "Concerning the relationship between nature and grace", pp. 297-317.

TI 2 (London: Darton, Longman and Todd, 1963).
 – "The resurrection of the body", pp. 203-216.

TI 4 (London: Darton, Longman and Todd; New York: Seabury, 1966, 1974)
 – "The concept of mystery in Catholic theology", pp. 36-73.
 – "On the theology of the Incarnation", pp. 105-120.
 – "Nature and Grace", pp. 165-188.
 – "The theology of the symbol", pp. 221-252.

TI 5 (London: Darton, Longman and Todd, 1966).

- "Christology within an evolutionary view of the world'", pp. 157-192.
- "Dogmatic reflections on the knowledge and self-consciousness of Christ", pp. 193-215.

TI 9 (London: Darton, Longman and Todd, 1972).
- "Observations on the doctrine of God", pp. 127-144.

TI 11 (London: Darton, Longman and Todd, 1974).
- "The Experience of God Today", pp. 149-165.
- "The position of Christology in the Church between exegesis and dogmatics", pp. 185-214.
- "Christology in the setting of modern man's understanding of himself and of his world", pp. 215-229.

TI 13 (London: Darton, Longman and Todd, 1975).
- "Experience of self and experience of God", pp. 122-132.
- "The quest for approaches leading to an understanding of the mystery of the God-man Jesus", pp. 195-200.
- "Remarks on the importance of the history of Jesus for Catholic dogmatics", pp. 201-212.

TI 16 (London: Darton, Longman and Todd, 1979).
- "Experience of the spirit and existential commitment", pp. 24-34.
- "Anonymous and explicit faith", pp. 52-59.
- "The hiddenness of God", pp. 227-243.
- "The mystery of the Holy Trinity", pp. 255-259.

TI 17 (London: Darton, Longman and Todd, 1981).
- "Jesus' Resurrection", pp. 16-23.
- "Christology today?" pp. 24-38.
- "Religious feeling inside and outside the Church", pp. 228-242.
- "Some clarifying remarks about my own work", pp. 243-248.

TI 18 (London: Darton, Longman and Todd, 1983, 1984).
- "What does it mean today to believe in Jesus Christ?" pp. 143-156.
- "Following the crucified", pp. 157-170.
- "The death of Jesus and the closure of revelation", pp. 132-142.
- "On the importance of the non-Christian religions for salvation", pp. 288-295.

TI 19 (London: Darton, Longman and Todd, 1983, 1984).
- "Self-realisation and taking up one's cross", pp. 253-257.

TI 21 (London: Darton, Longman and Todd, 1988).
  – "Natural science and reasonable faith", pp. 16-55.
  – "The present situation of Catholic theology", pp. 70-77.
  – "The specific character of the Christian concept of God", pp. 185-195.
  – "Jesus Christ – the meaning of life", pp. 208-219.
  – "Brief observations on systematic Christology today", pp. 228-238.
  – "The Christian understanding of redemption", pp. 239-254.
TI 22 (London: Darton, Longman and Todd, 1984, 1991).
  – "Book of God – book of human beings", pp. 214-224.
Rahner, K. *The Church and the Sacraments*, W.J. O'Hara trans., (London: Burns and Oates, 1963, 1974).
Rahner, K. *On Heresy*, W.J. O'Hara trans., (Freiburg: Herder, London: Burns and Oates, 1964).
Rahner, K. *Belief Today*, (London: Sheed and Ward, 1965, 1973).
Rahner, K. *The Trinity*, J. Donceel trans., (London: Burns and Oates, 1967, 1970).
Rahner, K ed. *Sacramentum Mundi: An Encyclopedia of Theology*, Vol. 5, (London: Search Press, 1970).
Rahner, K. "Christology Today" in K. Rahner and W. Thüsing, *A New Christology*, (London: Burns and Oates, 1972, 1980), pp. 3-17.
Rahner, K. ed. *Encyclopedia of Theology: The Concise Sacramentum Mundi*, (London: Burns and Oates, 1975, 1993):
  – "Dogma", pp. 352-356.
  – "Dogmatics", pp. 366-370.
  – "Grace", pp. 587-595.
  – "Incarnation", pp. 690-699.
  – "Jesus Christ: history of dogma and theology", pp. 751-772.
  – "Mystery", pp. 1000-1004.
  – "Theology", pp. 1686-1701.
  – "Transcendental theology", pp. 1748-1751.
  – "Trinity, Divine", pp. 1755-1764.
  – "Word of God and theology", pp. 1827-1829.
Rahner, K. *Foundations of Christian Faith: An Introduction to the Idea of Christianity*, W.V. Dych trans., (New York: Crossroad, 1976, 1978)

Rahner, K. *I Remember: An Autobiographical Interview with Meinhold Krauss*, H.D. Egan trans., (London: SCM Press, 1984, 1985).

Rahner, K. *The Great Church Year: The Best of Karl Rahner's Homilies, Sermons and Meditations*, A. Raffelt ed.; (New York: Crossroad, 1987, 1993).

Rahner, K. "Experiencing the spirit" in G.B. Kelly ed. *Karl Rahner: Theologian of the Graced Search for Meaning*, (Edinburgh: T and T, Clark, 1992), pp. 218-238.

Rahner, K. *Prayers for a Lifetime*, A. Raffelt ed., (New York: Crossroad, 1984, 1995).

Rahner, K. *Karl Rahner: Spiritual Writings*, P. Endean ed., (Maryknoll: Orbis Books, 2004).

Raschke, C. "Mark C Taylor" in D.W. Musser and J.L. Price eds., *A New Handbook of Christian Theologians*, (London: SCM Press, 1996), pp. 434-439.

Reid, D. *Energies of the Spirit: Trinitarian Models in Eastern Orthodox and Western Theology*, (Atlanta: Scholars Press, 1997).

Reno, R.R. *The Ordinary Transformed: Karl Rahner and the Christian Vision of Transcendence*, (Grand Rapids: Eerdmans, 1995).

Richardson, A. and Bowden J. eds. *A New Dictionary of Christian Theology*, (London: SCM Press, 1983).

Ries, J.C. "The concept of 'sacramental anxiety': A Kierkegaardian locus of transcendence?" in L. Boeve and L. Leijssen eds., *Sacramental Presence in a Postmodern Context*, (Leuven: Leuven University Press, 1997), pp. 310-324.

Roberts, J.M. *The Triumph of the West*, (London: British Broadcasting Company, 1985).

Rubenstein, M. "Unknow thyself: apophaticism, deconstruction, and theology after ontotheology", *Modern Theology*, 19 (2003), pp. 388-417.

Rorty, R. *Philosophy and the Mirror of Nature*, (Princeton: Princeton University Press, 1979).

Rorty, R. "Philosophy as a kind of writing: An essay on Derrida", *Consequences of Pragmatism (Essays, 1972-1980)*, (Sussex: Harvester Press, 1982), pp. 90-109.

Rorty, R. *Contingency, irony and solidarity*, (Cambridge: Cambridge University Press, 1989).

Rorty, R. "Wittgenstein, Heidegger, and the reification of language", in
C. Guignon ed., *The Cambridge Companion To Heidegger*, (Cambridge: Cambridge University Press, 1993), pp. 337-357.

Rorty, R. "Anti-clericalism and atheism" in M.A. Wrathall ed., *Religion After Metaphysics*, (Cambridge: Cambridge University Press, 2003), pp. 37-46.

Ruether, R.R. *Sexism and God-Talk: Towards a Feminist Theology*, (London: SCM Press, 1983).

Scanlon, M.J. "A deconstruction of religion: On Derrida and Rahner" in J.D. Caputo and M.J. Scanlon eds., *God, The Gift, And Postmodernism*, (Bloomington and Indianapolis: Indiana University Press, 1999), pp. 223-228.

Scanlon, M.J. "The humiliated self as the rhetorical self", in J.D Caputo, M.D. Dooley and M.J. Scanlon eds., *Questioning God*, (Bloomington: Indiana University Press, 2001), pp. 263-273.

Schelling, F.W.J. *Schelling's Philosophy of Mythology And Revelation*, V.C. Hayes trans., (Armidale: AASR, 1995).

Schillebeeckx, E. *Church: The Human Story of God*, (New York: Crossroad, 1989, 1990).

Schweitzer, A. *The Quest of the Historical Jesus*, first complete edition, J. Bowden ed., (London: SCM Press, 1906, 1913, 2000).

Scott J.W. "After History?" *History and the Limits of Interpretation: A Symposium*, (Draft: Feb 20, 1996), pp. 1-15.

Solomon, R.C. *Continental Philosophy Since 1750: The Rise and Fall of the Self*, (Oxford: Oxford University Press, 1988).

Solomon, R.C. "subjectivity", OCP, p. 857.

Spencer, L. "Postmodernism, modernity, and the tradition of dissent", in S. Sim ed., *Postmodern Thought*, (Cambridge: Icon Books, 1998), pp. 158-173.

Steiner, G. *Real Presences*, (Chicago: University of Chicago Press, 1989).

Steiner, G. *Grammars of Creation*, (London: Faber and Faber, 2001).

Sykes, S.W. "Systematic Theology", NDCT, pp. 560-562.

Swinburne, R.G. "God", OCP, pp. 314-315.

Taylor, C. "Closed World Structures" in M.A. Wrathall ed., *Religion After Metaphysics*, (Cambridge: Cambridge University Press, 2003), pp. 47-68.

Taylor, M.C. *Erring: A Postmodern A/theology*, (Chicago and London: Chicago University Press, 1984, 1987).

Taylor, M.C. *About Religions: Economies of Faith in Virtual Culture*, (Chicago and London: Chicago University Press, 1999).

Tarnas, R. *The Passion of the Western Mind*, (London: Pimlico, 1991).

Thatcher, A. *The Ontology of Paul Tillich* (Oxford: Oxford University Press, 1978).

Thompson, I.E. *Being and Meaning: Paul Tillich's Theory of Meaning, Truth and Logic*, (Edinburgh: Edinburgh University Press, 1981).

Thornhill, J. *Modernity: Christianity's Estranged Child Reconstructed*, (Cambridge: Eerdmans, 2000).

Toulmin, S. *Cosmopolis: The Hidden Agenda of Modernity*, (Chicago: University of Chicago Press, 1990, 1992).

Tillich, P. *The Construction of the History of Religion in Schelling's Positive Philosophy: Its Presuppositions and Principles,* V. Nuovo trans., (Lewisburg: Bucknell University Press, London: Associated University Presses, 1910).

Tillich, P. *The System of the Sciences: According to its Objects and Methods*, P. Wiebe trans., (Lewisburg: Bucknell University Press, 1923, 1981).

Tillich, P. *On the Boundary: An Autobiographical Sketch*, (New York: Charles Scribner's Sons, 1936, 1964, 1966).

Tillich, P. *The Shaking of the Foundations*, (Middlesex: Penguin Books, 1949).

Tillich, P. *The Protestant Era*, J.L. Adams trans. and ed. (London: Nisbet, 1951).
  - "Philosophy and fate", pp. 3-17.
  - "Kairos", pp. 37-58.
  - "Realism and faith", pp. 74-92.
  - "Philosophy and theology", pp. 93-104.
  - "Nature and sacrament", pp. 105-125.

Tillich, P. *Systematic Theology*, Vols. 1-3, (London: SCM Press, 1951, 1957, 1963, 1978).

Tillich, P. *The Courage to Be*, (Glasgow: William Collins, 1952).

Tillich, P. *Love, Power and Justice: Ontological Analyses and Ethical Applications*, (Oxford: Oxford University Press, 1954).

Tillich, P. *Biblical Religion and the Search for Ultimate Reality*, (Chicago: University of Chicago Press, 1955).

Tillich, P. *The New Being*, (London: SCM Press, 1956).

Tillich, P. *The Dynamics of Faith*, (New York: Harper and Row, 1957).

Tillich, P. *Theology of Culture*, R.C. Kimball ed., (Oxford: Oxford University Press, 1959).
  - "The two types of philosophy of religion", pp. 10-29.
  - "The nature of religious language", pp. 53-67.

Tillich, P. "The religious symbol" in R. May ed., *Symbolism in Religion and Literature*, (New York: George Braziller, 1960), pp. 75-98.

Tillich, P. "Reply to interpretation and criticism" in C.W. Kegley and R.W. Bretall eds., *The Theology of Paul Tillich* Vol I, (New York: MacMillan Co, 1961), p. 330.

Tillich, P. *The Eternal Now*, (New York: Charles Scribner's Sons, 1963).

Tillich, P. *Christianity and the Encounter of World Religions*, (Minneapolis: Fortress Press, 1963, 1991).

Tillich, P. *Ultimate Concern: Tillich in Dialogue*, (London: SCM Press, 1965).

Tillich, P. *My Search for Absolutes*, (New York: Simon and Schuster, 1967).

Tillich, P. *Perspectives on 19th and 20th Century Protestant Theology*, C. Braaten ed., (London: SCM Press, 1967).

Tillich, P. *A History of Christian Thought: From its Judaic and Hellenistic Origins to Existentialism*, C. Braaten ed., (New York: Simon and Schuster, 1967, 1968).

Tillich, P. *Paul Tillich: Theologian of the Boundaries*, Taylor, M.K. ed., (London: Collins, 1987).

Tillich, P. "Symbol and knowledge: a response by Paul Tillich" in J. Clayton ed., *Paul Tillich: Mainworks*, Vol. 4, (Berlin and New York: *De Gruyter-Evangelisches Verlagswerk* GmbH, 1987), pp. 273-276.

Tillich, P. *Theology of Peace*, R. H. Stone ed., (Louisville: Westminster/John Knox Press, 1990).

Tillich, P. *The Irrelevance and Relevance of the Christian Message*, D. Foster ed., (Cleveland: Pilgrim Press, 1996).

Tillich, P. *Against the Third Reich: Paul Tillich's Wartime Radio Broadcasts into Nazi Germany*, R. H. Stone ed. and M.L. Weaver ed. and trans., (Louisville: Westminster/John Knox Press, 1998).

Tracy, D. *The Analogical Imagination: Christian Theology and the Culture of Pluralism*, (London: SCM Press, 1981).

Vahanian, G. *The Death of God: The Culture of Our Post-Christian Era*, (New York: George Braziller, 1957, 1959, 1960, 1961).

Van Beeck, F.J. *Christology Proclaimed: Christology as Rhetoric*, (New York: Paulist Press, 1979).

Van Hoozer, K.J. "Theology and the condition of postmodernity: a report on knowledge (of God)" in K.J. VanHoozer ed., *The Cambridge Companion to Postmodern Theology*, (Cambridge: Cambridge University Press, 2003), pp. 3-25.

Van Inwagen, P. "Quam Dilecta" in T.V. Morris ed., *God and the Philosophers: The Reconciliation of Faith and Reason*, (New York and Oxford: Oxford University Press, 1994), pp. 31-60.

Vass, G. *A Theologian in Search of a Philosophy: Understanding Karl Rahner*, Vol. 1., (Westminster, London: Christian Classics, Sheed and Ward, 1985).

Vorgrimler, H. *Understanding Karl Rahner: An Introduction to his Life and Thought*, (London: SCM Press, 1985, 1986).

Ward, G. "Introduction" in G. Ward ed., *The Postmodern God*, (Oxford: Blackwell Publishing, 1997), pp. xv-xlvii.

Ward, G. "Deconstructive theology" in K.J. Vanhoozer ed., *Postmodern Theology*, (Cambridge: Cambridge University Press, 2003), pp. 76-91.

Watson, P. *A Terrible Beauty: The People and Ideas that Shaped the Modern Mind*, (London: Phoenix Press, 2000).

Weibe, P. "From system to systematics: the origin of Paul Tillich's theology" in J.J. Carey ed., *Kairos and Logos: Studies in the Roots and Implications of Tillich's Theology*, (Mercer: Mercer University Press, 1978, 1984).

Weisbaker, D.R. "Aesthetic elements in Tillich's theory of symbol" in J. J. Carey ed., *Kairos and Logos: Studies in the Roots and Implications of Tillich's Theology*, (Mercer: Mercer University Press, 1984), pp. 241-259.

Westphal, M. "Divine excess: the God who comes after", in J.D. Caputo ed., *The Religious*, (Oxford: Blackwell Publishers, 2002), pp. 259–276.

Wildman, W.J. *Fidelity with Plausibility: Modest Christologies in the Twentieth Century*, (New York: State University of New York Press, 1998).

Wittgenstein, L. *Philosophical Investigations*, G.E.M. Anscombe trans., (Oxford: Blackwell Publishing, 1974).

Wolff, H.W. *Joel and Amos*, W. Janzen, S.D. McBride and E.A. Muenchaw trans. S.D. McBride ed. (Philadelphia: Fortress Press, 1969, 1977).